Reading and Dyslexia in Different Orthographies

This book provides a unique and accessible account of current research on reading and dyslexia in different orthographies. While most research has been conducted in English, this text presents cross-language comparisons to provide insights into universal aspects of reading development and developmental dyslexia in alphabetic and non-alphabetic languages.

The book brings together contributions from a group of leading literacy researchers from around the world. It begins by examining the development of language skills in monolingual speakers of alphabetic and non-alphabetic languages; it then explores literacy acquisition in bilingual children learning to read in languages with different spelling–sound rules, including English, French, Greek, Welsh and Japanese. The second section is devoted to developmental dyslexia in monolingual and bilingual speakers of different languages and examines the impact of variations in orthography on the symptoms and aetiology of dyslexia. The final section explores the contribution of brain imaging to the study of impaired and unimpaired reading, giving an up-to-the-minute picture of how the brain deals with different languages and writing systems.

This is ideal reading for advanced undergraduates and postgraduates who have an interest in language acquisition, reading and spelling, as well as speech and language therapists, teachers and special educational needs professionals.

Nicola Brunswick is Senior Lecturer in Psychology at Middlesex University. Her research explores cognitive and psychophysiological aspects of reading development and developmental dyslexia in children and adults. She is a trustee of the British Dyslexia Association.

Siné McDougall is Professor of Psychology at Bournemouth University. Her research examines the phonological and memory skills that children need to learn to read successfully, and how difficulties with reading acquisition might be overcome through appropriate intervention. Her work has also examined factors influencing the way we interpret the icons, symbols and signs that we encounter in our everyday lives.

Paul de Mornay Davies is Senior Lecturer in Psychology at Middlesex University. His research is focused on acquired disorders of language following brain damage, and in particular on how the surface structure of the spoken language impacts on the ability to access meaning from sound and print.

Reading and Dyslexia in Different Orthographies

**Edited by Nicola Brunswick,
Siné McDougall and
Paul de Mornay Davies**

Psychology Press
Taylor & Francis Group
HOVE AND NEW YORK

First published in 2010
by Psychology Press
27 Church Road, Hove, East Sussex BN3 2FA

Simultaneously published in the USA and Canada
by Psychology Press
270 Madison Avenue, New York NY 10016

Psychology Press is an imprint of the Taylor & Francis Group, an Informa business

© 2010 Psychology Press

Typeset in Times New Roman by
RefineCatch Limited, Bungay, Suffolk
Printed and bound in Great Britain by
TJ International Ltd, Padstow, Cornwall
Cover design by Design Deluxe

This publication has been produced with paper manufactured to strict
environmental standards and with pulp derived from sustainable
forests.

British Library Cataloguing in Publication Data
A catalogue record for this book is available from the British Library

Library of Congress Cataloging-in-Publication Data
Reading and dyslexia in different orthographies / edited by Nicola
Brunswick, Siné McDougall and Paul de Mornay Davies.
   p. cm.
   Includes bibliographical references and index.
   1. Reading disability.   2. Dyslexic children—Education.
I. Brunswick, Nicola, 1970–   II. McDougall, Siné 1958–
III. De Mornay Davies, Paul, 1967–
   LB1050.5.R36 2010
   371.33'44678—dc22

                                          2009032288

ISBN: 978–1–84169–712–3 (hbk)

Contents

List of figures   vii
List of tables   xi
List of editors and contributors   xii
Acknowledgements   xiv
Foreword   xv
UTA FRITH

SECTION 1

The development of reading skills in different orthographies   1

1   Reading and dyslexia in different orthographies:
    An introduction and overview   3
    SINÉ McDOUGALL, NICOLA BRUNSWICK AND
    PAUL DE MORNAY DAVIES

2   A psycholinguistic grain size view of reading
    acquisition across languages   23
    USHA GOSWAMI

3   Phonological development from a cross-linguistic
    perspective   43
    LYNNE G. DUNCAN

4   Letter position encoding across deep and
    transparent orthographies   69
    MARIA KTORI AND NICOLA J. PITCHFORD

5   Differences in reading ability between children
    attending Welsh- and English-speaking primary schools
    in Wales   87
    J. RICHARD HANLEY

6 Writing a language that you can't hear 109
TEREZINHA NUNES, DIANA BURMAN, DEBORAH EVANS AND
DANIEL BELL

SECTION 2
Developmental dyslexia in different orthographies 129

7 Unimpaired reading development and dyslexia
across different languages 131
NICOLA BRUNSWICK

8 Reading acquisition and dyslexia in Spanish 155
ROBERT A. I. DAVIES AND FERNANDO CUETOS

9 Lexical reading in Italian developmental
dyslexic readers 181
DESPINA PAIZI, PIERLUIGI ZOCCOLOTTI AND CRISTINA BURANI

10 Dyslexia in Chinese: Implications for
connectionist models of reading 199
I-FAN SU, KATHRIN KLINGEBIEL AND BRENDAN S. WEEKES

11 Dyslexia in biscriptal readers 221
JOHN EVERATT, DINA OCAMPO, KAZUVIRE VEII,
STYLIANI NENOPOULOU, IAN SMYTHE, HAYA AL MANNAI AND
GAD ELBEHERI

SECTION 3
Neuroimaging studies of reading in different orthographies 247

12 Cross-cultural differences in unimpaired and
dyslexic reading: Behavioural and functional anatomical
observations in readers of regular and irregular orthographies 249
ERALDO PAULESU, NICOLA BRUNSWICK AND
FEDERICA PAGANELLI

13 Lexical retrieval in alphabetic and non-alphabetic
scripts: Evidence from brain imaging 273
BRENDAN S. WEEKES

Glossary 291
Author index 299
Subject index 307

Figures

1.1 North American Indian drawing of an
    exploratory expedition 4
1.2 The Yukaghir 'love letter' 5
1.3 Example of Sumerian cuneiform writing 7
1.4 Examples of logographic, syllabic and alphabetic scripts 8
2.1 Schematic depiction of the hierarchical structure
    of the syllable, illustrated using the sounds in the spoken
    word *captain* 28
3.1 The hierarchical internal structure of the syllable 44
3.2 Mean percentage accuracy at common unit
    identification for each age group of French and English
    speaking participants in Study 1 55
3.3 Mean percentage accuracy at common unit
    identification at the beginning (Time 1) and end (Time 2) of
    the first year of instruction for each language group in
    Study 2 57
4.1 Schematic illustration of the stimulus display used
    for (a) skilled adult readers and (b) developing readers in an
    experimental trial of the visual search task 70
4.2 Visual search functions produced by skilled
    readers of different orthographies 72
4.3 Letter search function produced by English and
    Greek (a) 6-year-old, (b) 9-year-old and (c) skilled readers
    when searching for native letters 77
4.4 Search functions produced by English and Greek
    (a) 6-year-old, (b) 9-year-old and (c) skilled readers when
    searching for non-native letters 78
4.5 Search functions produced by Greek–English
    adult bilingual readers when searching for first- (Greek) and
    second- (English) acquired letters 80
5.1 The number of words read correctly by English
    and Welsh children at three phases (November, March and
    June) during their first year of formal reading instruction 92

5.2   The mean number of English words read correctly
      (max = 110) by Welsh and English readers in the four quartile
      groups   96
5.3   The mean number of (a) English and (b) Welsh
      non-words read correctly by Welsh and English readers in the
      four quartile groups   98
5.4   Performance on the (a) accuracy, (b)
      comprehension and (c) speed measures from the Neale (1989)
      reading test in the four quartile groups   99
5.5   Performance on the phonological awareness tests
      as a function of quartile group: (a) rhyme; (b) first phoneme;
      (c) last phoneme   100
5.6   Performance on the Raven's Matrices test of
      non-verbal ability as a function of quartile group   101
6.1   An example of the way the items in the Raven's
      Matrices are structured   119
6.2   A schematic representation of the specific
      percentage of differences between deaf children in reading
      comprehension explained by suffix spelling after controlling
      for the other factors   121
6.3   A schematic representation of the specific
      percentage of differences between deaf children in writing
      skills explained by suffix spelling after controlling for the
      other factors   122
7.1   Word and non-word reading by English and
      Italian adults   138
7.2   The estimated incidence of dyslexia across
      different languages   141
7.3   Phonetic and semantic Chinese characters   145
7.4   The incidence of dyslexia in languages that differ
      in transparency and granularity   148
8.1   The dual-route cascaded (DRC) model of visual
      word recognition and reading aloud   158
8.2   The 'triangle model'   159
9.1   Mean reaction times (a) and errors (b) for the
      reading of morphological and simple non-words by reader
      group   191
9.2   Mean reaction times (a) and errors (b) for the
      reading of derived and simple words by reader group   193
10.1 (a) Model of reading in Chinese; (b) the dual-route
      cascade model of reading   210
10.2 The lexical constituency (LC) model of reading in
      Chinese   211
11.1 Comparative phonological awareness weaknesses
      (represented by z-scores away from the norm of zero) shown

by groups of children with poor literacy skills across four
languages   226

11.2   Average scores for word reading in Herero and
English across the grades   233

11.3   Average scores for non-word reading in Herero and
English across the grades   233

11.4   Average scores produced by the good and poor
English literacy children on the measure of phoneme
awareness in each of the languages of testing (English and
Filipino)   237

11.5   Average performance of groups of monolingual
non-dyslexic adults, monolingual dyslexic adults and
bilingual non-dyslexic adults (with up to 7 years of English
experience, or more than 7 years' experience) on the reading
tasks   238

11.6   Average performance of groups of monolingual
non-dyslexic, monolingual dyslexic and bilingual non-
dyslexic adult college-level students on the fluency tasks   239

11.7   Average performance of groups of monolingual
non-dyslexic, bilingual non-dyslexic and monolingual
dyslexic adult college-level students on the rapid naming
tasks   239

11.8   Profile of a Namibian Herero–English bilingual
child presenting evidence of difficulties in literacy skills in
both languages   240

11.9   Profile of a Filipino Tagalog–English bilingual
child presenting evidence of difficulties primarily in English   241

12.1   (a) Regions of brain activity in skilled readers
during a visual feature detection (implicit reading) task; (b)
a map of Brodmann areas (BAs) for the identification of
specific regions in the brain   254

12.2   Regions of common activation during reading;
greater activation in English readers than Italian readers
during non-word reading; and greater activation in Italian
readers than English readers regardless of word type   257

12.3   Effect size (*z*-scores) of the differences between
English, French and Italian dyslexic and control readers on
the tests of reading and phonological processing   261

12.4   Regions of normal brain activation and reduced
activation in English, French and Italian dyslexic readers
during the reading of concrete nouns   262

13.1   Diagram of the human brain showing the four
lobar divisions   274

13.2   Brain images showing contrasts between (a) early-
acquired and late-acquired words; (b) late-acquired and

early-acquired words; and (c) low-frequency words and
high-frequency words   276
13.3 Framework for oral reading and picture naming in
Chinese   278
13.4 Example items used in Weekes et al. (2005)   282
13.5 Brain activation decreases and increases in the
identity, phonological and orthographic conditions   284

Tables

1.1	Classification of languages in accordance with orthographic depth and complexity of syllabic structure	10
2.1	Data from the COST A8 study of grapheme–phoneme recoding skills for monosyllables in 14 European languages	38
3.1	Summary of Gombert's (1992) theory of meta-linguistic development	45
3.2	Key to the main tasks used to assess children's phonological awareness	47
3.3	Mean chronological age and vocabulary score for each participant group in Study 1	53
3.4	Mean chronological age and Raven's Matrices raw score for each participant group in Study 2	56
3.5	Classification of responses in Fox and Routh's Word Segmentation task according to whether the 'little bit of' the disyllabic word produced was a dictionary-defined syllable or just any valid sound	61
5.1	The percentage of words read correctly by Welsh and English children	90
5.2	The percentage of non-words read correctly by Welsh and English children, and percentage of words correct on a test of phoneme counting	91
5.3	Number of words read correctly and mean reading speed as a function of regularity and frequency	94
6.1	Mean correct in the Schonell Spelling Test and Suffix Spelling Task of hearing and deaf children	116
6.2	Pre- and post-test means by group on each of the intervention outcome measures	124
10.1	Description of Chinese writing	200
10.2	Types of dyslexia in Chinese	205
11.1	Measures used with Filipino–English bilingual children	228
11.2	Measures used with Namibian Herero–English bilingual children	229
11.3	Measures used with UK adult students	229

Editors and contributors

Haya al Mannai, University of Bahrain, PO Box 32038, Sakhir, Bahrain

Daniel Bell, Department of Educational Studies, University of Oxford, 15 Norham Gardens, Oxford, OX2 6PY, UK

Nicola Brunswick, Department of Psychology, School of Health and Social Sciences, Middlesex University, The Burroughs, Hendon, London, NW4 4BT, UK

Cristina Burani, Istituto di Scienze e Tecnologie della Cognizione (ISTC) del CNR, Via San Martino della Battaglia 44, 00185, Roma, Italy

Diana Burman, Department of Educational Studies, University of Oxford, 15 Norham Gardens, Oxford, OX2 6PY, UK

Fernando Cuetos, Facultad de Psicologia, Universidad de Oviedo, Plaza Feijoo, s/n, Oviedo 33003, Asturias, Spain

Robert A. I. Davies, Department of Psychology, Oxford Brookes University, Headington Campus, Gipsy Lane, Oxford, OX3 0BP, UK

Paul de Mornay Davies, Department of Psychology, School of Health and Social Sciences, Middlesex University, The Burroughs, Hendon, London, NW4 4BT, UK

Lynne G. Duncan, Department of Psychology, University of Dundee, Dundee, DD1 4HN, UK

Gad Elbeheri, Center for Child Evaluation and Teaching, Al Surra, Block 4, Street 14, PO Box 5453, Safat 13055, Kuwait

Deborah Evans, Department of Educational Studies, University of Oxford, 15 Norham Gardens, Oxford, OX2 6PY, UK

John Everatt, School of Literacies and Arts in Education, College of Education, University of Canterbury, Dovedale Avenue, Private Bag 4800, Christchurch 8140, New Zealand

Uta Frith, Institute of Cognitive Neuroscience, University College London, Alexandra House, 17 Queen Square, London, WC1N 3AR, UK

Usha Goswami, Faculty of Education, University of Cambridge, 184 Hills Road, Cambridge, CB2 8PQ, UK

J. Richard Hanley, Department of Psychology, University of Essex, Colchester, CO4 3SQ, UK

Kathrin Klingebiel Department of Psychology, Pevensey Building, University of Sussex, Falmer, BN1 9QH, UK

Maria Ktori, School of Psychology, University of Nottingham, University Park, Nottingham, NG7 2RD, UK

Siné McDougall, Psychology Department, School of Design, Engineering & Computing, Bournemouth University, Talbot Campus, Fern Barrow, Poole, Dorset, BH12 5BB, UK

Styliani Nenopoulou, c/o Department of Psychology, University of Surrey, Guildford, GU2 7XH, UK

Terezinha Nunes, Department of Educational Studies, University of Oxford, 15 Norham Gardens, Oxford, OX2 6PY, UK

Dina Ocampo, College of Education, University of the Philippines, Diliman, Quezon City 1105, Metro Manila, Philippines

Federica Paganelli, Dipartimento di Psicologia, Università degli Studi di Milano Bicocca, Piazza dell' Ateneo Nuovo 1, Stanza 428, Milan, Italy

Despina Paizi, Istituto di Scienze e Tecnologie della Cognizione (ISTC) del CNR, Via San Martino della Battaglia 44, 00185, Roma, Italy

Eraldo Paulesu, Dipartimento di Psicologia, Università degli Studi di Milano Bicocca, Piazza dell' Ateneo Nuovo 1, Stanza 428, Milan, Italy

Nicola J. Pitchford, School of Psychology, University of Nottingham, University Park, Nottingham, NG7 2RD, UK

Ian Smythe, Ibis Creative Consultants Ltd, 34 Collingwood Road, Sutton, Surrey, SM1 2RZ, UK

I-Fan Su, Division of Speech & Hearing Sciences, University of Hong Kong, Sai Ying Pun, Hong Kong

Kazuvire Veii, 17105 Queen Victoria Court 202, Gaithersburg, MD 20877, USA

Brendan Weekes, Division of Speech & Hearing Sciences, University of Hong Kong, Sai Ying Pun, Hong Kong

Pierluigi Zoccolotti, Department of Psychology, Sapienza University of Rome, Via dei Marsi 78, 00176 Rome, Italy

Acknowledgements

When we hosted a two-day workshop on *The role of orthographies in reading and spelling* at Middlesex University, we did not expect it to lead to this book. However, the enthusiasm of those who attended the workshop and the cutting-edge nature of the research they presented convinced us that we ought to share our experience with a wider audience. The research reported in this book explores how differences between orthographies can shape the way in which we acquire reading skills, and the difficulties that speakers of different languages are likely to encounter when reading. The emerging consensus suggests that the manner in which a particular orthography maps onto the sounds of the spoken language affects not only literacy acquisition in children but also adults' reading. We believe that this book provides a celebration of the many writing systems in use around the world and shows how systematic comparisons of reading across different orthographies may furnish us with better knowledge and understanding of how skilled reading is attained.

We would particularly like to thank those who contributed chapters. They have been generous with their time and effort, and their varied and innovative research has been an inspiration to us. We would also like to thank Middlesex University, London (particularly Professor Ray Iles), and the Experimental Psychology Society, who jointly supported our *Orthographies* workshop. Without them there would have been no basis for this text. Thanks must also go to Drs Bahman Baluch and Ilhan Raman, who helped us to organize and run the workshop, to Sharla Plant, our editor from Psychology Press, who has been nothing but patient and supportive throughout the whole editorial process, and to four anonymous reviewers who read an earlier version of this manuscript and made many helpful suggestions as to how it might be improved.

If there are any errors remaining, we are sure they are mostly ours, but we would like the idiosyncratic orthography of the English language to shoulder at least some of the blame!

Nicola Brunswick
Siné McDougall
Paul de Mornay Davies
June 2009

Foreword

Uta Frith

In the world of politics the lingua franca of our day is English. The language of science is English, and the vast majority of papers published in science are written in English. At the same time, English is not the native language of most of its users, and many users experience English solely as a written language. This is a phenomenon whose implications are still largely unexplored. Furthermore, it has been suggested that in the future the lingua franca may well be Chinese. In this case, it is likely that an entirely different writing system would come to dominate. Would this radically change our awareness and experience of communication? This book suggests that it might.

For this reason alone, the present volume is timely. It provides a much-needed platform for sharing knowledge of how we read and write in different languages. The expert contributors have taken stock of what we know about clashes and synergies that arise from the use of different writing systems. And there are multitudes of systems: over 400 orthographies are in use today. Among the most prominent of these are the alphabetic ones. The alphabet provides one of the most elegant and simple solutions to turn spoken language into written language. This solution is based on the brain's ability to segment speech and to map the segments to graphic symbols. With an astoundingly minimal set of just 26 letters, the alphabet provides a powerful code for translating between sounds and symbols.

The alphabetic principle has been remarkably successful in being adopted by many languages of the world. The 26 letters often prove to be too small a set for the variable number of speech sounds that can be said to be in use in different languages. Thus, there are arrangements such as digraphs, accents or umlauts to produce more detailed mappings between sounds and letters. There are other arrangements that extend the apparent limitations of the alphabet. When alphabets have been in use for a particular language for centuries, then there are likely to be many changes in spoken language and even in the meaning of words. Writing systems, like ships at sea, tend to take on extra cargo and end up encrusted in barnacles. This changes their efficiency but also gives them character and history. English orthography is one of the 'ships' that exemplifies a writing system that has grown to be particularly complex and historically rich.

This has a downside, however, which is only slowly beginning to be realized: it is an extremely complex writing system to learn. English speakers take longer to become literate than do speakers of other languages. Furthermore, the level of skill reached by English readers and writers is more variable than that of other readers and writers. Dyslexic readers are doubly hit. First, because their brains work in such a way that it is apparently harder for them to segment the sounds of speech, they find it difficult to learn the mapping between these sounds and letters. This applies to any writing system that uses the alphabet, however simple and transparent. However, in English they have to make sense of an orthography that is not only very complex but has quirky sets of rules and exceptions. No wonder that dyslexia is particularly prominent in English-speaking countries. No wonder either that dyslexia research is particularly well developed in these countries. But, as this book makes clear, dyslexia researchers who only focus on English miss out.

The comparison of languages yields rich insights. Such comparisons enlighten not just the study of dyslexic readers who struggle to learn, or of beginning readers on their way to becoming skilled readers. Comparisons between Italian and English skilled readers have told us what the reading process is like in the mind and in the brain. Skilled reading in both languages means making instant links between the sound, appearance and meaning of words. The brain does this by capitalizing on its evolutionarily ancient language system, and by slotting in a component that links automatically to the visual form of words. Thus, in a triangular connection, a written word instantly evokes its meaning and its sound; the meaning of a word evokes its sound and written form; and the sound of a word evokes its written form and its meaning. By skimming through text, the triangular connections are made even faster than by listening to spoken words.

In spite of these similarities, research has shown that skilled readers of Italian read differently, by giving more weight to one of the links in the triangle, while English readers give more weight to another link. Moreover, we know that the physiology that underlies their reading reflects this difference. The brain areas of the reading system of the Italian reader are configured in such a way that one component, the component that is involved in mapping sound to letters, is more active than the component that is involved in mapping words to meaning. The reverse is true for highly skilled English readers. This makes sense, since in English the meaning of the word is a key to its sound. How else is one to read ambiguous words such as *cough*, *bough* and *through*? Nevertheless, both English and Italian readers use all the components of the reading system, and they use them in concert. It is the dyslexic readers who fail in this respect. They are unable to reconfigure the language system of the brain in the way that skilled readers are apparently able to do. Instead, they have to rely on tricks to remember words and their spellings and to use the effortful mapping of letters to sound.

Comparisons of beginning readers in different European countries have also provided more detailed knowledge of how the mind/brain processes language. Readers of different European languages, who all use the alphabet, show remarkable differences in the speed with which they acquire their reading and writing skills. The concept of grain size of the different languages has been a major advance in explaining these differences. Thus, small grain, as in *la, ba, ga*, goes together with transparent orthographies, which are easier to learn. Large grain, as in languages with many rhyming words such as *jump, lump, hump*, goes together with complex orthographies. Complex orthographies are, in turn, hard to learn and reward only those who have no difficulty in memorizing whole spelling patterns. Other readers are likely to stumble. Sadly, the standards set for the speller in different orthographies tend to be extremely high. For reasons that are not entirely clear, there is little tolerance for less than totally accurate reproduction of spellings. This hits dyslexic readers hard.

One of the most unexpected effects of reading in an alphabetic system is that it promotes and even creates awareness of speech sounds. In this sense, written language changes the way we process spoken language. Users of the alphabet acquire something akin to a hearing aid that makes speech sound more staccato-like than it actually is. Speech is forever ready to be translated into discrete letters. In fact, the alphabet is one of the most striking examples of how culture insidiously and irrevocably changes minds and brains.

Deaf users of sign language, who do not have primary access to the sounds of speech, have also contributed to our understanding of written language. In this book we are faced with the puzzle of how a person who does not speak can learn to use the alphabetic writing system that is entirely based on speech. We learn that deaf children are faced with a similar problem to immigrant children who need to learn a second language through learning to read. Bilingual readers are increasingly common in a mobile world. They face the problem of flexibility and need to be able to reconfigure reading processes as the situation demands.

Much has been written about awareness of speech sounds and its role in learning to read. Conversely, difficulties in awareness of speech sounds, as experienced by a significant minority of children, have been linked to dyslexia. This volume contains a welcome update of this important theoretical issue and warns us of the dangers of a purely alphabet-centric perspective. Clearly, the alphabet is not always an elegant and a simple means of making language visible. For instance, syllabic or logographic writing systems may prove to be a more user-friendly system, at least in some languages.

By putting a searchlight on Chinese, the classic non-alphabetic writing system, this volume offers important insights that go well beyond the studies carried out in a European context. Is the same reading system of the brain used in this writing system as in alphabetic systems? Remarkably, the answer is no. Here the basic units are not the sounds of speech. Instead, the basic unit is meaning, and this entails a huge set of symbols. All these symbols, which are complex characters consisting of exquisitely configured strokes, have to be learned, and this places huge demands on visual and sensorimotor memory. The advantage of such a script is clear. People speaking vastly different languages still share the same set of meanings, and therefore written language allows them to communicate these meanings directly.

In the complex alphabetic orthography of English we find a small analogy. Here some words can only be read once you know what they mean and what they sound like. But, as in Chinese, there are useful clues to the meaning and to the pronunciation, and these act as reminders. Even in a perfectly transparent orthography such as Italian, in multisyllabic words it is not always clear on which syllable the stress should be placed. Prior knowledge of the word's meaning and sound is required even here. In the logographic system of Chinese, this requirement takes on paramount importance. True, clues to sound and meaning are contained in the form of the character. Nevertheless, this only slightly mitigates the burden of remembering the exact sound and meaning of the whole character. Again, as in the demands on spelling in other systems, there is an extremely high standard for total accuracy.

How do dyslexic readers fare in a writing system that is strongly based on prior knowledge, and where on-line decoding of sounds from characters is treacherous or impossible? There are suggestions that many different types of problems might be seen, including those that argue that the processing of speech as well as meaning are critical areas where difficulties can arise, but far fewer studies exist than in the case of alphabetic writing systems. If there is increasing demand for Chinese as a global language, then it would be necessary to fill this gap in our knowledge. At the very least, the present book will promote greater awareness of the different burdens that different writing systems impose. It will thus serve the noble goal of promoting global communication.

The unique perspective shared by the reading researchers represented in this volume is that they are aware of the machinery that the brain uses to understand language, but they are also aware of the cultural context in which reading and writing are embedded. Thus the way we understand our world is more and more through the written word. It is the most efficient way to transmit knowledge at vast distances of space and time. To learn from other human beings is so much more effective than to learn from our own mistakes. It is because of the pivotal nature of knowledge transmission through the written medium that the study of literacy is so hugely important.

Section 1

The development of reading skills in different orthographies

1 Reading and dyslexia in different orthographies: An introduction and overview

Siné McDougall, Nicola Brunswick and Paul de Mornay Davies

Introduction

In the May 2009 edition of *New Scientist*, Andrew Robinson wrote about trying to decipher ancient lost languages. He stated that 'Writing is one of the greatest inventions in human history. . . . Without writing, there could be no accumulation of knowledge, no historical record, no science—and of course no books, newspapers or internet.' However, writing is no use if we are not able to read it. To decipher an ancient script, experts need to be able to link what they discover through archaeology with a known language, or at least one with which they are familiar. The research presented in this book shows that children learning to read are going through a similar deciphering process. Furthermore, the way that they learn to read is determined in no small part by the writing system that they are trying to decode. Even as adult skilled readers, the way that we read is constrained by the nature of the written code that we use.

There are over 400 writing systems, or orthographies, used around the world (Coulmas, 1989). The word *orthography* is derived from the Greek words *orthós* meaning 'correct' and *gráphein* meaning 'to write'. An orthography is therefore the accepted usage of a set of symbols to represent a given language in a written form. When discussing the factors involved in creating new orthographies for unwritten languages, Cahill and Karan (2008) stipulated the following:

> Not just any orthography will do; it needs to be effective. That is, it needs to be (a) linguistically sound, (b) acceptable to all stakeholders, (c) teach-able, and (d) easy to reproduce. These roughly can be thought of as scientific, political, educational, and technical aspects (p. 3).

In contrast to the careful and systematic approach that can be taken when developing new orthographies, extant writing systems have evolved in a way which means that these reasonable requirements are rarely met. What follows is a brief overview of factors that have influenced the evolution of current orthographies to provide some insight into how the effectiveness of orthographies may fall short of these ideals, and the challenges they present to readers as a result.

Orthographies: A historical perspective

Pictograms and ideograms

Cave drawings and paintings from the late Palaeolithic period (35–15,000 BC) have been found in many locations including France, India, Zimbabwe and Sweden. Some linguists and historians see these as the earliest precursors of writing. Others view them as straightforward pictorial representations of the world, but it is harder to see later collections of 'picture writing' by North American Indians—for example, those published by Mallery (1893) and Schoolcraft (1851)—as being purely pictorial. Figure 1.1 shows an example from Schoolcraft's collection of drawings by Indian guides that tells the story of an exploratory expedition to the source of the Mississippi.

This drawing tells that there were 16 people on the expedition. Of these, two were American Indian guides and 14 were white men (denoted by the hats). The officer in charge is denoted by the sword on the far right. Next to him is the secretary of the party, who has a book in his hand. The figures at the top are infantry soldiers, and the muskets with which they were armed are shown beside them. At the bottom of the picture are a prairie hen and a tortoise, which had been caught the previous day.

This drawing is largely pictorial although we need to make several inferences (e.g., linking the muskets to the men to infer that they are infantry soldiers, and inferring the status of the officer in charge from the sword in his hand) to understand its full meaning.

Figure 1.1 North American Indian drawing of an exploratory expedition (from Schoolcraft, 1851).

Such drawings are often referred to as pictograms because they use a series of culturally accepted, fairly literal drawings of people and objects to tell a story. Over time, however, drawings gradually became more abstract and less pictorial—they became *ideographic*—representing mainly ideas and concepts rather than objects. In ideograms the relationship between what is depicted and what is meant is much more oblique, and viewers need to learn the meaning of individual symbols before they can grasp the concepts that they represent. One of the most famous examples of ideographic writing is the Yukaghir 'love letter' (see Figure 1.2). The Yukaghir tribe from north-eastern Siberia carved ideograms on birch bark to communicate affairs of the heart. In this particular image, the arrow shapes are believed to represent individual people (four adults and two children), and the solid and broken lines that connect them represent current and previous relationships between the adults (although see Unger, 2003, for an alternative view of this image). Even though these ideograms might superficially be regarded as pictorial, they

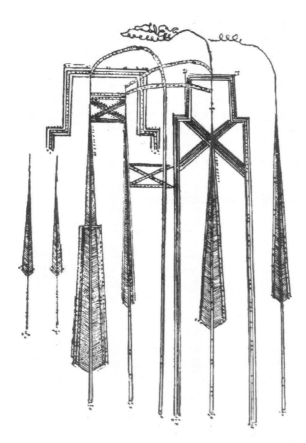

Figure 1.2 The Yukaghir 'love letter' (from Shargorodskii, 1895).

were actually highly stylized, represented complex ideas, and required considerable interpretation.

Although earlier writers (e.g., Diringer, 1947; Gelb, 1963) thought it a reasonable assumption that pictograms and ideograms formed the basis of subsequent writing, later researchers (e.g., Coulmas, 1985; DeFrancis, 1989) have been rather more sceptical. There were two main difficulties with the initial research. One was that although cultural meanings and interpretation were required to understand pictograms and ideograms, information was represented *semasiographically*. This means that there was no direct mapping between symbols and words, and no set of rules that related symbols to meaning, so the picture could be 'read' equally well in a number of different ways.

The second problem was that it was difficult to form a direct historical link between these early pictures and later writing. Many now think that the roots of true writing can be traced to the use of *tallies*, or early accounting systems, where the links between the written symbols and exactly what they meant was clearer. Meticulous research carried out by Schmandt-Besserat (1978, 1979) suggests that the roots of writing lie in early record-keeping and the use of tokens to record transactions. Stone clay tokens were kept in sealed containers called *bullae*. To identify the contents, the shape of each token was imprinted on the outside of the container. The crucial part of Schmandt-Besserat's work was the discovery that the impressions of the tokens were graphically identical to the earliest form of what would become one of the most important early scripts: Sumerian cuneiform writing. In this way, her research formed a much-needed link between the earliest forms of writing and a later, fully fledged, written script.

Logographic, syllabic and alphabetic orthographies

Sumerian cuneiform writing: A logographic orthography

The Sumerians lived in southern Mesopotamia (modern-day Iraq). Excavations in this area, from sites at Uruk, Jemdet Nasr, Ur and Babylon, have brought to light traces of a great civilization, including thousands of clay tablets written in cuneiform script (see Figure 1.3). To produce this script, impressions were made in clay with a wedge made out of reeds that had a triangular tip (hence the name *cuneiform*, which derives from the Latin *cuneus*, meaning 'wedge'). This technique produced linear pictograms, because the wedge impression was the fundamental component.

Over time, however, writing became progressively more stylized and less pictorial, until only those who were trained and had knowledge of the script could decipher what the symbols meant. This early form of writing is logographic (derived from the Greek *logos*, meaning 'word') because one symbol represented each word. In adopting a rule-based approach in which the relationship between a symbol and its meaning was prescribed, the guesswork

Figure 1.3 Example of Sumerian cuneiform writing.

involved in interpreting semasiographic scripts was avoided; writing thus became an effective way of representing a multiplicity of meanings rather than being restricted to limited meanings in particular contexts.

In later writing, logographic systems were adapted to represent syllables and, later still, consonants and vowels. The development of syllabaries and alphabets is largely the product of borrowing from earlier logographic writing systems and changing them to suit the needs of a particular language or culture (Olson, 1989).

Akkadian: A syllabic orthography

One of the first true syllabaries, Akkadian was derived from the Sumerian script around 2800 BC. The Akkadian people of Mesopotamia adapted the cuneiform script to represent the sounds of the syllables in their own language, so the logographic cuneiform script evolved into a syllabic writing system.

The development of the alphabet

It is now generally agreed that the Phoenicians in Northern Syria used the first alphabetic writing system around 1500 BC; this was derived from a combination of adapted Egyptian hieroglyphics and the Akkadian script. In the Phoenician language the emphasis was on consonants rather than vowel sounds, and 26 of the 28 characters were consonants. For this reason, Phoenician is known as a consonantal alphabet.

The transition from consonantal to alphabetic writing occurred when these scripts were adapted for use in Greek. Like English and many other European languages, Greek is a language in which a change in vowel sounds changes the meaning of the word (e.g., *cat, cot, cut*); it is therefore important to represent those sounds in writing so that we can differentiate one word from another. To fill the 'vowel gap', Phoenician characters that represented sounds unknown in Greek were borrowed to represent vowels. It is this addition of vowel sounds that enabled the Greek script to become the root for many European languages, including English.

Contemporary writing systems

Figure 1.4 shows examples of contemporary logographic, syllabic and alphabetic writing systems (Chinese, Cherokee and Greek). Continued use of each type of script reflects to some extent the goodness-of-fit between a script and the language it is meant to represent.

Logographic script		Syllabic script		Alphabetic script	
Chinese		Cherokee		Greek	
木	*mu* tree	**G** *tsa*		α	*a*
茶	*chá* tea	**V** *tse*		ε	*e*
聞	*wén* to hear	**Iт** *tsi*		ϕ	*f*
海	*hai* sea	**G** *wa*		μ	*m*
中	*zhong* middle	**ɖ** *we*		π	*p*
		Ɵ *wi*		τ	*t*

Figure 1.4 Examples of logographic, syllabic and alphabetic scripts (adapted from Campbell, 1997).

Logographic writing systems

The early development of a strong written tradition in China has tended to preserve and maintain the initial logographic writing system, although 80–90 per cent of characters now include both a semantic element that provides information about the meaning of the character, and a phonetic element that provides information about its pronunciation (DeFrancis, 1989; Sampson, 1985; Zhou, 1978).

One reason why this combination of semantic and phonetic information within the character is so useful is because there are, on average, 11 homophones (words that sound the same but differ in meaning) for every single-syllable word in Chinese Mandarin (Beijing Language Institute, 1986). These homophonic words can be distinguished relatively easily on the basis of the visual cue provided by the semantic element of the character. Similarly, in English homophones are almost always visually distinguishable—for example, *pair, pare* and *pear; raise, raze* and *rays*.

Syllabic writing systems

There are many syllabic scripts, including Japanese, Korean, Hindi and Cherokee. Figure 1.4 shows examples of the Cherokee script in which 85 symbols are used to denote combinations of consonant–vowel sounds that comprise the syllables of the language. This syllabary is one of the most famous American Indian writing systems and was invented in 1821 by Sequoyah, a half-Cherokee Indian, for his native language. The simplicity of the writing system meant that it could be learned easily, and it was soon adopted throughout the Cherokee nation. Aside from its simplicity, a syllabary was ideally suited to the Cherokee language, in which concepts are represented by a series of prefixes and suffixes added to an original stem word.

Alphabetic writing systems

In the simplest and most straightforward alphabetic writing systems, such as Finnish or Turkish, each symbol or letter (grapheme) represents a single sound (phoneme) (Öney & Durgunoğlu, 1997; Seymour, Aro, & Erskine, 2003). In these languages 'sounding out' individual letters to read and pronounce them is a successful strategy. In Cahill and Karan's (2008) terms, these scripts might be seen as meeting the requirements of an effective writing system since they are linguistically transparent as well as being easy to teach and reproduce. However, this one-to-one match, where graphemes map onto phonemes and vice versa, is not common. In most alphabetic languages more intricate and unpredictable letter–sound relationships appear. For example:

1   Several letters (complex graphemes) may represent a single phoneme (e.g., in *light* and *sight*, the letters '*ght*' represent the final sound in the word).
2   Spelling of words may signal related lexical identities (e.g., *sign* and *signature* derive from the same orthographic root, as do *bomb* and *bombard*; see Venezky, 1970).
3   Spelling of words may provide a visual contrast for homophones (e.g., *pair, pear* and *pare*).
4   Letter–sound relationships may depend on the context in which they appear (e.g., a *tear* rolled down his cheek; a *tear* appeared on her sleeve).
5   Spelling may be simplified for morphological functions (e.g., adding an 's' to pluralize *robes* and *roses* is much simpler than writing *robz* and *rosiz*; see Ellis, 1993).

The degree to which such variations occur in a language reflects its *orthographic depth*. Shallow, or transparent, orthographies (such as Finnish) are at one extreme while deep, or opaque, orthographies (such as English) are at the other (see Table 1.1).

Seymour et al. (2003) suggested that the complexity of syllables in a language (i.e., its *linguistic complexity*) is also important in determining the level of its *orthographic* complexity. Most Romance languages, such as Italian and Spanish, have simple syllables consisting of consonants and vowels (CV syllables) with few initial or final consonant clusters, as exemplified by the words *pasta* and *costa*. In contrast, Germanic languages (e.g., German, Danish, English) have numerous closed CVC syllables and complex consonant clusters, as exemplified by the word *entschuldigen* in German. Given the number of sounds in complex syllables, it is not surprising that they are not easily represented in an alphabetic script and that they require more letters and more complex letter combinations.

Logically, it might seem better to explore the possibility of representing Germanic languages using a syllabic script. However, if we take English as an

Table 1.1 Classification of languages in accordance with orthographic depth and complexity of syllabic structure

Syllabic structure	Orthographic depth				
	Shallow ⟵			⟶	Deep
Simple	Finnish	Greek Italian Spanish	Portuguese	French	
Complex		German Norwegian Icelandic	Dutch Swedish	Danish	English

Adapted from Seymour, Aro, and Erskine (2003).

example, the number of possible syllables is huge. Frost (2005) noted that not only are there many possible syllable structures (CV, VC, CVC, CCVC, CVCC, etc.), there are also 24 consonant sounds and 15 vowel sounds. This means that one would need approximately 15,000 syllable symbols which would not exactly be effective as a means of representation. It therefore seems that some languages are more difficult to represent optimally, and some degree of 'lack of fit' is inevitable. However, it is worth noting that for English at least, the closeness of the relationship between what is said and what is written has waxed and waned across the centuries (Scragg, 1974). What tended to make letter–sound relationships (or the lack of them) more permanent was the introduction of the printing press in the fifteenth century followed by the publication of the first dictionaries in the sixteenth and seventeenth centuries.

The effect of these dictionaries was to establish 'correct' spellings, and later changes in pronunciation are therefore not reflected in current spelling practice. The divergence between earlier phonemic spellings and our current pronunciations is seen in many words that begin with a silent *h*; this was still pronounced in some words (such as *honest, honour* and *heir*) until the eighteenth century. Interestingly, the word *herb* is currently undergoing this divergence—in American English the *h* is no longer pronounced, while in British English it is still pronounced.

Contemporary research

It is apparent that, for a variety of historical reasons, some orthographies are considerably more complex than others, but as yet there is no formal measure of orthographic complexity. In an attempt to address this issue, Seymour and colleagues (2003) produced the classification shown in Table 1.1 following their survey of experts from several European countries (for a discussion of possible orthographic complexity metrics, see also Ziegler, Stone, & Jacobs, 1997).

Research has shown that the rate at which children learn to read (and the difficulties that dyslexic readers experience) corresponds approximately to the orthographic complexity of the language that they speak (see Caravolas, 2005; and Ziegler & Goswami, 2005, for reviews). The precise nature of this relationship and the reasons for it are explored in the chapters that follow.

This volume is divided into three sections: Section 1 considers the skills required for learning to read in different orthographies and the differences in developmental trajectory resulting from the nature of the mapping between spoken language and the writing system. Section 2 explores the way in which the symptoms and aetiology of dyslexia vary as a result of differences between orthographies. Section 3 shows how neuroimaging studies inform our understanding of the role of orthography in reading. A brief summary and overview of each section is given below.

Section 1: The development of reading skills in different orthographies

The first two chapters in Section 1 provide differing theoretical perspectives on the nature of the relationship between language and orthography and how this shapes children's progress in learning to read. Usha Goswami (chapter 2) presents a psycholinguistic grain size view of reading across languages. In this chapter she sets out a theoretical framework that seeks to explain how as children acquire literacy they form mappings between their knowledge of the phonological units, or grains, of language (syllables, rimes and phonemes) and the way the language is written. Only once children have developed an effective understanding of how component sounds in their spoken language map onto units of their written language can their reading progress success-fully. The framework therefore provides a way of explaining differences in the ease and speed of reading acquisition across orthographies. A key assump-tion is that children develop an awareness of the larger grains of words first (i.e., syllables and rime) and then progressively of smaller grains (i.e., phon-emes and individual letter sounds). Goswami argues that this 'large-to-small progression' in awareness is universal across languages although there may be variation in the speed at which it occurs.

Lynne Duncan's approach in the following chapter (chapter 3) shares much with that taken by Goswami. Her review of the literature also high-lights ways in which reading development is shaped by the nature and com-plexity of mappings between language and orthography. However, she takes issue with one of Goswami's key assumptions—that progression in awareness follows a uniform pathway from large to small phonemic units. On the basis of her research examining acquisition of skills in the first year of reading across several European languages, Duncan argues that very different 'grain size' routes are taken by speakers of different languages. For example, despite their relatively poor awareness of syllables and rime, English speakers' awareness of initial phonemes is just as good as that of their French, Icelandic, Portuguese and Spanish counterparts. This suggests that English readers may proceed straight to awareness of smaller grain sizes without developing anything more than a superficial awareness of larger units. She therefore concludes that, rather than there being a universal 'large-to-small progression', learning paths in phonological development are shaped by native language, orthography and reading instruction.

In attempting to reconcile the data reported in these two chapters, it should be noted that apparent differences in findings and subsequent theory can hinge on the way in which children's knowledge and understanding of phon-ology is assessed. At the heart of the debate between Duncan and Goswami is Duncan's use of tasks designed to assess *implicit* (holistic) phonological understanding and *explicit* (analytic) phonological understanding. Duncan argues that English speakers develop only an implicit understanding of larger units before progressing to an explicit understanding of phonemes. No such distinction is made by Goswami. For this reason, it is worth looking at

Duncan's helpful table of phonological tasks (Table 3.2) and comparing the implicit and explicit tasks before reading both chapters carefully and drawing your own conclusions. Whatever conclusion you come to, it is worth bearing in mind that *both* viewpoints are influential in shaping current views of reading acquisition.

The remaining chapters in this section describe research examining differences in rates of reading acquisition that result from orthographic variation. Maria Ktori and Nicola Pitchford used a visual search paradigm to simulate how individuals scan words to identify letters and their positions (chapter 4). They showed that as children learn to read, a specialized system for doing this quickly emerges that is shaped by the orthography to which the children are exposed. When Ktori and Pitchford compared readers of Greek (a very transparent orthography) with readers of English, they found systematic differences in patterns of visual search that became progressively more marked as reading skills developed (see Figures 4.4 and 4.5). These patterns of visual search appear to reflect differences in underlying orthographic processing. Skilled English readers tend to search for, and identify, the first and last letters in a word; this is in line with whole-word parallel (or lexical) processing. However, while they are still learning to read, English children rely more heavily on identifying letters serially from left to right. This pattern is much more similar to that adopted by Greek readers, who tend to favour sequential decoding because of the transparency of the Greek orthography. The particular balance of processing in visual search is dependent on the demands of the orthography being used. These findings pose a challenge to existing models of letter position encoding, which assume either serial position encoding or parallel encoding. This chapter is a good example of how comparing and contrasting different orthographies helps to advance our understanding of the fundamental cognitive processes underpinning reading development. It also demonstrates that the orthographic mapping process requires specialist visual, as well as linguistic, processing. Not unrelated is the finding by Bosse, Tainturier, and Valdois (2007) that dyslexic children may have deficits in their visual attention span. The next logical step in research using the visual search paradigm may therefore be to explore the role of visual attention span in different orthographies in order to investigate whether or not this is related to the specialist visual search processing implicated in Ktori and Pitchford's study.

The research reported by Rick Hanley in chapter 5 resulted from the situation where two languages coexist in one geographical area. In Wales, some children receive reading instruction in Welsh (a transparent orthography), while others receive instruction in English. Hanley found that children learning the transparent Welsh orthography did better than their peers on phoneme awareness tasks, and they learned to read more quickly. He argues that such differences cannot be easily attributed to cultural differences since the children are drawn from the same area of Wales. Of particular interest is the finding that, in the original longitudinal sample, the most profound differences between Welsh- and English-speaking children emerged in the lowest quartile of readers. This suggests that children who experience reading difficulties have more trouble creating mappings between language and orthography when the orthography is inconsistent and opaque. This suggestion was borne out when, in a neat addition to the original work, another sample was tested several years later, after the development of a national phonics-based literacy strategy for English speakers. By this time, the lag in performance between the poorest readers in English and their Welsh counterparts had diminished considerably. Thus, while poor readers may encounter greater difficulties with less consistent and more complex orthographies, these difficulties can at least be partially overcome by intensive phonics instruction.

The final chapter in this section (chapter 6), by Terezinha Nunes, Diana Burman, Deborah Evans and Daniel Bell, considers the case of children who are deaf. These children have particular difficulty creating mappings between language and orthography, although, as this chapter shows, they may be able to use the indirect connection between oral and written language via meaning. Morphemes are the units in words that convey meaning. For example, the word *cars* consists of two morphemes, a stem *car* and the affix *s* to indicate the plural. The first study that Nunes and colleagues report shows that deaf children's understanding of morphology makes an important contribution to their reading skills. In the second study, children were given a short intervention consisting of exercises to promote their awareness of morphemes, along with specially designed story books. This enhanced not only the children's use of morphology in spelling but also their reading comprehension and writing skills. These findings have two major implications. First, that a simple intervention can substantially help deaf children to strengthen the tenuous and uncertain connection between British Sign Language and English orthography. Second, that we access orthography not only via phonology, but also via morphology. This latter finding is entirely congruent with other research that emphasizes the role of morphology in reading, particularly as children progress beyond the initial stages of learning (Castles & Nation, 2008; Nunes & Bryant, 2006, 2009).

To summarize, Section 1 provides an overview of current theoretical perspectives on how orthography shapes the rate and trajectory of reading development. It also shows that our ability to deal with orthography may rely not only on creating mappings between phonology and orthography, but also on the degree to which our visual processing and morphemic skills map onto the orthography that we use. The chapters by Hanley (chapter 5) and by Nunes and colleagues (chapter 6) also show how effective phonological and morphological interventions can be in determining final outcomes in learning to read.

Section 2: Developmental dyslexia in different orthographies

A great deal of what we know about the nature and incidence of developmental dyslexia comes from studies in English and may therefore be as idiosyncratic as the orthography from which it is derived. Section 2 broadens this perspective.

Nicola Brunswick begins this section (chapter 7) with a review of skilled and impaired reading in different orthographies. Initially the orthographic depth hypothesis suggested that readers of transparent orthographies such as Spanish or Italian rely primarily on sub-lexical phonological recoding to read words, while readers of opaque languages such as Danish or English are much more likely to use whole-word lexical strategies (e.g., Katz & Frost, 1992). However, research findings have now accumulated which show that all readers, irrespective of orthography, use a combination of lexical and sub-lexical processing. This has led to the development of weaker versions of the orthographic depth hypothesis. The latest instantiation of this is the psycholinguistic grain size theory outlined by Goswami in chapter 2. Brunswick then presents evidence to show that the incidence of dyslexia depends upon a combination of the degree of granularity of the language and the transparency of the orthography (see Figure 7.4). This sets the scene for the remaining chapters in this section, which explore the nature and incidence of dyslexia in Spanish (Davies & Cuetos, chapter 8), Italian (Paizi, Zocolotti, & Burani, chapter 9), Chinese (Su, Klingebiel, & Weekes, chapter 10) and other deep and shallow languages (Everatt et al., chapter 11).

The findings of both Davies and Cuetos and Paizi and colleagues add weight to Brunswick's contention that readers of transparent orthographies use a combination of sub-lexical and lexical processing. Dyslexic readers of Spanish and Italian do read more slowly, but they also show the lexical effects that are evident in more skilled readers, so these findings suggest that reading in Italian and Spanish is affected by morphology and semantics as well as by phonology. In this context, Davies and Cuetos' suggestion that there is a convergence in processing mechanisms across orthographies in adult readers seems plausible. It is apparent from the research presented here that adult readers, irrespective of orthography, combine multiple forms of representation and processing to produce skilled reading. However, it is clear from Su and colleagues' chapter that the balance of processing is likely to be different for the reading of logographic scripts such as Chinese. They argue that while there are similarities between dyslexia in Chinese and dyslexia in alphabetic languages, the difficulties experienced by these two groups of dyslexic readers cannot be identical because the orthographies are so different. For those of us used to dealing only with alphabetic scripts, the sheer complexity of the mappings required between language and orthography in Chinese is bewildering. The table describing Chinese writing (Table 10.1) is particularly helpful to the reader and, along with the description in the text, provides fascinating insights into the challenge of reading in Chinese.

In contrast to previous chapters, the authors of these three chapters situate their findings within connectionist models of reading such as the dual-route cascade (DRC) model (Coltheart, Rastle, Perry, Langdon, & Ziegler, 2001), the connectionist dual processing (CDP+) model (Perry, Ziegler, & Zorzi,

2007), the polysyllabic multiple-trace (ACV98) model (Ans, Carbonnel, & Valdois, 1998) and, for reading in Chinese, the lexical constituency (LC) model (Perfetti, Liu, & Tan, 2005). Davies and Cuetos' review of connectionist theories, combined with their developmental approach, helps the reader to bring together these perspectives on the reading of both skilled adults and early learners.

The strain of existing connectionist models is almost palpable as these researchers seek to explain their findings. It is therefore not surprising that Davies and Cuetos put forward a model that combines connectionist principles with the self-teaching mechanism proposed by Share (1995) through which language-orthographic mappings emerge to allow successful reading. Su and colleagues utilize a new model of reading in Chinese to explain their findings (see Klingebiel & Weekes, 2008): this model allows for the complex representations of orthographic, phonological and semantic (lexical and morphemic) information in Chinese to interact to produce speech. It is clear that one of the challenges ahead in reading research is to provide computational models which are more developmental in their perspective and which specify more fully the nature and interaction of developing representational frameworks for reading.

In the final chapter of this section, Everatt and colleagues report an examination of dyslexia across several orthographies including English, Hungarian, Arabic, Chinese and Herero. While the measurement of phonological skills appears to be important in predicting reading difficulties across a variety of scripts, it is also clear that predictors of reading difficulty vary according to the nature of the script being learned. When bilingual children with reading difficulties were simultaneously learning to read one transparent and one opaque orthography, the predictors of literacy deficits in the less transparent language re-emerged as predictors of literacy in the more transparent language. Moreover, phonological skills in one language appeared to be good predictors of reading ability in both languages. This finding raises the issue of the degree to which common processes are being used in each language and the extent to which common representational structures—rather than individual representations—support bilingual reading.

The final section of this volume shows how neuroimaging research, by combining behavioural data with brain scanning (fMRI, PET and MEG), has been able to address these issues.

Section 3: Neuroimaging studies of reading in different orthographies

In a review of neuroimaging studies of skilled reading and dyslexia across languages, Paulesu, Brunswick and Paganelli show that several areas of the brain support reading. This multi-component reading system appears to be similar across languages although the extent to which different brain areas are implicated depends on the transparency of the orthography. This finding reflects a common theme running through the chapters in this book. A good example of this is provided by Paulesu et al.'s (2000) study, which compared PET scan data from Italian and English participants during reading. While both groups showed common activation in the classical language areas of the perisylvian cortex, Italian readers showed greater activation of the left planum temporale, which has been implicated in phonological processing. English readers, in contrast, showed greater activation in the left posterior inferior temporal cortex and the anterior inferior frontal gyrus, areas associated with word retrieval during reading and naming. Neuroimaging studies have also been able to provide convergent evidence of a phonological deficit underlying the reading deficits in dyslexia. Several studies have provided evidence for abnormal activation of, and connectivity between, areas of the brain associated with phonological processing, naming and sub-lexical processing. Also apparent is the brain's ability to respond to reading remediation. Paulesu and colleagues review a number of studies in which improved reading performance has been reflected in increased activation of associated brain regions. These findings are encouraging, suggesting that reading difficulties are not immutable.

The final chapter, by Brendan Weekes (chapter 13), shows that brain imaging can help to tease out the nature of lexical processing in alphabetic and non-alphabetic scripts in a way that has not previously been possible in behavioural studies of word recognition. One of the great debates has been the extent to which the speed and accuracy of word reading are determined by the frequency with which we have previously encountered the word (e.g., *say*, a frequent word vs. *sty*, an infrequent word) and the age at which we acquired it (e.g., *sun*, an early-acquired word vs. *sop*, a late-acquired word; Morrison, Ellis, & Quinlan, 1992; Oldfield & Wingfield, 1965). In addition, the extent to which word frequency and age of acquisition effects are independent of one another (since typically words that are more frequent are also those that we are likely to acquire earlier) has also been the subject of much debate. Weekes reports work that he and his colleagues have conducted in which they capitalize on the nature of Chinese orthography to vary frequency and age of acquisition orthogonally. When fMRI was used in conjunction with a lexical decision task, frequency and age of acquisition showed independent effects on brain activity during reading, with activation in different loci for words that differ in frequency compared to words that differ in age of acquisition. These findings are comparable to those reported for German by Fiebach, Friederici, Müller, von Cramon, and Hernandez (2003).

Weekes's chapter also explores the mapping between orthography and phonology in Chinese. His findings suggest that orthographic and phonological representations may be underpinned, at least in part, by different neural mechanisms in Chinese readers' brains, making the development of connectivity between loci important in reading acquisition (see Paulesu, Frith, Snowling, & Gallagher, 1996, for an early brain scanning study showing the importance of brain connectivity in reading). He draws on these findings to inform current models of word reading and picture naming in Chinese.

The themes of localized neural activation and inter-region connectivity, which are central to current brain-based explanations of learning, emerge strongly from both chapters in this section, and it is clear that they will be at the heart of future studies examining reading acquisition across languages (Goswami, 2008).

Conclusion

The research reported here demonstrates the rapid advances that have been made in recent years in our understanding of how reading develops; it is a current collection of work in a tradition of cross-linguistic studies of reading that has spanned over three decades. This cross-linguistic thread can be traced in research collections from the 1980s (Henderson, 1984; Kavanagh & Venezky, 1980), the 1990s (Frost & Katz, 1992; Harris & Hatano, 1999; Taylor & Olson, 1995) and through the 2000s (Joshi & Aaron, 2006; Smythe, Everatt, & Salter, 2004). As we have already noted, current theoretical debates, new methodologies and ever-widening orthographic populations are included in this volume.

As well as indicating what we already know, this book also specifies where further research is required. In our view, there are four main areas that need to be addressed. These are:

Theory development

The work reported in this book shows that cross-language research has the potential to inform theoretical debates, particularly with respect to connectionist models (see chapters by Davies and Cuetos, Paizi et al. and Su et al.). A focus on research that specifically tests the assumptions of opposing models will help to develop our theoretical (as well as practical) understanding of reading. Examples of such research are now beginning to emerge (see, for example, Rastle, Havelka, Wydell, Coltheart, & Besner, 2009).

Information about the later stages of reading development

Research has traditionally focused on the very earliest stages of reading development, but this leaves a large gap in our understanding of how the child who can slowly read a few words becomes the skilled adult reader who reads automatically and effortlessly. This gap is now beginning to be filled by research examining morphemic and orthographic development (see Castles & Nation, 2008; Nunes & Bryant, 2006, 2009; Nunes et al., chapter 6).

Adopting a flexible and multi-causal approach

What is apparent from the research reported in this volume is that tactics that individuals adopt to help them to read are based on a multi-strategic and problem-solving approach. While developing an effective mapping between phonology and orthography is clearly critical, it is also apparent that other basic processes support our reading. An example of this is the nuanced visual scanning developed by readers in response to different orthographies (see Ktori and Pitchford, chapter 4). Similarly, it is still an open question as to whether or not the learning mechanisms that underlie visual and verbal paired-associate learning contribute to learning, particularly in languages with opaque and complex orthographies (for a discussion, see Lervåg, Bråten, & Hulme, 2009).

Reliable and replicated fMRI studies

Brain scanning techniques such as fMRI clearly have enormous potential, not only to provide evidence in support of existing behavioural data but also to extend our understanding of the brain mechanisms involved in reading. In reading research, as in other areas of psychology, there is a need to show reliable and replicable findings from these studies which typically have a small number of participants and large assumptions built into the data analysis.

Research in all of these areas is only likely to be meaningful if it goes beyond the idiosyncratic and constrained confines of English orthography to embrace the advantages that can be found in comparing and contrasting reading and its development across languages.

References

Ans, B., Carbonnel, S., & Valdois, S. (1998). A connectionist multi-trace memory model of polysyllabic word reading. *Psychological Review, 105*, 678–723.

Beijing Language Institute. (1986). *Xiandai hanyu pinlu cidian* [Modern Chinese frequency dictionary]. Beijing, China: Beijing Language Institute Press.

Bosse, M.-L., Tainturier, M. J., & Valdois, S. (2007). Developmental dyslexia: The visual attention span deficit hypothesis. *Cognition, 104*, 198–230.

Cahill, M., & Karan, E. (2008). *Factors in designing effective orthographies for unwritten languages* (SIL Electronic Working Papers 2008–001: 16). Cahill, Karan, & SIL International. http://www.sil.org/silewp/abstract.asp?ref=2008-001

Campbell, G. L. (1997). *Handbook of scripts and alphabets*. London: Routledge.

Caravolas, M. (2005). The nature and causes of dyslexia in different languages. In M. J. Snowling & C. Hulme (Eds.), *The science of reading: A handbook* (pp. 336–356). Oxford, UK: Blackwell.

Castles, A., & Nation, K. (2008). Becoming a good orthographic reader. *Journal of Research in Reading, 31*, 1–7.

Coltheart, M., Rastle, K., Perry, C., Langdon, R., & Ziegler, J. (2001). The DRC model: A model of visual word recognition and reading aloud. *Psychological Review, 108*, 204–256.

Coulmas, F. (1989). *The writing systems of the world*. Oxford, UK: Blackwell.

DeFrancis, J. (1989). *Visible speech: The diverse oneness of writing systems*. Honolulu, HI: University of Hawai'i Press.

Diringer, D. (1947). *The alphabet: A key to the history of mankind.* London: Hutchinson.

Ellis, A. W. (1993). *Reading, writing and dyslexia: A cognitive analysis* (2nd ed.). Hove, UK: Lawrence Erlbaum Associates.

Fiebach, C. J., Friederici, A. D., Müller, K., von Cramon, D. Y., & Hernandez, A. E. (2003). Distinct brain representations for early and late learned words. *NeuroImage, 19,* 1627–1637.

Frost, R. (2005). Orthographic systems and skilled word recognition processes in reading. In M. J. Snowling & C. Hulme (Eds.), *The science of reading: A handbook* (pp. 272–295). Oxford, UK: Blackwell.

Frost, R., & Katz, L. (Eds.). (1992). *Orthography, phonology, morphology and meaning.* Amsterdam: Elsevier.

Gelb, I. J. (1963). *A study of writing* (2nd ed.). London: The British Library.

Goswami, U. (2008). Reading, complexity and the brain. *Literacy, 42,* 67–74.

Harris, M., & Hatano, G. (Eds.). (1999). *Learning to read and write: A cross-linguistic perspective.* Cambridge, UK: Cambridge University Press.

Henderson, L. (1984). *Orthographies and reading: Perspectives from cognitive psychology, neuropsychology and linguistics.* London: Lawrence Erlbaum Associates.

Joshi, R. M., & Aaron, P. G. (2006). *Handbook of orthography and literacy.* Mahwah, NJ: Lawrence Erlbaum Associates, Inc.

Katz, L., & Frost, R. (1992). The reading process is different for different orthographies: The orthographic depth hypothesis. In R. Frost & L. Katz (Eds.), *Orthography, phonology, morphology and meaning* (pp. 67–84). Amsterdam: Elsevier.

Kavanagh, J. F., & Venezky, R. L. (Eds.). (1980). *Orthography, reading, and dyslexia.* Baltimore: University Park Press.

Klingebiel, K., & Weekes, B. S. (2008). Developmental dyslexia in Chinese: Behavioural, genetic and neuropsychological issues. In S. P. Law, B. S. Weekes, & A. Wong (Eds.), *Disorders of speech and language in Chinese* (pp. 220–273). San Diego, CA: Plural Publishing.

Lervåg, A., Bråten, I., & Hulme, C. (2009). The cognitive and linguistic foundations of early reading development: A Norwegian latent variable longitudinal study. *Developmental Psychology, 45,* 764–781.

Mallery, G. (1893). Picture-writing of the American Indians. *Tenth Annual Report of the Bureau of Ethnology to the Secretary of the Smithsonian Institution, 1888–1889.* Washington, DC: US Government Printing Office.

Morrison, C. M., Ellis, A. W., & Quinlan, P. T. (1992). Age of acquisition, not word frequency, affect object naming, not object recognition. *Memory and Cognition, 20,* 705–714.

Nunes, T., & Bryant, P. (2006). *Improving literacy through teaching morphemes.* London: Routledge.

Nunes, T., & Bryant, P. (2009). *Children's reading and spelling: Beyond the first steps.* London: Wiley.

Oldfield, R. C., & Wingfield, A. (1965). Response latencies in naming objects. *Quarterly Journal of Experimental Psychology, 17,* 273–291.

Olson, D. (1989). *The world on paper: The conceptual and cognitive implications of writing and reading.* Cambridge, UK: Cambridge University Press.

Öney, B., & Durgunoğlu, A. Y. (1997). Beginning to read in Turkish: A phonologically transparent orthography. *Applied Psycholinguistics, 18,* 1–15.

Paulesu, E., Frith, U., Snowling, M., & Gallagher, A. (1996). Is developmental dyslexia a disconnection syndrome? Evidence from PET scanning. *Brain, 119,* 142–157.

Paulesu, E., McCrory, E., Fazio, F., Menoncello, L., Brunswick, N., Cappa, S. F., et al. (2000). A cultural effect on brain function. *Nature Neuroscience, 3,* 91–96.

Perfetti, C. A., Liu, Y., & Tan, L. H. (2005). The lexical constituency model: Some implications of research on Chinese for general theories of reading. *Psychological Review, 12,* 43–59.

Perry, C., Ziegler, J. C., & Zorzi, M. (2007). Nested incremental modeling in the development of computational theories: The CDP+ model of reading aloud. *Psychological Review, 114,* 273–315.

Rastle, K., Havelka, J., Wydell, T. N., Coltheart, M., & Besner, D. (2009). The cross-script length effect: Further evidence challenging PDP models of reading aloud. *Journal of Experimental Psychology: Learning, Memory, and Cognition, 35,* 238–246.

Robinson, A. (2009, May). Decoding antiquity: What do you do when you dig up an ancient inscription but don't know what it means? *New Scientist, 202,* 24–30.

Sampson, G. (1985). *Writing systems: A linguistic introduction.* London: Hutchinson.

Schmandt-Besserat, D. (1978, June). The earliest precursor of writing. *Scientific American, 238,* 50–59.

Schmandt-Besserat, D. (1979). An archaic recording system in the Uruk-Jemdet Nasr period. *American Journal of Archaeology, 83,* 19–48.

Schoolcraft, H. R. (1851). *Historical and statistical information respecting the history, condition and prospects of the Indian tribes of the United States.* Philadelphia: Lippincott, Grambo & Company.

Scragg, D. J. (1974). *A history of English spelling.* Manchester, UK: Manchester University Press.

Seymour, P. H. K., Aro, M., & Erskine, J. M. (2003). Foundation literacy acquisition in European orthographies. *British Journal of Psychology, 94,* 143–174.

Share, D. L. (1995). Phonological recoding and self-teaching: Sine qua non of reading acquisition. *Cognition, 55,* 151–218.

Shargorodskii, S. (1895). Ob lukagirskikh pis'menakh [On Yukaghir writing]. *Zemlevedenie, 2–3,* 135–148.

Smythe, I., Everatt, J., & Salter, R. (Eds.). (2004). *The international book of dyslexia.* London: Wiley.

Taylor, I., & Olson, D. R. (1995). *Scripts and literacy: Reading and learning to read alphabets, syllabaries, and characters.* Dordrecht, The Netherlands: Kluwer Academic.

Unger, J. M. (2003). *Ideogram: Chinese characters and the myth of disembodied meaning.* Honolulu, HI: University of Hawai'i Press.

Venezky, R. L. (1970). *The structure of English orthography.* Mouton, The Netherlands: The Hague.

Zhou, Y. G. (1978). To what extent are the "phonetics" of present-day Chinese characters still phonetic? *Zhonggou Yuwen, 146,* 172–177.

Ziegler, J. C., & Goswami, U. (2005). Reading acquisition, developmental dyslexia, and skilled reading across languages: A psycholinguistic grain size theory. *Psychological Bulletin, 131,* 3–29.

Ziegler, J. C., Stone, G. O., & Jacobs, A. M. (1997). What's the pronunciation for -OUGH and the spelling for /u/? A database for computing feedforward and feedback inconsistency in English. *Behavior Research Methods, Instruments, and Computers, 29,* 600–618.

2 A psycholinguistic grain size view of reading acquisition across languages

Usha Goswami

Introduction

The 'learning problem' faced by a child acquiring reading is similar across languages, even though a striking variety of rather different symbol systems have been invented to represent spoken language. These symbol systems include alphabetic systems like English and Italian, and character-based systems like Japanese and Chinese. We call these visual codes for spoken language *orthographies*, and the efficient use of these visual codes *reading*. Efficient readers can look at pages of symbols and understand the communicative messages intended by the writers of the symbols.

To read, the child essentially has to understand speech when it is written down. Although reading must be taught, reading acquisition also requires some cognitive prerequisites on the part of the child. These cognitive prerequisites are rather similar across languages. Factors that affect the development of speech processing also affect the acquisition of reading. Examples of such factors include vocabulary development, structural aspects of vocabularies in different languages (e.g., word length, and the ways in which words sound similar to each other), individual differences in awareness of the phonological structure or sound-structure of words (the sounds comprising the words, and the order in which they occur) and characteristics of syllable structure in different languages. Although skilled readers appear to access meaning directly from visual codes, in fact phonological activation is mandatory for both the beginning reader and the skilled reader (see Ziegler & Goswami, 2005). This is because the orthographic lexicon is parasitic on the speech processing system (the brain has evolved not to read but to understand communicative messages conveyed by spoken language). This mandatory phonological activation is revealed, for example, by brain imaging work on the *visual word form area* (VWFA; Cohen & Dehaene, 2004; see also chapter 12, this volume). This area of visual cortex stores links between the visual form of a word (orthography) and its spoken sound (phonology).

These links can be either at the whole-word level or at sub-word levels, called here psycholinguistic *grain sizes* (e.g., many English words can be segmented into syllables, and so the VWFA will store orthographic representations for these syllables as well as for the whole words). As the development of the VWFA depends on orthographic learning, so it will also reflect the orthographic units used in different languages. For example, Japanese characters (called *kana*) represent individual syllables, and so the VWFA for Japanese readers will store kana–syllable connections. The alphabet represents smaller sound elements in spoken words called *phonemes*, and so the VWFA will learn both grapheme–phoneme connections (e.g., the written letters/letter strings *ph* and *f* to the spoken sound 'f'), body–rime connections (e.g., the written letters *eek* and *eak* to the spoken sound 'eek') and orthography–syllable connections (the written words *beak* and *break* to the spoken words 'beak' and 'break'). Even within alphabetic orthographies, there are differences in the consistency of correspondence between symbols and sounds (*orthographic transparency*): Italian has high transparency as there are one-to-one mappings between graphemes and phonemes, English has low transparency as there are many-to-one mappings between graphemes and phonemes. These different lexical, phonological and structural factors will all contribute to explaining cross-language differences in reading acquisition by children and are captured by psycholinguistic grain size theory (Ziegler & Goswami, 2005).

Phonological awareness and reading

Phonological awareness prior to reading

As the brain evolved to understand communicative messages conveyed by spoken language, developmental aspects of the acquisition of spoken language will affect the acquisition of reading. One key factor is phonological awareness, which is the child's ability to detect and manipulate the component sounds that comprise words, at different grain sizes. As noted, the development of phonological awareness prior to acquiring reading is affected by a number of factors. These include structural factors to do with the vocabularies that comprise different languages, structural factors to do with how syllables are made in different languages and speech perception factors that contribute to individual differences in acquiring phonological awareness.

Prior to the teaching of reading, phonological awareness develops as a natural part of language acquisition. In order to acquire spoken language, babies and children need to learn the sounds and combinations of sounds that are permissible in the language that they are learning. As they learn these sounds, their brains develop *phonological representations* of the sound structure of individual words. Phonological representations depend on both language comprehension and language production, as the act of producing words yourself is important for representing phonological structure. Both processes require extensive development, and between the ages of 1 and 6 years children acquire more than 14,000 words (Dollaghan, 1994). The acquisition process is supported by powerful neural learning mechanisms, such as *statistical learning*, where the infant brain effectively computes probabilities, such as conditional probabilities, between the sounds that make up the words that it hears. Hence it will learn that the sound sequence 'atn' is more likely to occur at a word boundary (e.g., 'at night') than within a word. The individual sound elements comprising words that we call *phonemes* depend on physical changes in the speech signal, such as devoicing (when the vocal cords do not vibrate). However, the points in the speech signal where languages place phonetic boundaries are not random (Kuhl, 1986). These acoustic changes are also distinguished by animals, which can perform phoneme categorization tasks even though they do not speak a language (Kuhl, 2004). This may explain why at birth infants are sensitive to the acoustic boundaries that correlate with phoneme boundaries (e.g., the spoken 'b' versus 'd') for *all* the phonemes used in human languages. Rapid sensory learning during the first year then leads the infant brain to specialize in the phonemes particular to their language. The infants are tracking the distributional properties of the sounds in the language/s that they hear, using implicit statistical learning, and are learning the acoustic features that co-occur regularly together. These relative *distributional frequencies* then yield the sound categories that we approximate with the term *phonemes* (Kuhl, 2004).

Infants also need to group together the phonemes that comprise individual words and to learn which phonemes belong to one word and which phonemes belong to the next word. The rules that govern the sequences of phonemes used to make words in a particular language are called *phonotactics*. By tracking the transitional probabilities between different phonemes, infants learn the phonotactics of their language, and this is also well under way during the first year of life (e.g., Jusczyk & Aslin, 1995). Phonotactic learning is facilitated by prosodic cues (speech rhythm and stress), as changes in stress help infants to pick out word boundaries (Echols, 1996). We talk to babies in a particular way (called *motherese*, or *infant-directed speech*). Infant-directed speech exaggerates prosodic cues, and this appears to have a learning function. It also uses heightened pitch, increased duration and exaggerated rhythm and intonation to help babies to pick out words in the speech stream (e.g., Fernald & Mazzie, 1991). Prosodic cues are also important for phonotactic learning because when words are multi-syllabic, these cues carry important information about *how* sounds are ordered into words. Experimental research has shown that by the end of the first year infants are developing phonological representations of potential word forms that encode both lexical stress (e.g., that *doctor* has stronger stress on the first syllable) and segmental information (e.g., the individual sound elements in *doctor*; see Curtin, Mintz, & Christiansen, 2005).

Structural vocabulary factors that affect phonological development

Prior to reading, a challenge to the learning brain is posed by the massive number of vocabulary items acquired by children. Each word in the mental lexicon will have a unique sound and a unique meaning. Sometimes meaning will depend on stress alone (e.g., *CONtent* and *conTENT* share the same phonemes but have different meanings, which are conveyed by stressing). More usually, changes in meaning are signalled by changes in one or more phonemes comprising the word form. Hence words that sound highly similar phonologically, such as *back* and *bag*, or *dip* and *tip*, must be represented as distinct forms. Language-specific factors based on the structure of the words comprising spoken vocabulary can help to explain why some words are more difficult to represent phonologically than others. Two important language-specific factors are *sonority profile* and *phonological neighbourhood density*. Sonority profile refers to the types of sounds in words. Vowels are the most sonorant sounds that we can make, followed in decreasing order by glides (e.g., /w/), liquids (e.g., /l/), nasals (e.g., /n/) and obstruents or plosive sounds (e.g., /p/). Phonological neighbours are words that sound similar to each other, usually because they differ by one phoneme (Luce, Pisoni, & Goldinger, 1990). For example, the neighbours of the target word *ram* include *ramp, am* and *rim*. If many words resemble the target, the neighbourhood is said to be dense; if few words resemble the target, the neighbourhood is said to be sparse. Both sonority profile and phonological neighbourhood density affect the development of phonological representations.

For example, French is a more sonorant language than English. Whereas the majority of syllables in English (almost 40 per cent) end with obstruents, the majority of syllables in French (almost 50 per cent) either end in liquids or have no final consonant phoneme/s (coda) at all. Regarding phonological neighbourhood density, an example of a dense neighbourhood in English is words that rhyme with *seen* (e.g., *keen, lean, mean*), while an example of a sparse neighbourhood in English is words that rhyme with *love* (e.g., *shove, glove, Guv*). Words with many neighbours tend to have high-probability phonotactics (Vitevitch, Luce, Pisoni, & Auer, 1999). Experiments in psycholinguistics show that children develop better phonological awareness of words in dense neighbourhoods (e.g., De Cara & Goswami, 2003) and also retain words in dense neighbourhoods better in phonological memory tasks (e.g., Thomson, Richardson, & Goswami, 2005). Density in English is intimately connected with rhyme because English has lots of words that rhyme with each other: typically, around 60 per cent of words in a dense phonological neighbourhood will rhyme (De Cara & Goswami, 2002). Rhyme awareness is a very important aspect of phonological awareness in English (e.g., Bradley & Bryant, 1983). Hence structural linguistic factors linked to vocabulary such as sonority profile and neighbourhood density affect the development of phonological awareness during the pre-school period.

Syllable structure effects on phonological development in different languages

Syllable structure refers to the number of sound elements that comprise a syllable in a particular language. These sound elements can be either consonants (C) or vowels (V). The simplest syllable is a single vowel, but usually syllables are called *simple* when they are CV units, and *complex* when they comprise a number of C and V units. In English, single syllables can be V (*a*), CV (*go*), CVC (*cat*), CCVC (*pram*), CVCC (*hold*), CCVCC (*stamp*), CCCVC (*spread*) and CCCVCC (*sprained*). For many of the world's languages, the most frequent syllable type is CV. Languages like Japanese, Chinese, Spanish, Italian, Finnish and Turkish contain predominantly CV syllables. In other languages, like English and German, syllable structure is more complex. The most frequent syllable type in English is CVC: this structure accounts for 43 per cent of monosyllables (e.g., *tip, dog, bowl*; see De Cara & Goswami, 2002). There are also many CCVC syllables in English (15 per cent of monosyllables, e.g., *trip, spin*), CVCC syllables (21 per cent of monosyllables, e.g., *fast, jump*) and some CCVCC syllables (6 per cent, e.g., *crust*). Although a language like German has fewer monosyllables overall (approximately 1400 compared to approximately 4000 for English), phonological structure is similar. German has syllables with complex onsets, like *Pflaume* [*plum*], and with complex codas, like *Sand* [*sand*].

A priori, it seems plausible that it would be easier to become *phonologically aware* of sounds in syllables that have a simple structure (e.g., consonant–vowel or CV) than of sounds in syllables that have a complex structure (e.g., CCVCC). *A priori*, it should also be easier to become phonologically aware of the constituent sounds in syllables when consonant phonemes are less sonorant (e.g., *at* should be easier to segment than *am*). Although both predictions are broadly true, they apply in general to the grain size of the phoneme. Otherwise, cross-language studies show more similarities than differences in the development of phonological awareness. This is because phonological awareness develops at three different linguistic levels: the grain size of the *syllable*, the grain size of *onset-rime* (the onset comprises any sounds before the vowel, such as the /tr/ sound in *trip*; the rime comprises the vowel and any following sounds, such as the /amp/ sound in *stamp*) and the grain size of the *phoneme*. According to linguistic theory, each syllable in a word can be decomposed into onsets, rimes and phonemes in a hierarchical fashion (e.g., Treiman, 1989). This is shown in Figure 2.1. To find the onset-rime division of the syllable, the sound pattern of the word must be divided at the vowel. For English, words like *seat, sweet* and *street* all share the same rime sound but have different-length onsets. The onset of *seat* is /s/, the onset of *sweet* is /sw/ and the onset of *street* is /str/. These onsets comprise one, two and three phonemes, respectively, and the rime pattern (*eet*) comprises two phonemes. For English syllables, further segmentation of onsets and rimes is usually required to reach the grain size of the phoneme. Contrast this with

Syllable

Onset-rime

Phonemes

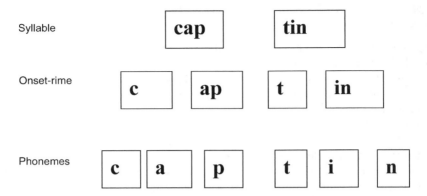

Figure 2.1 Schematic depiction of the hierarchical structure of the syllable, illustrated using the sounds in the spoken word *captain*.

languages like Spanish and Italian, where syllable structure is simple. When syllables are CV units, onsets, rimes and phonemes are equivalent. Each onset and each rime that comprises the syllable is also a single phoneme.

The hierarchical structure shown in Figure 2.1 is developmentally meaningful, as the development of phonological awareness appears to follow this hierarchical sequence across languages. Children first gain awareness of syllables, and they can usually demonstrate this awareness in cognitive tasks by around age 3 (although, of course, research with babies shows that they can distinguish syllables such as /ba/ and /ga/ perceptually within the first month of life). Next, children gain awareness of onset-rime units and can usually demonstrate this awareness in cognitive tasks by around the age of 3–4 years. Finally, children become aware of phonemes. Phoneme awareness emerges at different ages in different languages. This cross-language variation appears to depend on (a) the syllable structure of the language, and (b) the transparency with which the orthography represents phonemes. It may also depend on morphology (the study of meaning in individual units of language, see Goswami & Ziegler, 2006).

Levels of phonological awareness in different languages

Becoming aware of syllables

Among the cognitive tasks designed to measure syllable awareness, counting and tapping tasks are particularly frequent. For example, Liberman, Shankweiler, Fischer, and Carter (1974) devised a tapping task to measure syllable awareness in pre-reading children. They gave American children aged from 4 to 6 years a small stick and asked them to tap once for words that had one syllable (*dog*), twice for words that had two syllables (*tur-key*) and three times for words that had three syllables (*pres-i-dent*). A criterion of six correct responses in a row was required in order for children to be accorded syllabic awareness. This criterion was passed by 46 per cent of the 4-year-olds, 48 per cent of the 5-year-olds and 90 per cent of the 6-year-olds. The 4- and 5-year-olds were pre-readers, and the 6-year-olds had been learning to read for about a year.

Another measure used to assess syllabic awareness in young children is the counting task. In the counting task, children are given plastic counters and are asked to use them to represent the number of syllables in words of increasing length (Elkonin, 1963). Treiman and Baron (1981) gave a syllable counting task to 5-year-old American pre-readers. For example, if the experimenter said *rabbit*, the child had to set out two counters. Treiman and Baron (1981) reported good syllable awareness in these pre-readers. Treiman and Zukowski (1991) devised a same–different task to assess syllable-level skills, using a puppet who felt happy when he heard two words that had some of the same sounds in them. The children had to listen to pairs of words like *hammer—hammock* and *compete—repeat*, repeat them and then decide whether the puppet would like them. As the first pair of words shares the first syllable and the second pair of words shares the second syllable, the puppet should like both of these pairs. Treiman and Zukowski found that 100 per cent of 5-year-olds, 90 per cent of 6-year-olds and 100 per cent of 7-year-olds succeeded in this task.

Similar evidence of success at the syllable level has been found in deletion tasks (deleting a syllable from a word, e.g., *party—part*, see Bruce, 1964); in tasks requiring children to say 'just a little bit' of a word (e.g., *Peter—Pete*, see Fox & Routh, 1975); and in blending tasks (blending together two syllables to form a word, e.g., *sis + ter* makes *sister*, Anthony et al., 2002). Data from these different tasks converge to suggest that syllable awareness has developed in young children before they learn to read. Absolute success level seems to vary with the different tasks, which is probably due to their differing cognitive demands. For example, same–different judgement tasks appear to be easier than tapping tasks. Nevertheless, at the syllable level, children as young as 3 years perform at above-chance levels in *all* of these tasks.

Children learning to read in more transparent languages such as Italian, Turkish and Norwegian show similar proficiency with syllables. For example, Cossu, Shankweiler, Liberman, Katz, and Tola (1988) asked Italian pre-readers (4- to 5-year-olds) and Italian children learning to read (7- to 8-year-olds) to tap out the number of syllables in words like *gatto* [*cat*], *melone* [*melon*] and *termometro* [*thermometer*]. Criterion was reached by 67 per cent of the 4-year-olds, 80 per cent of the 5-year-olds and 100 per cent of the school-age sample. Durgunoğlu and Öney (1999) gave a similar tapping task to Turkish kindergartners. Performance was 94 per cent correct. The Norwegian study used a syllable counting task in which children were asked to make pencil marks for each syllable in a word (e.g., *telephone* = 3 marks). Høien, Lundberg, Stanovich, and Bjaalid (1995) reported that Norwegian pre-schoolers performed at 83 per cent correct. German pre-schoolers (81 per cent correct) and French kindergartners (69 per cent correct) perform at similar high levels in syllable counting tasks (Demont & Gombert, 1996; Wimmer, Landerl, Linortner, & Hummer, 1991). Syllable awareness appears universally present prior to children receiving instruction in literacy. Hence this 'large' grain size is particularly easy to detect across languages.

Becoming aware of onsets and rimes

The *nursery rhyme* is an intimate part of an English-speaking childhood. This suggests that onset-rime awareness might also be well developed in young children prior to schooling. Popular nursery rhymes have strong rhythms that emphasize syllabification (e.g., *HUMP-ty DUMP-ty sat on a wall*), and many nursery rhymes contrast rhyming words in ways that distinguish the onset from the rime (e.g., *Twinkle Twinkle Little Star* rhymes *star* with *are; Incy Wincy Spider* rhymes *spout* with *out*). One task that is used to measure onset-rime awareness in pre-school children is the oddity task or odd-man-out task (Bradley & Bryant, 1978). Children listen to an experimenter saying three or four words and are asked to select the 'odd word out' on the basis of either the initial sound (*bus, bun, **rug***), the medial sound (***pin**, bun, gun*) or the final sound (*top, **doll**, hop*). For example, Bradley and Bryant (1983) gave the oddity task to approximately 400 pre-school English children aged 4 and 5 years. They reported that average performance was well above chance levels (33 per cent correct), at 56 per cent correct for onsets (initial sound task) and 71 per cent correct for rimes (medial and final sound tasks). The same–different judgement task devised by Treiman and Zukowski (1991) can also be used at the onset-rime level. For example, word pairs like *steam* and *stop* share the onset, and words like *spin* and *win* share the rime. Treiman and Zukowski (1991) reported that 56 per cent of their 5-year-olds, 74 per cent of their 6-year-olds and 100 per cent of their 7-year-olds could judge which pairs of words the puppet would like. Another measure of rime awareness is to ask children to complete nursery rhymes. For example, Bryant, MacLean, Bradley, and Crossland (1990) asked 3-year-olds to complete familiar nursery rhymes such as *Jack and Jill went up the? [hill]*. They reported that the mean score out of 10 for the group was 4.5. Only one child (out of 64) was unable to complete any nursery rhymes. Data from these different tasks suggest that onset-rime awareness, too, has developed in young English-speaking children before they learn to read.

Again, a similar developmental picture is found in other languages. For example, the oddity task has been given to pre-readers learning German, Chinese, Norwegian and Greek. Wimmer, Landerl, and Schneider (1994) reported that for German kindergartners, group performance was 44 per cent correct with onsets and 73 per cent correct with rimes. Ho and Bryant (1997) reported that Chinese 3-year-olds performed at a group level of 68 per cent correct in the rime oddity task. Høien et al. (1995) found that their Norwegian pre-schoolers were 91 per cent correct in a rhyme task using a match-to-sample format in which the children select one picture out of three that rhymes with a target picture such as *fish*. For Greek children, Porpodas (1999) reported that first-grade children scored 90 per cent correct in a rime oddity task based on sets of four words. Onset-rime awareness, like syllable awareness, appears to be universally present prior to children receiving instruction in literacy. The ability to divide the syllable into two constituents by segmenting at the vowel, another 'large' grain size, is again present across languages.

Becoming aware of phonemes

As noted above, phoneme awareness does not appear to be universal in its developmental trajectory. Rather, phoneme awareness emerges at different ages in different languages, depending on factors like the syllable structure of the language and the transparency with which the orthography of the language represents phonemes (Ziegler & Goswami, 2005). In terms of development this is not really surprising, because despite its utility as an abstract concept for explaining reading development, the phoneme is not a natural speech unit. The concept of a phoneme is an averaged description of the physical stimulus rather than the physical stimulus itself. For example, the *p* phoneme in *spoon* and *pit* is not the same physical sound. The differences between these two physical sounds can be described in terms of acoustic features, such as voicing, which determine phonetic differences.

Sounds that overlap in many acoustic features are called *allophones* and are essentially similar but non-identical sounds that the brain groups together as *prototypes* of the sound element /p/. This abstracted similarity is described as a *phoneme*. This means that children cannot learn about phonemes such as /p/ simply by analysing their own speech. In fact, as shown by the work of Charles Read on the earliest spelling attempts made by pre-readers (*invented spellings*), if children do proceed in this way, then they will group together allophones that are not recognized in the orthographic representation of phonemes (Read, 1986). For example, pre-reading children think that the sounds at the beginning of *chicken* and *track* require the same orthographic representation. However, orthographic convention tells us that the sound at the beginning of *track* is more similar to the sound at the beginning of *tip*—even though acoustically this is not the case.

Empirical research suggests that the primary mechanism for learning about the abstract unit of the phoneme is learning about letters. Accordingly, the development of phoneme awareness depends in part on the consistency with which letters symbolize phonemes in different orthographies. This can be demonstrated by cross-language investigations of the development of phono-logical awareness. However, the complexity of phonological syllable structure will also contribute to how rapidly children can develop an awareness of phonemes. These factors lead to cross-language divergence in the rate of development of phonemic awareness.

Most of the studies mentioned above for syllable awareness also measured phoneme awareness using a range of cognitive tasks. Phoneme counting tasks were used by Wimmer et al. (1991) in their German study, Demont and Gombert (1996) in their French study and Høien et al. (1995) in their Norwegian study. Phoneme tapping tasks were used by Durgunoğlu and Öney (1999) in their Turkish study, and by Cossu et al. (1988) in their Italian study. Performance in the different languages varied widely among pre-school children. The German pre-school children performed at 51 per cent correct, the French children at 2 per cent correct, the Norwegian children at 56 per cent correct and the Turkish children at 67 per cent correct. The Italian children were required to reach a criterion of six consecutive correct responses in phoneme tapping. Criterion was reached by 13 per cent of the 4-year-olds and 27 per cent of the 5-year-olds. In English, the same criterion was reached by none of the 4-year-olds and 17 per cent of 5-year-olds studied by Liberman et al. (1974).

This language-specific variation in the ease with which pre-readers can identify individual phonemes in words is also found in children who are already learning to read. When English- and Italian-speaking children were compared directly in the phoneme tapping task during their first year of reading instruction in the United States versus Italy, 97 per cent of the Italian sample were able to tap out phonemes compared to 70 per cent of the English-speaking sample. Similar performance levels for English-speaking first-grade children (71 per cent correct) were reported in Australia by Tunmer and Nesdale (1985), and in the United States by Perfetti, Beck, Bell, and Hughes (1987) who studied second-grade children (65 per cent correct). When languages have a higher degree of orthographic consistency than English, children who are learning to read tend to score at levels more comparable to the Italian children tested by Cossu et al. (1988). For example, in phoneme counting tasks Turkish first-graders scored 94 per cent correct, Greek first-graders scored 100 per cent and German first-graders scored 92 per cent correct (see Durgunoğlu & Öney, 1999; Harris & Giannouli, 1999; Wimmer et al., 1991). French is a less orthographically transparent language, and accordingly phonemic awareness in French children is more similar to that of English-speaking children. For example, by the end of Grade 1, Demont and Gombert (1996) reported group performance of 61 per cent correct in their phoneme counting measure. Therefore, the rate at which phoneme awareness develops in different languages is highly variable.

However, these differences can be explained systematically in terms of orthographic consistency and syllable structure. Languages like Turkish, Italian and Greek are very transparent and also have a simple syllable structure. These two factors help children to perform close to ceiling levels with phonemes. It is easy to segment these syllable structures, and letters provide a consistent guide to phonemes. English and German both have a complex syllable structure, but German is a transparent orthography. German children were also performing close to ceiling level, suggesting that orthographic consistency makes an enormous difference to how rapidly phoneme awareness emerges as children learn to read and to spell. Wimmer et al. (1991) found that German children scored above 90 per cent correct in their first year of reading tuition, compared to around 70 per cent correct for English-speaking children (e.g., Tunmer & Nesdale, 1985). This is discussed in greater detail in the next section.

Orthographic effects on learning to read

Orthographic effects on phonological awareness as captured by psycholinguistic grain size theory

According to our psycholinguistic grain size theory, there are a variety of language-dependent reasons for the cross-language variation found in the development of both phoneme awareness and reading acquisition (Ziegler & Goswami, 2005, 2006). One important factor is syllable structure. For languages like Italian and Spanish, onset-rime segmentation of the syllable is equivalent to phonemic segmentation. An Italian child who segments an early-acquired word like *Mamma* at the onset-rime level will also arrive at the phonemes comprising this word (e.g., /m/ /a/ /m/ /a/). Only 5 per cent of English monosyllables follow the CV pattern (see De Cara & Goswami, 2002; examples are *go* and *me*). For languages like English and German, onset-rime segmentation is usually not equivalent to phoneme segmentation. For words like *tip, spoon, jump* and *crust*, both onsets and rimes can contain clusters of phonemes. Accordingly, another cognitive step is required to reach the phoneme level for English. Complex onsets like *sp* and complex rimes like *ump* must be segmented further. Also important are linguistic factors such as the sonority profile of syllables. For example, it should be more difficult to separate sonorant consonant phonemes, like /l/, from vowels than to separate obstruent phonemes, like /t/, from vowels (e.g., it should be more difficult to segment *ill* than *it*).

As also mentioned earlier, alphabets represent phonemes with more consistency in some languages than in others. For example, Italian, Greek and Spanish are all highly consistent in their spelling–sound correspondences and hence are termed *transparent*. In these languages, one letter makes only one sound. English, Danish and French are much less consistent in their letter–sound correspondences. In these languages, one letter can make multiple sounds. For example, the letter *a* in English makes different sounds in the highly familiar words *man, make, car* and *walk*.

In order to try to study the effects of these different factors systematically, it is necessary to devise language comparisons where all factors except one can be held constant. As languages vary naturally in many dimensions, this is difficult to do. However, English and German offer a very interesting pair of languages for experiments on reading acquisition and phonological awareness because these languages are essentially identical in their phonological structure. Indeed, lots of words are the same in the two languages (e.g., *wine* [*Wein*], *house* [*Haus*], *sand* [*Sand*]). However, the two languages differ considerably in orthographic consistency. German is a highly consistent orthography with one-to-one mappings between graphemes and phonemes (a grapheme is a letter or group of letters that make a single sound, as in *ph* or *f* for the phoneme /f/). English is not a highly consistent orthography. Experimentally, therefore, we can ask whether the largely consistent spelling–sound relations learned by German children impact on the development of phonological representation in a different way from the largely inconsistent spelling–sound relations learned by English children. According to psycholinguistic grain size theory (Ziegler & Goswami, 2005), the kinds of internal representations (the *psycholinguistic units*) that will develop in a child exposed to a consistent orthography will differ from the kinds of internal representations that will develop if the same child is exposed to an inconsistent orthography.

We tested one aspect of this prediction in a cross-language study of pre-reading children and children who were just beginning to learn to read, in English and German (Goswami, Ziegler, & Richardson, 2005). We compared rime awareness to phoneme awareness and investigated whether phonological awareness differed for words that had consistent spelling patterns and those with inconsistent spelling patterns, in each language. English children will be acquiring many inconsistent orthographic relations for individual phonological rimes (e.g., *pear, chair, stare, where*), as well as for phonemes (as in the example given above for *a* in *make, walk, man, car*). Hence orthographic consistency might be expected to affect both onset-rime awareness and phoneme awareness as the children learn to read. Prior to learning to read, however, phonological awareness should depend on spoken language factors only. As the spoken language has the same phonological characteristics in English and German, *pre-readers* would be expected to show equivalent performance in both the rime awareness and the phoneme awareness tasks.

To test these ideas, Goswami et al. (2005) used an oddity task to test both rime and phoneme awareness (thus equating task difficulty across linguistic level). Children listened to word triples that either had a different rime (e.g., *house, mouse, kiss*), or a different vowel phoneme (e.g., *house, loud, path*). These examples have consistent orthographic representations for the rime and the shared vowel phoneme, respectively. Children were also tested with word triples where orthographic representations were inconsistent, for example, *boat, note, root* (*boat* and *note* share the common rime /oːt/ but *root* does not), and *dawn, fork, rice* (in Received Standard English, *dawn* and *fork* share a common rime but *rice* does not). In the rime awareness task the pre-reading children performed at the same overall level across language, and there was no effect of orthographic consistency. The children who were beginning to read also showed the same accuracy levels across language, but there was a marked effect of orthographic consistency for the English children only. Rime consistency improved performance in the rime oddity task by 19.5 per cent (the comparable rime consistency effect for German was 0.7 per cent). In the phoneme awareness task, the pre-reading children again performed at the same overall level across language, and there was no effect of orthographic consistency. However, for the children who were beginning to read, there was a marked effect of orthographic consistency, this time for the German children only. Phoneme consistency improved performance in the phoneme oddity task by 14.2 per cent (the comparable phoneme consistency effect for English was 2.3 per cent). The German children were also significantly better at identifying the shared phonemes in the word triples than were the English children.

These data show that spelling consistency affects phonological awareness both in terms of the whole language system and in terms of specific items or words in that system. As predicted by psycholinguistic grain size theory, the German children became sensitive to phoneme units more quickly than did the English children, because of the overall consistency of grapheme–phoneme correspondences in German (a system-level or whole lexicon effect). Regarding item-specific effects, the German readers made fewer accurate phonological judgements when words shared phonemes but used inconsistent spellings for those phonemes (as in *dawn* and *fork*), whereas the English readers made fewer accurate phonological judgements when words shared rimes but used inconsistent spellings for those rimes (as in *boat* and *note*). These interactions between orthographic consistency and phonological grain size suggest that consistency only affects the most salient phonological units within each language—at least, at the beginning of learning to read. The fact that consistency effects were only found for *readers* in both languages suggests that the source of the consistency effect in phonological processing is indeed orthographic.

Orthographic effects on mapping sounds to letters

The data discussed so far show clear effects of orthographic transparency on phonological development. However, according to psycholinguistic grain size theory, orthographic transparency will also affect reading acquisition. This is because the different grain sizes salient in the spoken language, and the consistency with which these grain sizes are represented in the written language, are bound to affect learning. According to psycholinguistic grain size theory, both the grain size of lexical representations and the reading strategies that children develop for decoding will show systematic differences across orthographies (Ziegler & Goswami, 2005).

Orthographic transparency can be hypothesized to affect at least three aspects of learning symbol–sound mappings: availability, consistency and granularity. The *availability* problem has already been partially discussed and essentially reflects the fact that not all phonological units are equally accessible prior to reading. For example, syllables are more accessible than phonemes, and so we can predict that a Japanese child who is learning visual symbols that represent syllables (an early-developing grain size), will be at an advantage compared to an English child who is learning letters that represent phonemes (a later-developing grain size). Phonemes in particular may be inaccessible to pre-readers, and the rate of development of phoneme awareness differs as reading is acquired, with faster acquisition in more consistent orthographies.

The *consistency* problem refers directly to linguistic differences in transparency. Clearly, the alphabet represents phonemes with more transparency in some languages than in others. Languages like Greek, German, Spanish and Italian have a one-to-one mapping between letters and sounds. In these languages, letters correspond consistently to one phoneme. Languages like English, Danish and French have a one-to-many mapping between letters and sounds. Some letters or letter clusters can be pronounced in more than one way: for example, the *o* in *do* and *so*, the *ea* in *clean* and *break* and the *g* in *magic* and *big* (see Berndt, Reggia, & Mitchum, 1987; Ziegler, Stone, & Jacobs, 1997). It is easier for a child to become aware of phonemes if one letter consistently maps to one and the same phoneme. It is relatively difficult to learn about phonemes if a letter can be pronounced in multiple ways (see Ziegler & Goswami, 2005, 2006, for more detailed arguments). Sound–spelling consistency also varies across languages. Although most alphabetic languages are inconsistent for *sound–spelling* correspondence, with one sound corresponding to more than one letter (a one-to-many relationship), some languages are consistent for both spelling and reading (e.g., Italian, Serbo-Croatian). Inconsistency from spelling to sound, or *feedforward inconsistency*, seems to be the most important factor in slowing initial reading acquisition (see Ziegler & Goswami, 2005). In fact, English has an unusually high degree of feedforward inconsistency (for example, it has words like *though*, *cough*, *through*, and *bough*).

The *granularity* problem refers to the absolute number of mappings that need to be learned. Clearly, there are more orthographic units to learn when access to the phonological system is based on larger grain sizes like syllables. This is because there are more words than there are syllables in any language, there are more syllables than there are rimes, there are more rimes than there are graphemes and there are more graphemes than there are letters. We have argued that reading proficiency in a particular language will reflect a language-dependent resolution of all of these problems (see Ziegler & Goswami, 2005, 2006, for details). As an example, children who are learning to read in English need to develop multiple strategies in parallel if they are to become successful readers. They need to develop whole-word recognition strategies so that they can read words like *choir* and *yacht*, they need to develop rhyme analogy strategies so that they can read irregular words like *light*, *night* and *fight* and they need to develop grapheme–phoneme recoding strategies so that they can read regular words like *tip*, *fat* and *dog*. Cross-language data on reading acquisition are consistent with the prediction that learning to recode orthographic symbols to sound will take longer in orthographically inconsistent languages like English and French compared to orthographically consistent languages like Spanish, German and Italian.

Orthographic effects and the rate of reading acquisition

For many of the world's languages, the main task facing children who are acquiring reading is to develop grapheme–phoneme recoding strategies. Languages like Finnish, German, Italian, Greek and Turkish can be read very successfully by learning graphemes and learning how to convert them into phonemes. Empirical studies of children learning to read in these languages suggest that they develop efficient levels of grapheme–phoneme recoding within the first months of learning to read (e.g., Cossu, Gugliotta, & Marshall, 1995; Durgunoğlu & Öney, 1999; Wimmer, 1996). One empirical approach is to use the different cognitive 'hallmarks' of a reliance on grapheme–phoneme recoding.

The first of these is a *length effect*: when words are longer, children who are applying grapheme–phoneme correspondences should take longer to read them. Reliable length effects are indeed found in children who are learning to read consistent orthographies like Greek compared to children who are learning to read inconsistent orthographies like English (e.g., Goswami, Porpodas, & Wheelwright, 1997).

A second cognitive hallmark is *skilled non-word reading*: if you are reading by applying grapheme–phoneme correspondences, then it should not matter whether words have semantic content or not. Children who are recoding graphemes into phonemes in a sequential manner should be as efficient at reading letter strings that do not correspond to real words as letter strings that do correspond to real words (e.g., *grall, tegwump,* vs. *ball, wigwam*). Cross-language comparisons show consistently that children who are learning to read transparent orthographies like German are better at reading non-words like *grall* than are English children (Frith, Wimmer, & Landerl, 1998).

A third hallmark of a reliance on grapheme–phoneme correspondences is the *absence of a rime familiarity effect* in non-word reading. Logically, a non-word like *grall* can be read by analogy to a familiar real word like *ball* (as well as by applying sequential grapheme–phoneme correspondences). Empirical comparisons show that readers of consistent orthographies, like German, show no difference in reading accuracy for non-words that can be read by analogy compared to non-words that cannot be read by analogy. Readers of inconsistent orthographies, like English, do show a difference. English children are more accurate at reading non-words that can be read by analogy to real English words, like *dake* [*cake*] and *murn* [*burn*], in comparison to phonologically matched non-words that have no analogies (e.g., *daik, mirn*; see Goswami, Ziegler, Dalton, & Schneider, 2003). Children who are learning to read consistent orthographies like German do not show a reading advantage for non-words that have rime analogies. Readers of consistent orthographies also read non-words very efficiently when different types of non-word (large-grain-size non-words like *dake* and small-grain-size non-words like *daik*) are mixed together in the same list. Readers of inconsistent orthographies like English show a strategy-switching cost, apparently alternating between using a rime analogy reading strategy for the large-grain-size non-words [*make–dake*] and using a grapheme–phoneme recoding strategy for the small-grain-size non-words [*d-ai-k*] (see Goswami et al., 2003).

Another empirical measure is to compare the efficiency of grapheme–phoneme recoding strategies in children who are learning to read different languages using closely matched items. Relevant studies show a clear advantage for children who are learning to read consistent alphabetic orthographies from the first year of reading instruction. For example, the largest cross-language study carried out to date compared simple word and non-word reading in first grade speakers of 14 European Union (EU) languages (Seymour, Aro, & Erskine, 2003). All children selected were attending schools using *phonics*-based-(grapheme–phoneme-based) instructional programmes. There was careful matching of the word and non-word items across languages, and the length of time during which the children had received tuition in reading was also equated. As children in different EU countries begin school at different ages, however, the ages of the children differed (e.g., the English-speaking children were 5-year-olds, the German-speaking children were 6-year-olds, the Finnish children were 7-year-olds). The data collected by Seymour et al. (2003) are shown in Table 2.1.

When the languages are ordered in terms of orthographic transparency, it can be seen that the efficiency of grapheme–phoneme recoding was close to ceiling for most of the European languages (recall that this is during the first

Table 2.1 Data from the COST A8 study of grapheme–phoneme recoding skills for monosyllables in 14 European languages

Language	Familiar real words	Non-words
Greek	98	97
Finnish	98	98
German	98	98
Austrian German	97	97
Italian	95	92
Spanish	95	93
Swedish	95	91
Dutch	95	90
Icelandic	94	91
Norwegian	92	93
French	79	88
Portuguese	73	76
Danish	71	63
Scottish English	34	41

Note. Percentage correct.
Adapted from Seymour, Aro, and Erskine (2003).

year of receiving tuition). The table shows that children who were learning to read languages like Italian, Spanish, German and Greek read both words and non-words with accuracy levels above 90 per cent. In contrast, rather lower levels were achieved by children learning to read French (79 per cent correct), Danish (71 per cent correct) and Portuguese (73 per cent correct). This is in accord with psycholinguistic grain size theory and reflects the reduced orthographic consistency of these languages. The slowest rates of acquisition were shown by the children learning to read in English, who managed to read 34 per cent of the simple words correctly and 41 per cent of the simple non-words. These children were only 5 years old. However, they were followed up a year later, when they had been receiving two years of reading instruction. Accuracy levels were now 76 per cent for real words and 63 per cent for non-words. Clearly, this still falls short of the early efficiency shown by the Italian and German children. Again, this is consistent with the predictions made by psycholinguistic grain size theory. The English-speaking children are having to learn an alphabetic orthography with high inconsistency. Furthermore, to use grapheme–phoneme recoding strategies, they have to work with grapheme–phoneme correspondences that map onto complex syllables. The combined effects of phonological complexity and orthographic transparency make it more difficult to acquire efficient reading skills in a language like English.

Conclusion: Learning to read in different languages—a universal problem with language-specific solutions

Psycholinguistic grain size theory offers a systematic framework for considering how different lexical, phonological and structural factors can contribute to explaining cross-language differences in reading acquisition. As shown, there is an apparently universal developmental sequence of phonological awareness across languages with the acquisition of larger grain sizes like syllables, onsets and rimes preceding the acquisition of smaller grain sizes such as phonemes. Children learning very different spoken languages (e.g., English vs. Chinese) show similar developmental trajectories, developing syllable and onset-rime awareness prior to schooling and phoneme awareness as reading is taught. Cross-language divergence occurs, however, in the rate at which phonemic awareness then develops. Phoneme awareness develops more rapidly in children who are segmenting simple syllables with a CV phonological structure. Phoneme awareness also develops more rapidly in children who are learning to read transparent or consistent alphabetic orthographies. Such children also learn to decode faster than children who are learning to read less consistent orthographies. This is because they can rely on a grapheme–phoneme recoding strategy to yield efficient recoding of symbols to sound. For reading, the nature of the symbol system itself affects cognitive development. This is captured by the role of orthographic factors. For typically developing children, however, such cognitive differences are transient in nature. Most children learn to read whether they are learning a consistent alphabetic orthography, an inconsistent alphabetic orthography or a non-alphabetic orthography. They may achieve fluency at different rates, but by the age of around 9 to 10 years most children are recoding symbols to sound with high efficiency, whatever orthography they are required to learn. Psycholinguistic grain size theory offers a cognitive framework for explaining why this is so.

References

Anthony, J. L., Lonigan, C. J., Burgess, S. R., Driscoll, K., Phillips, B. M., & Cantor, B. G. (2002). Structure of pre-school phonological sensitivity: Overlapping sensitivity to rhyme, words, syllables, and phonemes. *Journal of Experimental Child Psychology*, *82*, 65–92.

Berndt, R. S., Reggia, J. A., & Mitchum, C. C. (1987). Empirically derived probabilities for grapheme-to-phoneme correspondences in English. *Behavior Research Methods, Instruments, and Computers*, *19*, 1–9.

Bradley, L., & Bryant, P. (1978). Difficulties in auditory organization as a possible cause of reading backwardness. *Nature*, *271*, 746–747.

Bradley, L., & Bryant, P. E. (1983). Categorising sounds and learning to read: A causal connection. *Nature*, *310*, 419–421.

Bruce, D. J. (1964). The analysis of word sounds by young children. *British Journal of Educational Psychology*, *34*, 158–170.

Bryant, P. E., MacLean, M., Bradley, L., & Crossland, J. (1990). Rhyme and alliteration, phoneme detection, and learning to read. *Developmental Psychology*, *26*, 429–438.

Cohen, L., & Dehaene, S. (2004). Specialization within the ventral stream: The case for the visual word form area. *NeuroImage*, *22*, 466–476.

Cossu, G., Gugliotta, M., & Marshall, J. C. (1995). Acquisition of reading and written spelling in a transparent orthography: Two non-parallel processes? *Reading and Writing*, *7*, 9–22.

Cossu, G., Shankweiler, D., Liberman, I. Y., Katz, L., & Tola, G. (1988). Awareness of phonological segments and reading ability in Italian children. *Applied Psycholinguistics*, *9*, 1–16.

Curtin, S., Mintz, T. H., & Christiansen, M. H. (2005). Stress changes the representational landscape: Evidence from word segmentation. *Cognition*, *96*, 233–262.

De Cara, B., & Goswami, U. (2002). Statistical analysis of similarity relations among spoken words: Evidence for the special status of rimes in English. *Behavior Research Methods and Instrumentation*, *34*, 416–423.

De Cara, B., & Goswami, U. (2003). Phonological neighbourhood density: Effects in a rhyme awareness task in five-year-old children. *Journal of Child Language*, *30*, 695–710.

Demont, E., & Gombert, J. E. (1996). Phonological awareness as a predictor of recoding skills and syntactic awareness as a predictor of comprehension skills. *British Journal of Educational Psychology*, *66*, 315–332.

Dollaghan, C. A. (1994). Children's phonological neighbourhoods: Half empty or half full? *Journal of Child Language*, *21*, 257–271.

Durgunoğlu, A. Y., & Öney, B. (1999). A cross-linguistic comparison of phonological awareness and word recognition. *Reading and Writing*, *11*, 281–299.

Echols, C. H. (1996). A role for stress in early speech segmentation. In J. L. Morgan & K. Demuth (Eds.), *Signal to syntax: Bootstrapping from speech to grammar in early acquisition* (pp. 151–170). Hillsdale, NJ: Lawrence Erlbaum Associates, Inc.

Elkonin, D. B. (1963). The psychology of mastering the elements of reading. In B. Simon & J. Simon (Eds.), *Educational psychology in the USSR* (pp. 165–179). Stanford, CA: Stanford University Press.

Fernald, A., & Mazzie, C. (1991). Prosody and focus in speech to infants and adults. *Developmental Psychology, 27*, 209–221.

Fox, B., & Routh, D. K. (1975). Analyzing spoken language into words, syllables and phonemes: A developmental study. *Journal of Psycholinguistic Research, 4*, 331–342.

Frith, U., Wimmer, H., & Landerl, K. (1998). Differences in phonological recoding in German- and English-speaking children. *Scientific Studies of Reading, 2*, 31–54.

Goswami, U., & Ziegler, J. C. (2006). Fluency, phonology and morphology: A response to the commentaries on becoming literate in different languages. *Developmental Science, 9*, 451–453.

Goswami, U., Porpodas, C., & Wheelwright, S. (1997). Children's orthographic representations in English and Greek. *European Journal of Psychology of Education, 3*, 273–292.

Goswami, U., Ziegler, J. C., Dalton, L., & Schneider, W. (2003). Nonword reading across orthographies: How flexible is the choice of reading units? *Applied Psycholinguistics, 24*, 235–247.

Goswami, U., Ziegler, J., & Richardson, U. (2005). The effects of spelling consistency on phonological awareness: A comparison of English and German. *Journal of Experimental Child Psychology, 92*, 345–365.

Harris, M., & Giannouli, V. (1999). Learning to read and spell in Greek: The importance of letter knowledge and morphological awareness. In M. Harris & G. Hatano (Eds.), *Learning to read and write: A cross-linguistic perspective* (pp. 51–70). Cambridge, UK: Cambridge University Press.

Ho, C. S.-H., & Bryant, P. (1997). Phonological skills are important in learning to read Chinese. *Developmental Psychology, 33*, 946–951.

Høien, T., Lundberg, L., Stanovich, K. E., & Bjaalid, I. K. (1995). Components of phonological awareness. *Reading and Writing, 7*, 171–188.

Jusczyk, P. W., & Aslin, R. N. (1995). Infants' detection of the sound patterns of words in fluent speech. *Cognitive Psychology, 29*, 1–23.

Kuhl, P. K. (1986). Reflections on infants' perception and representation of speech. In J. Perkell & D. Klatt (Eds.), *Invariance and variability in speech processes* (pp. 19–30). Norwood, NJ: Ablex.

Kuhl, P. K. (2004). Early language acquisition: Cracking the speech code. *Nature Reviews Neuroscience, 5*, 831–843.

Liberman, I. Y., Shankweiler, D., Fischer, F. W., & Carter, B. (1974). Explicit syllable and phoneme segmentation in the young child. *Journal of Experimental Child Psychology, 18*, 201–212.

Luce, P. A., Pisoni, D. B., & Goldinger, S. D. (1990). Similarity neighbourhoods of spoken words. In G. T. M. Altmann (Ed.), *Cognitive models of speech processing: Psycholinguistic and computational perspectives* (pp. 122–147). Cambridge, MA: MIT Press.

Perfetti, C. A., Beck, I., Bell, L., & Hughes, C. (1987). Phonemic knowledge and learning to read are reciprocal: A longitudinal study of first grade children. *Merrill-Palmer Quarterly, 33*, 283–319.

Porpodas, C. D. (1999). Patterns of phonological and memory processing in beginning readers and spellers of Greek. *Journal of Learning Disabilities, 32*, 406–416.

Read, C. (1986). *Children's creative spelling*. London: Routledge.

Seymour, P. H. K., Aro, M., & Erskine, J. M. (2003). Foundation literacy acquisition in European orthographies. *British Journal of Psychology, 94*, 143–174.

Thomson, J., Richardson, U., & Goswami, U. (2005). Phonological similarity neighbourhoods and children's short-term memory: Typical development and dyslexia. *Memory and Cognition, 33*, 1210–1219.

Treiman, R. (1989). The internal structure of the syllable. In G. Carlson & M. Tanenhaus (Eds.), *Linguistic structure in language processing* (pp. 27–52). Dordrecht, The Netherlands: Kluger.

Treiman, R., & Baron, J. (1981). Segmental analysis: Development and relation to reading ability. In G. C. MacKinnon & T. G. Waller (Eds.), *Reading research: Advances in theory and practice* (Vol. 3, pp. 159–198). New York: Academic Press.

Treiman, R., & Zukowski, A. (1991). Levels of phonological awareness. In S. Brady & D. Shankweiler (Eds.), *Phonological processes in literacy* (pp. 67–83). Hillsdale, NJ: Lawrence Erlbaum Associates, Inc.

Tunmer, W. E., & Nesdale, A. R. (1985). Phonemic segmentation skill and beginning reading. *Journal of Educational Psychology, 77*, 417–527.

Vitevitch, M. S., Luce, P. A., Pisoni, D. B., & Auer, E. T. (1999). Phonotactics, neighbourhood activation and lexical access for spoken words. *Brain and Language, 68*, 306–311.

Wimmer, H. (1996). The non-word reading deficit in developmental dyslexia: Evidence from children learning to read German. *Journal of Experimental Child Psychology, 61*, 80–90.

Wimmer, H., Landerl, K., Linortner, R., & Hummer, P. (1991). The relationship of phonemic awareness to reading acquisition: More consequence than precondition but still important. *Cognition, 40*, 219–249.

Wimmer, H., Landerl, K., & Schneider, W. (1994). The role of rhyme awareness in learning to read a regular orthography. *British Journal of Developmental Psychology, 12*, 469–484.

Ziegler, J. C., & Goswami, U. (2005). Reading acquisition, developmental dyslexia and skilled reading across languages: A psycholinguistic grain size theory. *Psychological Bulletin, 131*, 3–29.

Ziegler, J. C., & Goswami, U. (2006). Becoming literate in different languages: Similar problems, different solutions. *Developmental Science, 9*, 429–453.

Ziegler, J. C., Stone, G. O., & Jacobs, A. M. (1997). What's the pronunciation for -OUGH and the spelling for /u/? A database for computing feedforward and feedback inconsistency in English. *Behavior Research Methods, Instruments, and Computers, 29*, 600–618.

3 Phonological development from a cross-linguistic perspective

Lynne G. Duncan

Introduction

The research presented in this chapter examines phonological development during the transition to early reading in a range of European languages. Although no reading data are presented, the work directly addresses two issues that are central to the understanding of reading development: (1) the question of the *availability* of phonology at the outset of learning to read (Ziegler & Goswami, 2005); and (2) the influence of orthography and instruction in shaping phonological development during and after the transition to literacy (Gombert, 1992; Morais, Cary, Alegria, & Bertelson, 1979; Read, Zhang, Nie, & Ding, 1986). While it has been suggested that European languages show a universal sequence of phonological development (Ziegler & Goswami, 2005, p. 9), I argue instead that phonological development can take different paths according to the characteristics of a child's native language and the context of learning to read.

Theories of phonological development

The availability of phonology at the outset of learning to read has been identified by Ziegler and Goswami (2005) as one of the three main problems of reading acquisition. These authors state that the '*availability problem* reflects the fact that not all phonological units are consciously (explicitly) accessible prior to reading. Thus, connecting orthographic units to phonological units that are not yet readily available requires further cognitive development' (p. 3). Several theories of phonological development have offered competing accounts of the phonological units that are available to the beginning reader, and these theories are reviewed below.

Evidence from the literature on how speech is perceived implies that during development the level of detail that is used in remembering and recognizing speech becomes gradually more refined (Nittrouer, 1992; Walley, Smith, & Jusczyk, 1986). Nittrouer (1992) concluded that within the cognitive system for speech perception, the representations of speech used by young children are organized around an articulatorily defined syllable. Later in development, the organization of the system changes and Jusczyk (1986) suggests that this happens in successive steps according to the hierarchical structure of the syllable (see Figure 3.1). Once syllables are established, the sounds within the syllable gradually become more salient such that the speech system represents spoken words using the *onset* (any initial consonants) and the *rime* (the vowel plus any following consonants) in order to distinguish the words more accurately. The final phase of development is when speech is fully represented at the most detailed level of discrimination involving individual phonemes.

The idea that the phonological representations for speech become more segmental during early to middle childhood is consistent with a large body of literature that reports a large-to-small transition in phonological awareness (see Goswami & Bryant, 1990, for a review). Treiman (1987, 1992) linked this to the linguistic structure of the syllable by suggesting that awareness develops progressively down the syllable hierarchy, from large units (syllables) through intermediate units (onset-rime) to small units (phonemes), and this hypothesis has received broad support from a recent analysis by Anthony, Lonigan, Driscoll, Phillips, and Burgess (2003).

The lexical restructuring theory (Metsala & Walley, 1998) has attempted to integrate these two strands of research through the proposal that the status of underlying representations in the speech system has a direct effect on the emergence of phonological awareness and, by implication, on the process of reading acquisition. The idea is that the restructuring of the representations within the speech perception system produces a large-to-small sequence of development in phonological awareness tasks, culminating in an explicit ability to segment spoken words into phonemes. If this is indeed the case, an understanding of the factors that drive the restructuring process will be essential for the study of normal and impaired reading development.

Some insight comes from a review by Fowler (1991) which pieces together evidence that the restructuring of the phonological representations in the speech system is driven by vocabulary growth which creates a pressure for representations to become less holistic and more segmental in nature in order to accurately discriminate between vocabulary items (Menyuk & Menn, 1979;

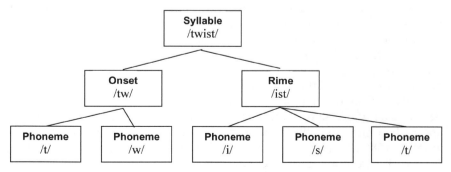

Figure 3.1 The hierarchical internal structure of the syllable.

Walley, 1993) and from later findings that change is *item-specific* rather than system-wide (Garlock, Walley, & Metsala, 2001; Metsala, 1997).

Nevertheless, preliminary findings are equivocal as to whether vocabulary growth really is the major driving force behind this process of segmental restructuring and, hence, behind the emergence of small-unit (phoneme) awareness. While McBride-Chang, Wagner, and Chang (1997) reported that vocabulary and phoneme awareness were related in the performance of children beginning to read, both Elbro, Borstrom, and Petersen (1998) and Garlock et al. (2001) failed to replicate this finding. Further, Elbro et al. (1998) and Snowling (2000) noted that one implication of the theory— namely, that children with reading disabilities will have poor spoken vocabularies—is not borne out by experimental findings 'since the "classic" dyslexic pattern is poor reading and phonological awareness in combination with good receptive vocabulary skills' (p. 60).

An alternative account of meta-linguistic development by Gombert (1992) provides a different perspective. A summary of this four-phase sequence can be viewed in Table 3.1. For the purposes here, it is sufficient to know that Gombert's theory has its roots in an earlier model formulated by Karmiloff-Smith (1986) in which the type of linguistic representations discussed in the introduction undergo successive redescriptions, allowing the emergence of new levels of organization within the speech system. The feature of this process that is most relevant to the present work is that Gombert makes a distinction between the representation of knowledge in the speech system in an implicit and instance-based format, and knowledge that has been redescribed into a more explicit and flexible format that can be generalized for use in new linguistic contexts. Thus, Gombert is contrasting epi-linguistic

Table 3.1 Summary of Gombert's (1992) theory of meta-linguistic development

Phase of development		Description
Phase 1	Acquisition of first linguistic skills	Correspondences between linguistic forms and reinforced pragmatic contexts are stored in an implicit and instance-bound format.
Phase 2	Acquisition of epi-linguistic control	The need to resolve new problems of communication triggers an internal reorganization of linguistic information in a multi-functional format that remains inaccessible to conscious awareness.
Phase 3	Acquisition of meta-linguistic awareness	A demand for intentional control elicits a conscious (*meta*) awareness of elements of the organization established in Phase 2.
Phase 4	Automation of the meta-process	Reductions in cognitive load are achieved by automation of aspects of *meta* functioning.

(implicit) knowledge that is inaccessible to conscious reflection with meta-linguistic (explicit) knowledge that is available to conscious manipulation.

Several aspects of Gombert's model merit contrast with Metsala and Walley's (1998) position in the lexical restructuring theory. First, the catalyst for the redescription process is not limited to vocabulary growth but, rather, varies according to the child's phase of development. For example, change from Phase 1 to Phase 2 is driven by interaction with the linguistic environment, whereas movement into Phase 3 is dependent on specific demands to establish meta-linguistic control over phonology, such as might occur in the context of learning to read.

This gives rise to a second point of difference between the models. Although Phases 1 and 2 in Gombert's model are obligatory, Phase 3 is seen as an optional development. This appears to explain why illiterate adults have failed to develop an explicit awareness of phonemes (Morais et al., 1979).

Third, in contrast to the large-to-small sequence described by Metsala and Walley (1998), movement through the phases can proceed independently for each unit of sound, leaving open the possibility that a child could be in the (explicit) meta-phase for phoneme awareness but remain in the (implicit) epi-phase for rhyme awareness (Duncan, Seymour, & Hill, 1997).

Finally, whereas a large-to-small sequence has been described as a universal pathway for European languages (Ziegler & Goswami, 2005), Gombert's model has the potential for multiple routes to meta-linguistic awareness according to the characteristics of the child's linguistic environment, such as the nature of the native language in both spoken and written form.

Does the evidence support a large-to-small sequence of phonological development in English?

Many influential studies have been directed at assessing children's early awareness of the larger units in the syllable hierarchy (see Figure 3.1). A summary of the main phonological awareness tasks that have been used in this literature is provided in Table 3.2. With syllables, a picture of early competence emerges from studies using matching tasks (Treiman & Zukowski, 1991) and blending tasks (Goldstein, 1976; Lonigan, Burgess, Anthony, & Barker, 1998). In relation to rime units, young English-speaking children appear very sensitive to rhyming words in oddity tasks (e.g., Bowey & Francis, 1991; Bradley & Bryant, 1983; Bryant, MacLean, & Bradley, 1990a; Bryant, MacLean, Bradley, & Crossland, 1990b; MacLean, Bryant, & Bradley, 1987) and in matching tasks (Lenel & Cantor, 1981; MacLean et al., 1987; Read, 1978; Stanovich, Cunningham, & Cramer, 1984; Stuart & Coltheart, 1988; Treiman & Zukowski, 1991; Yopp, 1988).

However, when sensitivity to syllables and rimes is compared, opinion is divided over whether children show an earlier sensitivity to syllables than to rimes, as predicted in Metsala and Walley's (1998) framework. Carroll, Snowling, Hulme, and Stevenson (2003) did not find any difference in

Table 3.2 Key to the main tasks used to assess children's phonological awareness

Task[a]	Instructions	Sound unit	Example
Matching	The experimenter reads out each word-pair, and the child judges whether the words had some of the same sounds in them or not (e.g., Treiman & Zukowski, 1991).	Syllable Rime Phoneme	'com*pete*–re*peat*' → 'yes'; 'delight–unique' → 'no' 'sp*it*–w*it*' → 'yes'; 'rail–snap' → 'no' 'smo*ke*–ta*ck*' → 'yes'; 'twist–brain' → 'no'
Oddity	The experimenter says 3 or 4 words, and the child detects the odd word (e.g., Bradley & Bryant, 1983).	Rime	'pin . . . win . . . sit . . . fin' → 'sit'
Blending	The experimenter says a sequence of sounds, and the child combines those sounds to make a new word or non-word (e.g., Lonigan et al., 1998).	Syllable Phoneme	'light . . . bulb' → 'lightbulb' 'b . . . a . . . t' → 'bat'
Tapping	The experimenter says a word, and the child has to tap out the number of sounds in the word (e.g., Liberman et al., 1974).	Syllable Phoneme	'dinner' → the child taps two times 'red' → the child taps three times
Segmentation	The experimenter says a word and asks the child to split up the words into smaller sounds (e.g., Goldstein, 1976).	Syllable Phoneme	'kangaroo' → 'kan . . . ga . . . roo' 'tea' → 't . . . ea'
Deletion	The experimenter says a word and then asks the child to say what is left if a particular sound is taken away (e.g., Anthony et al., 2003).	Syllable Phoneme	'Say "candy" without the "dy" ' → 'can' 'Say "hat" without the "h" ' → 'at'
Common unit	The experimenter reads out a word-pair, and the child responds with the bit of the word that sounds the same (Duncan et al., 1997).	Rime Phoneme	'Which bit sounds the same in "boat–goat"?' → 'oat' 'Which bit sounds the same in "face–food"?' → 'f'

a Note that these tasks are administered as *oral* language games: the children are never shown the words in written form.

performance between syllables and rimes in a matching task over a four-month period during pre-school. In contrast, a large-scale study of children aged between 2 and 6 years conducted by Anthony et al. (2003) revealed an overall advantage for syllables over rimes from analyses of blending and deletion data.

Much may depend on the size of the syllables and rimes that are compared. Although syllables are regarded as larger than rimes in the large-to-small sequence, this is not *necessarily* the case, as rimes can also be similar in size to syllables (e.g., *chant* vs. *antler*) or larger than syllables (e.g., *ramp* vs. *amber*). Observations that children are sensitive to the degree of phonological similarity between items when performing matching tasks (e.g., Byrne & Fielding-Barnsley, 1993; Cardoso-Martins, 1994; Carroll & Snowling, 2001; Treiman & Baron, 1981; Treiman & Breaux, 1982; Treiman & Zukowski, 1991) suggest that larger sounds may be more salient by reason of their size rather than their linguistic status (i.e., syllable vs. rime). Treiman and Zukowski (1996) examined kindergartners' sensitivity to syllable and rime units of *equivalent* size in a matching task. Target word-pairs for syllables (e.g., *repeat–compete*) and rimes (e.g., *amused–confused*), in which the shared sound contained three phonemes, had to be discriminated from foil word-pairs sharing no sounds (e.g., *delay–inject*). They found no advantage for syllables over rimes in disyllabic words, and it was only after substituting nonsense stimuli that a small superiority for syllables emerged. Thus, syllables and rimes appear to have a very similar salience in matching tasks when unit size is equalized.

Other support for the large-to-small view of phonological development has come from comparisons of rime and phoneme awareness in English. Evidence showing strong rhyming skills among pre-school children (Bradley & Bryant, 1983; Lenel & Cantor, 1981; Read, 1978; Stanovich et al., 1984) contrasts with studies showing that phoneme awareness is relatively poor prior to school entry (e.g., Bruce, 1964; Liberman, Shankweiler, Fischer, & Carter, 1974; Snowling & Perin, 1983). However, this comparison contains not just a contrast in sound (rimes vs. phonemes) but also a concurrent contrast in task (rime oddity or rime matching vs. phoneme deletion or phoneme segmentation).

Both Morais (1991) and Gombert (1992) have proposed that oddity and matching tasks can be accomplished on the basis of *holistic* (implicit) sensitivity to global sound similarity, whereas tests such as deletion or segmentation require more *analytic* (explicit) skills. This is illustrated by the examples in Table 3.2, where it can be seen that in the tasks towards the top of the table the child is required to make a judgement at the word level, whereas in the tasks towards the bottom of the table more analysis is required, and the child has to identify a particular unit of sound. As a result, it is unclear whether the correct interpretation of the above studies should be that rimes are more salient than phonemes or simply that oddity and matching tasks are easier than segmentation or deletion tasks. In the next section a series of studies is reviewed that have attempted to use the same task to measure different units of sound at both the implicit and explicit levels to examine phonological development more systematically.

Distinguishing between different types of phonological awareness

Duncan et al. (1997; Duncan, Seymour, & Hill, 2000) followed a group of children during nursery and the first two years of primary school. An implicit oddity task and an explicit common unit task were administered using both rimes and phonemes in each task. At nursery, the children exhibited the classic pattern of advantage for larger rime units (e.g., *wall–hall–duck*) over smaller phonemic units (e.g., *mop–man–dish*) in an oddity task. On transfer to primary school, investigation of explicit phonological skills revealed that, despite their excellent implicit rhyming skills, the children were mostly unable to identify the large unit of sound shared by rhyming word-pairs like *boat–goat* in the common unit task. This contrasted markedly with their accuracy on pairs such as *face–food*, which shared a smaller phonemic unit. This finding has since been replicated by Seymour, Duncan, and Bolik (1999) and by Goswami and East (2000).

Roberts and McDougall (2003) made a similar comparison of rime and phoneme awareness in three sets of tasks: implicit tasks, production and discrimination tasks and segmentation and blending tasks. The results for the implicit tasks were broadly similar to those of Duncan et al. (1997) in that an advantage was observed for rimes over phonemes among 4- and 5-year-olds in their first school year. The children showed no difference in performance between the sound units in the production and discrimination tasks, but they were better with rimes than phonemes in the segmentation and blending tasks (cf. Seymour & Evans, 1994). Nevertheless, one issue to be borne in mind in interpreting these results is that different sets of tests were sometimes used to assess awareness at the rime and phoneme levels. This was particularly noticeable in the final and most demanding set of tasks where segmentation and blending tests were administered for both rimes and phonemes but a deletion test was also incorporated as an additional measure of phoneme awareness alone. This difference in assessment method may account for the lower mean accuracy in response to phonemes in this set of tasks.

A later study by Savage, Blair, and Rvachew (2006) compared performance in just two tasks: the (implicit) matching task and the (explicit) common unit task. These tasks were administered using a carefully controlled set of stimuli that controlled for the size and position of sound units within words. Pre-readers displayed an advantage for larger over smaller units in the matching task. This contrasted with performance in the common unit task where initial phonemes tended to be identified better than final phonemes and larger rime units. Other pre-school children who had already developed some early reading skills showed more sensitivity to initial phonemes in both the implicit and explicit tasks, including a clear advantage for initial and final phonemes over rimes in the common unit task.

Two conclusions are suggested by this body of work: (1) awareness of sound can take different forms (implicit and explicit), according to the degree of conscious control that can be exerted over speech sounds; and (2) meta-phonological development does not necessarily progress in a large-to-small sequence and may at times follow a small-to-large path. It is difficult to account for such findings in Metsala and Walley's (1998) model since there is no provision for small-unit processing to emerge before large-unit processing. However, both conclusions are compatible with the ideas advanced by Gombert (1992).

A cross-linguistic perspective on phonological development

Cross-linguistic studies of European languages allow investigation of another important question raised earlier in this chapter: namely, whether there is a universal pathway in phonological development (Ziegler & Goswami, 2005). A universal pathway is also implied in Metsala and Walley's (1998) theory, but Gombert's (1992) model appears to argue against a fixed pathway, given the overt dependence of meta-phonological development on the native language environment and on the demands placed on the child during reading instruction.

When phonological development is examined in languages other than English, the findings suggest considerable cross-linguistic variation. Caravolas and Bruck (1993) reported that English-speaking and Czech-speaking beginning readers differed in their ability to isolate or delete phonemes from consonant–consonant–vowel (CCV) and consonant–vowel–consonant (CVC) structures. These differences were interpreted as reflecting the greater frequency of words beginning with complex consonant clusters in Czech. Durgunoğlu and Öney (1999) found that Turkish kindergartners and first-graders were better at syllable and phoneme tapping than their US counterparts, especially with syllable items. The authors attributed this to the salience and clarity of syllable boundaries in Turkish, which contrasts with the ambiguous syllable boundaries that are typical of English. Cossu, Shankweiler, Liberman, Katz, and Tola (1988) made a similar comparison between Italian and English (using data from Liberman et al., 1974). Syllable tapping was consistently better in Italian, which, according to the authors, reflects the simpler syllable structure of Italian, where syllables tend to end in a vowel (open syllables) and there are fewer syllable and vowel types. Differential effects of language were also observed among French and English beginning readers in the identification of *body* units (e.g., CV, CCV), which correspond to open syllables and occur more frequently in French than in English (Duncan, Gombert, Seymour, & Martinot, reported in Duncan, 2004).

The complexity and clarity of syllable structure appear to be implicated in the cross-linguistic variation described in the studies above. One aspect of language that is closely associated with syllable structure is speech rhythm (Ramus, Nespor, & Mehler, 1999), which refers to the temporal rhythm that characterizes each spoken language. The timing of the rhythmic beats in speech depends on different features in different languages. In English, a *stress-timed* language, lexical stress is critical to the timing of speech, whereas in French, a *syllable-timed* language, speech rhythm is based on the syllable (Abercrombie, 1967). Such differences raise the interesting possibility that the rhythmic characteristics of a child's language might influence phonological development. Infants appear to tune in quickly to the rhythm of their native language (Nazzi, Bertoncini, & Mehler, 1998), leading to the hypothesis that speech rhythm might be one aspect of the early linguistic environment that could play a role in shaping different paths in phonological development. This is consistent with the influence attributed to *first linguistic skills* in Gombert's (1992) model but less compatible with the idea of a universal large-to-small sequence of development. In the remainder of this chapter, two studies that investigate explicit phonological skills cross-linguistically are presented. The aims are two-fold: (1) to examine the emergence of *explicit* awareness of syllables, rimes and phonemes longitudinally; and (2) to establish the extent to which explanations in terms of native language and the experience of reading instruction can give an account of the sequence of development that is observed. A comparison of English and French is presented in Study 1 and a wider range of European languages is explored in Study 2.

Study 1: The development of explicit awareness among English and French monolinguals (Duncan, Colé, Seymour, & Magnan, 2006)

As previously mentioned, French is regarded as a syllable-timed language and English as a stress-timed language on the basis that the languages differ in terms of speech rhythm. Several contrasting features of the two languages may underlie the different rhythms: (a) syllable structure: syllables tend to have open structures (e.g., CV) in French and closed structures (e.g., CVC) in English; (b) prosody: lexical stress is contrastive in English, with each word having a characteristic pattern of stress (e.g., *construct* has a different meaning in English according to whether it is stressed on the first syllable, in which case it is a noun, or the second syllable, in which case it is a verb); in French, the stress pattern of a word can vary in connected speech without affecting meaning; and (c) vowel reduction: vowels tend to be reduced in unstressed syllables in English (e.g., *mature* and *meringue* are both pronounced with the same reduced vowel in the first syllable), but this feature is not typical of French.

One consequence of these differences associated with speech rhythm is that infants from native language environments that differ in speech rhythm are thought to use different linguistic cues when they start to try to divide up the speech that they hear around them into individual words (Ramus et al., 1999). These cues are thought to be syllable-based in French but stress-based in English. Although this creates the expectation that French and English children may differ in their sensitivity to phonological syllables, the experimental evidence from the only existing comparison of English and French syllable processing does not fully resolve this issue. Bruck, Genesee, and Caravolas (1997) found equivalent accuracy in the performance of French and English kindergarten children in syllable matching, which suggests similar implicit sensitivity to large units of sound. The French speakers, however, did show a small but significant advantage over the English speakers (80 vs. 74 per cent) in syllable counting where the *number* of syllables in one-, two- and three-syllable non-words had to be distinguished. This difference in the more explicit test of syllable awareness is consistent with an effect of speech rhythm, but given that the difference in performance was relatively small and that overall performance was relatively high in both groups, we decided to take a closer look at explicit awareness of syllables in English and French. Sensitivity to syllables, rimes and phonemes during the transition to literacy was assessed using common unit identification rather than counting in order to circumvent concerns about the influence of basic counting skills on the performance of nursery-age children. Furthermore, the common unit task requires the precise identification of shared units of sound and so might be more likely to uncover differences in syllable clarity arising from speech rhythm.

Concerning the availability of phonology in pre-school children, Gombert's (1992) theory predicts that the differing speech rhythms are likely to lead to an advantage for French speakers in explicit awareness of syllables, although there would be no reason to expect explicit awareness of rimes or phonemes in either group at pre-school. At school, however, all children will be learning to read an alphabetic orthography via a method of instruction that places emphasis on letters and sounds and this would be expected to boost explicit awareness of phonemes (independently of other units) in both languages, but especially in the case of the more transparent French orthography (Cossu et al., 1988).

In contrast, Metsala and Walley (1998) argue that language development rather than general meta-cognitive ability or reading experience has the greatest influence on the course of phonological development. For this reason, their lexical restructuring theory predicts a similar large-to-small sequence in both French and English during the transition to literacy. It is possible that development through this large-to-small sequence might be accelerated in the more transparent French orthography (Anthony & Francis, 2005), but explicit phoneme awareness will not emerge in either language until this large-to-small sequence is complete.

The French- and English-speaking children were matched on chronological age (see Table 3.3 for group characteristics). Although it was established that vocabulary skills were normal for age in each language group, it was not possible to use the same vocabulary test in both countries: a test of receptive vocabulary, The British Picture Vocabulary Scale (BPVS)[1] was used in English, and a test of expressive vocabulary, the Vocabulary subtest from the WPPSI(R) or WISC(R),[2] depending on the age of the child, was used in French. All of the children attended schools with an average SES catchment area. However, the educational systems of France and the United Kingdom differ in that instruction is introduced at the age of 5 years in the United Kingdom, a year earlier than in France. Three types of phonological common

Table 3.3 Mean chronological age and vocabulary score for each participant group in Study 1

Age	Language	N	Chronological age	Vocabulary (standard score)	
				BPVS	*WPPSI(R)/ WISC(R)*
4 years	English	22	4.58 (0.25)	98 (12)	—
	French	20	4.58 (0.25)	—	8.75 (0.78)
5 years	English	23	5.58 (0.25)	103 (13)	—
	French	35	5.50 (0.42)	—	10.51 (1.31)
6 years	English	22	6.92 (0.25)	107 (12)	—
	French	33	6.58 (0.25)	—	9.26 (1.46)

Note: Standard deviations in parentheses.

unit were assessed within the first CV or CVC syllable of disyllabic words according to the following conditions: syllables (e.g., *canal–cassette*; *confuse–control*), rimes (e.g., *baboon–career*; *bamboo–campaign*) and initial phonemes (e.g., *hello–hooray*; *sardine–submit*). There was no inconsistency in the spellings of the phonological common units. As can be seen from the examples, all of the English items had iambic stress in order to match the obligatory stress pattern of French. There were four items per condition in each language. Children were asked in their own language: 'Which bit sounds the same in ____?' and were then asked to repeat the word-pair and to identify the common sound. The order of administration of the conditions was counter-balanced, with each session taking place on a separate (usually successive) day.

At age 4 years, English performance was close to floor level on all units, while the French children were very accurate at identifying shared syllables (86 per cent correct). The French syllable advantage persisted at ages 5 and 6 years and is consistent with an early and lasting effect of linguistic environment on phonological development (Gombert, 1992). Excellent syllable awareness did not, however, stimulate the emergence of an explicit awareness of either rimes or initial phonemes among the French pre-schoolers. Phoneme identification accuracy increased sharply at age 5 in English (64 per cent), and there was a comparable abrupt improvement in phonemic skills at age 6 in French. These differential effects can be related to the start of formal literacy instruction in the United Kingdom (at age 5) and in France (at age 6). Little evidence emerged that the French children made any more progress in explicit phoneme awareness during the first year at school than did the English speakers.

The results did not conform to a large-to-small progression in either language: the sequence in English was phoneme→syllable/rime, and in French it was syllable→phoneme→rime. This contradicts the expectation from the lexical restructuring theory that there would be a large-to-small sequence of development in each language. The evidence for differing paths in the development of explicit phonological awareness in different languages is most consistent with the views of Gombert (1992), who emphasized the influence of the external linguistic environment on the nature of subsequent phonological development. From infancy, the spoken syllable is a more salient sound in the syllable-timed French language than in the stress-timed English language, and these results show that explicit awareness of syllables develops earlier among French than among English speaking children. Furthermore, in keeping with Gombert's ideas about the impact of letter-sound-based reading instruction, both groups were observed to develop an explicit awareness of phonemes after school entry (see Figure 3.2).

Study 2: Phonological development in English, French, Icelandic, Portuguese and Spanish (Duncan et al., 2009)

The second study of phonological development formed part of a larger European investigation of reading acquisition and reading disability. The data described here contain a replication of the French–English comparison using French speaking participants from Belgium rather than from France. These data are reported together with findings from three other languages (Icelandic, Portuguese and Spanish), which are introduced to further explore the effects of speech rhythm and orthography.

As previously discussed, English and French differ in terms of lexical stress, vowel reduction and syllable structure, and these parameters have been quantified by Ramus et al. (1999) in an attempt to establish a measurable basis for the stress-timed versus syllable-timed contrast. By using the proportion of time allotted to vowels in spoken sentences and the variability in the duration of consonant sequences, Ramus et al. found that English and French could be clearly distinguished. When they used this metric to classify other languages, stress-timed and syllable-timed languages could be seen to fall into different clusters: English was similar to other Germanic languages like Dutch, and French clustered with other Romance languages like Italian, and also Spanish.

Ramus et al. (1999) commented that it remained unclear whether languages were classifiable into a small number of rhythm classes or whether some languages might fall into intermediary categories, as if distributed along a continuum. Unfortunately, Icelandic and Portuguese were not examined by Ramus et al. (1999), but their metric has subsequently been applied to (European) Portuguese by Frota and Vigário (2001). Portuguese was observed to overlap with both the stress-timed and the syllable-timed language clusters in the previous study and seemed therefore to constitute one of the intermediary languages referred to by Ramus et al. This would fit with the characteristics of Portuguese, which, despite being considered a Romance language, has a variable stress pattern with vowel reduction like English (a Germanic language), although, like French, Portuguese has a predominance of open syllables. Icelandic has not yet been investigated in this way and so

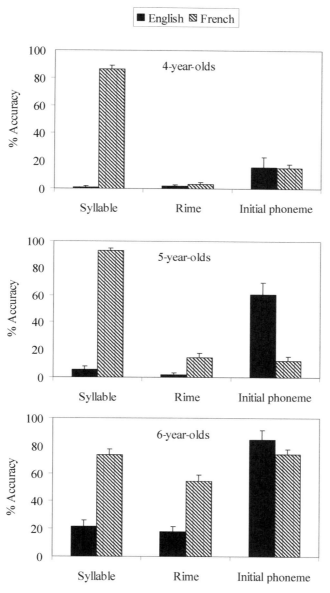

Figure 3.2 Mean percentage accuracy at common unit identification for each age group of French and English speaking participants in Study 1.

cannot be classified into a rhythm category with any certainty. Nevertheless, Icelandic also appears to occupy an intermediate position on some of the key parameters. Icelandic is considered a Germanic language but differs from English in that it has a fixed stress pattern and does not show vowel reduction. While in these respects Icelandic is more similar to French, syllable structure appears more complex in Icelandic than in French. Thus, some of the languages in the study are easily classifiable into two distinct groupings on the basis of speech rhythm: English is stress-timed, whereas French and Spanish are syllable-timed. There may also be an intermediate class of rhythmically mixed languages, Portuguese and Icelandic, which share characteristics with both of the other rhythm classes.

As in the previous study, the predictions contrast Gombert's (1992) view that different types of meta-awareness develop independently in response to the language environment and the experience of learning to read, with Metsala and Walley's (1998) prediction of a large-to-small progression in phonological development. If speech rhythm influences levels of explicit syllable awareness, then the following outcome might be expected in terms of performance accuracy: French, Spanish > Icelandic, Portuguese > English. If orthographic depth is important in the rate at which explicit phoneme awareness is acquired, then the analysis provided by Seymour et al. (2003) suggests the following outcome: Spanish, Icelandic > Portuguese > French > English.

These possibilities were examined in a longitudinal study of the first year of schooling. Children were selected from schools with an average SES catchment area in each of five participating countries (Belgium, Iceland, Portugal, Spain and the United Kingdom). The English speakers were younger than the other children due to differences in the age of schooling between the United Kingdom (5 years) and the other European countries (6 years). However, all of the groups experienced instruction that emphasized the relationship between letters and sounds at the phoneme level. Mean chronological ages and Raven's Coloured Progressive Matrices (Raven, 1973)[3] scores for each group can be seen in Table 3.4. In line with the age differences, the Raven's raw scores were lowest in the UK group, although the scores for the Portuguese group were more similar to those of the UK group than to the other 6-year-olds in the study.

The common unit task followed a format similar to Study 1. Each country produced a parallel set of disyllabic materials with the common unit in the first CV or CVC syllable to form eight conditions, each with four items. English examples are as follows: syllables (e.g., *button–bubble*, *window–winter*);

Table 3.4 Mean chronological age and Raven's Matrices raw score for each participant group in Study 2

Language	N	Chronological age	Raven's Matrices
English	33	5.31 (0.32)	17.82 (3.40)
Icelandic	27	6.18 (0.30)	25.81 (4.40)
Portuguese	22	6.29 (0.32)	18.23 (4.72)
Spanish	62	6.21 (0.29)	21.23 (4.71)
French	20	6.50 (0.33)	24.65 (5.58)

Note: Age in years. Standard deviations in parentheses.

rimes (e.g., *hammer–saddle*, *panther–bandage*); phonemes (e.g., **wallet–woman**, **garden–guilty**). The test was part of a large assessment that took place during the first month of schooling (Time 1) and was then repeated at the end of the school year, when the Raven's Matrices test was also administered (Time 2).

Group percentage accuracy at common unit identification is illustrated in Figure 3.3. At Time 1, statistical analysis showed cross-linguistic differences in sensitivity to the three units of sound. With *syllables*, the pattern observed in Study 1 was replicated, with French speakers performing extremely well at syllable identification and English speakers performing very poorly. In line with the predictions based on speech rhythm, the languages formed three levels of accuracy with respect to syllables: French = Spanish > Icelandic =

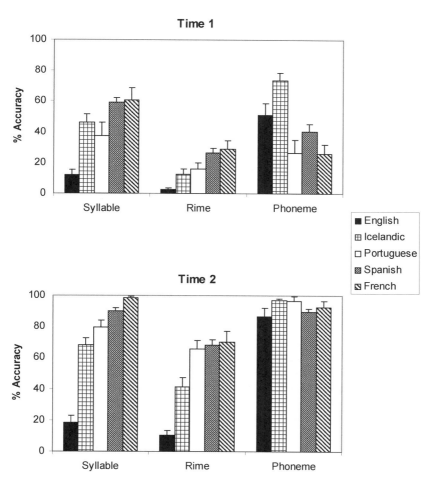

Figure 3.3 Mean percentage accuracy at common unit identification at the beginning (Time 1) and end (Time 2) of the first year of instruction for each language group in Study 2.

Portuguese > English. The only exception to this pattern was that Icelandic also overlapped with the syllable-timed languages (French and Spanish). Responses to *rimes* showed that English-speakers were also worse in this condition than the Spanish and French groups, but no other group differences emerged. Of greatest interest, however, are the contrasting abilities of the language groups in response to *phonemes* just after reading instruction had begun. The Icelandic children performed significantly above the level of any other group, followed closely by the English speakers, who were better than the French and the Portuguese groups, although they did not differ significantly from the Spanish children. Therefore, the correspondence with the predictions based on orthographic depth is poor, since phonemic skills in Spanish (most transparent) and English (least transparent) were indistinguishable.

By Time 2, the pattern showed some important changes, especially in relation to phonemes. With *syllables*, however, the children's performance was very similar to Time 1, with speakers of the syllable-timed languages (French and Spanish) the best and speakers of the stress-timed language (English) the worst. Icelandic and Portuguese speakers performed at an intermediate level, but this time it was the Portuguese children who overlapped with the syllable-timed languages, being similar in accuracy to Spanish speakers although significantly less accurate than French speakers. With rimes, performance was lowest among the English speakers, and although the Icelandic children were more accurate, they did not attain the same level of performance as the remaining three language groups, who scored well (and equivalently). Finally, it was phoneme identification that showed the greatest improvement at the end of the first year of schooling, since all of the groups scored at ceiling level with no variation in relation to orthographic depth.

As it has been suggested that cross-linguistic differences may serve to accelerate development through a large-to-small sequence (Anthony & Francis, 2005), the patterns of phonological development in the data will be set out in greater detail. Throughout the year, the English and Icelandic groups were consistently better at explicit identification of phonemes than of syllables. In contrast, the Spanish and French children were more sensitive to syllables than phonemes at Time 1 but by the end of the year identified both units of sound with equivalent accuracy. Portuguese children showed a unique pattern of initially being equally sensitive to syllables and phonemes but by Time 2 showing an advantage for phonemes over syllables. In all cases, rimes were the least accurately identified unit, sometimes in conjunction with another type of sound, but always among the most difficult sounds to identify explicitly. This outcome contrasts with the suggestion that rimes have an intermediate status in phonological development (Metsala & Walley, 1998), at least with respect to *explicit* awareness of sound.

Overview

The results of the two cross-linguistic studies reported here show a complex and changing pattern of phonological sensitivity between the ages of 4 and 7 years. The results are more compatible with Gombert's (1992) flexible system of shifts from implicit to explicit awareness according to the external demands placed upon the child than with a universal large-to-small progression in phonological development. The discussion focuses on the two key questions linking phonological development and reading acquisition that were identified in the Introduction: (1) the availability of phonology at the outset of learning to read; and (2) the subsequent effects of orthography and instruction in shaping further phonological development.

The availability of phonological awareness as reading instruction begins

The experimental work described here was designed to address the *availability* question raised by Ziegler and Goswami (2005). Study 1 (Duncan et al., 2006) revealed a major cross-linguistic disparity in the ability of French and English speaking children to manipulate syllables explicitly. The English speakers were unexpectedly poor at explicitly identifying shared syllables, while the French children performed close to ceiling from the age of 4 years. This French–English contrast was successfully replicated in Study 2 (Duncan et al., 2009) using French speakers from Belgium rather than from France.

One interpretation of this result is that the French–English contrast has its origin in the differing speech rhythms of the two languages. Syllables are considered more salient in French, a syllable-timed language, than in English, a stress-timed language. The performance of the language groups in Study 2 gives some support to this suggestion. Meta-awareness of syllables in Spanish, a syllable-timed language like French, was excellent and statistically equivalent to that of the French speakers at each test point. Performance by the only established stress-timed language in the study, English, was consistently less accurate than that of any other group. An intermediate category emerged between these distinct rhythm groupings containing Icelandic and Portuguese, as was predicted from observations that these two languages possess qualities associated with both syllable- and stress-timing.

Cross-linguistic differences were also observed in children's meta-awareness of phonological rimes. In both studies, the English speakers were poor at explicitly identifying common rime units at the outset of reading instruction. Both language groups in Study 1 exhibited floor performance on rimes at pre-school, and in Study 2 rimes were among the most difficult sounds to identify explicitly for beginning readers in each language (for similar results in tasks measuring explicit awareness of monosyllabic rimes, see Duncan et al., 1997; Geudens & Sandra, 2003; Goswami & East, 2000; and Savage et al., 2006). No clear pattern of association with speech rhythm emerged for rime awareness, although performance was not completely inconsistent with this explanation. English speakers proved to be worse than the French and Spanish groups at each testing point, but there was no other differentiation in the data except at the end of the school year, when the Icelandic children proved to be better than the English speakers but worse than any of the other three groups.

The variation observed in awareness of larger units among school-aged children appears surprising if viewed in relation to theories in which syllables and rimes are positioned early in the sequence of phonological development (e.g., Metsala & Walley, 1998) and considered to be universally available at the outset of reading acquisition in European languages (Ziegler & Goswami, 2005). The argument being offered here is that this apparent discrepancy can be understood if task demands and native language variation are considered.

It was noted in the Introduction that syllable and rime awareness is usually assessed using epi-linguistic (implicit) tasks such as oddity or matching that can be solved on the basis of global sound similarity. In English, as in other languages, performance in these more implicit tasks appears to be sensitive to unit size, which favours larger over smaller units regardless of their linguistic status (Byrne & Fielding-Barnsley, 1993; Cardoso-Martins, 1994; Carroll & Snowling, 2001; Treiman & Baron, 1981; Treiman & Breaux, 1982; Treiman & Zukowski, 1991, 1996). The results described in the present chapter differ from these earlier findings because the common unit task is a measure of *explicit* awareness which demands the conscious manipulation of sound (Gombert, 1992).

One problem in addressing the issue of differing task demands, however, is that it is not straightforward to classify each phonological task on Gombert's (1992) implicit–explicit dimension. The extreme ends of this dimension corresponding to *global sound similarity* versus *conscious manipulation of units of sound* seem reasonably clear, but there is an element of uncertainty between these two limits. Roberts and McDougall (2003) attempted to do this by classifying phonological tasks according to the processes involved and then using this analysis to place the tasks in order of increasing difficulty: implicit awareness → production and discrimination → segmenting and blending. However, the status of some tasks remains difficult to establish: for example, tapping tasks, which have shown an early advantage for syllables over phonemes (Liberman et al., 1974; but see Backman, 1983, for a contrary result). Although the task appears to be analytic and to fulfil the requirement for greater conscious control, it has been suggested that the rhythmic aspect of tapping may circumvent these meta-demands (Treiman & Baron, 1981). For the purpose of the present argument, it may be more important to note that tapping does not require the precise identification of syllables and that it seems to be this latter ability that poses problems for English speakers (Duncan et al., 2006).

Studies that have demanded this type of analysis for sounds other than phonemes are rare, but those that do exist in English suggest that performance becomes more variable as the demands for greater precision increase.

Goldstein (1976) reported that pre-school segmentation was better for syllables than for phonemes; however, responses were scored correct if they constituted 'a sequence of sounds which corresponded one-to-one with the sequence of segments in a word' (p. 682). Duncan et al. (2006, Experiment 1) have shown that pre-school children can be very good at dividing English disyllables into two correct sequential parts but that these parts do not always correspond to syllables. This finding has a resonance with earlier work by Fox and Routh (1975) in which children were provided with disyllables and monosyllables and simply asked 'to say just a little bit of' each item. While children were expected to provide syllables and phonemes, respectively, this was not always the case, leading the authors to classify responses to disyllables in two ways: any correct portion of the disyllable or a conventional (dictionary-defined) syllable. Results differed according to these two scoring methods, as can be seen in Table 3.5, which illustrates the lower level of meta-awareness when one insists that the sound provided corresponds to a syllable (see Seymour & Evans, 1994, for a similar finding with onset-rime segmentation).

Since 25 per cent of Fox and Routh's stimuli were compound words (e.g., *maybe*, *someone*), which possess unusually clear syllable boundaries, even this analysis may overestimate ability. Rosner and Simon (1971) found that 80 per cent of kindergartners could perform final syllable deletion (e.g., *birthday* → *birth*), but only 50 per cent were successful at initial syllable deletion (e.g., *carpet* → *pet*) and none could delete the medial syllable (e.g., *reproduce* → *reduce*).[4] The results from initial or medial segment deletion in this task may reflect meta-awareness of sound more accurately than final segment deletion because correct responses in the latter task can be generated simply by interrupting the motor activity of articulation (Morais, Alegria, & Content, 1987).

According to these observations, the view that English speaking children

Table 3.5 Classification of responses in Fox and Routh's Word Segmentation task according to whether the 'little bit of' the disyllabic word produced was a dictionary-defined syllable or just any valid sound

Age	*Child's response*[a] *(% of responses)*	
	Any valid sound	*Syllable*
3 years	62.50	42.75
4 years	~100	57.88
5 years	~100	44.13
6 years	~100	66.25
7 years	~100	75.00

Note: Fox and Routh's Word Segmentation task: Fox and Routh (1975). Child's response as percentage of responses.
a Note that the two response categories are overlapping as a syllable response would also be a valid sound response.

display a high level of syllable awareness from an early age may more accurately reflect epi-linguistic (implicit) awareness than meta-linguistic (explicit) awareness. This may seem like a technical point, but the importance of what is claimed about the availability of sounds lies in the inferences that can be drawn about how children might use these sounds in the reading task. The results presented here suggest that young children have a good implicit sensitivity to larger units of sound but that this may not be sufficient to support the use of large units in reading. This is precisely the conclusion reached with respect to rimes by Duncan et al. (1997, 2000). The research described in this chapter suggests that poor explicit awareness of syllables may prevent English-speaking children from exploiting syllables as units in reading, just as the evidence of excellent syllable awareness in French is consistent with reports of syllable use in French children's reading (Colé, Magnan, & Grainger, 1999).

The interaction between literacy acquisition and phonological development

Each of the language groups in Studies 1 and 2 received reading instruction that emphasized the correspondence between print and sound at the letter (phoneme) level. The common unit results from Study 1 confirmed that an explicit awareness of phonemes coincided with the introduction of reading instruction at age 5 in the United Kingdom and at age 6 in France. In Study 2, which examined the period from the first introduction of reading instruction to the end of the first year of reading, the language groups showed varying degrees of explicit awareness of phonemes at the outset of the study. It was not the case that speakers of languages with the best syllabic skills also had the best phonemic skills (cf. Anthony & Francis, 2005), since the English speakers, whose explicit awareness of syllables and rime was poor, were second only to the Icelandic speakers in explicit awareness of phonemes, and significantly better than the French speakers in this respect. Neither did it seem that orthographic depth could explain the initial language group differences in phoneme awareness, but, as ceiling effects had obscured any group variation by Time 2, more regular testing during the first school year may be necessary to assess the influence of this factor fully. Another issue that needs to be pursued is whether the pace of introduction of letter–sound instruction differed between the language groups at the beginning of the school year.

No obvious pattern of association emerged between syllable or rime awareness and literacy acquisition. The cross-linguistic differences observed early in schooling remained largely unchanged at the end of the year, despite improvements in accuracy. Nevertheless, Gombert's (1992) theory predicts that the external demands placed upon the children during development must have differed in relation to syllables. One possibility is that the findings are simply an effect of pre-school teaching, as the pre-schoolers in Study 1 regularly took part in language games that involved the manipulation of 'large' units. This mainly took the form of rhyming games and, in France, syllables were sometimes included as well, but our measures show that these games apparently made no difference to either group's meta-awareness of rimes. As this weakens the argument that this explanation can account for the syllable results, it may be that other factors associated with speech rhythm and early language use lead to the emergence of meta-awareness of syllables.

The outcome reinforces the longstanding view that learning to read has a profound impact on the development of a meta-awareness of phonemes. In each of the five countries in Study 2, explicit awareness of phonemes improved to ceiling level in the course of the first year of reading instruction that introduced the children to letters and their sounds. Hence, instructionally generated letter-sounding strategies appear to have a direct impact on the organization of the phonological system, although exactly how these processes might interact remains unclear and is a topic for future research (Bråten, 1993; Ceci & Nightingale, 1990; Clark & Karmiloff-Smith, 1993; Rumelhart, Smolensky, McClelland, & Hinton, 1986; Smolensky, 1988).

Conclusion

The work presented in this chapter examines the idea of a universal large-to-small progression in phonological development and yields evidence instead of differing pathways, varying in the sequence and level of awareness of large and small units and seemingly shaped by native language and reading instruction. As well as emphasizing the benefits of a cross-linguistic perspective, this outcome illustrates the importance of taking the meta-cognitive demands of phonological tasks into account in drawing conclusions about the availability of sound at the beginning of the reading process.

Notes

1 The child must select which picture out of four presented matches the word spoken by the experimenter.
2 The Wechsler Pre-School & Primary Scale of Intelligence—Revised [WPPSI(R)] and the Wechsler Intelligence Scale for Children—Revised [WISC(R)]. The child must provide definitions for words spoken by the experimenter.
3 A test of non-verbal intelligence in which participants are presented with six images and must select the correct image that completes a logical sequence.
4 These initial and final deletion data are each based on only one item in the Auditory Analysis Test, and where performance was most accurate (final syllable deletion) that item had a compound structure.

References

Abercrombie, D. (1967). *Elements of general phonetics*. Edinburgh, UK: Edinburgh University Press.

Anthony, J. L., & Francis, D. J. (2005). Development of phonological awareness. *Current Directions in Psychological Science, 14*, 255–259.

Anthony, J. L., Lonigan, C. J., Driscoll, K., Phillips, B. M., & Burgess, S. R. (2003). Phonological sensitivity: A quasi-parallel progression of word structure units and cognitive operations. *Reading Research Quarterly, 38*, 470–487.

Backman, J. (1983). The role of psycholinguistic skills in reading acquisition—a look at early readers. *Reading Research Quarterly, 18*, 466–479.

Bowey, J. A., & Francis, J. (1991). Phonological analysis as a function of age and exposure to reading instruction. *Applied Psycholinguistics, 12*, 91–121.

Bradley, L., & Bryant, P. E. (1983). Categorizing sounds and learning to read—a causal connection. *Nature, 301*, 419–421.

Bråten, I. (1993). Cognitive strategies: A multi-componential conception of strategy use and strategy instruction. *Scandinavian Journal of Educational Research, 37*, 217–243.

Bruce, D. J. (1964). The analysis of word sounds by young children. *British Journal of Educational Psychology, 34*, 158–170.

Bruck, M., Genesee, F., & Caravolas, M. (1997). A cross-linguistic study of early literacy acquisition. In B. Blachman (Ed.), *Foundations of reading acquisition and dyslexia* (pp. 145–162). Mahwah, NJ: Lawrence Erlbaum Associates, Inc.

Bryant, P., MacLean, M., & Bradley, L. (1990a). On rhyme, language, and children's reading—comments. *Applied Psycholinguistics, 11*, 449–450.

Bryant, P. E., MacLean, M., Bradley, L. L., & Crossland, J. (1990b). Rhyme and alliteration, phoneme detection, and learning to read. *Developmental Psychology, 26*, 429–438.

Byrne, B., & Fielding-Barnsley, R. (1993). Recognition of phoneme invariance by beginning readers—confounding effects of global similarity. *Reading and Writing, 5*, 315–324.

Caravolas, M., & Bruck, M. (1993). The effect of oral and written language input on children's phonological awareness—a cross-linguistic study. *Journal of Experimental Child Psychology, 55*, 1–30.

Cardoso-Martins, C. (1994). Rhyme perception—global or analytical. *Journal of Experimental Child Psychology, 57*, 26–41.

Carroll, J. M., & Snowling, M. J. (2001). The effects of global similarity between stimuli in performance on rime and alliteration tasks. *Applied Psycholinguistics, 22*, 327–342.

Carroll, J. M., Snowling, M. J., Hulme, C., & Stevenson, J. (2003). The development of phonological awareness in preschool children. *Developmental Psychology, 39*, 913–923.

Ceci, S. J., & Nightingale, N. N. (1990). The entanglement of knowledge and process in development: Toward a tentative framework for understanding individual differences in intellectual development. In W. Schneider & F. E. Weinert (Eds.), *Interactions among aptitudes, strategies, and knowledge in cognitive performance* (pp. 29–46). New York: Springer-Verlag.

Clark, A., & Karmiloff-Smith, A. (1993). The cognizer's innards: A psychological and philosophical perspective on the development of thought. *Mind and Language, 8*, 487–519.

Colé, P., Magnan, A., & Grainger, J. (1999). Syllable-sized units in visual word recognition: Evidence from skilled and beginning readers of French. *Applied Psycholinguistics, 20*, 507–532.

Cossu, G., Shankweiler, D., Liberman, I. Y., Katz, L., & Tola, G. (1988). Awareness of phonological segments and reading ability in Italian children. *Applied Psycholinguistics, 9*, 1–16.

Duncan, L. G. (2004). Influence de l'apprentissage de la lecture et de la langue maternelle sur le développement phonologique: Une perspective inter-langues [The impact of literacy and native language on phonological development: A cross-linguistic study]. In S. Valdois, P. Colé, & D. David (Eds.), *Apprentissage de la lecture et dyslexies développementales: De la théorie á la practique orthophonique et pédagogique* (pp. 15–41). Marseille, France: SOLAL.

Duncan, L. G., Colé, P., Seymour, P. H. K., & Magnan, A. (2006). Differing sequences of metaphonological development in French and English. *Journal of Child Language, 33*, 369–399.

Duncan, L. G., Seymour, P. H. K., Baillie, S., Genard, N., Leybaert, J., Lund, R., et al. (2009). *Phonological development in English, French, Icelandic, Portuguese and Spanish: Tracing the effects of speech rhythm and literacy acquisition.* Manuscript in preparation.

Duncan, L. G., Seymour, P. H. K., & Hill, S. (1997). How important are rhyme and analogy in beginning reading? *Cognition, 63*, 171–208.

Duncan, L. G., Seymour, P. H. K., & Hill, S. (2000). A small to large unit progression in metaphonological awareness and reading? *Quarterly Journal of Experimental Psychology, 53A*, 1081–1104.

Durgunoğlu, A. Y., & Öney, B. (1999). A cross-linguistic comparison of phonological awareness and word recognition. *Reading and Writing, 11*, 281–299.

Elbro, C., Borstrom, I., & Petersen, D. K. (1998). Predicting dyslexia from kindergarten: The importance of distinctness of phonological representations of lexical items. *Reading Research Quarterly, 33*, 36–60.

Fowler, A. E. (1991). How early phonological development might set the stage for phoneme awareness. In S. A. Brady & D. P. Shankweiler (Eds.), *Phonological processes in literacy* (pp. 97–117). Hillsdale, NJ: Lawrence Erlbaum Associates, Inc.

Fox, B., & Routh, D. K. (1975). Analyzing spoken language into words, syllables, and phonemes: A developmental study. *Journal of Psycholinguistic Research, 4*, 331–342.

Frota, S., & Vigário, M. (2001). On the correlates of rhythmic distinctions: The European/Brazilian Portuguese case. *Probus, 13*, 247–275.

Garlock, V. M., Walley, A. C., & Metsala, J. L. (2001). Age-of-acquisition, word frequency, and neighbourhood density effects on spoken word recognition by children and adults. *Journal of Memory and Language, 45*, 468–492.

Geudens, A., & Sandra, D. (2003). Beyond implicit phonological knowledge: No support for an onset-rime structure in children's explicit phonological awareness. *Journal of Memory and Language, 49*, 157–182.

Goldstein, D. M. (1976). Cognitive-linguistic functioning and learning to read in preschoolers. *Journal of Educational Psychology, 68*, 680–688.

Gombert, J. E. (1992). *Metalinguistic development.* London: Harvester Wheatsheaf.

Goswami, U., & Bryant, P. E. (1990). *Phonological skills and learning to read.* Hillsdale, NJ: Lawrence Erlbaum Associates, Inc.

Goswami, U., & East, M. (2000). Rhyme and analogy in beginning reading: Conceptual and methodological issues. *Applied Psycholinguistics, 21*, 63–93.

Jusczyk, P. W. (1986). Toward a model of the development of speech perception. In

J. Perkell & D. H. Klatt (Eds.), *Invariance and variability in speech perception* (pp. 1–19). Hillsdale, NJ: Lawrence Erlbaum Associates, Inc.

Karmiloff-Smith, A. (1986). From meta-processes to conscious access—evidence from children's metalinguistic and repair data. *Cognition, 23*, 95–147.

Lenel, J. C., & Cantor, J. H. (1981). Rhyme recognition and phonemic perception in young children. *Journal of Psycholinguistic Research, 10*, 57–67.

Liberman, I. Y., Shankweiler, D., Fischer, F. W., & Carter, B. (1974). Explicit syllable and phoneme segmentation in the young child. *Journal of Experimental Child Psychology, 18*, 201–212.

Lonigan, C. J., Burgess, S. R., Anthony, J. L., & Barker, T. A. (1998). Development of phonological sensitivity in 2- to 5-year-old children. *Journal of Educational Psychology, 90*, 294–311.

MacLean, M., Bryant, P., & Bradley, L. (1987). Rhymes, nursery rhymes, and reading in early-childhood. *Merrill-Palmer Quarterly: Journal of Developmental Psychology, 33*, 255–281.

McBride-Chang, C., Wagner, R. K., & Chang, L. (1997). Growth modelling of phonological awareness. *Journal of Educational Psychology, 89*, 621–630.

Menyuk, P., & Menn, L. (1979). Early strategies for the perception and production of words and sounds. In P. Fletcher & M. Garman (Eds.), *Language acquisition* (pp. 49–70). Cambridge, UK: Cambridge University Press.

Metsala, J. L. (1997). An examination of word frequency and neighborhood density in the development of spoken-word recognition. *Memory and Cognition, 25*, 47–56.

Metsala, J. L., & Walley, A. C. (1998). Spoken vocabulary growth and the segmental restructuring of lexical representations: Precursors to phonemic awareness and early reading ability. In J. L. Metsala & L. C. Ehri (Eds.), *Word recognition in beginning literacy* (pp. 89–120). Mahwah, NJ: Lawrence Erlbaum Associates, Inc.

Morais, J. (1991). Phonological awareness: A bridge between language and literacy. In D. J. Sawyer & B. J. Fox (Eds.), *Phonological awareness in reading: The evolution of current perspectives* (pp. 31–71). New York: Springer-Verlag.

Morais, J., Alegria, J., & Content, A. (1987). The relationships between segmental analysis and alphabetic literacy: An interactive view. *European Bulletin of Psychology, 7*, 415–438.

Morais, J., Cary, L., Alegria, J., & Bertelson, P. (1979). Does awareness of speech as a sequence of phones arise spontaneously? *Cognition, 7*, 323–331.

Nazzi, T., Bertoncini, J., & Mehler, J. (1998). Language discrimination by newborns: Toward an understanding of the role of rhythm. *Journal of Experimental Psychology: Human Perception and Performance, 24*, 756–766.

Nittrouer, S. (1992). Age-related differences in perceptual effects of formant transitions within syllables and across syllable boundaries. *Journal of Phonetics, 20*, 351–382.

Ramus, F., Nespor, M., & Mehler, J. (1999). Correlates of linguistic rhythm in the speech signal. *Cognition, 73*, 265–292.

Raven, J. C. (1973). *Coloured progressive matrices*. London: H.K. Lewis & Co.

Read, C. (1978). Children's awareness of language with emphasis on sound systems. In A. Sinclair, R. J. Jarvella, & W. J. M. Levelt (Eds.), *The child's conception of language* (pp. 65–92). New York: Springer-Verlag.

Read, C., Zhang, Y. F., Nie, H. Y., & Ding, B. Q. (1986). The ability to manipulate speech sounds depends on knowing alphabetic writing. *Cognition, 24*, 31–44.

Roberts, L., & McDougall, S. (2003). What do children do in the rime-analogy task? An examination of the skills and strategies used by early readers. *Journal of Experimental Child Psychology, 84*, 310–337.

Rosner, J., & Simon, D. P. (1971). The auditory analysis test: An initial report. *Journal of Learning Disabilities, 4*, 384–393.

Rumelhart, D. E., Smolensky, P., McClelland, J. L., & Hinton, G. E. (1986). Schemata and sequential thought processes in PDP models. In D. E. Rumelhart & J. L. McClelland (Eds.), *Parallel distributed processing: Explorations in the microstructure of cognition* (Vol. 2, pp. 7–57). Cambridge, MA: MIT Press.

Savage, R., Blair, R., & Rvachew, S. (2006). Rimes are not necessarily favored by prereaders: Evidence from meta- and epilinguistic phonological tasks. *Journal of Experimental Child Psychology, 94*, 183–205.

Seymour, P. H. K., Aro, M., Erskine, J. M., Wimmer, H., Leybaert, J., Elbro, C., et al. (2003). Foundation literacy acquisition in European orthographies. *British Journal of Psychology, 94*, 143–174.

Seymour, P. H. K., Duncan, L. G., & Bolik, F. M. (1999). Rhymes and phonemes in the common unit task: Replications and implications for beginning reading. *Journal of Research in Reading, 22*, 113–130.

Seymour, P. H. K., & Evans, H. M. (1994). Levels of phonological awareness and learning to read. *Reading and Writing, 6*, 221–250.

Smolensky, P. (1988). On the proper treatment of connectionism. *Behavioural and Brain Sciences, 11*, 1–23.

Snowling, M. J. (2000). *Dyslexia*. Oxford, UK: Blackwell.

Snowling, M. J., & Perin, D. (1983). The development of phoneme segmentation skills in young children. In D. Rogers & J. A. Sloboda (Eds.), *The acquisition of symbolic skills* (pp. 155–162). New York: Plenum Press.

Stanovich, K. E., Cunningham, A. E., & Cramer, B. B. (1984). Assessing phonological awareness in kindergarten children—issues of task comparability. *Journal of Experimental Child Psychology, 38*, 175–190.

Stuart, M., & Coltheart, M. (1988). Does reading develop in a sequence of stages? *Cognition, 30*, 139–181.

Treiman, R. (1987). On the relationship between phonological awareness and literacy. *Cahiers de Psychologie Cognitive, 7*, 524–529.

Treiman, R. (1992). The role of intrasyllabic units in learning to read and spell. In P. B. Gough, L. C. Ehri, & R. Treiman (Eds.), *Reading acquisition* (pp. 1–70). Hillsdale, NJ: Lawrence Erlbaum Associates, Inc.

Treiman, R., & Baron, J. (1981). Segmental analysis ability: Development and relation to reading ability. In G. E. MacKinnon & T. G. Waller (Eds.), *Reading research: Advances in theory and practice* (Vol. 3, pp. 159–198). New York: Academic Press.

Treiman, R., & Breaux, A. M. (1982). Common phoneme and overall similarity relations among spoken syllables—their use by children and adults. *Journal of Psycholinguistic Research, 11*, 569–598.

Treiman, R., & Zukowski, A. (1991). Levels of phonological awareness. In S. A. Brady & D. P. Shankweiler (Eds.), *Phonological processes in literacy: A tribute to Isabelle Y. Liberman* (pp. 67–84). Hillsdale, NJ: Lawrence Erlbaum Associates, Inc.

Treiman, R., & Zukowski, A. (1996). Children's sensitivity to syllables, onsets, rimes, and phonemes. *Journal of Experimental Child Psychology, 62*, 432–455.

Walley, A. C. (1993). The role of vocabulary development in children's spoken word recognition and segmentation ability. *Developmental Review, 13*, 286–350.

Walley, A. C., Smith, L. B., & Jusczyk, P. W. (1986). The role of phonemes and syllables in the perceived similarity of speech sounds for children. *Memory and Cognition, 14*, 220–229.

Yopp, H. K. (1988). The validity and reliability of phonemic awareness tests. *Reading Research Quarterly, 23*, 159–177.

Ziegler, J. C., & Goswami, U. (2005). Reading acquisition, developmental dyslexia, and skilled reading across languages: A psycholinguistic grain size theory. *Psychological Bulletin, 131*, 3–29.

4 Letter position encoding across deep and transparent orthographies

Maria Ktori and Nicola J. Pitchford

Introduction

The orthographic structure of languages varies widely. In languages with a transparent orthography, such as Greek and Spanish, the mappings between letters and sounds are highly consistent: given the rules, all words can be read successfully. However, in languages with a deep orthography, such as English and Danish, the letter-to-sound correspondence in words is less consistent: many words have irregular spellings (e.g., *yacht*) and learning their unusual pronunciations is the only way to read them correctly. Empirical evidence from cross-linguistic studies suggests that the variation in the orthographic structure of languages may significantly affect the development of word recognition skills and of reading in general (e.g., Frith, Wimmer, & Landerl, 1998; Patel, Snowling, & de Jong, 2004; Seymour, Aro, & Erskine, 2003; see also Ziegler & Goswami, 2005, for a review). Orthographic structure may also influence the initial stages of written word recognition in which letter identity and position are encoded.

The successful recognition of written words begins with letter-based orthographic processing, which involves identification of the letters within a letter string and encoding of their relative position (Coltheart, Rastle, Perry, Langdon, & Ziegler, 2001; Plaut, McClelland, Seidenberg, & Patterson, 1996). For example, children learning to read often say letter sounds out loud ('duh–oh–guh' for *dog*) to try to make sense of words they have not encountered. Even as adults we tend to do this for difficult words, like *procrastinate*. Encoding the letters in a word relative to each other is an important process as it enables readers to distinguish between anagrams, such as *dog* and *god*, or *coincidental* and *nondialectic*. Recent research has investigated how early orthographic processing occurs in written word recognition, and several computational models of letter position encoding have been developed (see Davis & Bowers, 2006; Grainger, 2008; and Whitney, 2008, for reviews). Most of this research has, however, been conducted in English and in other fairly deep orthographies, such as French. Consequently relatively little is known about early orthographic encoding in transparent orthographies, such as Greek and Spanish, and whether or not it differs from that of deep orthographies.

Research on skilled readers of English has revealed positional biases in early orthographic processing. In English, the first and last letters of words or letter strings (e.g., the 'b' and 'k' in *blank*) are identified faster than are interior letters (e.g., the 'l' 'a', or 'n' in *blank*; Hammond & Green, 1982; Humphreys, Evett, Quinlan, & Besner, 1987; Jordan, Thomas, Patching, & Scott-Brown, 2003a, 2003b; Peressotti & Grainger, 1995). Furthermore, letters appearing at the left of a word or letter string (e.g., 'b' and 'l' in *blank*) are processed faster than letters appearing at the right (e.g., 'n' and 'k' in *blank*) (e.g., Hammond & Green, 1982; Harcum & Nice, 1975; Humphreys, Evett, & Quinlan, 1990). This may reflect the need for both parallel (whole-word or lexical) and serial (letter-by-letter or sub-lexical) processing of letter strings in deep orthographies that enable irregular words (e.g., *yacht*) and novel or nonsense words (e.g., *tellop*) to be read successfully (Coltheart et al., 2001). However, for transparent orthographies with consistent letter-to-sound correspondences, successful word recognition can occur purely by serial (sub-lexical) processes. Therefore, skilled readers of transparent orthographies may rely to a greater extent on serial processes in written word recognition than do skilled readers of a deep orthography (Katz & Frost, 1992; Paulesu et al., 2000), and this may also be reflected in the initial stages of reading when readers identify individual letters and note their position within the written word.

In this chapter we describe experimental work that has used a visual search task to explore early orthographic processing in skilled adult readers and developing readers. In a standard visual search task readers are required to determine whether or not a previously cued character (letter or non-letter symbol) is present as a target in a subsequently presented array of five different random characters. The task allows careful manipulation of the position in which the target appears in the test array (see Figure 4.1 for an illustration of the task). Response time to detect a target appearing in each of the five

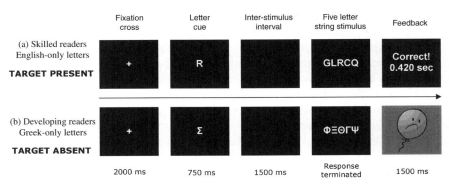

Figure 4.1 Schematic illustration of the stimulus display used for (a) skilled adult readers and (b) developing readers in an experimental trial of the visual search task.

positions of the array produces a search function that is thought to reflect the processes utilized by participants during the task.

Although this task is a relatively distal measure of orthographic processing compared to more direct measures such as lexical decision, a growing body of evidence suggests that letter search performance taps into specialized processes used in written word recognition. First we review previous research that has used this task to investigate early orthographic processing. Then we describe our own studies, which have shown differential letter search performance across skilled and developing readers of deep (English) and transparent (Greek) orthographies. We end by considering the theoretical implications of letter search data for contemporary models of letter position encoding and suggest how future research may use this task in conjunction with other measures of orthographic processing to explore different patterns of reading behaviour in a multilingual context.

Review of previous research with the visual search task

The visual search task first became popular in the late 1970s and 1980s as a method for exploring positional biases in early orthographic processing (e.g., Hammond & Green, 1982; Mason, 1975, 1982; Mason & Katz, 1976). The task was initially used to investigate whether letter string processing utilizes specialized mechanisms associated with written word recognition or whether similar attentional processes are used for a variety of visual stimuli (such as letters and other non-letter shapes). As research with skilled and developing readers of English suggested that letter search performance reflected dedicated processes used in recognizing English words, the task was later extended to skilled readers of different orthographies that vary from English in structure in order to explore how orthographic structure impacts on search performance.

Visual search performance of skilled and developing readers of English

Previous studies that have used the visual search task to investigate ortho-graphic processing have shown that skilled English readers identify cued letters that appear at the ends (Positions 1 and 5) and centre (Position 3) of a 5-letter array faster than neighbouring letters in Positions 2 and 4, and response time increases from the left to the right of the array. Performance of skilled readers of English produces an upward sloping M-shaped search function which is characterized by significant linear (upward slope) and quartic (M-shape) components (as illustrated in Figure 4.2). This performance pattern has been taken to reflect the two processes involved with recognizing English words. First, the faster identification of letters at the ends of the array (Positions 1 and 5) relative to the neighbouring letters (Positions 2 and 4) has been taken to reflect the influence of parallel (whole-word or lexical) processes engaged in written word recognition. Second, the faster identification

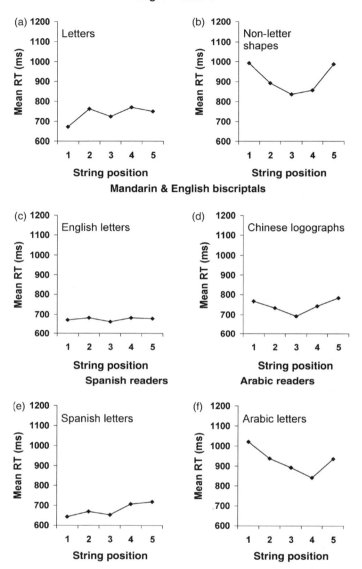

Figure 4.2 Visual search functions produced by skilled readers of different orthographies. Data plotted from Hammond and Green (1982) for (a) skilled English readers searching for English letters, showing a left-to-right upward-sloping M-shaped function in which identification of the initial and final letters is facilitated relative to neighbouring letters, and (b) non-letter shapes, showing a U-shaped function in which end characters are recognized slowest. Data plotted from Green et al. (1996) for biscriptal Mandarin–English readers when searching for (c) English letters, showing an upward-sloping M-shaped function, and (d) Chinese characters, showing a U-shaped function. Data plotted from Green and Meara (1987) for (e) Spanish readers searching for Spanish letters, showing an upward-sloping Z-shaped function in which recognition of the final letter is *not* facilitated, and (f) Arabic readers searching for Arabic letters, showing a U-shaped function sloping from right to left.

of target letters appearing at the left (Positions 1 and 2) compared to the right (Positions 4 and 5) of the array is thought to reflect serial (letter-by-letter or sub-lexical) processing in line with the left-to-right direction for decoding English words (Green, Hammond, & Supramaniam, 1983; Hammond & Green, 1982; Pitchford, Ledgeway, & Masterson, 2008).

Facilitation of exterior letters in the test string, revealed by skilled English readers, is thought to reflect genuine orthographic processes rather than better visual discrimination of these letters relative to interior letters in the string (interior letters might be perceived as being crowded together, so leading to poorer performance). This is because response times of skilled English readers correlate significantly with positional letter frequency (i.e., the frequency with which different letters appear in different positions of words of a specified length) for the exterior letters, such that more frequent letters are identified faster than less frequent letters in the initial and final positions, suggesting an influence from lexical processes (Pitchford et al., 2008). Also, skilled English readers are slowest to detect other non-letter stimuli that appear in the exterior positions of a test string comprised of random non-letter shapes (Hammond & Green, 1982; Mason, 1982). When searching for non-letter shapes, skilled readers of English are faster at identifying targets appearing in the medial position of the test array; they become increasingly slower as the target moves further from the centre of the string. This response pattern reveals a U-shaped search function that is characterized by a significant quadratic component and reflects a centre-out scanning process (Hammond & Green, 1982), as illustrated in Figure 4.2.

For both letters and non-letter shapes skilled English readers tend to fixate at the medial position of the test array (Wagstaffe, Pitchford, & Ledgeway, 2005), showing a bias at the centre of the visual field where visual acuity is sharpest. Thus, skilled readers tend to focus at the centre (Position 3) of the test array, as this optimizes perception of characters (letters and non-letter shapes) within the array. Hence, the critical difference between identifying letter and non-letter targets on this task lies in the exterior positions of the test string and the advantage to letter (but not shape) stimuli presented to the left of the array.

These studies suggest that the letter search performance of skilled readers of English reflects engagement with a specialized system for processing written words that is not utilized when searching for non-letter shapes. Accordingly, search patterns for letters and non-letter shapes should differ across development as children learn to read. To investigate this hypothesis, Green et al. (1983) gave English beginner readers (5-year-olds) and developing readers (7-year-olds) visual search tasks comparing letter and non-letter-shaped stimuli. They showed that the developing readers, when identifying cued letters embedded in a random 5-letter array, produced search functions that sloped upward from the left to the right of the array. This linear component became more prominent with age: 5-year-old children did not reveal a significant linear component in their search performance whereas 7-year-old children did. Furthermore, both groups of children produced a qualitatively different function when searching for non-letter shapes, as they responded more slowly to letter targets in the exterior positions of the test string than to those presented in the medial position. These findings led the authors to conclude that different processes are utilized when searching for letters and shapes on the visual search task, and that the positional biases shown in the letter search function reflect processes typically engaged in written word recognition that become more established with age.

Visual search performance of readers of different writing systems

A series of investigations has shown how letter search performance varies according to different orthographic systems. The Chinese writing system is radically different from that of English. While English has an alphabetic writing system and combinations of letters are required to represent a word, Chinese has a logographic system in which characters are either comprised of a semantic element and a phonetic element which together provide meaning, or a single character can represent a complete lexical concept (see chapter 10, this volume). When searching for Chinese characters, Chinese readers have been shown to produce a U-shaped search function similar to the non-letter-shaped function produced by English readers (Green & Meara, 1987). Furthermore, biscriptal readers of Mandarin and English seem to vary their search performance depending on the nature of script they are given; the same readers produced an upward-sloping M-shaped function when searching for English letters and a U-shaped function when searching for Chinese characters (Green, Liow, Tng, & Zielisnki, 1996), as illustrated in Figure 4.2.

The Arabic writing system, although alphabetic, has noticeable differences from English, the most prominent being reading direction. Arabic is read from right to left, in contrast to English which is read from left to right. When searching for Arabic letters, skilled readers of Arabic produce a U-shaped search function, with response times showing a tendency to increase from right to left, reflecting the direction of reading Arabic script (Green & Meara, 1987). These studies show that performance on the visual search task is sensitive to the nature of the orthographic input to which readers are exposed. Thus, even though the visual search task does not involve processing of words or pronounceable non-words, it appears to engage with orthographic processes utilized in written word recognition.

Visual search performance of readers of orthographies varying in transparency

In order to investigate whether the letter search function generated by skilled readers of English reflects specific strategies required for processing a deep orthography, Green and Meara (1987) investigated letter search performance in skilled readers of Spanish, a transparent orthography. Native Spanish readers produced a letter search function that was highly similar to that produced by English readers, leading the authors to conclude that orthographic transparency has little effect on the processes utilized in the letter search task.

This conclusion may be unwarranted, however, as the Spanish participants recruited to Green and Meara's study could read English fluently, and exposure to English orthography may have influenced their search performance. Also, the letter search function of Spanish readers demonstrated a significant cubic (Z-shape) component, as they did not show facilitation of letter targets appearing in the final position of the test string relative to the fourth position, as is typical of skilled English readers (see Figure 4.2). It has been suggested that facilitation of the final letter may reflect the influence of parallel (lexical) processes utilized in written word recognition on the early orthographic processing of letter strings because response times to identify letter targets in the final position correlate with the frequency with which letters appear in the final position of 5-letter English words (Pitchford et al., 2008). As Spanish readers failed to show such facilitation, this may suggest that their performance on this task is influenced by lexical processes to a lesser extent than readers of a deep orthography. Thus, the extent to which orthographic transparency influences the identification of letters and encoding of their relative position within letter strings has yet to be determined.

Recent research investigating the effect of orthographic transparency on letter search performance in skilled and developing readers

In this section we describe recent research that we have carried out to examine whether orthographic transparency influences letter search performance. We summarize two cross-linguistic investigations, one with skilled readers (Ktori & Pitchford, 2008) and one with developing readers (Ktori & Pitchford, 2009) of Greek (transparent) and English (deep) orthography. Greek is considered to be a very transparent orthography (Seymour et al., 2003), with a highly consistent relationship between spelling and sound. The spelling of written words therefore determines how they are pronounced (Chitiri & Willows, 1994). Thus, Greek is an ideal orthography in which to explore the effects of orthographic transparency on letter identification and position encoding by comparing it to English which is one of the most opaque orthographies.

Both of our studies used a letter search task to compare how readers of English or Greek process letter identity and encode letter order. We adopted a standard visual search paradigm in which participants were required to identify a cued letter in a subsequently presented random array of five different letters, as illustrated in Figure 4.1. The visual search task consisted of three sets of letter stimuli. One set of stimuli comprised 10 letters (A, B, E, H, I, K, M, N, P, T) that are shared by both alphabets (English and Greek). Another set of stimuli comprised 10 letters (C, G, J, L, Q, R, S, U, V, W) found only in the English alphabet (English-only). A third set of stimuli comprised 10 letters (Γ, Δ, Θ, Λ, Ξ, Π, Σ, Φ, Ψ, Ω) found only in the Greek alphabet (Greek-only). This enabled us to compare the performance of English and Greek readers when searching for letters of their native orthography to letters of their non-native orthography, and thus the effects of stimulus familiarity on search performance could also be investigated. The length of time required to identify a target letter correctly in different positions of the test array enabled comparisons to be made between critical letter positions.

To investigate the pure effect of orthographic transparency on letter search performance, we suggest that comparisons need to be performed between monolingual readers who have no knowledge (spoken or written) of an additional language. Thus, we compared the performance of a group of skilled monolingual adult readers of either English or Greek who were matched for age and education. To investigate the development of letter position processing over these two orthographies, we compared the performance of 6- and 9-year-old children learning to read in either English or Greek who could not speak or read in another language.

We predicted that when searching for letters from their native orthographies (i.e., English-only and English and Greek letters combined for English readers; Greek-only and English and Greek letters combined for Greek readers), skilled monoscriptal readers of English should show an upward-sloping M-shaped function in which both the initial (Position 1) and final (Position 5) letters in the string are recognized faster than the neighbouring letters (Positions 2 and 4), as illustrated in Figure 4.2. In contrast, skilled monoscriptal readers of Greek should show an upward-sloping Z-shaped function in which the initial (but *not* the final) letter is identified faster than the neighbouring letter (Position 2), similar to Spanish readers in Figure 4.2. Furthermore, if performance on the letter search task genuinely reflects processes utilized in written word recognition, then these functions should emerge with development as children gain more exposure to, and skill in reading, their native orthography. Thus, we expected to see the letter search functions become increasingly defined across development for each of the two orthographies. For non-native letters (Greek-only for English readers; English-only for Greek readers), we envisaged similar performance patterns across skilled and developing readers of both orthographies which should resemble the search function for non-letter shapes (illustrated in Figure 4.2), as these letters should have been unfamiliar to the participants.

Results are shown in Figures 4.3 (native letters) and 4.4 (non-native letters). As is clearly shown, when searching for native letters, skilled and developing readers of English produced an upward-sloping M-shaped function in which both the initial and final letters were recognized faster than the neighbouring letters in Positions 2 and 4, respectively (see Figure 4.3). Thus, our data are consistent with previous research (e.g., Hammond & Green, 1982), as illustrated in Figure 4.2. Effect size analyses showed that initial (Position 1 vs. Position 2) and final (Position 4 vs. Position 5) letter facilitation became more

Native letters

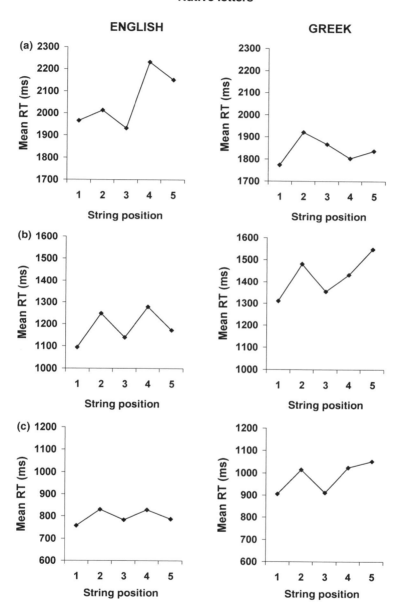

Figure 4.3 Letter search function produced by English (left column) and Greek (right column) (a) 6-year-old, (b) 9-year-old and (c) skilled readers when searching for native letters. For each of the orthographies, data show emergent characteristic upward-sloping M-shaped (English) and Z-shaped (Greek) search functions with development.

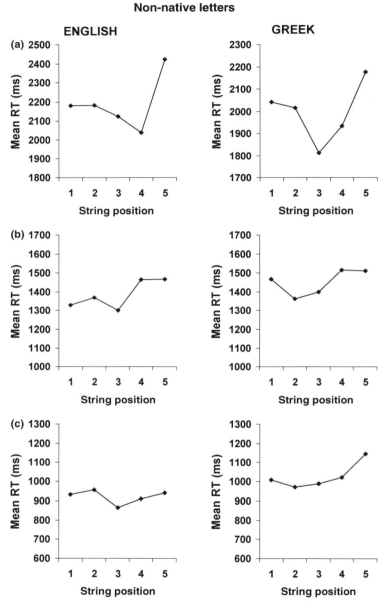

Figure 4.4 Search functions produced by English (left column) and Greek (right column) (a) 6-year-old, (b) 9-year-old and (c) skilled readers when searching for non-native letters. For each of the orthographies, data show similar U-shaped search functions across development, in which recognition of end letters is not significantly speeded relative to neighbouring letters.

pronounced with age, increasing from a small to a medium effect size across the three reader groups (initial letter facilitation effect sizes were 0.1, 0.6 and 0.5, and final letter facilitation effect sizes were 0.2, 0.4 and 0.3, for 6-year-old, 9-year-old and skilled readers, respectively). In contrast, the magnitude of the upward slope became less marked with age, as evidenced by effect sizes for left-to-right (Position 1 vs. Position 5) letter facilitation decreasing from medium to small with age (left-to-right facilitation effect sizes were 0.4, 0.3 and 0.2, for 6-year-old, 9-year-old and skilled readers, respectively).

A qualitatively different performance pattern was found for skilled and developing Greek readers when searching for native letters, as they produced an upward-sloping Z-shaped function, which differed from the M-shaped function produced by English readers primarily in that the final letter was *not* recognized faster than the neighbouring letter in Position 4 of the test string (see Figure 4.3). This processing pattern is highly similar to the letter search function produced by skilled (bilingual) readers of Spanish reported by Green et al. (1996), as shown in Figure 4.2. Thus, the lack of a final letter advantage on the letter search task appears to characterize readers of a highly transparent orthography. As with the English readers, the search function of Greek readers for native letters became more pronounced with age. Effect sizes for initial letter facilitation (Position 1 vs. Position 2) increased from small to medium across the three reader groups (0.3 for 6-year-olds, 0.6 for 9-year-olds and 0.5 for skilled adult readers). Similarly, effect sizes for left-to-right facilitation (Position 1 vs. Position 5) increased with age, from small–medium to medium–large (0.4 for 6-year-olds, 0.7 for 9-year-olds and 0.6 for skilled adult readers). In contrast, small effect sizes were found for final letter encoding (Position 4 vs. Position 5) for each of the three Greek reader groups (0.1, 0.3 and 0.1, for 6-year-old, 9-year-old and skilled adult readers, respectively), and for each age group letter targets appearing in the fourth position of the test array were recognized faster than those appearing in the fifth position.

For non-native letters, qualitatively different search functions were produced by skilled and developing readers of English and Greek (see Figure 4.4) compared to the search functions they produced for native letter stimuli (see Figure 4.3). Furthermore, all reader groups produced a similar U-shaped function when searching for unfamiliar letters, which resembled the function produced by skilled readers when searching for non-letter shapes (as shown in Figure 4.2). This U-shaped function is characterized by faster identification of non-native letter targets presented centrally, with slower recognition of non-native letters presented at the ends of the stimulus array. Only the 9-year-old and skilled English readers diverted from this U-shaped function at the initial position, as they identified non-native letters faster in Position 1 than in Position 2. However, this difference was not significant, and the effect size was very small (0.1 in both cases) compared to the medium effect size produced when identifying native letters in these positions (0.6 and 0.5 for 9-year-old and skilled adults readers, respectively). This is consistent with previous research reporting visual search performance for non-letter shapes (e.g., Hammond & Green, 1982).

Thus, our data suggest that a specialized system for identifying letters and encoding their position within letter strings emerges with development, as children become experienced with processing their native orthography. The English data suggest that, as children gain experience in reading English words, they learn to encode initial and final letters faster than neighbouring letters, in line with parallel (whole-word or lexical) processes. Furthermore, as children advance from relying on a decoding (sounding-out or sub-lexical) strategy for reading English words as they become skilled readers, so the extent to which they encode letters serially (from left to right) decreases. In contrast, the Greek data suggest that readers of a transparent orthography rely almost exclusively on serial (left-to-right) processes for letter identification and position encoding and receive very little benefit from parallel (whole-word or lexical) processes.

We also investigated letter search performance in a group of skilled bilingual readers whose first-acquired (native) language was Greek. This group of adults had all learned English from the age of 10 years on and were being educated in English at the University of Nottingham at the time of investigation. They were thus all highly proficient in speaking and reading English (their second-acquired language). Comparing search performance for this group of bilingual readers when identifying letters from their native (first-acquired) language compared to their non-native (second-acquired) language enabled us to assess the impact that learning to encode letter identity and position in a transparent orthography (Greek) has on the later acquisition of letter encoding processes in a deep orthography (English) and vice versa.

The results, shown in Figure 4.5, revealed that the bilingual readers applied

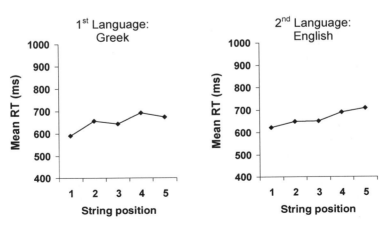

Figure 4.5 Search functions produced by Greek–English adult bilingual readers when searching for first- (Greek) and second- (English) acquired letters.

similar strategies when searching for letters from both their first-acquired (Greek) and second-acquired (English) orthography. For both sets of stimuli, the group of bilingual readers identified letter targets in the initial position faster than those in the neighbouring second position of the test array, although the effect size was greater for Greek (0.5) than for English (0.2) letters. When searching for first- and second-acquired letter targets presented at the end (Positions 4 and 5) of the stimulus array, the group of bilingual readers produced marginally different performance patterns. For Greek letters, the bilingual readers were slightly faster at identifying letters in the fifth compared to the fourth position, whereas for English letters they showed the opposite pattern.

However, for both letter sets these differences were not significant, and effect sizes were very small (0.1 for both sets of stimuli), illustrating that the effect of final letter processing in this group of bilingual readers was not very robust. In contrast, medium effect sizes were found for left-to-right processing of the string as bilingual readers were faster at identifying letter targets presented in the initial position (1) compared to the final position (5) of the stimulus string for both Greek (0.5) and English (0.6) stimuli. Interestingly, the magnitude of left-to-right letter facilitation shown by the bilingual readers for both sets of letters was similar to that shown by the group of Greek monoscriptal readers when searching for Greek (native) letters (0.6), but it was much greater than the effect size shown by the English monoscriptal readers when searching for English (native) letters (0.2), as reported above (see also Figure 4.3). This suggests that the serial encoding of letters in strings by readers of a transparent, first-acquired orthography has lasting effects on letter position processing and generalizes to the processing of letters in a deep, later-acquired orthography that is not typically characterized by such marked serial processes.

Theoretical implications and future developments for research with the visual search task

Our research using the letter search task to investigate the effect of orthographic transparency on early orthographic processing, in which letter identity and position is encoded, has revealed qualitative differences across readers of a deep (English) compared to a transparent (Greek) orthography. While readers of both English and Greek showed an advantage for identifying letters in the initial position of the string, differences were found across orthographies for encoding letters in the final position and the magnitude of left-to-right processing across the letter string. English readers showed speeded recognition of the final letter in the test string, consistent with parallel (whole-word or lexical) processes, where Greek readers did not. In contrast, Greek readers showed greater left-to-right facilitation of letters across the stimulus string, consistent with serial (sub-lexical) processes, than readers of English. Furthermore, these positional biases emerged with reading development, reflecting the acquisition of a dedicated system for letter identification and position encoding that is adaptive to the nature of the script to which the reader is exposed while learning to read.

Effects of orthographic transparency on reading acquisition have been shown in numerous recent developmental studies (see chapter 3, this volume; for a review, see also Ziegler & Goswami, 2005). This research has shown that the development of word and non-word reading occurs at a more rapid rate in children who are learning to read in a transparent orthography (e.g., Greek) compared to children learning to read in a deep orthography (e.g., English). This is thought to occur because the nature of a transparent orthography, which is characterized by a consistent set of simple letter-to-sound correspondences, promotes rapid development of sub-lexical decoding skills (Seymour et al., 2003). As most unfamiliar words can be read successfully with sub-lexical decoding skills in a highly transparent orthography, rapid acquisition of letter–sound decoding skills will lead to greater reading success than in a deep orthography, where the application of decoding skills to some unfamiliar words (i.e., irregular and inconsistent words) will lead to inaccurate pronunciations. Consequently, children learning to read in a transparent orthography are thought to rely on serial decoding skills to a greater extent than children learning to read a deep orthography (Katz & Frost, 1992; Paulesu et al., 2000; Share, 1999, 2004). Our research has shown that learning to read in a transparent orthography also promotes serial processing of letter strings to a greater extent than is typical of learning to read in a deep orthography. This has lasting effects across development.

Our investigations have important implications for theories and models of orthographic processing that describe and simulate how letter identity and position are encoded. Our results suggest that a specialized system for identifying letters and encoding their position within written words and letter strings emerges during the early stages of reading development. Furthermore, this system appears to be adaptive to the nature of orthography to which the reader is exposed. Different positional biases exist for readers of a deep compared to a transparent orthography that may reflect the extent to which parallel (whole-word or lexical) and serial (sub-lexical) processes influence early orthographic processing. Models of letter position encoding need to be able to account for these data to be considered comprehensive.

Recently, several models of letter position encoding have been proposed that differ in the extent to which they can accommodate our data (e.g., the SOLAR model, Davis, 1999; the SERIOL model, Whitney, 2001; and the open-bigram model, Grainger & van Heuven, 2003). The consistent left-to-right letter facilitation shown across both English and Greek readers reflects the utilization of serial processes, in line with reading direction of these orthographies. Our data thus support models of letter position encoding that operate in serial (Davis, 1999; Whitney, 2001) rather than in parallel (Grainger & van Heuven, 2003). However, at present, neither the SOLAR (Davis, 1999) nor the SERIOL (Whitney, 2001) model, both of which operate in a serial fashion, can capture the difference in magnitude of left-to-right processing shown by our Greek and English readers.

Furthermore, none of the current models of letter position encoding can account adequately for the differences in positional biases, especially for the final letter, in letter string processing shown by our groups of English and Greek readers. For example, the open-bigram model (Grainger & van Heuven, 2003), which operates in parallel, predicts no advantage for encoding letters in different string positions. In contrast, the SOLAR model (Davis, 1999), which operates on a spatial coding scheme, promotes earlier encoding of the initial, but not the final, letter in the string. Also, the SERIOL model (Whitney, 2001), which operates according to a temporal coding scheme in line with reading direction, benefits encoding of the initial letter in a string but also boosts final-letter processing due to reduced lateral inhibition from the absence of neighbouring letters in the terminal position. Accordingly, the exterior letters in a string receive stronger activation than do the internal letters. While the SERIOL model provides the most comprehensive account of our English data, the SOLAR model is more compatible with our Greek data.

Clearly, the differential pattern of final letter processing and the difference in magnitude of left-to-right processing of letters across a string, found in both developing and skilled readers of orthographies that vary in transparency, poses a major challenge to all contemporary models of letter position encoding. Further research using different tasks of letter perception and orthographic processing, with readers of orthographies that vary in structure, is needed to verify our findings. For example, using a direct measure of orthographic processing, such as lexical decision, we expect to see sensitivity to the frequency of initial letters in words for both readers of English and Greek, but only readers of English (and other deep orthographies) may show sensitivity to the frequency of final letters in words. Furthermore, exaggerated length effects should be observed by skilled readers of Greek compared to skilled readers of English when recognizing words in a lexical decision task, and bilingual readers of Greek and English should show differential effects of length on tasks of visual word recognition when processing Greek and English words. We are currently exploring these hypotheses in our laboratory. Together with the letter search data described in this chapter, these tasks will help us to gain a better understanding of how orthographic structure influences the early stages of orthographic processing.

References

Chitiri, H., & Willows, D. M. (1994). Word recognition in two languages and orthographies: English and Greek. *Memory and Cognition, 22*, 313–325.

Coltheart, M., Rastle, K., Perry, C., Langdon, R., & Ziegler, J. C. (2001). DRC: A dual route cascaded model of visual word recognition and reading aloud. *Psychological Review, 108*, 204–256.

Davis, C. J. (1999). The self-organising lexical acquisition and recognition (SOLAR) model of visual word recognition (Doctoral dissertation, University of New South Wales, Sydney, New South Wales, Australia, 1999). *Dissertation Abstracts International, 62*, 594.

Davis, C. J., & Bowers, J. S. (2006). Contrasting five theories of letter position coding. *Journal of Experimental Psychology: Human Perception and Performance, 32*, 535–557.

Frith, U., Wimmer, H., & Landerl, K. (1998). Differences in phonological recoding in German- and English-speaking children. *Scientific Studies of Reading, 2*, 31–54.

Grainger, J. (2008). Cracking the orthographic code: An introduction. *Language and Cognitive Processes, 23*, 1–35.

Grainger, J., & van Heuven, W. (2003). Modelling letter position encoding in printed word perception. In P. Bonin (Ed.), *The mental lexicon* (pp. 1–24). New York: Nova Science Publishers.

Green, D. W., Hammond, E. J., & Supramaniam, S. (1983). Letters and shapes: Developmental changes in search strategies. *British Journal of Psychology, 74*, 11–16.

Green, D. W., Liow, S. J. R., Tng, S. K., & Zielisnki, S. (1996). Are visual search procedures adapted to the nature of the script? *British Journal of Psychology, 87*, 311–326.

Green, D. W., & Meara, P. (1987). The effects of script on visual search. *Second Language Research, 3*, 102–117.

Hammond, E. J., & Green, D. W. (1982). Detecting targets in letter and non-letter arrays. *Canadian Journal of Psychology, 36*, 67–82.

Harcum, E., & Nice, D. (1975). Serial processing shown by mutual masking icons. *Perceptual and Motor Skills, 40*, 399–408.

Humphreys, G. W., Evett, L. J., & Quinlan, P. T. (1990). Orthographic processing in visual word recognition. *Cognitive Psychology, 22*, 517–560.

Humphreys, G. W., Evett, L. J., Quinlan, P. T., & Besner, D. (1987). Orthographic priming: Qualitative differences between priming from identified and unidentified primes. In M. Coltheart (Ed.), *Attention and performance XII: The psychology of reading* (pp. 105–125). Hillsdale, NJ: Lawrence Erlbaum Associates, Inc.

Jordan, T., Thomas, S., Patching, G., & Scott-Brown, K. (2003a). Assessing the importance of letter pairs in initial, exterior and interior positions in reading. *Journal of Experimental Psychology: Learning, Memory, and Cognition, 29*, 883–893.

Jordan, T., Thomas, S., Patching, G., & Scott-Brown, K. (2003b). Assessing the importance of letter pairs in reading—parafoveal processing is not the only view: Reply to Inhoff, Radach, Eiter and Skelly (2003). *Journal of Experimental Psychology: Learning, Memory, and Cognition, 29*, 900–903.

Katz, L., & Frost, R. (1992). Reading in different orthographies: The orthographic depth hypothesis. In R. Frost & L. Katz (Eds.), *Orthography, phonology, morphology and meaning* (pp. 67–84). Amsterdam: North Holland.

Ktori, M., & Pitchford, N. J. (2008). Effect of orthographic transparency on letter position encoding: A comparison of Greek and English monoscriptal and biscriptal readers. *Language and Cognitive Processes, 23*, 258–281.

Ktori, M., & Pitchford, N. J. (2009). Development of letter position processing: Effects of age and orthographic transparency. *Journal of Research in Reading, 32*, 180–198.

Mason, M. (1975). Reading ability and letter search times: Effects of orthographic structure defined by single-letter positional frequency. *Journal of Experimental Psychology: General, 104,* 146–166.

Mason, M. (1982). Recognition time for letters and non-letters: Effects of serial position, array size and processing order. *Journal of Experimental Psychology: Human Perception and Performance, 8,* 724–738.

Mason, M., & Katz, L. (1976). Visual processing of non-linguistic strings: Redundancy effects and reading ability. *Journal of Experimental Psychology: General, 105,* 338–348.

Patel, T. K., Snowling, M. J., & de Jong, P. F. (2004). A cross-linguistic comparison of children learning to read in English and Dutch. *Journal of Education of Psychology, 96,* 785–797.

Paulesu, E., McCrory, E., Fazio, F., Menoncello, L., Brunswick, N., Cappa, S. F., et al. (2000). A cultural effect on brain function. *Nature Neuroscience, 3,* 91–96.

Peressotti, F., & Grainger, J. (1995). Letter-position coding in random consonant arrays. *Perception and Psychophysics, 57,* 875–890.

Pitchford, N. J., Ledgeway, T., & Masterson, J. (2008). Effect of orthographic processes in letter position encoding. *Journal of Research in Reading, 31,* 97–116.

Plaut, D. C., McClelland, J. L., Seidenberg, M. S., & Patterson, K. (1996). Understanding normal and impaired word reading: Computational principles in quasi-regular domains. *Psychological Review, 103,* 56–115.

Seymour, P. H. K., Aro, M., & Erskine, J. M. (2003). Foundation literacy acquisition in European orthographies. *British Journal of Psychology, 94,* 143–174.

Share, D. L. (1999). Phonological recoding and orthographic learning: A direct test of the self-teaching hypothesis. *Journal of Experimental Child Psychology, 72,* 95–129.

Share, D. L. (2004). Orthographic learning at a glance: On the time course and developmental onset of self-teaching. *Journal of Experimental Child Psychology, 87,* 267–298.

Wagstaffe, J. K., Pitchford, N. J., & Ledgeway, T. (2005). Does central fixation account for medial letter facilitation in visual search? *Perception, 34*(Suppl.), 150.

Whitney, C. (2001). How the brain encodes the order of letters in a printed word: The SERIOL model and selective literature review. *Psychonomic Bulletin and Review, 8,* 221–243.

Whitney, C. (2008). Supporting the Serial in the SERIOL Model. *Language and Cognitive Processes, 23,* 824–865.

Ziegler, J. C., & Goswami, U. C. (2005). Reading acquisition, developmental dyslexia and skilled reading across languages: A psycholinguistic grain size theory. *Psychological Bulletin, 131,* 3–29.

5 Differences in reading ability between children attending Welsh- and English-speaking primary schools in Wales

J. Richard Hanley

Introduction

The first half of this chapter reviews the main findings from a research programme that my colleagues and I completed in 2004, in which we examined the acquisition of reading skills in children living in Wales (Hanley, Masterson, Spencer, & Evans, 2004; Spencer & Hanley, 2003, 2004). In this investigation, the ease of learning to read the notoriously opaque English orthography was compared with learning to read Welsh (a highly transparent alphabetic orthography). Wales offers a unique opportunity to compare the effects of a transparent and opaque orthography on reading development because children in Wales are taught to read in either Welsh- or English-speaking primary schools. Consequently, it is possible to compare the acquisition of a shallow and deep orthography in children of a similar age in the same country and education system. There are therefore a number of methodological advantages associated with studies of learning to read in Wales compared with other investigations of the effects of orthographic transparency on learning to read. As will become evident, the results from our research clearly demonstrate that the single-word reading and phonological awareness skills of the children who were learning to read the transparent Welsh orthography developed much more quickly than did those of children who were learning to read English.

The second half of the chapter considers some issues that have not been explored in the papers referred to above. These include:

- whether boys are disadvantaged relative to girls when learning to read a transparent orthography;
- the precise characteristics of the underachieving 'tail' of English readers relative to the poorest Welsh readers;
- whether the differences in reading ability between Welsh and English readers have diminished following the advent of the National Literacy Strategy in England;
- the optimal ways of selecting reading materials when comparing the ability to read words in different writing systems.

Welsh orthography

The Welsh writing system originated approximately 400 years ago. There is a Welsh Academy (*Academi Gymreig*) that regulates the spelling of Welsh words. Consequently, new words entering the language (e.g., technical terms and foreign words, such as *quantum mechanics* and *taxi*) are given a standardized spelling to reflect the rules of the Welsh writing system (e.g., *mecaneg cwantwn* and *tacsi*). Welsh spelling was standardized in 1928 and again in 1977, when many words whose spellings were inconsistent with Welsh letter–sound correspondences ('irregular words') were reformed. It is now a highly transparent orthography.

The Welsh alphabet contains 21 letters of the Roman alphabet (k, q, v, x, z are missing). Eleven consonants are represented by digraphs (ch, dd, ff, ll, ng, nn, ph, rh, rr, si, th), and the eight that children are most likely to encounter in print are explicitly taught to children in schools as letters. Diphthongs (vowel sounds in which the tongue changes position to produce the sound of two vowels) are also represented by digraphs (ai, ae, aw, au, ei). Only very rarely, as in the name of the town *Bangor*, do these vowel or consonant digraphs represent two distinct phonemes when they appear together in a word. In addition, each letter or digraph almost always represents the same phoneme in every word in which it appears. Those exceptions that do exist are almost entirely predictable from the position of the letter in the word. For example, some letters represent vowels that are different when they appear at the start of a syllable and when they represent the middle of a syllable. Moreover, unlike transparent orthographies such as Greek, where vowel phonemes have more than one possible spelling, there is only one way in which phonemes can be written in Welsh. This means that Welsh is also highly transparent for the purposes of writing.

Rationale for our study

In the 1990s, several studies demonstrated that the word recognition skills of children learning to read transparent orthographies such as Turkish (e.g., Öney & Durgunoğlu, 1997), German (e.g., Wimmer & Hummer, 1990) and Italian (e.g., Cossu, Shankweiler, Liberman, & Gugliotta, 1995) developed more rapidly than those of children learning to read English. Young readers of transparent orthographies, even 'poor' readers, made very few reading errors by the end of their first year of formal instruction. More recently, Seymour, Aro, and Erskine (2003) reported the results of a comprehensive study of single-word reading skills at the end of first year of formal reading instruction in 14 European languages. Children learning English read fewer words correctly than did any of the other nationalities. Children learning transparent orthographies are also more likely to adopt phonologically based strategies when reading. For example, their reading errors are more likely to be phonologically similar non-words (e.g., *cave* → *cav*) than visually similar words (e.g., *cave* → *come*), suggesting that they are more likely than English children to pronounce unfamiliar words by using letter–sound associations. They also perform better than children learning English on tests of phoneme awareness (e.g., counting the number of phonemes in spoken words).

However, there are a number of cultural differences between the United Kingdom and Continental Europe that make direct comparisons slightly difficult to interpret. Reading instruction starts at 4–5 years in the United Kingdom, but at 6–7 years across most of Continental Europe. Children in the United Kingdom are therefore at least a year younger at the end of their first year of reading instruction than are most other children in Europe. The structure of English syllables is also more complex than in European languages such as Italian or Spanish. For example, clusters of consonants can appear before and after the vowel in English syllables but not in Spanish or Italian syllables. Also, there are a larger number of different vowel sounds in English. These differences (sometimes referred to as *phonotactic* differences) might be responsible for superior phonological awareness skills and hence might produce differences in rates of reading acquisition in different languages, regardless of orthographic transparency.

An investigation of learning to read in Wales makes it possible to overcome such difficulties. In Wales, the reading performance of children learning to read a deep orthography can be compared with that of children learning to read a transparent orthography who are similar in age, amount of schooling, educational system and geographical location. Furthermore, the structure of Welsh syllables is much closer to English than it is to Spanish or Italian. Consequently, there is no apparent reason for the superior phonological awareness skills in Welsh speakers, other than the transparent nature of the Welsh orthography.

Participants in our research

All of our participants were children living in Wales. Children that we will refer to as 'Welsh' came from Welsh-speaking families and were attending a Welsh-medium primary school in Denbighshire in North Wales. 'English' children came from English-speaking families and were attending an English-medium primary school in Denbighshire. Welsh was the main language spoken in the home by all of the families of the Welsh children, and English was the main language spoken in the home by all of the families of the English children. Several Welsh- and English-speaking schools in Denbighshire were used in the study. None of the effects that we discovered appeared to be explicable in terms of differences in age, spoken vocabulary, non-verbal ability or short-term memory between the Welsh and English children.

The schools told us that phonics instruction played a large part in the way that the children were taught to read. The Welsh schools said that they 'taught phonics via the Welsh alphabet'. The English schools used commercially available phonics schemes such as *Jolly Phonics*.

Native adult speakers of Welsh are almost always fluent speakers of English and are more likely to be bilingual than are Welsh adults whose first language is English. However, there is no evidence that Welsh children in their first or second year of formal reading instruction are bilingual. We do not therefore believe that our results are explicable in terms of Welsh children being 'more bilingual' than English children (see Spencer & Hanley, 2003, for further discussion of this issue).

The second and third years of formal reading instruction

A study of children's reading during their second and third year of formal reading instruction was carried out between 1996 and 1998 (Spencer & Hanley, 2003). We initially tested 74 Welsh-speaking children and 88 English-speaking children in 1996/7, when they were 6 years old and in their second year of formal reading instruction. We re-tested 70 of the Welsh children and 75 of the English children a year later.

The first reading test (List 1) that we administered to the English children comprised 15 common regular words (e.g., *on*, *happy*, *day*) whose pronunciation is predictable according to the 'rules' of English, and 15 common irregular words (e.g., *of*, *shoe*, *good*). These words do not follow the most common rules of English, whereby, for example, the word *good* would be pronounced to rhyme with *food* and *mood*. We asked the Welsh children to read the Welsh translations of these words (e.g., *ar*, *ddim*, *gosod*, *da*, *cerdyn*, *gweld*). There is some controversy regarding the best way to compare word recognition in different orthographies, and this is an issue that is discussed further in a later section of this chapter. In case the children found the original lists to be too easy, a more difficult 30-word list (List 2) was also generated for use with the 7-year-olds containing items such as *brandy/brandi* and *castle/castell*.

The results are shown in Table 5.1. It is clear that the Welsh children read very many more words correctly than did the English children. The differences were most marked for the words that were irregular in English when compared with their Welsh equivalents (which are, of course, regular in Welsh). Nevertheless, the differences between the Welsh and English children were

Table 5.1 The percentage of words read correctly by Welsh and English children

List	Age	Words	Welsh children	English children
List 1	6 years	All	81	59
		Regular	78	67
		Irregular	84	52
List 2	7 years	All	86	47
		Regular	86	53
		Irregular	86	41

statistically significant even for regular words. This result suggests that both the sight vocabulary (written words that they have learned to recognize relatively automatically) and the decoding skills of the English children lagged behind those of the Welsh children.

These differences in decoding skills were confirmed when we compared the children's ability to read a set of 18 non-words. Following Wimmer and Goswami (1994), the non-words were created from English and Welsh number words. English examples included *gwine, sen, feven* (based on *nine, ten* and *seven*); Welsh examples included *gump, ffeg, haith* (based on *pump* [five], *deg* [ten] and *saith* [seven]). We asked all children to read both the Welsh and the English set and allowed any response that was correct according to either Welsh or English grapheme–phoneme rules. The results in Table 5.2 reveal a substantial advantage for the Welsh children. They are more accurate than the English children even at reading the English-based non-words.

We also compared the phonological awareness abilities of our two samples by asking them to count the number of phonemes in spoken words (Liberman, Shankweiler, Fischer, & Carter, 1974). As the bottom panel of Table 5.2 shows, the Welsh children performed more accurately on this task than did the English children, not only with the Welsh words but also with the English words.

We were not the only researchers to have compared reading acquisition in Welsh- and English-medium primary schools during the second year of formal reading instruction. Ellis and Hooper (2001) examined the ability of 20 Welsh and 20 English children from primary schools in Wrexham, North Wales, to read a list of real words matched for frequency of occurrence in English and Welsh. They also reported significantly better performance by the children learning to read Welsh than by the children learning to read English.

Performance during the first year of formal reading instruction

The next issue that we examined was the point at which the differences in reading and phonological awareness abilities between Welsh and English children start to emerge. To investigate this issue, we compared reading

Table 5.2 The percentage of non-words read correctly by Welsh and English children, and percentage of words correct on a test of phoneme counting

		6-year-olds		7-year-olds	
		Welsh	*English*	*Welsh*	*English*
Reading non-words	English	68	44	71	62
	Welsh	78	33	89	46
Phoneme counting (words)	English	76	63	84	71
	Welsh	87	51	95	56

performance at three points during the first year of formal reading instruction at a Welsh- and at an English-speaking primary school. Our sample consisted of 22 English children and 29 Welsh children, and we used the same word list and phonological awareness tests that were given to the 7-year-old children in our previous study. The school year ran from September to July, and the children were tested in November, March and June.

The children's scores on the reading test are shown in Figure 5.1. It can be seen that differences were fairly small in November, with the Welsh children reading on average just over 4/30 words correctly and the English children being unable to read any words at all. By March, the Welsh children's reading had improved substantially, and it improved by a similar amount between March and June. By contrast, the English children's reading improved at a much slower rate. By the end of the school year, they were reading approximately the same number of words as the Welsh children could read at the start of the year.

Performance at phoneme counting, in which the children had to indicate the number of phonemes in spoken words, showed a similar pattern. The Welsh children showed substantial improvement in both March and June relative to earlier testing sessions. The English children started at a lower point and improved somewhat between November and March but did not improve again between March and June. It appears likely that these improvements in phonological awareness are a direct consequence of the greater improvements

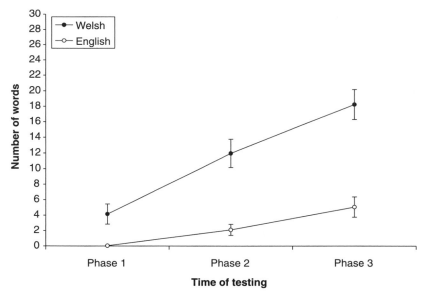

Figure 5.1 The number of words read correctly by English and Welsh children at three phases (November, March and June) during their first year of formal reading instruction.

in reading shown by the Welsh children. Interestingly, the ability to recognize written letters showed significant improvement throughout the year, but at no point was there any significant difference between the performance of the Welsh and the English children.

It is therefore clear that large differences in reading ability are not present at the start of formal reading instruction. None of the children could read more than a very small number of words at this point. Very rapidly during the first year of instruction, however, the reading and phonological awareness of the Welsh children improved at a much greater rate than did those of the English children.

It is also clear that the Welsh children continued to make reading errors even at the end of the first year of reading instruction. This is different from what is typically observed when children are learning to read transparent orthographies in Continental Europe (Seymour et al., 2003). The critical point to bear in mind, however, is that children are at least a year younger when reading instruction commences in Wales compared with those in countries such as Germany and Greece. Therefore it is likely to be the relative immaturity of the Welsh readers that prevents them from reading quite as well as their European counterparts at the end of their first year of reading instruction.

Reading at 10 years of age

We have so far seen that differences in reading and phonological awareness between Welsh and English children increase substantially over the course of the first year of formal reading instruction and are very strong during the second and third year. Will such differences remain when the children are older? In 2001/2, in an attempt to answer this question, we re-tested 46 of the Welsh children and 52 of the English children whom we had originally tested in 1996. In 2001/2, the average age of these children was 10 years.

When we gave them a new set of 24 non-words to read, the average scores obtained by the Welsh and English children (20.7 and 20.1 out of 24, respectively) did not differ significantly. This finding suggested that in terms of their decoding skills, the English children had caught up with their Welsh counterparts. One of the most interesting results of this investigation emerged when we examined reading accuracy on a set of 60 words that varied according to their regularity and their frequency (i.e., how often they occur in written English). For example, the words *horse* [*ceffyl*], *tooth* [*dant*] and *grill* [*gril*] are regular words of high-, medium- and low-frequency, and *bowl* [*bowlen*], *glove* [*maneg*] and *sword* [*cleddyf*] are irregular words of high-, medium- and low-frequency. The English children read all of the regular words and high-frequency irregular words as accurately as did the Welsh children (see Table 5.3). Significantly superior performance by the Welsh children was only observed on the medium- and low-frequency irregular words. The lower-frequency irregular words will have been encountered less often in print and many of them do not yet appear to be part of the English children's sight

Table 5.3 Number of words read correctly and mean reading speed as a function of regularity and frequency

Words	Frequency	Accuracy (max = 10)				Latency (ms)			
		English children		Welsh children		English children		Welsh children	
		N	SD	N	SD	M	SD	M	SD
Regular	High	9.10	2.07	8.78	1.26	876	290	884	335
	Mid	8.19	2.17	9.04	1.24	953	289	928	316
	Low	8.19	2.6	8.07	2.25	1014	326	1082	411
Irregular	High	9.00	2.07	9.48	1.13	859	319	874	317
	Mid	7.15	2.41	9.11	1.12	944	242	904	355
	Low	4.73	1.99	8.46	1.87	1005	304	1030	470

Note: Number of words read correctly in the first language. For the Welsh children, 'irregular' refers to Welsh translations of words that are irregular in English.

vocabulary. If English children try to use decoding skills to read those words that they do not recognize, they will pronounce them incorrectly. The absence of irregular words in Welsh means that Welsh children will be able to read aloud correctly the Welsh equivalents of these words even though they are equally unlikely to have encountered them in print very often.

We also measured the length of time that it took the children to read words aloud. These reading latencies showed no overall differences in reading speed between the Welsh and English children. However, it was interesting to note that both groups of children showed a significant effect of frequency on reading times. That is, all children, both Welsh and English, read familiar words significantly more quickly than less familiar words. If the children were reading simply on the basis of letter–sound associations, one might not have expected to see such a strong effect of word frequency. What this finding suggests is that the Welsh children, despite the transparency of their orthography, had memorized the visual form of frequently encountered words, and this enabled them to be read more quickly than less familiar words. In both Welsh and English, therefore, it seems that even when competence at decoding has been achieved, less common words are being added to a learner's sight vocabulary when they are encountered in print sufficiently often to become familiar. Even at the age of 10, in their sixth year of formal reading instruction, the learning process is not complete for good readers. This is an important issue for the acquisition of the English writing system because orthographic irregularity means that unfamiliar written words are much less likely to be read correctly in English than in Welsh, even if the child is a skilful reader.

At 10 years of age, the Welsh children displayed better phoneme awareness than did the English children—they showed superior performance at phoneme counting with both Welsh and English words. Interestingly though, a slightly more complex pattern of results emerged when we compared performance on phoneme awareness and rhyme awareness tasks. Children saw two pictures at the same time as they heard the names of the pictures spoken aloud. Materials were selected such that the words were the same in both English and Welsh. On 16 trials the children were asked whether the words contained the same first phoneme (e.g., *tank*, *desk*); on 16 trials they were asked whether the words contained the same final phoneme (e.g., *sink*, *flag*); and on 16 trials they were asked whether the words rhymed (e.g., *bus*, *jug*). The English children performed just as accurately as did the Welsh children on the rhyme test and first-phoneme (alliteration) test, but they were significantly less accurate on the last-phoneme test. The Welsh children performed just as accurately on the phoneme tests as on the rhyme awareness test. It appears, therefore, that learning a transparent orthography improves phoneme awareness performance from the first grade of formal reading instruction right through to at least the fifth grade, when the children are aged 10. Rhyme awareness, by contrast, seems to be much less influenced by the nature of the orthography.

When the children were 10 years old, we corrected one glaring omission from our previous studies in Wales by examining, for the first time, reading comprehension. We were surprised to observe that the English children were significantly better than the Welsh children at answering comprehension questions about three short stories from the Neale (1989) reading test[1] that they had been asked to read aloud. This suggests that a transparent orthography may not confer any advantages as far as reading comprehension is concerned. As comprehension is clearly the goal of reading, this finding is potentially reassuring for teachers of English. Nevertheless, on the Neale test, the tester corrects children when they read a word incorrectly, and so many of the advantages of a transparent orthography are negated. It would also be more reassuring if relatively good reading comprehension could be demonstrated in younger English readers at a point when their decoding skills lag behind those of their Welsh counterparts. The fact that the comprehension score of the English children actually exceeded the score of the Welsh children might have been because semantic processing occurs more automatically in an opaque orthography. This is because it may often be necessary in an opaque orthography to access a word's meaning in order to retrieve its pronunciation from memory. It is also possible, however, that *oral* reading (which the Neale test requires) may itself lead readers of a transparent orthography to neglect a semantic reading strategy. It would certainly be interesting to investigate whether superior performance by the English children would be observed on tests of reading comprehension following *silent* reading.

The underachieving tail of English readers

A finding that we have consistently observed in our data is that it is the least able readers who appear to be the most disadvantaged by learning to read an opaque orthography (e.g., Spencer & Hanley, 2003). Although the top

75 per cent of English readers consistently performed at a lower level than did their Welsh counterparts at recognizing familiar words, it is in the bottom 25 per cent of the English readers that the most striking differences in reading ability emerge. The Welsh children at the bottom end of the distribution of reading ability perform relatively well compared with the more able readers of Welsh. Even the least able Welsh reader read 83/110 words correctly, whereas the lowest English score was only 19/110. There appeared to be an underachieving tail among the English readers that did not exist among the Welsh readers. The remainder of this section examines in much more detail the underachieving tail of English readers (i.e., the worst-performing 25 per cent) at age 10.

This bottom 25 per cent comprised 13 readers, of whom 8 were boys and 5 were girls. We will compare them with the 12 Welsh readers who read the fewest words on the equivalent test of Welsh reading. A series of comparisons was made between the performance of all four quartile groups of Welsh and English readers on a series of tests.

Overall, there was no significant difference in the number of English words from the 110-word list that were read correctly by the Welsh and English readers. However, as Figure 5.2 suggests, the highest quartile of English readers read significantly more English words correctly than did the highest quartile of Welsh equivalents. Conversely, the lowest quartile of English readers actually read significantly fewer English words correctly than were read by their Welsh equivalents.

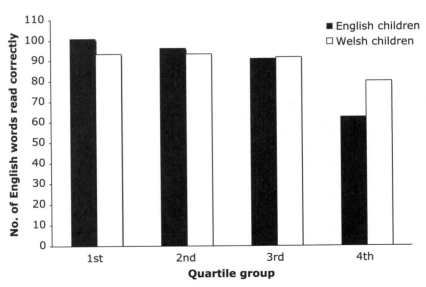

Figure 5.2 The mean number of English words read correctly (max = 110) by Welsh and English readers in the four quartile groups. The first quartile are the best readers and the fourth quartile are the worst readers.

This is a particularly striking result because it means that the *English* reading skills of the underachieving English readers are even worse than those of the weakest Welsh readers who are reading in their second language. Learning a transparent orthography seems to allow even the weakest Welsh readers to develop sufficient literacy skills to enable them to learn to read English successfully, even though it is their second language.

A similar pattern of results was obtained on the tests of non-word reading. On the English version of the test there was no significant difference between the English and Welsh children in the first three quartiles. But in the lowest quartile, the Welsh readers read the non-words more accurately than did the English readers. On the Welsh non-word reading test, the Welsh children outperformed the English children in all four quartiles, but as Figure 5.3 indicates, the differences were greatest for the lowest quartile.

There was also particularly poor performance by the lowest English quartile on the accuracy measure of the Neale (1989) reading test, where the Welsh readers were reading in their first language. Only in the lowest quartile of readers was there a significant advantage for the Welsh over the English children (see Figure 5.4 for more details). The significant advantage for the English readers in comprehension that we discussed in the previous section was present for the best two quartiles but was not present in the two lowest quartiles (see Figure 5.4). In fact, Figure 5.4 shows that the English children in the lowest quartile performed somewhat worse at comprehension than did their Welsh counterparts.

On the Neale reading speed measure, there was a significant advantage for the English children. The greater reading speed achieved by the English readers is not particularly important, as word length was not balanced in the English and Welsh versions of the test, but it is interesting that reading speed seems to decline at an approximately equivalent rate in the Welsh and English readers as we move from the most to the least accurate readers (see Figure 5.4).

On the tests of phonological awareness (where the same words were used in the Welsh and English versions of the task), the Welsh children performed significantly better overall than did the English children. Although the highest two quartiles of English readers performed at a similar level to their Welsh counterparts, both the third and the fourth quartiles performed worse than their Welsh counterparts. Figure 5.5 demonstrates how the lowest quartile performed strikingly worse than did their Welsh counterparts on the first phoneme, final phoneme and the rhyme matching tasks.

In summary, the conclusions that were drawn in the previous section need to be tempered somewhat. There it was argued that by age 10 the reading skills of the English children have caught up with their Welsh counterparts, and it is only because of the existence of lower frequency irregular words that the English children read real words less accurately than do Welsh children. This section makes it clear that this optimistic prognosis cannot be applied to the poorest readers of English. This underachieving English tail continues to perform worse than their Welsh counterparts even on tasks such as word and

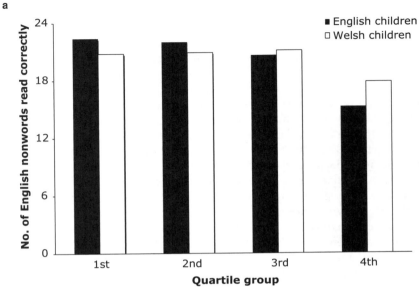

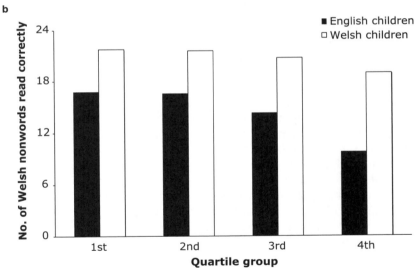

Figure 5.3 The mean number of (a) English and (b) Welsh non-words read correctly by Welsh and English readers in the four quartile groups.

non-word reading and rhyme awareness, where there were no differences between the full sample of Welsh and English children. Even on the Neale comprehension test, where the English children overall outperformed the Welsh children, there was no advantage for the weakest English readers who

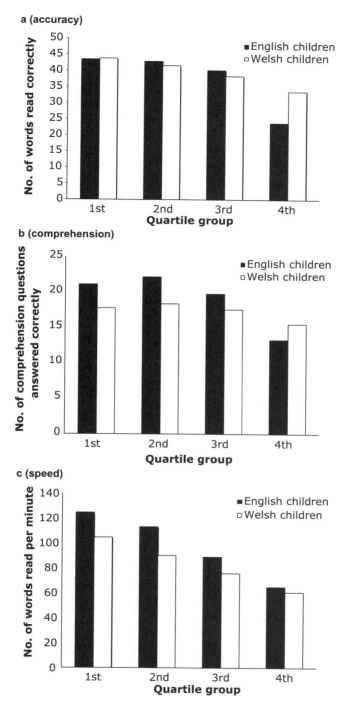

Figure 5.4 Performance on the (a) accuracy, (b) comprehension and (c) speed measures from the Neale (1989) reading test in the four quartile groups.

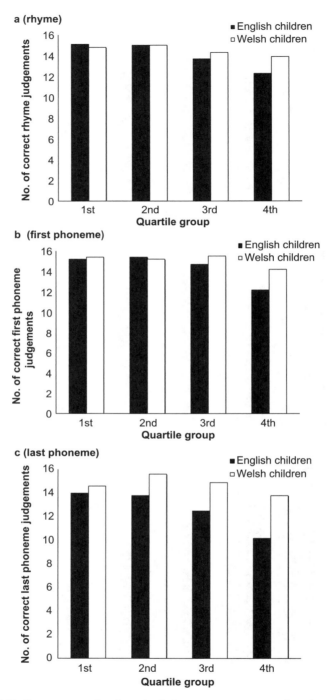

Figure 5.5 Performance on the phonological awareness tests as a function of quartile group: (a) rhyme; (b) first phoneme; (c) last phoneme.

performed slightly more poorly than did their Welsh counterparts. The lowest 25 per cent of English readers were worse even at reading real English words than were the poorest Welsh readers. It is very clear that the under-performing English readers still lag well behind Welsh children who have learned to read a transparent orthography, on a variety of reading and reading-related measures.

None of the differences between the two groups can be explained in terms of general verbal ability. This is because the Welsh and English children performed similarly on a measure of receptive vocabulary (the British Picture Vocabulary Scale [BPVS]; Dunn, Dunn, Whetton, & Burley, 1997), and there was no significant difference between the performance of the four quartile groups on the BPVS. The lowest performing readers of English did, however, perform worse on Raven's Matrices (a test of non-verbal ability; Raven, 1982) than did their Welsh counterparts. However, it cannot be the case that the poor performance of the lowest quartile on the other tests that we have reported in this section can be explained simply in terms of general ability. This is because the Raven's score of the lowest two English quartiles was virtually identical, yet it was only the lowest quartile of English children that consistently performed significantly worse than did their Welsh counterparts (see Figure 5.6).

Finally in this section, it is interesting to note that the inventors of the Initial Teaching Alphabet (ITA) in the early 1960s had also been aware of the potential difficulties that English-speaking children face in learning their opaque orthography (Pitman, 1961). The solution that they proposed was that young children should at first learn a transparent version of the English alphabet. ITA therefore contained 44 distinct graphemes, so that there was a discrete symbol to represent each English phoneme in a consistent fashion. The children were eventually transferred to the standard orthography once

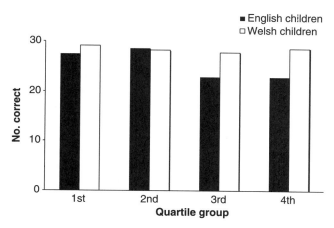

Figure 5.6 Performance on the Raven's Matrices test of non-verbal ability as a function of quartile group.

decoding skills had been acquired by learning ITA. Unfortunately, some children encountered difficulties in the transition to standard orthography (Vernon, 1967). Nevertheless many children made rapid advances in reading the new script (Downing, 1967). A particularly important problem that Downing noted was that ITA seemed to be helpful for the most skilled readers, but the least able readers appeared to derive relatively little benefit. Consequently, it is particularly interesting to note that in direct contrast to what was observed with ITA, it is the weakest Welsh readers who appear to benefit the most from their transparent orthography. Precisely why this should be the case is unclear.

Are there sex differences in learning to read a transparent orthography?

It is well known that in the United Kingdom, the reading attainment of primary school boys lags behind that of girls from a relatively early age (e.g., Gorard, Rees, & Salisbury, 2001). An interesting question is whether sex differences in reading are as apparent when children are taught a transparent orthography as when they are taught an opaque orthography. Moss (2000) has suggested that boys react more negatively than girls to judgements made in classrooms about their reading skills. Consequently, she suggests, they may become more likely than girls to disengage from the learning process, and their reading proficiency may suffer as a consequence. Moss suggests that classroom criticism of an individual's reading proficiency may be less likely to occur when learning a transparent orthography because the learning process is more straightforward. She tentatively suggests that as a consequence boys may perform as well as girls when learning to read a transparent orthography.

The data that we collected make it possible to examine this suggestion. We compared the reading performance of 42 Welsh girls, 34 Welsh boys, 50 English girls and 38 English boys during their second year of formal reading instruction in 1996/7. The test was the set of 15 regular and 15 irregular words reported previously (Table 5.1). Would the girls outperform the boys by the same amount in the Welsh sample as in the English sample?

Overall, the girls performed significantly more accurately than did the boys. As anticipated, these results demonstrate superior performance overall by the girls compared with the boys. The crucial finding was that the advantage that the girls enjoyed over the boys was at least as great in the Welsh sample (mean score for girls = 25.9, mean score for boys = 22.1) as in the English sample (mean score for girls = 18.9, mean score for boys = 16.1). There is therefore no evidence from our study that the effects of sex on word recognition ability are in any way mediated by the transparency of the orthography that is being learned. Girls appear to perform better than boys to the same extent in transparent orthographies as in opaque orthographies.

The selection of word lists in cross-cultural comparisons

In the studies described in this chapter, the materials used to compare Welsh and English reading have primarily been *translation pairs*. Essentially, what we have done is to compare reading performance of English words with the equivalent words translated into Welsh. The advantage of this approach is that by definition translation pairs mean the same thing and are matched for semantic variables that are known to affect reading such as imageability (the capacity of a word to arouse sensory experiences) and concreteness (the extent to which a word refers to what is experienced in the physical world). They will also be matched for part of speech (their grammatical role) and are very likely to be matched for their frequency and their age of acquisition (the age at which the word was learned). Indeed Fear (1997) has shown that the familiarity ratings of English words and their Welsh equivalents are highly correlated. The same is true for imageability ratings, age of acquisition ratings and concreteness ratings (Fear, 1997).

A different approach was taken by Ellis and Hooper (2001) in their comparison of Welsh and English reading. They stated that there is 'no guarantee that translation pairs are equally frequent in their respective languages' (p. 572). It is true that there is no guarantee that translation pairs are of equal frequency, but Fear's (1997) study shows that translation pairs are very likely to be of similar frequency as far as Welsh and English are concerned. Moreover, if there are any differences in frequency between individual pairs of words, they are unlikely to favour one orthography over the other in any systematic way.

Nevertheless, Ellis and Hooper decided instead to use a technique that, in their opinion, represents an important methodological advance over studies that use translation pairs. They produced entirely separate English and Welsh words lists that were matched for frequency. Each list contained 100 words that comprised 10 words in 10 different frequency bands ranging from the highest (e.g., *the*) to the lowest (e.g., *moped*) levels of frequency. For each frequency band words were selected at random from the entire corpus of each language.

Ellis and Hooper made no attempt to control any other variable such as part of speech, age of acquisition, concreteness, orthographic regularity or word length. Indeed, almost all of the first 30 words in their English list were function words (e.g., *the*, *of*, *and*), because these are the most common words in English. As Ellis and Hooper put it, once frequency has been controlled 'everything to do with language should be freed to vary' (p. 574).

Such an approach has some logic. If one wants to discover whether orthography *X* is more difficult to learn than orthography *Y*, then if one controls for certain variables, one may control out the very variable that makes orthography *X* more difficult to learn than orthography *Y*. Unfortunately however, if one uses this approach then there is a danger that one might select, by chance, sets of words that differ on one or more variables that affect reading performance. This may not seem likely to be a particular problem when lists of words contain 100 items each. However, if one is comparing reading performance by children of a particular age who are reading different orthographies, many of the words will be either too easy (very frequent) or too difficult (very infrequent) to produce any differences between the two writing systems. That is, children are likely to read, respectively, all of them or none of them correctly. It is likely to be a relatively small subset of the words that is crucial in determining whether performance in the two groups of readers is significantly different. Therefore the chance that this subset of items in the two orthographies will differ in terms of one or more of these uncontrolled variables is actually quite high.

Furthermore, word lists chosen in this way are unlikely to contain any irregular Welsh words because there are hardly *any* irregular words in Welsh. By contrast, there were several irregular words in Ellis and Hooper's (2001) English list (e.g., *people*, *moment*). Such an experimental design makes it very hard to determine whether the relative difficulties that English children experience occur only on irregular words or on both regular and irregular words. By using translation pairs and manipulating the regularity of the English set, one can answer this important question. Overall, no approach to matching materials cross-culturally is immune from methodological problems. However, contrary to the views of Ellis and Hooper (2001), there appears to be no reason to believe that matching solely on the basis of word frequency represents any sort of methodological advance over using translation pairs.

Reading in Wales in 2001/2

The National Literacy Strategy was introduced to all primary schools in England in September 1998. The Strategy required that phonics instruction plays a major role in teaching word recognition skills to children. The National Literacy Strategy was not formally implemented in Wales. Nevertheless, it is our view that it has had a major impact on the way in which reading is taught in English-medium primary schools in Wales. Informally, teachers in Denbighshire have told us that there has been a greater reliance on phonics-based teaching methods than was previously the case. We have no information about whether these methods emphasize synthetic phonics (the teaching of letter sounds and blending these sounds together), as advocated by the National Literacy Strategy and by Rose (2006), whose report set out to examine best practice in teaching reading in the United Kingdom.

One particularly important question is whether the disadvantages in learning to read an opaque alphabetic writing system can be reduced or even overcome completely if children receive extensive phonics instruction. Our research in Wales cannot provide a definitive answer to this question because we have never directly compared English-medium primary schools that placed more or less emphasis on phonics instruction. Nevertheless in 2001/2 we did examine the reading performance of a group of 34 children from an

English-medium primary school in Wales when they were on average 5 years of age and coming towards the end of their first year of formal reading instruction. These children had all been non-readers 12 months earlier. The children were asked to read the same 15 regular and 15 irregular words that we had asked our original sample of children to read when they were 6 years old (see Table 5.1).

The results of this comparison were very striking. In 2001/2, the new sample of 5-year-old English readers read 83 per cent of the regular words correctly and 52 per cent of the irregular words correctly. Table 5.1 reveals that in 1996/7, our 6-year-olds read only 67 per cent of the regular words correctly and 52 per cent of the irregular words correctly. In fact, performance on the regular words was no worse than performance by the 6-year-old Welsh children on their Welsh translations (see Table 5.1). Only on irregular words did the 5-year-old English children perform poorly relative to the 6-year-old Welsh children, and, of course, it is unlikely that phonics-based instruction could ever make irregular words as easy for children to read as regular words. The performance of the children at phoneme counting in 2001/2 was also strikingly better than that of our earlier sample: they were correct on 83 per cent of the English words.

As we had not tested children from this primary school previously, we attempted to replicate these findings by administering the same reading test in the English-medium primary schools that we had used in our earlier studies. To allow closer comparison with our previous results, we tested 26 6-year-old children from these schools in 2001/2. These children read 83 per cent of the regular words correctly and 63 per cent of the irregular words correctly. Performance was therefore much better than by children of a similar age in our original study (see Table 5.2) in these primary schools.

These new figures represent a substantial improvement in reading performance relative to performance five years earlier. We believe that this improvement is probably the consequence of increased teaching of phonics in English-medium primary schools in Wales, although we certainly cannot prove that to be the case. In light of these findings, it is encouraging to note that it does appear that the disadvantages associated with learning to read an opaque alphabetic orthography can be substantially reduced in the early stages of learning to read. It would be extremely interesting to conduct a new study that investigates the extent to which decoding skills in other English-medium primary schools in Wales have now reached the levels that can be found in Welsh-medium schools. A future study that also investigates the precise relationship between any improvements in reading skill in Wales and the amount and type of instruction in phonic skills that children receive would be extremely valuable.

Note

1 This is a standardized test in which children read aloud short passages of text that relate to an image on the opposite page and then answer questions about the text.

Acknowledgements

The work reported in this chapter was funded by the ESRC in the form of a project grant (No. R000238437) and an earlier research studentship to Llinos Spencer. I am grateful to Llinos Spencer, Jackie Masterson and Dylan Evans for the contribution that they made to the research discussed in this chapter. I would also like to thank the teachers and staff of a number of primary schools in Denbighshire, North Wales, for permission to test the children in their classes.

References

Cossu, G., Shankweiler, D., Liberman, I. Y., & Gugliotta, M. (1995). Visual and phonological determinants of misreadings in a transparent orthography. *Reading and Writing*, *7*, 237–256.

Downing, J. (1967). *Evaluating the initial teaching alphabet*. London: Cassell.

Dunn, L. M., Dunn, L. M., Whetton, C., & Burley, J. (1997). *British Picture Vocabulary Scale* (2nd ed.). Windsor, UK: NFER-Nelson.

Ellis, N. C., & Hooper, A. M. (2001). It is easier to learn to read in Welsh than in English: Effects of orthographic transparency demonstrated using frequency-matched cross-linguistic reading tests. *Applied Psycholinguistics*, *22*, 571–599.

Fear, W. J. (1997). Ratings for Welsh words and their English equivalents. *Behavior Research Methods, Instruments and Computers*, *29*, 425–445.

Gorard, S., Rees, G., & Salisbury, J. (2001). Investigating the patterns of differential attainment of boys and girls at school. *British Educational Research Journal*, *27*, 125–139.

Hanley, J. R., Masterson, J., Spencer, L., & Evans, D. (2004). How long do the advantages of learning to read a transparent orthography last? An investigation of the reading skills and incidence of dyslexia in Welsh children at 10 years of age. *Quarterly Journal of Experimental Psychology*, *57A*, 1393–1410.

Liberman, I. Y., Shankweiler, D., Fischer, F. W., & Carter, B. (1974). Explicit syllable and phoneme segmentation in the young child. *Journal of Experimental Child Psychology*, *18*, 201–212.

Moss, G. (2000). Raising boys' attainment in reading: Some principles for intervention. *Reading*, *34*, 101–106.

Neale, M. D. (1989). *Neale Analysis of Reading Ability*. Windsor, UK: NFER-Nelson.

Öney, B., & Durgunoğlu, A. Y. (1997). Beginning to read in Turkish: A phonologically transparent orthography. *Applied Psycholinguistics*, *18*, 1–15.

Pitman, J. (1961). *Learning to read*. London: Initial Teaching Alphabet Foundation.

Raven, J. C. (1982). *Revised manual for Ravens Progressive Matrices and Vocabulary Scale*. Windsor, UK: NFER-Nelson.

Rose, J. (2006). *Independent review of the teaching of early reading*. London, UK: Department for Education and Skills.

Seymour, P. H. K., Aro, M., & Erskine, J. M. (2003). Foundation literacy acquisition in European orthographies. *British Journal of Psychology, 94*, 143–174.

Spencer, L., & Hanley, J. R. (2003). The effects of orthographic consistency on reading development and phonological awareness: Evidence from children learning to read in Wales. *British Journal of Psychology, 94*, 1–28.

Spencer, L., & Hanley, J. R. (2004). Learning a transparent orthography at 5 years old: Reading development of children during the first year of formal reading instruction in Wales. *Journal of Research in Reading, 27*, 1–14.

Vernon, M. D. (1967). Evaluations. In J. Downing (Ed.), *The ITA symposium*. Hove, UK: King Thorne & Stace.

Wimmer, H., & Goswami, U. (1994). The influence of orthographic consistency on reading development: Word recognition in English and German children. *Cognition, 51*, 91–103.

Wimmer, H., & Hummer, P. (1990). How German-speaking first-graders read and spell: Doubts on the importance of the logographic stage. *Applied Psycholinguistics, 11*, 349–368.

6 Writing a language that you can't hear

Terezinha Nunes, Diana Burman, Deborah Evans and Daniel Bell

Introduction

An orthography is a notational system for a language. The word *system* in this context indicates that there is a finite number of elements (e.g., letters) with a distinct form and meaning that can be copied and identified; these elements are combined according to specific rules to produce an interpretable notation (Goodman, 1976; Harris, 1995; Tolchinsky, 2003). The word *notation* indicates that orthographies enable oral languages to be encoded, recorded, transported and reproduced in a systematic way. Orthographies are powerful tools: with a limited set of letters, we can write all the existing words in a language, and even new ones, invented much later than the orthography. Just think of words like *computer*, *rocket* and *software*, and you will see how these are so much younger than English orthography.

This notational conception of orthographies when applied to English emphasizes the fact that letters represent sounds: there is a direct connection between the surface of the oral language (i.e., the sounds we hear) and the surface of the written language (i.e., the letters we write). It is easy for most people to understand that this connection exists and to see its significance for learning to read and write.

However, letter–sound correspondences do not tell the whole story of the connection between oral and written language. In many orthographies writing represents different aspects of the language. For example, if the word *magician* were spelled as *migishen* or *mugishon*, we could pronounce it and would know what was written, but this spelling would not reveal its connection to the word *magic*. The linguist Jean-Pierre Jaffré (adopting a modified version of Vachek's, 1973, definition) proposes that orthographies often combine two principles: phonographic and semiographic (Jaffré, 1997).

The phonographic principle is manifested by correspondences between meaningless units of spoken language (phonemes or syllables) and meaningless units of written language (phonograms or syllabograms). The semiographic principle encompasses the units [of meaning] and their functions in the linguistic elements of written language. These units are

> determined by the morphological structure of the languages in question
> . . . and by the way in which the written words are assembled (p. 9).

So we write *magician* in this way because this spelling is the result of putting together two units, '*magic*' and '*ian*'. These units are called morphemes, which are defined as the smallest units of meaning in a language. The principal morpheme in a word is the stem: in the case of *magician*, the stem is 'magic', and 'ian' is a suffix. Other words can have a prefix—that is, a morpheme that comes before the stem: for example, *dissatisfied* has the prefix '*dis*', which usually indicates a negation.

The suffix 'ian' is used to form nouns that refer to agents. There is another suffix in English, 'ion', which is used to form abstract nouns. These two suffixes have a vowel that is not clearly articulated, so the two words sound exactly the same at the end. This vowel sound they have at the end is called a *schwa* vowel. So the words *magician* and *confession* sound exactly the same at the end, but their endings are spelled differently because *confession* is the result of putting a different suffix at the end of the stem, the suffix 'ion'. When children understand that there is a connection between these units of meaning, morphemes and spelling, we say that they understand the representation of morphology in spelling.

The semiographic principle goes beyond spelling *per se*. It involves an interpretation of what was said in the choice of how the sequence of sounds is represented. Here is a puzzle for the reader. At a conference that had both hearing and deaf participants, the expert writer of subtitles for deaf participants produced the following subtitle:

'Aspirin says Diana said . . .'

We leave this puzzle for you here, but point out that the issue is about what was said, not about a correct transcription of the sounds. The transcription is excellent, and native speakers of English will recognize it when they understand the meaning of what was said.

In this chapter, we will refer to the letter–sound correspondences, which are so important in the notational view of orthography, as the *direct connection* between oral and written language. The connection between oral and written language based on the semiographic principle, which goes beyond the representation of sounds by letters, will be referred to as the *indirect connection* between oral and written language. The reasons for calling it 'indirect' will become clearer in the subsequent section of the chapter where we explore it further.

The aim of this chapter is to consider what it means to read and write a language that you can't quite hear (see also Mayer & Wells, 1996). Since the pioneering work of Bryant and his colleagues (e.g., Bradley & Bryant, 1983), there is little doubt that phonological skills are important for hearing children learning to read. Many of the subtle phonological distinctions required for correct spelling are outside the range of sounds that severely and profoundly deaf children can access. As a result, the direct connection between oral and written language is difficult for deaf children to master. Given a degraded oral language input, could deaf children use the indirect connection between oral and written language, the connection through meaning, to boost their literacy achievement? Are deaf readers currently using this connection through meaning to read and spell? Could appropriately targeted teaching help?

The chapter starts with a brief discussion of the importance of the indirect connection between oral and written language and explores the difficulties that deaf children might encounter. This is followed by a summary of three studies. In the first, deaf and hearing children of the same age level are compared in their use of the indirect connection between oral and written language. The second study explores the value of a measure of deaf children's use of the indirect connection for predicting deaf children's reading comprehension. Finally, an intervention study and its educational implications are presented.

The indirect connection between oral and written language and the deaf child

In order to consider whether deaf children might find this indirect connection difficult to learn, it is necessary to consider how it works in English. We explore here two aspects of this connection: the importance of syntax and the importance of morphology, which we analyse here by focusing mostly on suffixes.

First, the indirect connection between oral and written language is important for the organization of words into sentences. Many linguists, among them the prominent Noam Chomsky (1965), have argued that meaning is expressed in languages not only in words but also in the way words relate to each other in sentences. The meaning of a sentence is not the sum of the meanings of the words that compose it. Its meaning is understood also by the connection that the sentence has with an implicit grammar that represents simpler sentences. The sentences *the boy chased the dog* and *the dog chased the boy* are composed of the same words, but they do not mean the same thing. In English, the order in which the words appear determines who did what to whom: in this case, who did the chasing. Chomsky argued that we recognize ambiguities in sentences because we connect the same sentence to different, simpler sentences. To use one of his examples, the sentence *I had a book stolen* could mean that *I had a book; someone stole it* or *I asked someone to steal a book; this person did it*. The sentences that we hear are referred to as 'the surface of the language'; the underlying grammar to which we refer in order to understand sentences is referred to as 'the deep structure' or the 'syntax' of the language.

We suggest that to transcribe and understand written language, we refer to the surface of the language and also to the underlying syntax. If you have not understood by now the subtitle 'Aspirin says Diana said . . .', you will now give it meaning by reading another transcription of the same sequence of sounds:

'As Princess Diana said . . .'

When you pronounced the sounds by reading the first transcription, you may have thought that this phrase just did not make sense. You could not find a simpler sentence that would correspond to it. The second transcription can be immediately connected to a syntactic form in the deep structure of the English language.

Why might written English syntax be difficult for deaf children? It is possible, but by no means certain, that deaf children educated orally have an advantage over deaf children educated in British Sign Language (BSL) in this respect. Even though children educated orally are acquiring language in a medium that is difficult for them to access, the words that they learn will correspond to the words that are presented on paper, and so will the organization of words into sentences. In contrast, deaf children educated primarily in BSL use a language that does not have a one-to-one sign-to-written word correspondence in English. BSL is a multichannel language and can express different words by one sign alongside a facial expression: the same sign accompanied by different expressions means 'like' and 'don't like'. BSL can also use one sign when we use more than one word in English (e.g., *I ask you* is three words and only one sign, where the movement from the speaker to the listener denotes the subject–object relationship). BSL can also use two signs when we use one word in English (e.g., *magician* is signed as 'magic' and 'man'). Finally, BSL is an independent language and has its own syntax. If a native English-speaker were to learn a large number of BSL signs but did not learn its syntax, this learner would not be able to communicate in BSL. Both comprehension and production of BSL sentences would elude this learner (see Sutton-Spence & Woll, 1998). This means that it is not sufficient for deaf learners to memorize lots of written English words in order to learn to read. Like the hearing learner of BSL, they would not be able to understand written English only from knowing isolated written words.

A second aspect of the indirect connection between oral and written language is the use of inflections in marking different aspects of syntax. Past tense and plural, for example, are marked by inflections in English, not necessarily by more words in the sentence. These inflections are spelled in the same way in regular forms, irrespective of how they are pronounced. Regular verbs in the past, for example, are spelled with the ending 'ed', but they are never pronounced in this way: *kissed* is pronounced as /kist/, *killed* is pronounced as /kild/ and *wanted* is pronounced as /wantid/ (see Nunes, Bryant, & Bindman, 1997). Similarly, regular plurals are marked in English by the letter 's' at the end of words, irrespective of whether the ending sounds like /s/, as in *cats*, or like /z/, as in *dogs*. When the 'ed' spelling appears in a verb, the reader knows that this is something that happened in the past; when the 's' is added to a noun, the reader knows that this is a plural.

Chomsky argued that we are all innately equipped with a language acquisition device (LAD) that provides all humans with the necessary basis for learning the grammar of any language; this, of course, applies also to deaf children. This device is used to learn the specific grammar of the language that we are exposed to. Deaf children use it exceedingly well to learn signed languages but have trouble in using it to learn oral languages because they get a degraded stimulus, not because they lack a language acquisition device. Think of the sentences *I visit my parents on Sundays* and *I visited my parents on Sunday*. If you could not distinguish the endings of the words *visited* and *visit* and could not distinguish the endings of the words *Sunday* and *Sundays*, you could not distinguish between these two sentences. The word order is the same and you could not access the grammatical differences between past and present, and between singular and plural. This could well be the situation of many deaf children. Lip-reading the difference between *Sunday* and *Sundays* and between *visit* and *visited* may not be an easy task. For them, the meaning of these two sentences would not be clear.

Deaf children educated orally or primarily in BSL may not be in a very different position when it comes to understanding these inflections. If a deaf child is educated orally and cannot access the differences between the non-inflected and the inflected forms, the child would not understand the difference between these two sentences. If the child is educated primarily in BSL, the reason for the difficulty might be different. BSL uses inflections differently from English because it has its own syntax. For example, English uses the final 's' in spelling to mark plurals; this 's' is a bound morpheme (a morpheme that cannot appear on its own as a separate word). BSL, in contrast, may use a repetition of the sign (the sign for *child* repeated in different locations means *children*) or use quantifiers (e.g., a number, the sign for *lots of*). Quantifiers may appear before and after the plural word (see Sutton-Spence & Woll, 1998, for a fuller description). So a deaf child educated primarily in BSL would need to learn about English inflections to understand written English, just as a hearing learner has to learn about BSL syntax to understand BSL.

This brief analysis highlights the importance of finding out how deaf children manage to use the indirect connection between oral and written language when learning English literacy. There is much research on deaf children's and adults' use (or not) of phonology in reading and spelling (e.g., Beech & Harris, 1997; Campbell, 1992; Conrad, 1977, 1979; Gates & Chase, 1926; Harris & Moreno, 2004, 2006; see also Alegria, 2004; Marschark & Harris, 1996; Musselman, 2000; Perfetti & Sandak, 2000, for excellent reviews about reading by deaf children), so this direct connection will not be discussed here. There is comparatively little on deaf children's use of morphology in reading and spelling (a notable exception is Leybaert & Alegria, 1995), but there is a growing awareness of the possibility that knowledge of morphology might be an important avenue for improving deaf children's literacy (e.g., Gaustad, 2000).

Our studies provide an initial analysis of the use of this indirect connection by deaf children in reading and writing. It is hypothesized that deaf children, irrespective of whether they are educated orally or in sign, do not find the use of the indirect connection between oral and written language easy to master. If they have a hearing loss that is more than mild, they receive a degraded input that gives them less access to morphology and syntax than is available to hearing children. It is also hypothesized that deaf children are quite able to learn the meaning distinctions that are marked by morphology and syntax if they receive explicit teaching about the connection between these meanings and written English. We summarize here results from three studies that were carried out to test these hypotheses.

The use of suffixes in spelling by deaf children

Suffix spelling is one of the measures that can be used to assess children's use of the indirect connection between oral and written language. Past research (Beers & Beers, 1992; Deacon & Bryant, 2005; Nunes & Bryant, 2006; Nunes et al., 1997) shows that suffix spelling is difficult for hearing children. Hearing children typically succeed with the suffixes that are spelled phonetically, such as the 's' for plurals when it sounds like /s/, but many suffixes are not spelled phonetically, including the 's' plural in some cases: for example, after long vowels the 's' is pronounced as /z/, as in the words *fleas* (pronounced as /fleaz/) and *bees* (pronounced as /beez/). Kemp and Bryant (2003) found that hearing children have difficulties with the 's' for plurals when the ending of the word sounds like a /z/. They asked children aged from 5 to 8 years to write plural words that ended in a /z/ sound. The children made many mistakes in spelling the ending of the plural words in which the sound immediately preceding the /z/ ending was a long vowel (e.g., *fleas*), and managed to spell it correctly only 73 per cent of the time. They spelled 20 per cent of these plural endings either as '-ze' or as '-se': these are the incorrect markers for the plural. Hearing children have even more difficulty with suffixes such as 'less' (*careless*), 'ion' (*emotion*) and 'ian' (*magician*), which cannot be spelled correctly only on the basis of phonology. There is no phonological reason for 'less' to have double 's' at the end, and the vowel sound in 'ion' and 'ian' is usually the same—it is an unclearly articulated schwa vowel. Thus a test of how children spell suffixes whose spelling cannot be predicted from the way they sound is a good measure of hearing children's use of morphology in spelling.

We decided to use suffix spelling to assess the extent to which deaf children use syntax and morphology in word spelling. In our Suffix Spelling Task, we asked children to spell 44 words, all of which have at least two morphemes: for example, *windows* has the stem 'window' and the 's' for the plural, *walks* has the stem and the 's' for the third person, *jumped* has the stem and the 'ed' for the past, *magician* has the stem and the 'ian' for agents. We used

11 suffixes, with four instances of each one. In order to administer this task, we showed the children a picture and presented them with a sentence in oral and signed language. The sentence was written on their answer sheet; the target word to be spelled was missing, and a line marked the place where the children should write it. Our pilot work showed that it was sometimes necessary to prompt the children with the initial letter in the word so that the correct target would be spelled: for example, when our target word was *measurement* and we wanted to score the spelling of 'ment', some children wrote *size* instead and did not produce the target word. Leybaert and Alegria (1995) used this method in French, and we found that it works well also with English. For example, the first sentence was 'These are windows.' The children were shown a slide with many windows, and their answer sheet read:

These are w . . .

There is much evidence that deaf children score lower than hearing children of the same age level in literacy tasks (see, for example, Conrad, 1977; Rodda & Eleweke, 2000; Traxler, 2000; Webster, 2000). If we were to compare deaf children with a hearing cohort of the same age, we would undoubtedly find that the deaf children are worse at spelling suffixes. In order to compare the deaf children in our sample with a sample of hearing children, we decided to use the reading-level match design (Bryant & Goswami, 1986). A comparison of deaf children with hearing children of the same age would only show that deaf children are behind their hearing peers in one more literacy task. In contrast, if the deaf children were to show poorer performance than the hearing children *of the same reading level*, this would suggest that spelling suffixes causes them surprisingly more difficulty than expected: their difficulty would be surprising exactly because the hearing children they were being compared to were of the same reading level.

In this study we used spelling scores rather than reading scores because our interest was in suffix spelling. Because there is no standardized word spelling test for deaf children, we developed our own adaptation. We chose the Schonell Spelling Test (Schonell & Goodacre, 1971) for this purpose. The procedure used in this test is to say the target word first by itself, then repeat it in the context of a sentence to ensure that the children know what the target word is, then say the word once again. This method does not necessarily work with deaf children, as they might write a different word. So we used the same method as in the Suffix Spelling Task: the children were shown a picture and presented with a sentence in oral and signed language, the sentence was written on their answer sheet and the target word's first letter was provided when we expected that they could write a different word. It was necessary to change some of the original words in the Schonell Test because their meanings could not be made clear by this method. When this was necessary the words had the same phonological difficulty as those that had been used originally in the Schonell Test: for example, *yet* was replaced with *wet*, and *sight* with *fight*.

We validated this adapted form of the Schonell Spelling Test by testing a sample of hearing children on the traditional and the adapted version on different occasions. The correlation between the two forms was as high as the test–retest correlation for the Schonell Test, and equal to .9.

Deaf and hearing children were recruited through primary schools: 249 deaf children from 29 schools (49 per cent from special schools for the deaf; 36 per cent from mainstream schools with units for the hearing impaired; 15 per cent from mainstream schools) and 72 hearing children (from one school that recruits children from a variety of socio-economic backgrounds) participated. All the deaf children had at least moderate hearing loss; 46 had received a cochlear implant. In all the special schools for the deaf, and mainstream schools with units, the deaf children were exposed both to BSL and English. The level of use of these languages varied across schools, but it is not possible to ascertain this variation without a detailed observational study of how the children themselves used BSL or English throughout the day and with different interlocutors. So we will not consider in our analyses which language was used most often by the children. Although we recognize its potential significance, it does not affect the internal validity of our study.

The deaf children's mean age was 10 years and 1 month; the age range was 6 years 2 months to 12 years and 6 months; the standard deviation was 1.3 years. The hearing children's mean age was 7 years 6 months; the age range was 6 years 2 months to 9 years 2 months; the standard deviation was 0.9 years. So the deaf children were older than the hearing children.

The assessments were administered either by the researchers or by a teacher who had received special training. The score for the Schonell Spelling Test is the number of correctly spelled words; for the Suffix Spelling Task it is the number of correctly spelled suffixes, irrespective of whether the stem was correct. The means and standard deviations by group in these two tasks are presented in Table 6.1.

t-Tests were used to compare the hearing and deaf children's scores in the reading and spelling tests. This statistical analysis showed that, even though the hearing children were younger, their results in the Schonell and the Suffix

Table 6.1 Mean correct in the Schonell Spelling Test and Suffix Spelling Task of hearing and deaf children

	Hearing children (N = 72)	*Deaf children (N = 249)*
Schonell Spelling (out of 50)[a]	35.82 (10.56)	24.93 (14.73)
Suffix Spelling (out of 44)[a]	25.69 (10.27)	11.24 (12.25)
Adjusted means for Suffix Spelling controlling for Schonell Spelling[b]	19.89 (0.82)	12.73 (0.43)

Note: Schonell Spelling Test adapted.
a Standard deviations in parentheses.
b Standard errors of mean in parentheses.

Spelling tests were significantly better than the results obtained by the deaf children—for the Schonell Spelling Test, $t(153.19) = 7.05$, $p < .001$; for the Suffix Spelling Task, $t(125.34) = 13.32$, $p < .001$.

These results demonstrate deaf children's poorer performance in both tests, but they do not test the hypothesis that the deaf children have unexpected difficulty in spelling suffixes. In order to say that their difficulty in spelling suffixes is unexpected, we need to compare the deaf children with hearing children who, in the general spelling test, have the same scores as the deaf children. The question really is whether the deaf children are worse in suffix spelling than the hearing children for their general level of spelling. Analysis of covariance was used to compare hearing and deaf children's scores in suffix spelling after taking into account how well they did on the Schonell Test. This statistical analysis allows for the calculation of an adjusted mean for each of the two groups on the Suffix Spelling Task, in view of the differences in their general spelling score. Just as it would be expected that younger children don't spell as well as older children, so it is also expected that the children who have lower scores in general spelling will also have lower scores in suffix spelling. Because there are more deaf than hearing children with lower scores in the Schonell Test, which assesses general spelling, one would also expect that the scores obtained by the deaf children in the Suffix Spelling Test would be lower. The means are then adjusted to give similar weights in the calculation of the mean to the deaf and hearing children who obtained similar scores in the Schonell Test, irrespective of the number of children who had similar scores. This allows for a fair comparison between the groups' suffix spelling scores because it does not lower the mean for the deaf children as a result of more deaf children having lower general spelling scores.

The adjusted means on the Suffix Spelling Task, after taking into account their performance on the Schonell Test, are shown in Table 6.1. The table shows that this adjusted mean is better for the deaf children than the mean obtained without the adjustment. This is due to the fact that the deaf children had performed significantly worse on general spelling. But the hearing children obtained a higher mean than the deaf children even after this adjustment. Analysis of covariance showed that the difference between the groups was significant ($F_{1,319} = 57.79$; $p < .001$) and thus can be interpreted as a real difference between the deaf and the hearing children. In brief, the deaf children did perform unexpectedly poorly in suffix spelling for their general spelling ability.

We conclude that above and beyond the problems that deaf children have in literacy due to their difficulty in accessing phonological information, they also have problems that result from their difficulty in using the representation of syntax and morphology in written English.

We now turn to the question of whether this difficulty is restricted to suffix spelling or whether this poor performance on suffix spelling reflects a more general difficulty in using syntax and morphology in written English.

Suffix spelling as a predictor of other literacy measures

Research has shown that, for hearing children, suffix spelling is a good measure of literacy in a broader sense. Deacon and Kirby (2004) and Nagy, Berninger, and Abbot (2006) independently found that measures of children's suffix spelling were good longitudinal predictors of their reading comprehension later on, even after controlling for the children's performance in phonological tasks (for a review, see Nunes & Bryant, 2009).

To test our hypothesis that suffix spelling is a measure of deaf children's use of syntax and morphology in literacy, we used a short-term longitudinal design. Our aim was to see whether there is a specific link between deaf children's use of the indirect connection in spelling and their performance in two important measures of literacy, reading comprehension and writing skill. In order to maintain that this specific link exists, it is necessary to show that suffix spelling predicts deaf children's reading comprehension and writing skills at a later time, after controlling for their scores on tests that assess their use of phonology in word reading and word spelling. The reasoning used here is the same as that used in the previous study. Children who are better at reading words in isolation are also better at understanding texts, and those who are better spellers are better at writing texts. So the question is whether suffix spelling, viewed as a measure of the deaf children's use of morphology in spelling, allows us to predict how well they understand and produce texts after controlling for their general word reading and spelling skills.

We decided to control also for their general intelligence. It is easy to see that children who are cognitively more able should be better at reading comprehension, writing texts and also at learning how to spell suffixes. If we did not control for their general cognitive ability in our analysis, we could find correlations between suffix spelling and the two literacy measures that are simply the result of the fact that cognitive ability influences each of these measures. We chose to use Raven's Progressive Matrices as the measure of intelligence because this is a more appropriate measure for deaf children.

Raven's Progressive Matrices is a measure of non-verbal intelligence in which the respondents are presented with pictures, arranged in rows and columns, but one of the pictures is missing. For example, in a two-by-two matrix, like the one presented in Figure 6.1, there are on the left column two figures, a circle on top and, underneath it, a circle with a cross inside. On the right, there is a square on top, and the figure underneath is missing; its place is indicated by a grey form. The respondents have to choose which, out of an array of six figures, would best fit into the empty place. The expected response in this case would be a square with a cross inside. The test starts with simple examples, and the visual analysis becomes progressively more difficult. The respondents are given one point for each correct answer. Their score is then transformed into an adjusted score that takes into account how well children of the same age do on the test.

The reading comprehension measure was adapted from Burman and

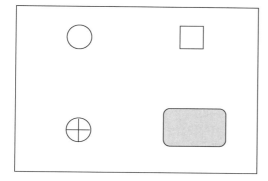

Figure 6.1 An example of the way the items in the Raven's Matrices are structured.

Pretzlik (2004), and shows a good distribution of scores for deaf primary school children. The children are asked to read two short texts, about a dog and a cat, and to answer some information and some inference questions. Children are given one point for each correct response.

The children's writing skills were assessed by a measure developed by Burman, Nunes, and Evans (Burman, Evans, & Nunes, 2008; Burman, Nunes, & Evans, 2007) in which the children are shown four pictures that show: (1) a person packing a bag; (2) the same person loading the bag into a car; (3) a family inside a car, on the road; and (4) two children playing on the sand by the ocean. The children are asked to write a story about the pictures. Children's writing is analysed by considering one aspect of their production at a time. For each aspect, a score between 0 and 4 is given. A total of 16 specific aspects are scored, with 10 items referring to grammar and 6 to the quality of the writing. For example, one of the grammar items considers whether the children use subject–verb–object order appropriately. The text is given a score of 0 if there is no evidence of the use of appropriate word order, and 4 if the text shows consistent use of appropriate word order. Deaf children might write 'suitcase man pack', using a word order that is fine in BSL but not in written English. If all their writing is of the same type, they would score 0. If they use correct English word order systematically, they would score 4. Different levels of variation between these extreme points are scored. The items that assess use of grammar focus on features that are obligatory for correct writing. The items on quality of the writing focus on optional aspects that improve text coherence and creativity. For example, one item analyses the use of pronouns instead of continuous repetition of the nouns, and another analyses whether the children added information beyond what is presented in the picture (e.g., one child wrote that the family was going to Spain for a holiday on the beach, thereby adding the location information, Spain, not contained in the picture). The assessment produces a single score by adding all the points across the 16 items.

These reading and writing assessments were chosen because the scores obtained by deaf primary school children show a wide distribution across the possible values. Other measures were tried out in our previous work (Burman et al., 2007), but there was little differentiation of the deaf children's performance. Their scores tended to be clustered at the lower values, and sometimes more than three quarters did not obtain a single point in the assessment.

The final measure used in this study was an adaptation of the Schonell Word Reading Test. The children are asked to read words, but instead of pronouncing them, they have a choice of four pictures to indicate what the word means. Severely and profoundly deaf children's pronunciation can be indistinct, and this makes their assessment through oral production less reliable. We gave the standard and the adapted version of this test to our sample of hearing children in the previous study to assess its validity. The correlation between the results in the two versions of the test was .85. Although this is not as high as the test–retest correlation for the Schonell Word Reading Test, it is sufficiently high to validate this adaptation for use with deaf children.

The participants in this study were some of the deaf children who had participated in the previous study and who were seen again in the subsequent school term. A total of 74 deaf children participated, covering the same age range as in the previous study. The remaining children participated in an intervention study, which is reported in the next section of this chapter.

At Time 1 (T1), the children were given the Raven's Progressive Matrices, the adaptations of the Schonell Word Spelling and Word Reading tests and the Suffix Spelling Task. At Time 2 (T2) they were given the reading comprehension and the writing skills tests described earlier. It must be recalled that we think there is a specific connection between the literacy measures, the reading comprehension and writing tests, and suffix spelling as a measure of the children's use of the indirect connection between oral and written language. So we need to exclude from our analysis the overlaps that exist between general cognitive ability (measured by the Raven's Matrices Test) and also the reading skills (measured by the Schonell Word Reading Test), which assess the reading ability based on the direct connection between oral and written language. In statistical terms, we say that we control for these factors before analysing how well the children's use of suffixes in spelling predicts their reading comprehension and writing skills.

Two regression analyses were used to test whether there is this specific connection between suffix spelling and the literacy outcome measures. One of the analyses considers how well suffix spelling predicts reading comprehension, the other how well it predicts the children's writing skills. Preliminary analyses showed that cochlear implants did not explain individual differences in the children's performance in the outcome measures of literacy in this study, so this factor is not analysed here. It is pointed out, however, that this does not mean that cochlear implants do not have an effect on children's literacy learning. The result we observed may be due to the fact that other differences between children should be controlled for before analysing the effect of cochlear implants, and this was not possible in the present study.

Figure 6.2 shows how well suffix spelling predicts reading comprehension after taking into account the children's age, general cognitive ability and word reading. These three factors together explain 57 per cent of the differences between deaf children in reading comprehension. Suffix spelling explains a further 13 per cent, after taking into account the differences in age, cognitive ability and word reading.

Figure 6.3 shows how well suffix spelling predicts the children's writing skills after taking into account the children's age, general cognitive ability and general spelling ability. These three factors together explain 75 per cent of the differences between deaf children in writing skill. Suffix spelling explained a further 2 per cent of the differences between the children. Although this may seem like a small addition, this was still a significant factor after the other three had been taken into account. This small value is due to the fact that there is a very close connection between general spelling ability and suffix spelling. When we later ran the analyses considering first suffix spelling and general spelling, we found that the first three factors—age, general cognitive ability and suffix spelling—together explained 70 per cent of the differences between the children in writing skills, and general spelling explained a further 6 per cent. This shows that the two measures of spelling are very closely related, but it is still possible to separate out their connection to writing skill using this statistical approach.

Thus there is strong evidence that knowledge of grapheme–phoneme correspondences and knowledge of morphemes make independent contributions

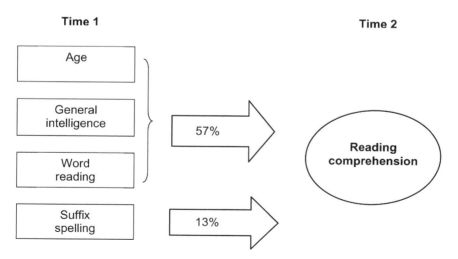

Figure 6.2 A schematic representation of the specific percentage of differences between deaf children in reading comprehension explained by suffix spelling after controlling for the other factors.

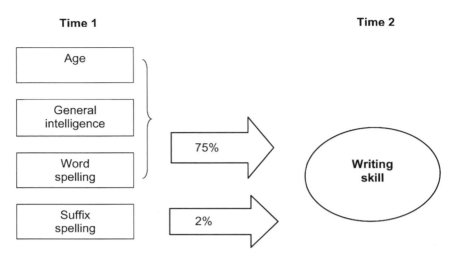

Figure 6.3 A schematic representation of the specific percentage of differences between deaf children in writing skills explained by suffix spelling after controlling for the other factors.

to deaf children's reading comprehension and writing skills. Although these two types of knowledge tend to go together, the fact that their contributions to children's reading comprehension and writing skill can be separated shows that it is important to pay attention to both when teaching literacy to deaf children.

Can deaf children's use of the indirect connection between oral and written language be promoted?

The schools that were involved in our first study provided participants for the second study, reported in the previous section, and for this intervention study. We used a waiting-list design according to which approximately half of the schools received the intervention materials in the first year and the other half received them in the second year; the latter formed the control group for this study.

Participants were 85 children in the intervention group (mean age 10 years and 4 months; $SD = 1.53$ years) and 88 children in the control group (mean age 10 years and 4 months; $SD = 1.34$ years); 17 children in the intervention group and 18 in the control group had cochlear implants. There were more profoundly deaf children in the intervention group than in the control group (37 vs. 23) and fewer who were severely deaf (9 vs. 20); the remaining levels of hearing loss had similar frequencies across the groups.

An intervention that had been developed for hearing children, and that had proved successful in improving their suffix spelling, was adapted for deaf children. It was implemented in the classroom by the teachers who participated in one day's training with the researchers. Teachers received further telephone and email support during implementation, and further materials as the children's work was returned for monitoring. The teachers used the materials at their own pace, taking as much time as they felt was needed and spreading it over differing numbers of days. The programme was implemented over four to seven months (mean: five months). The pre- and post-tests were administered during subsequent school terms.

The intervention contained IT-supported exercises to promote awareness of morphemes and grammar, games to offer the children extra practice in working with morphemes and specially designed story books that exposed children to the words in context and created the opportunity for further exercises. The first exercises focused on the structure of English sentences. The children were asked to produce sentences about each other saying what each person was doing (e.g., 'Tom reads'); this allowed them to learn about the use of the 's' ending for third person singular. They also practised sentences with a subject–verb–object structure and the past tense of regular verbs (i.e., verbs such as 'walk' that end in 'ed' in the past tense), creating the opportunity for English word order to become part of sentence writing. For example, in a teacher-led activity, the children were presented with (1) the sentence, 'He cleans the windows'; (2) a picture of a window-cleaner; and (3) the incomplete sentence 'Yesterday he ____ the windows'. The children had worksheets on which they were asked to complete the sentence. After they had finished, the teacher provided them with the correct answer.

Computer games were used to introduce new morphemes (e.g., the 's' for plurals, different suffixes for agents such as 'er' and 'ian'), and these were then used in books and sentence completion tasks. For example, one book reported Ben's walk to school during which he met several characters (a cleaner, a footballer, a swimmer, etc.). In the sentence completion task, the children were asked to identify peers who would fit certain descriptions (e.g., _____ *dances*; ____ *is a dancer*). Other games were also developed for further practice of the same morphemes. For example, in a dominoes game, the children had pieces that contained a word on one side and a picture on the other. The game was played in the same manner as a regular dominoes game, with children taking turns to place their pieces on the table. A child who had, for example, a drawing with two spoons would need to match this to the word *spoons* when this was on the table, and a child with the picture of one spoon would need to match it to the word *spoon*.

The children in the intervention and control groups were pre-tested on the assessments described in the previous studies: Raven's Matrices, Schonell Word Reading and Spelling (adapted for deaf children), Suffix Spelling, Reading Comprehension and Writing Skills. They were post-tested in Suffix Spelling, Reading Comprehension and Writing Skills. Table 6.2 presents the pre-test means for each group and the standard deviations on each measure.

There were small differences between the groups at pre-test, and these differences are consistently larger and in favour of the intervention group at

Table 6.2 Pre- and post-test means by group on each of the intervention outcome measures

Scores	Max. score	Intervention group		Control group	
		M	SD	M	SD
Pre-test					
Suffix spelling	44	9.54	11.12	11.57	12.90
Reading comprehension	22	10.34	5.49	8.00	5.14
Writing skill	64	26.43	12.47	22.73	11.65
Post-test					
Suffix spelling	44	18.98	13.46	12.82	13.60
Reading comprehension	22	12.58	5.09	8.48	5.42
Writing skill	64	28.70	13.06	22.52	11.24

post-test. In order to show that the intervention was effective in promoting the deaf children's use of morphology in reading and writing, we needed to show that the children in the intervention group had made more progress than had those in the control group. So the children in the intervention group were compared to control children who had similar results in the pre-test on the measures of general cognitive ability and on the relevant pre-test—that is, when we compared them in suffix spelling at post-test, we matched them on suffix spelling at pre-test. This way of asking the question is very similar to the way we have analysed the results of the previous study. It uses the analysis of covariance which considers the amount of progress between pre- and post-test in relation to the children's performance at pre-test.

We carried out three analyses. The first analysis compared the children's use of morphemes in the Suffix Spelling Test. This assessed whether we had succeeded in helping the children become more aware of morphemes in words. The mean for the intervention group was significantly higher than the mean for the control group (according to the analysis of covariance, $F_{1,168} = 67.67; p < .001$).

The second analysis tested whether this improvement in the children's knowledge of morphemes was accompanied by greater progress in reading comprehension by the children in the intervention group than by those in the control group. The intervention children had not received any specific instruction in reading comprehension, but they did make significantly more progress in reading comprehension than the control children (according to the analysis of covariance, $F_{1,168} = 20.86; p < .001$).

The third analysis tested whether the improvement in children's knowledge of morphemes was accompanied by greater progress in writing skills. Again, the children had not received specific instruction in writing during the intervention, but they did make significantly more progress than the control children (according to the analysis of covariance, $F_{1,164} = 4.79; p = .03$).

In brief, this study showed that it is possible to teach deaf children about English syntax and morphemes and help them understand that word order and the small 'bits' at the ends of written words convey specific meanings. When their awareness of syntax and morphemes in written English improves, their reading comprehension and writing skills also improve.

Conclusion

These studies show strong support for the idea that there are two connections between oral language and literacy: the first is a direct connection between the surface of oral language (the sounds) and the surface of written language (the letters), and the second is through the deep structure of the language (i.e., the simpler sentences that help us to understand more complex sentences), and through the units of meaning, called morphemes. Deaf children are unexpectedly weaker than hearing children of the same spelling level at using suffixes in word spelling, and this shows that they are less aware of the importance of morpho-syntax than hearing children are. Thus they seem to have a double disadvantage in learning literacy in comparison to hearing children: they have difficulty in accessing both the sounds and the deep structure of English.

Traditional measures of deaf children's word reading and spelling, which are based on phonological decoding and recoding, are significant predictors of their reading comprehension and writing skill, and so too is a measure of their ability to use morphemes in spelling. These measures make independent contributions to reading comprehension and to writing skill.

These findings could appear to be bad news for deaf children: This would be one more domain in literacy where they fall behind their hearing peers. However, even a short intervention delivered by teachers in the classroom can enhance deaf children's use of morphology in spelling and at the same time improve their reading comprehension and writing skills.

These results have extremely important implications for the education of deaf children. In the United Kingdom deaf children are not taught about English morphology and syntax as part of their language instruction. It is expected that their innate ability to learn languages will take care of their learning English morphology and syntax. This is a reasonable expectation because they do not need instruction in the grammar and morphology of BSL in order to learn it.

However, learning a written language is not the same as learning an oral or signed language. Hearing children's literacy learning is strongly related to their awareness of phonology and morphology, not to their use of oral language in everyday life. It may be appropriate to compare deaf children's learning of written English to the situation of second-language learners. DeKeyser (2005), in a recent analysis of hearing immigrants' difficulties in learning a second language, concluded:

Morphology in L2 [second language] is hard: Basic word-order is typically non-problematic past the initial stages of acquisition, but even the most basic morphology is often lacking from the speech of untutored immigrants and of classroom learners who are not able to monitor themselves effectively (p. 6).

DeKeyser argues that morphology is a weak cue in the initial stages of learning any second language (L2), and if it becomes stronger over time, this only happens in a very slow and gradual fashion through explicit tutoring and conscious monitoring of L2 morphology. Recent evidence for the importance of awareness in learning L2 morphology strongly supports this analysis (Ellis, 2006; Mackey, 2006). These remarks are in complete agreement with the point we have made about deaf children for whom morphology may be an even weaker cue than for hearing immigrants. The question would be whether anything can be done in the education of deaf students to help them to acquire and use explicit knowledge of written English morphology. Our results show that it is not only possible but also a responsibility of educators to help deaf children to become more aware of English syntax and morphology in order to improve their literacy outcomes.

Acknowledgements

The research reported in this chapter would not have been possible without generous support from the Nuffield Foundation, which was expressed in funding as well as in valuable advice and encouragement. We are very grateful to them and to all the teachers, head teachers and children, without whose collaboration research of this nature would be impossible. We also thank the parents who gave permission for their children's participation and who showed so much interest in the results.

References

Alegria, J. (2004). Deafness and reading. In T. Nunes & P. Bryant (Eds.), *Handbook of children's literacy* (pp. 459–489). Dordrecht, The Netherlands: Kluwer Academic Press.

Beech, J. R., & Harris, M. (1997). The prelingually deaf young reader: A case of reliance on direct lexical access? *Journal of Research in Reading, 20*, 105–121.

Beers, C. S., & Beers, J. W. (1992). Children's spelling of English inflectional morphology. In S. Tempelton & D. R. Bear (Eds.), *Development of orthographic knowledge and the foundations of literacy: A memorial Festschrift for Edmund H. Henderson* (pp. 230–252). Hillsdale, NJ: Lawrence Erlbaum Associates, Inc.

Bradley, L., & Bryant, P. (1983). Categorising sounds and learning to read—a causal connection. *Nature, 301*, 419–421.

Bryant, P. E., & Goswami, U. (1986). The strengths and weaknesses of the reading level design—comment on Backman, Mamen and Ferguson. *Psychological Bulletin, 100*, 101–103.

Burman, D., Evans, D., & Nunes, T. (2008). Assessing deaf children's writing in primary school: Grammar and story development. *Deafness and Education International, 10*, 93–110.

Burman, D., Nunes, T., & Evans, D. (2007). Writing profiles of deaf children taught through British Sign Language. *Deafness and Education International, 9*, 2–23.

Burman, D., & Pretzlik, U. (2004). Paths to literacy for deaf British Sign Language (BSL) users. In T. Nunes & P. Bryant (Eds.), *Handbook of children's literacy* (pp. 741–766). Dordrecht, The Netherlands: Kluwer Academic Press.

Campbell, R. (1992). Read the lips: Relations of lipreading to academic and cognitive development of deaf children. In M. Marschark, P. Siple, R. Campbell, D. Lillo-Martin, & V. Everhart (Eds.), *Relations of language and cognition: The view from deaf children's development* (pp. 110–146). New York: Oxford University Press.

Chomsky, N. (1965). *Aspects of the theory of syntax*. Cambridge, MA: MIT Press.

Conrad, R. (1977). The reading ability of deaf school-leavers. *British Journal of Psychology, 47*, 138–148.

Conrad, R. (1979). *The deaf school child: Language and cognitive function*. London: Harper & Row.

Deacon, S. H., & Bryant, P. (2005). What children do and do not know about the spelling of inflections and derivations. *Developmental Science, 8*, 583–594.

Deacon, S. H., & Kirby, J. R. (2004). Morphological awareness: just "more phonological"? The roles of morphological and phonological awareness in reading development. *Applied Psycholinguistics, 25*, 223–238.

DeKeyser, R. M. (2005). What makes learning second language grammar difficult? A review of issues. *Language Learning, 55*, 1–25.

Ellis, N. C. (2006). Selective attention and transfer phenomena in L2 acquisition: Contingency, cue competition, salience, interference, overshadowing, blocking, and perceptual learning. *Applied Linguistics, 27*, 164–194.

Gates, A. I., & Chase, E. H. (1926). Methods and theories of learning to spell tested by studies of deaf children. *Journal of Educational Psychology, 17*, 289–300.

Gaustad, M. G. (2000). Morphological analysis as a word identification strategy for deaf readers. *Journal of Deaf Studies and Deaf Education, 5*, 60–80.

Goodman, N. (1976). *Languages of art*. Indianapolis, IN: Hacket.

Harris, M., & Moreno, C. (2004). Deaf children's use of phonological coding: Evidence from reading, spelling, and working memory. *Journal of Deaf Studies and Deaf Education, 9*, 253–268.

Harris, M., & Moreno, C. (2006). Speech reading and learning to read: A comparison of 8-year-old profoundly deaf children with good and poor reading ability. *Journal of Deaf Studies and Deaf Education, 11*, 189–201.

Harris, R. (1995). *Signs of writing*. London: Routledge & Kegan Paul.

Jaffré, J. P. (1997). From writing to orthography: The functions and limits of the notion of system. In C. A. Perfetti, L. Rieben, & M. Fayol (Eds.), *Learning to spell. Research, theory, and practice across languages* (pp. 3–20). Mahwah, NJ: Lawrence Erlbaum Associates, Inc.

Kemp, N., & Bryant, P. (2003). Do beez buzz? Rule-based and frequency-based knowledge in learning to spell plural -s. *Child Development, 74*, 63–74.

Leybaert, J., & Alegria, J. (1995). Spelling development in deaf and hearing children: Evidence for the use of morpho-phonological regularities in French. *Reading and Writing, 7*, 89–109.

Mackey, A. (2006). Feedback, noticing and instructed second language learning. *Applied Linguistics*, *27*, 405–430.

Marschark, M., & Harris, M. (1996). Success and failure in learning to read: The special case (?) of deaf children. In C. Cornoldi & J. Oakhill (Eds.), *Reading comprehension difficulties: Processes and intervention* (pp. 279–300). Mahwah, NJ: Lawrence Erlbaum Associates, Inc.

Mayer, C., & Wells, G. (1996). Can the linguistic interdependence theory support a bilingual–bicultural model of literacy education for deaf students? *Journal of Deaf Studies and Deaf Education*, *1*, 93–107.

Musselman, C. (2000). How do children who can't hear learn to read an alphabetic script? A review of the literature on reading and deafness. *Journal of Deaf Studies and Deaf Education*, *5*, 9–31.

Nagy, W., Berninger, V. W., & Abbott, R. D. (2006). Contributions of morphology beyond phonology to literacy outcomes of upper elementary and middle-school students. *Journal of Educational Psychology*, *98*, 135–147.

Nunes, T., & Bryant, P. (2006). *Improving literacy through teaching morphemes*. London: Routledge.

Nunes, T., & Bryant, P. (2009). *Children's reading and spelling. Beyond the first steps*. Oxford, UK: Blackwell.

Nunes, T., Bryant, P., & Bindman, M. (1997). Morphological spelling strategies: Developmental stages and processes. *Developmental Psychology*, *33*, 637–649.

Perfetti, C. A., & Sandak, R. (2000). Reading optimally builds on spoken language: Implications for deaf readers. *Journal of Deaf Studies and Deaf Education*, *5*, 32–50.

Rodda, M., & Eleweke, C. J. (2000). Theories of literacy development in limited English proficiency deaf people: A review. *Deafness and Education International*, *2*, 101–113.

Schonell, F., & Goodacre, E. (1971). *The psychology and teaching of reading*. London and Edinburgh: Oliver & Boyd.

Sutton-Spence, R., & Woll, B. (1998). *The linguistics of British Sign Language. An introduction*. Cambridge, UK: Cambridge University Press.

Tolchinsky, L. (2003). *The cradle of culture and what children know about writing and numbers before being taught*. Mahwah, NJ: Lawrence Erlbaum Associates, Inc.

Traxler, C. B. (2000). The Stanford Achievement Test, 9th Edition: National norming and performance standards for deaf and hard-of-hearing students. *Journal of Deaf Studies and Deaf Education*, *5*, 337–348.

Vacheck, J. (1973). *Written language: General problems and problems of English*. The Hague, The Netherlands: Mouton.

Webster, A. (2000). An international research review of literacy intervention strategies for children with severe to profound deafness. *Deafness and Education International*, *2*, 128–141.

Section 2

Developmental dyslexia in different orthographies

7 Unimpaired reading development and dyslexia across different languages

Nicola Brunswick

Introduction

Much of what we know about unimpaired reading development and developmental dyslexia derives from studies of English speakers, and attempts have been made to generalize from models based on these studies' findings to other alphabetic languages. This has led some to make potentially unfounded assumptions about the development and nature of reading in languages that differ from English in terms of their structure and complexity. This chapter explores the structure and complexity of different languages, primarily distinguishing between *shallow* (transparent) and *deep* (opaque) languages, and the impact that orthographic complexity has on reading development in these languages. It then considers the occurrence and presentation of developmental dyslexia in speakers of different alphabetic and non-alphabetic languages. Theoretical models of unimpaired reading and dyslexia are discussed, and the universality (or otherwise) of skilled and impaired reading processes is considered.

Orthographic depth

English is not a 'typical' language. It is irregular and unpredictable, with complex grapheme–phoneme rules that are frequently ambiguous and often difficult to learn. The 40 sounds of spoken English may be represented by somewhere in the region of 1120 possible letters or letter combinations (Nyikos, 1988). Consider, for example, the word pairs *mint/pint, clove/love, cough/bough* and *gave/have*. Many of the more unusual English spellings have their origin in other languages—including Latin (e.g., *aegis*), Greek (e.g., *psychology*), French (e.g., *blancmange*) and German (e.g., *abseil*)—each of which has its own particular spelling–sound rules. This ready assimilation of foreign words into English has led to the justified description of English spelling as 'a pseudo-historical and anti-educational abomination' (Jespersen, 1982) or, more simply, 'the world's most awesome mess' (Pei, 1967). In rather more scientific terms, English is described as having a *deep* orthography.

While English is undoubtedly an important language to study, being the world's *lingua franca*, research with English readers is only one very small part of a much larger story, and the last few decades have witnessed an increase in reading research in other alphabetic and non-alphabetic languages. In contrast with English, many of these languages, including Italian, Finnish, Spanish, Serbo-Croatian and Japanese kana, have more regular, predictable and consistent grapheme–phoneme rules, which make learning to read and spell in these languages a relatively straightforward process. The 25 sounds of spoken Italian, for example, are represented by just 33 letters or letter combinations (Lepschy & Lepschy, 1981). In the ultimate example of a regular language, each of the 33 individual written letters of Serbo-Croatian can only be pronounced in one way, and each spoken sound can only be written in one way (Frost, 2005). These languages are described as having a *shallow* orthography.

Young children are generally quick to learn the fundamental grapheme–phoneme rules of shallow languages and make rapid progress with their reading development. Italian children, for example, are able to achieve almost 100 per cent word reading accuracy after only a few months of reading instruction (Cossu, Gugliotta, & Marshall, 1995a; Orsolini, Fanari, Tosi, De Nigris, & Carrieri, 2006). Young would-be readers of deep languages, however, only begin to unravel the 'abominable mess' of their orthographies with considerable time and effort. The difficulties that unimpaired readers of deep orthographies face are magnified in dyslexic readers, who, as described in this chapter, continue to experience particular difficulty with the irregularity of deep orthographies.

Learning to read in shallow and deep orthographies

It is unsurprising that the orthographic depth of a language has a direct bearing on the ease with which children learn to read. Those whose native languages are shallow are generally able to learn the grapheme–phoneme rules that underpin reading and spelling in their languages rapidly and easily. By contrast, the inconsistency of deep languages makes the learning of generalizable grapheme–phoneme rules in these languages a much more difficult and protracted process.

This has been demonstrated by Seymour, Aro and Erskine's (2003) cross-language research project in which they compared the acquisition of foundation literacy—letter knowledge and the reading of simple, familiar words and non-words—in 5- to 7-year-old children from 14 European countries. The results of this project showed that word reading accuracy by the end of the first year of school was almost 100 per cent in Finnish, Greek and German-speaking (German and Austrian) children; it was around 92–95 per cent for Italian, Spanish, Swedish, Dutch, Icelandic and Norwegian children; 70–80 per cent for French, Portuguese and Danish children, and 34 per cent for English-speaking children. Similar findings emerged for the reading of non-words: By the end of the first year of school, around 90–95 per cent of Norwegian, Finnish, Greek and German-speaking children could read non-words accurately, as could 82–89 per cent of Italian, Spanish, Swedish, Dutch, Icelandic and French children, 77 per cent of Portuguese children, 54 per cent of Danish children and 29 per cent of English-speaking children.

Even by the end of the second year at school, the English-speaking children were only able to read 76 per cent of simple, real words and 64 per cent of non-words, indicating that the development of foundation literacy skills in English-speaking children occurs twice as slowly as in non-English-speaking European children. This finding is particularly striking as by the end of the first school year the English-speaking children were able to identify individual letters with an accuracy of 94 per cent, rising to 96 per cent by the end of Year 2—a finding comparable with the results from the non-English-speaking children.

These results mirror what would be predicted on the basis of the regularity of the languages. Further support comes from a follow-up study by the same research group in which around one third of Finnish children had already learned to read 'spontaneously' from playing with letters before they started school and received formal reading instruction. Furthermore, the ease and speed with which Finnish children learn to read are demonstrated by the finding that almost 90 per cent are able to read within the first school semester (Lyytinen et al., 2004).

Children whose native languages are irregular and inconsistent experience much greater difficulty learning the spelling–sound rules of their languages than do children whose native languages are regular and consistent. This is reflected in the accuracy of non-word reading across the 13 languages, and particularly in the English-speaking children.

Children in the United Kingdom start school from the age of 5, or sometimes shortly before their fifth birthday, and they immediately begin to receive reading instruction. This instruction builds upon basic literacy skills that they have learned in their pre-school years. This is in contrast to children from other countries, particularly the Scandinavian countries such as Finland and Norway, who typically do not begin formal reading instruction until they are 6 or 7 years old. Therefore, the word and non-word reading accuracy results reported above are actually comparing children of different ages. As English-speaking children are often one or two years younger than the non-English-speaking children, it is possible that their early reading difficulties actually reflect their relative immaturity rather than the complexity of their language *per se*. However, Danish children—who also need to learn a predominantly deep orthography—also experience difficulty in acquiring foundation literacy skills (Juul & Sigurdsson, 2005; Seymour et al., 2003). This is despite the fact that these children do not start school until the age of 7, traditionally having received very little reading instruction at home before this age. Furthermore, the English children's reading accuracy after two years at school, by which time they are 7 years old, is still considerably poorer than that of the other 7-year-old children at the end of their first year at school.

Although English-speaking (and Danish-speaking) children are considerably slower at developing these early literacy skills than are their non-English- (and non-Danish-) speaking counterparts, the good news is that they do catch up. While 7-year-old Finnish children are able to read with 90 per cent accuracy after around 10 weeks of reading instruction in school, English-speaking children may take four or five years to achieve this same level of reading accuracy, while Danish children may achieve a comparable level of skill within two or three years. Irrespective of the depth of orthography, the data suggest that the fundamental building blocks of reading are in place by this time, and differences in the reading ability of speakers of different languages have generally disappeared by the age of 12 or 13 years.

Reading in any language involves deriving meaning from printed symbols. Attempts to explain the means by which this process is achieved in different languages with different orthographic depths are represented by a number of cognitive models. Two of these models—the orthographic depth hypothesis and the psycholinguistic grain size theory—are considered below.

The orthographic depth hypothesis: The strong version

The orthographic depth hypothesis suggests that languages that differ in the complexity, or depth, of their grapheme–phoneme rules are read in different ways—that is, readers rely to different degrees on lexical (whole-word) and sub-lexical (phonological) reading processes (Benuck & Peverly, 2004; Frost, 1994; Katz & Frost, 1992; Seidenberg, 1992). The more regular the orthography, the more readers rely upon phonological recoding to provide access to the mental lexicon.

Speakers of orthographically shallow languages should always rely on a sub-lexical (phonological) route from print to sound when they read. As these languages have a clear and consistent (sometimes one-to-one) relationship between graphemes and phonemes, perfect reading accuracy of all words and non-words is possible through the real-time conversion of graphemes into phonemes. Readers of shallow orthographies have no need, therefore, to access the mental lexicon to achieve reading accuracy (Bridgeman, 1987; Katz & Feldman, 1983; Turvey, Feldman, & Lukatela, 1984).

By contrast, speakers of orthographically deep languages are unable to rely solely on sub-lexical processes when they read. As these languages have an obscure and inconsistent (one-to-many) relationship between graphemes and phonemes, perfect reading accuracy of irregular words and non-words is possible only through the involvement of a lexical, orthographic route from print to sound. Whole words are 'looked up' in the mental lexicon, and their meanings and pronunciations are obtained (Coltheart & Coltheart, 1997; Lukatela & Turvey, 1994; Rastle & Coltheart, 1999).

However, research does not entirely support this strong version of the orthographic depth hypothesis. It is unable, for example, to explain how readers of shallow languages are able to allocate stress to the correct syllable within multi-syllable words. Information regarding stress assignment is not available via the sub-lexical, phonological route. Yet some of the most consistent and regular languages, such as Italian, Spanish and Serbo-Croatian, have inconsistent and unpredictable stress patterns. In Italian, for example, stress is placed on the last syllable in approximately 4 per cent of words (e.g., *leggero*, meaning 'I will read'); on the second-to-last syllable in approximately 84 per cent of words (e.g., *leggere*, meaning 'light'); and on the third-to-last syllable in approximately 12 per cent of words (e.g., **leggere**, meaning 'to read') (Thornton, Iacobini, & Burani, 1997). Such inconsistencies would trip up readers of shallow orthographies if they had no access to the mental lexicon to tell them which syllable within a word should be stressed (Burani & Arduino, 2004; Colombo & Tabossi, 1992).

The importance of the mental lexicon to readers of shallow orthographies is also illustrated by reports of Italian aphasic and acquired dyslexic patients who are still able to read non-words and regularly stressed real words—those that are stressed on the second-to-last syllable—almost perfectly. They are significantly less accurate, however, at assigning stress to words that are stressed irregularly, on the third-to-last or last syllables (Cappa, Nespor, Ielasi, & Miozzo, 1997; Galante, Tralli, Zuffi, & Avanzi, 2000; Laganaro, Vacheresse, & Frauenfelder, 2002; Miceli & Caramazza, 1993). Similar results are reported for Dutch and German aphasic and acquired dyslexic readers who are able to read with almost perfect accuracy real words and non-words that follow the most consistent stress pattern of the language. However, like the Italian patients, these Dutch and German readers also show a strong tendency to regularize the stress assignments in the reading of irregularly stressed words (de Bree, Janse, & van de Zande, 2007; Janssen, 2003).

These findings have been interpreted as evidence that the regular stress pattern for words in each language is assigned by default unless information to the contrary is stored in the lexicon. Italian, Dutch and German patients with damage to their lexicon will, therefore, tend to produce regular stress patterns for words by default. Of course, in most cases this will be correct. However, what is particularly interesting about these findings is that these patients are still able to read irregularly stressed words correctly, albeit with lower rates of accuracy than regularly stressed words. This finding indicates that these readers are relying to some extent on information about stress assignment that is stored in the mental lexicon. This provides evidence that is contrary to the strong version of the orthographic depth hypothesis in which readers of shallow orthographies have no need to access the mental lexicon—or even to develop a lexical route—to achieve reading accuracy.

Further evidence against the strong version of the orthographic depth hypothesis is provided by the finding that readers of shallow languages, like readers of deep languages, demonstrate lexical priming effects in which a word such as *butter* is read faster and more accurately if it is preceded by the word *bread* than by the word *door*. Similar priming effects occur for the spelling of non-words. For example, the heard non-word [bo:p] (pronounced to rhyme with hope) is more likely to be spelled as *bope* following priming by the word *Vatican* because of its implicit association with the word *pope*; while it is more likely to be spelled as *boap* following priming by the word *detergent* because of its association with the word *soap* (Seymour & Dargie, 1990).

Lexical priming and lexical decision effects have been observed in several shallow languages, including Spanish (Cuetos, 1993; Sebastián-Gallés, 1991), Dutch (Assink, Van Bergen, Van Teeseling, & Knuijt, 2004), Greek (Plemmenou, Bard, & Branigan, 2002; Voga & Grainger, 2004), Persian (Baluch & Besner, 1991) and Italian (Barry & de Bastiani, 1997). If these readers were relying solely on a sub-lexical, phonological route to reading and spelling, then these effects would not be found. So, contrary to the predictions of the strong version of the orthographic depth hypothesis, the presence of these lexical effects indicates that these readers *are* able to access the mental lexicon during reading and spelling (see Besner & Smith, 1992).

The orthographic depth hypothesis: The weak version

A 'weaker' version of the orthographic depth hypothesis suggests that reading in all languages, deep or shallow, involves both sub-lexical and lexical processes. The difference between deep and shallow languages is seen in the *extent* to which readers rely on these different processes: readers of shallow languages are more likely to rely on phonological processes, while readers of deep languages are more likely to rely on orthographic processes.

Evidence for this hypothesis is provided by research showing that young readers of shallow languages such as German (Landerl, 2000; Wimmer & Goswami, 1994; Wimmer & Hummer, 1990), Welsh (Spencer & Hanley, 2003), Spanish (Defior, Martos, & Cary, 2002; Goswami, Gombert, & de Barrera, 1998), Italian (Cossu et al., 1995a; Cossu, Shankweiler, Liberman, & Gugliotta, 1995b), Turkish (Öney & Durgunoğlu, 1997) and Greek (Goswami, Porpodas, & Wheelwright, 1997; Porpodas, Pantelis, & Hantziou, 1990) are more accurate at reading—phonologically decoding—non-words than are readers of deep languages such as English or, to a lesser extent, French (Frith, Wimmer, & Landerl, 1998; Seymour et al., 2003; see also Ziegler & Goswami, 2005, for an excellent review of cross-language studies of reading development).

Further evidence for shallow readers' greater reliance on phonological decoding is provided by studies in which participants are asked to read pseudo-homophones such as *focks* or *dore*. In one such study, Goswami, Ziegler, Dalton, and Schneider (2001) showed 7- to 9-year-old German and English children real words in their own language (e.g., the German word *fünf* (meaning five) and the English word *fake*); pseudo-homophones based on these words (e.g., *fünv* and *faik*); phonologically and orthographically plausible non-words (e.g., *sünf* and *dake*); and implausible non-words (e.g., *zaudt* and *koog*). At all ages the English children showed a significant pseudo-homophone effect on this task—that is, they were better able to read the pseudo-homophones (63 per cent correct) than the plausible non-words (56 per cent correct) or the implausible non-words (43 per cent correct). By contrast, the German children showed little difference in their ability to read the pseudo-homophones (91 per cent), the plausible non-words (93 per cent) and the implausible non-words (84 per cent).

These data indicate that English children rely more than German children on whole-word 'top-down' processing of information from the lexicon. Their accuracy for the reading of pseudo-homophones is facilitated as these particular non-words resemble real words stored in the lexicon, although clearly the English children also use phonological recoding to support their reading of non-words. German children are, however, able to read real words, pseudo-homophones and non-words with a high degree of accuracy simply by relying on 'bottom-up' phonological decoding.

Other studies have shown that readers of shallow languages are significantly more likely than readers of deep languages to accept pseudo-homophones as real words in a lexical decision task (Di Filippo, De Luca, Judica, Spinelli, & Zoccolotti, 2006; Goswami et al., 2001; Marcolini, Burani, & Colombo, 2009). This finding suggests that readers of deep orthographies make more accurate lexical decisions on the basis of whole-word orthographic processing, so they are less likely to be tripped up by pseudo-homophones. By contrast, readers of shallow orthographies are impeded in their whole-word processing by the automatic activation of phonological processes, so they are far more likely to accept pseudo-homophones as real words.

One problem with cross-language studies of word reading and lexical processing is the difficulty in controlling for specific effects of participants and the words that are used. To control for these effects, Paulesu and colleagues compared English and Italian adults' reading of high-frequency regular words from their native language (e.g., *cabin, market, cottage; marmo, ponte, moto*); non-words based on these English and Italian words (e.g., *cagin, marnet, connage; margo, ponda, moco*); and familiar 'international' words that have the same spelling and meaning in both languages (Paulesu et al., 2000; see also chapter 12, this volume). Half of these international words conformed to English spelling patterns, the other half to Italian patterns. The 'English' words, *partner, basket* and *corner*, for example, contained clusters of consonants that do not appear in Italian (e.g., the 'rtn' in *partner*), the letter 'k', which is rare in Italian and only appears in words of foreign derivation, and all of the words ended in consonants (most Italian words end in vowels). The 'Italian' words, such as *coma, villa* and *pasta*, all ended in vowels (which is far rarer in English) and, unlike English words, their letters were consistently pronounced.

Paulesu et al. found that the Italian students were consistently faster at reading Italian real words, non-words derived from Italian words and non-words derived from English words than were the English students when reading English words, non-words derived from English words and non-words derived from Italian words (see Figure 7.1). This finding has been labelled by Uta Frith 'the Ferrari effect', referring to the speed of the Italian sports cars and the speed of Italian readers.

An interesting finding emerged for the reading of the international words in that the Italian readers were significantly faster at reading words that conformed to their own rules of spelling than those that conformed to the English rules. No such effect emerged for the English readers' reading of words that conformed to English rules and those that conformed to Italian rules (see Figure 7.1). Brain imaging data gathered from the same study showed more activity in the English readers' brains in the left posterior, inferior temporal gyrus and the anterior, inferior frontal gyrus—regions associated with whole-word reading/picture naming. Italian readers' brains showed more activity in left superior temporal regions associated with phonological processing (these findings are discussed in greater detail in chapter 12, this volume). This difference in the extent to which English and Italian readers rely on orthographic and phonological processes provides further support for the weak version of the orthographic depth hypothesis.

The psycholinguistic grain size theory

In a neat modification of the orthographic depth hypotheses, the grain size theory (described in detail in chapter 2) proposes that while reading in any language entails converting spelling into sound, the size of the letter strings—the 'grain size'—into which words are broken down depends on the depth of the language (Ziegler & Goswami, 2005). In shallow languages, in which single letters consistently and predictably represent single sounds, the grain size is very small (at the level of the individual grapheme). Children therefore

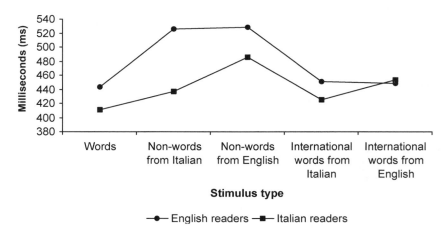

Figure 7.1 Word and non-word reading by English and Italian adults.

quickly learn that words and non-words can be decoded letter-by-letter. In deep languages children cannot rely solely on letter-by-letter reading if they are to avoid making frequent reading errors. Instead, these children need to learn how to convert psycholinguistic units of varying sizes (rimes, syllables and whole words) into their corresponding sounds to enable them to read efficiently and accurately.

Support for the grain size theory is provided by Goswami et al.'s (2001) study of German and English children, described above. In this study German readers' reading of words and non-words was predominantly influenced by the number of letters in the words and non-words—that is, they showed a significant word length effect. These children were significantly better at reading monosyllabic words (95 per cent correct) than bisyllabic words (90 per cent correct), and significantly better at reading bisyllabic words than trisyllabic words (84 per cent correct). The English children showed no such effect, being most accurate at reading bisyllabic words (66 per cent correct).

The English readers' reading was influenced more by the structure of the words and non-words—that is, they showed a significant pseudo-homophone effect and were better able to read plausible non-words (e.g., *loffee* that shares many of its letters with the real word *coffee*) than implausible non-words (e.g., *hixa* that bears little visual resemblance to any real words).

In a follow-up lexical decision task, Goswami et al. (2001) found that German children were significantly disadvantaged (in terms of response time and accuracy) by the presence of pseudo-homophones. English children were not disadvantaged in this way. This pattern of results suggests that the English children are making their lexical decisions based on the look of the whole word (its orthographic form). Words that do not look right may be rejected quickly. German children are, however, prevented from making quick and reliable lexical decisions based on the orthographic form of the words by their automatic recoding of graphemes into phonemes.

Together, these findings indicate that whereas German readers—as well as readers of other shallow orthographies—employ small grain, sub-lexical reading processes at the level of individual graphemes, English readers (and readers of other deep orthographies) are not restricted in this way but are able to employ a reading strategy based on a larger grain size, even up to the level of the whole word.

Unlike some of its predecessors, the grain size theory of reading is able to explain the development of different reading strategies in deep and shallow languages. It also explains differences in the incidence of dyslexia across languages, the topic of the next section.

Dyslexia across different languages

As the studies described in the preceding sections have shown, the ease with which children learn to read and spell depends to a great extent on the depth of their native language. This also determines the incidence of developmental dyslexia for speakers of that language, with estimates generally ranging between 5 and 15 per cent for readers of alphabetic languages. However, this figure masks some quite striking differences in the incidence of dyslexia across languages and orthographies (including Chinese and Japanese), as illustrated in Figure 7.2.

The languages in this figure are divided by their orthographic depth, with the deep languages (Chinese, Danish and English) at the top and the shallow languages at the bottom of the figure. There is a fairly clear distinction, with only one or two exceptions, between the incidence of dyslexia in the shallow and deep languages. However, such neat comparisons are hindered by the fact that dyslexia manifests itself in different ways in different languages, so countries necessarily differ in the way they define and assess dyslexia (Brunswick, 2009; Miles, 2004).

One point on which there is agreement, however, is that dyslexic readers of all languages experience phonological processing deficits. The extent to which these deficits impede the reading development of children in different countries depends on the depth of the language spoken.

Dyslexia in deep and shallow languages

The link between orthographic depth and the prevalence of dyslexia has long been recognized, although not always fully understood, as Critchley (1970) noted:

> Claiborne [writing in 1906] blamed dyslexia . . . upon the arbitrary pronunciation of the English language, and he seemed to doubt whether this disability ever occurred in those whose mother-tongue was Italian, Spanish or Russian. He was obviously not correct as experience has abundantly shown. None the less, the fact that English, like Chinese, and to a lesser extent French and Danish, is no logical orthographic language and is not necessarily spelt as it is pronounced, or pronounced as it is written, must erect certain barriers. It is not that dyslexia is unusually common in England, but rather that dyslexics are identified more readily and more early by dint of their failure to master our odd spelling. (p. 14)

While dyslexic readers of all orthographies have difficulty converting written letters into their corresponding sounds, those who need to translate between the spoken and written forms of complex, deep, irregular languages will be the ones who experience the greatest reading difficulty. Dyslexic readers of deep orthographies will be identifiable on the basis of their extremely slow and impaired reading, spelling and phonological processing. Dyslexic readers of shallow languages, however, may cope adequately with their daily reading, since their word and non-word reading accuracy is likely to be no poorer than that of non-dyslexic readers. Dyslexia in these readers is typically characterized by reading that is slower (but no less accurate) than expected, poor

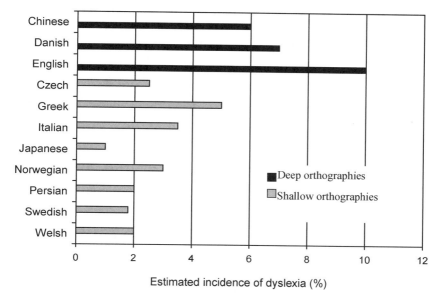

Figure 7.2 The estimated incidence of dyslexia across different languages.

spelling ability and effortful phonological processing (Barca, Burani, Di Filippo, & Zoccolotti, 2006; Caravolas & Volin, 2002; Paulesu et al., 2001). Readers of languages with a moderately shallow orthography (e.g., Dutch, Portuguese and German) may have little difficulty reading familiar words, but they may be slow and inaccurate reading unfamiliar words and non-words (van Daal & van der Leij, 1999; Wimmer, 1996). For this reason, while a measure of reading accuracy such as the National Adult Reading Test[1] (Nelson & Willison, 1991) may be usefully included in a dyslexia assessment for readers of English or Danish, such a test would reveal little about the abilities of dyslexic readers of Spanish or Italian.

Studies of German and English dyslexic readers offer a good opportunity to compare the abilities of readers of shallow (German) and deep (English) languages using words and non-words that are as orthographically and phonologically similar as possible. Because English and German developed from the same Germanic root, they share many words in common, such as the German words *Ball*, *Katze*, *Salat* and the English equivalents *ball*, *cat*, *salad*. The main difference in the pronunciation of these words lies in the vowels. Whereas the 'a' in each of the German words is pronounced consistently as a short 'a' sound (as in the English word *cat*), the 'a' in each of the English words is pronounced inconsistently, as an 'aw' sound in *ball*, as a short 'a' sound in *cat* and in the word *salad* as a short 'a' followed by an 'u' sound.

In one such cross-language study Landerl, Wimmer, and Frith (1997) tested the word and non-word reading ability of 12-year-old dyslexic and non-dyslexic children. Stimuli were selected to be as closely matched as possible in the two languages in terms of their spelling, pronunciation and meaning. While the German-speaking dyslexic children read the consistently spelled high-frequency German words (e.g., *jung* and *Mutter*) with around 97 per cent accuracy, English dyslexic readers of the same age read only 81 per cent of the inconsistently spelled high-frequency English equivalent words (e.g., *young* and *mother*) accurately. When these children were asked to read infrequent words (e.g., *Schwert*/*sword*, *Kamm*/*comb*), accuracy rates dropped to 89 per cent for the German-speaking children and 48 per cent for the English children. When they were asked to read non-words (e.g., *Hoot*, formed from the German words *Hand* and *Boot*, and *hoat*, formed from the English words *hand* and *boat*), accuracy dropped even further, to 77 per cent for the German children and 27 per cent for the English children.

Because of the consistency of the German language, reading in Germany and Austria is predominantly taught via the use of phonics-based methods that stress the sounds of letters rather than their names. Children are encouraged to assemble words from their constituent sounds and quickly learn which letters represent which sounds. This combination of orthographic consistency and an emphasis on phonics makes learning to read a relatively straightforward task for German-speaking dyslexic children—hence their almost perfect reading of real words and their above 75 per cent accuracy for the reading of non-words.

The English-speaking dyslexic children also read the high-frequency real words, which can be recognized by sight, with a reasonable degree of accuracy. However, their accuracy rates dropped below 50 per cent for the reading of low-frequency words and below 30 per cent for non-words. Low-frequency words and non-words need to be phonologically recoded as they cannot be recognized by sight; the inconsistency of English makes this recoding much less accurate for English-speaking dyslexic children.

While the consistency of the German language allows German-speaking dyslexic readers to develop fairly accurate reading skills, the difficulties of dyslexia manifest in these individuals in other ways. One of these is slow reading speed—in fact, dyslexic children's reading is described as being 'painstakingly slow' and laborious (Landerl, 2001). Bachmann (1927), for example, observed that when German dyslexic children read aloud a list of long words (of at least 11 letters each), they did so between one-and-a-half and six times as slowly as non-dyslexic readers of the same age. On average, the word *Strassenbahnhaltestelle* [*tram stop*] took a non-dyslexic child around 2–4 seconds to read, but a dyslexic child around 39 seconds. To illustrate further the difficulties of dyslexic readers, Bachmann described one 11-year-old dyslexic reader's attempts at reading the word *Handarbeitslehrerin* [*female handicraft teacher*]: after 20 seconds the child attempted 'Hander . . .'; after 40 seconds, 'Handbar . . .'; after 60 seconds, 'Handbarweisstellerin'; and finally, after 90 seconds, 'Handarbeitslehrerin'. More recently, others have reported that 12-year-old German and Spanish dyslexic children read at the same speed as typically developing 6- to 8-year-old children of the same reading age (Landerl et al., 1997; Serrano & Defior, 2008).

Other common manifestations of dyslexia in readers of shallow languages include reduced rapid automatized naming (RAN)[2] speed (Brizzolara et al., 2006; Holopainen, Ahonen, & Lyytinen, 2001) and poor phonological awareness (Paulesu et al., 2001; Ramus, 2003; Wolf & Bowers, 2000). Landerl et al. (1997), for example, found that their Austrian dyslexic children performed just as poorly as did English-speaking dyslexic children on a Spoonerism task[3] (with 63 vs. 73 per cent errors), despite the phonics-based reading instruction received by the German-speaking children. The presence of these specific difficulties, in the absence of overt reading difficulties, is further demonstrated by Paulesu et al.'s (2001) study of English, Italian and French adults. While the researchers had no difficulty identifying English and French dyslexic readers, Italian dyslexic readers proved extremely difficult to find. From screening 1200 students, it was possible to identify only 18 dyslexic readers, and these only on the basis of their extremely slow reading speed, slow digit naming and poor phonological awareness. The study found that the Italian dyslexic readers were consistently more accurate than the English and French dyslexic readers at reading words and non-words. However, all three dyslexic groups were significantly poorer at reading and at performing a Spoonerism task than were their non-dyslexic peers.

These and other results suggest that phonological deficits lie at the heart of dyslexia in readers of both deep and shallow languages. These phonological difficulties may have a common neuroanatomical origin (something that is explored in the final section of this volume), although they manifest themselves in different ways depending on the depth of the language. The combination of phonological difficulties and the inconsistency of deep languages causes dyslexic readers to read poorly and slowly, while the combination of phonological difficulties and the consistency of shallow languages enables dyslexic readers of these languages to read accurately, albeit slowly.

An interesting finding from studies with dyslexic children has shown that during the first few years of schooling, speakers of both shallow and deep languages experience phonological processing difficulties. For example, approximately 97 per cent of first-grade Greek unimpaired readers are able to read non-words correctly, but this figure drops to 93 per cent for children with dyslexia (Porpodas, 1999); for Austrian children, figures of 96 per cent and 60 per cent are reported (Wimmer, 1996); for French children, these figures are 90 per cent and 75 per cent (Sprenger-Charolles, Colé, Lacert, & Serniclaes, 2000); and for Norwegian children, around 84 per cent and 74 per cent (although the mean figure for the dyslexic children hides a broad range of abilities; Nergård-Nilssen, 2006). Some researchers have suggested that these difficulties disappear within a couple of years in readers of shallow languages, by which time the phonological abilities of dyslexic readers have 'caught up' with those of non-dyslexic readers (de Jong, 2003; López & Jiménez Gonzáles, 2000; Porpodas, 1999; Wimmer, 1993).

German-speaking dyslexic readers from the third grade are virtually perfect at spelling non-words, indicating that they have grasped the fundamental spelling–sound rules of the language (Wimmer, 1993, 1996). Similarly, while dyslexic Dutch pre-school children are poor at identifying which word out of three does not rhyme with the other two (i.e., they demonstrate simple phonological difficulties), they are able to perform this task by the end of first grade (de Jong, 2003; de Jong & van der Leij, 2003). More difficult tests of phonological awareness (e.g., 'Which word from *hat, cat, man, bat* ends in a different sound from the other three?' or 'What word remains when the middle sound is deleted from *memslos*?') are beyond the capabilities of dyslexic pre-school children. However, dyslexic children are able to perform this task as well as unimpaired readers by the end of sixth grade (Patel, Snowling, & de Jong, 2004). A combination of the shallow German and Dutch orthographies and systematic phonics-based reading instruction enables even dyslexic readers to overcome their early phonological difficulties, develop phonological awareness, learn grapheme–phoneme correspondences and become proficient—if relatively slow—readers.

A slightly different pattern has emerged for the development of phonological skills and reading in Czech dyslexic readers beyond the early school years. For example, the word and non-word spellings of 11-year-old Czech dyslexic readers have been classified as either phonologically accurate (so a word *sounds* correct even if the word is spelled incorrectly: for example, the word *please* might be spelled 'please', 'plees' or 'pleez') or phonologically inaccurate (not all the sounds of the word are represented: for example, the word *please* might be spelled as 'plays', 'pls' or 'bls'). Despite the consistency of their language, Caravolas and Volin (2002) found that these dyslexic Czech children produced significantly more phonologically inaccurate spellings than did their non-dyslexic peers, such that 19 per cent of the dyslexic children's spelling of words and 4 per cent of the non-dyslexic children's were classified as being phonologically inaccurate, while 28 per cent of the dyslexic children's spelling of non-words and 7 per cent of the non-dyslexic children's were classified as being phonologically inaccurate.

Czech dyslexic readers aged 7–12 years (Grades 3–7) are also poorer than chronological age-matched control readers on a phoneme deletion task (deleting the first, second or third sound from single-syllable words) and a Spoonerism task with one- and two-syllable words (Caravolas, Volin, & Hulme, 2005). In fact, the Czech dyslexic readers displayed phonological deficits on these tasks that were comparable to those of English dyslexic readers of the same age.

Together, these findings show that phonological difficulties are a consistent feature of dyslexia across deep and shallow alphabetic languages, at least through the primary school years (ages 4–11 years). The precise nature of these difficulties, however, varies with the depth of the language.

Dyslexic readers of shallow languages may learn to master relatively simple phonological skills, such as recognizing and producing rhyme and alliteration, within their first few years at school. More complex phonological skills, such as adding, deleting and swapping sounds within and between words, take longer to master. By contrast, dyslexic readers of deep languages continue to show poor phonological skills into adulthood. The phonological difficulties that these readers experience typically manifest themselves as slow and inaccurate reading (particularly of irregular words, such as *aisle*), inaccurate spelling and frequent mispronunciation of long words (such as *phenomenal*). The remainder of this chapter will consider the extent to which such difficulties might affect dyslexic readers of non-alphabetic languages.

Dyslexia in non-alphabetic languages

A common misconception about the Chinese script is that it is entirely pictographic. Some of its characters *do* represent entire words, and the shape of the character gives a clue to the word's meaning, but such characters are few. The majority of characters—around 90 per cent—are compounds (Kang, 1993). These include a semantic element that provides information about the meaning of the character, and a phonetic element that provides information about its pronunciation. For example, see the character for *mother* in Figure 7.3.

This compound character is composed of the symbol for *woman*, which provides the meaning, and the symbol for *horse*, which provides a clue to the word's pronunciation but no information about meaning. However, the phonetic information is, for the most part, ambiguous: only around 25 per cent of compound characters can be reliably pronounced on the basis of the phonetic element (Hoosain, 1991). While the sounds that represent *horse* and *mother* in Chinese are both *ma*, they are pronounced in subtly different ways. *Ma* meaning mother is pronounced with a constant high pitch, while *ma* meaning horse is pronounced with a low pitch that falls and then rises again. Confusingly, *ma* can also be pronounced with a medium pitch that rises (meaning *flax*), and with a high pitch that falls to a low pitch (meaning *to scold*). For this reason, Chinese is considered to be a deep orthography (for a more detailed description of the Chinese orthography see chapter 10).

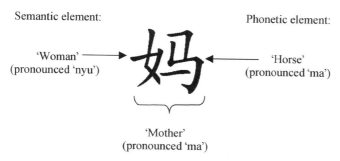

Figure 7.3 Phonetic and semantic Chinese characters.

The Japanese writing system has two forms: kanji and kana. Kanji is a pictographic script that was imported from China, and each kanji character can be pronounced in two ways. One way represents the original Chinese word form, the other the Japanese word form. Which of these is correct in any particular sentence is dictated by the context.

Kanji characters usually represent nouns (e.g., *horse*), and verb and adjective stems. For example, the kanji character that represents the verb *to see* cannot be changed to represent the past tense (*saw*), the future tense (*will see*) or the negative (*do not see*). Similarly, the character that represents the adjective *happy* cannot be changed into the comparative form (*happier*) or the adverb (*happily*). These modifications are indicated by the presence of a kana character that follows the stem.

Kana is a phonetic script that reliably represents syllables in the spoken language. In addition to providing verb endings (e.g., to indicate past tense), it is also used to write foreign names and words for which there is no kanji character. While kanji characters provide no clue to their pronunciation and so are considered to be orthographically deep, kana characters have a perfect correspondence between their written form and their pronunciation, so they are considered to be orthographically shallow.

Although learning to read Chinese requires less obvious phonological processing than that involved in learning to read alphabetic languages, some phonological skills are still necessary (Ho & Bryant, 1997). It is unsurprising, therefore, that Chinese dyslexic readers experience phonological difficulties similar to those of dyslexic readers of alphabetic languages: these include slower object naming (Ho, Chan, Tsang, & Lee, 2002; Ho & Lai, 1999), less accurate detection and production of rhymes (Ho & Lai, 1999; Ho, Law, & Ng, 2000), less accurate deletion of phonemes from spoken words (Huang & Zhang, 1997), poorer phonological memory (Ho & Lai, 1999; Ho et al., 2000) and less accurate repetition of non-words (Ho et al., 2000) compared to non-dyslexic age-matched readers. In one of the few studies to include reading-age- as well as chronological-age-matched control readers, Ho and colleagues (2000) found that dyslexic children with reading difficulties (but not writing difficulties) displayed significantly poorer phonological abilities (onset detection, rhyme detection, word and non-word repetition) than age-matched control readers. However, they performed similarly to younger children of the same reading age. This suggests that Chinese dyslexic readers, like dyslexic readers of alphabetic orthographies, have phonological deficits. These deficits prevent Chinese dyslexic children from benefiting from the phonological information provided by the phonetic elements of printed characters, thereby contributing to their reading difficulties.

Dyslexic readers tend to have difficulty analysing not only the sounds of words (phonology) but also the written forms of words (orthography). Given the complexity of Chinese written characters—most are formed out of some 9–11 individual strokes—dyslexic readers' orthographic difficulties are also likely to hinder their reading. This importance of visual (and phonological) skills has been explored in a large-scale study of dyslexic children in Hong Kong, reported by Ho et al. (2004). They found that relative to non-impaired readers of the same age, 57 per cent of the dyslexic children were significantly impaired at naming written digits (they displayed rapid naming deficits); 42 per cent showed significantly poorer knowledge of the structure of written characters (they displayed orthographic processing deficits); 29 per cent were significantly less able to detect onsets and rimes within words and to repeat words and non-words accurately (they displayed phonological processing deficits); and 27 per cent showed poorer visual perception and visual memory (they displayed visual perceptual deficits). Further analysis revealed a positive correlation between the severity of an individual's dyslexia and the extent of their rapid naming and orthographic processing impairments. On the basis of these findings the authors conclude that, for Chinese dyslexic readers, difficulties with orthographic processing and rapid naming 'pose an interrelated . . . problem in acquiring orthographic knowledge . . . and linking efficiently the orthographic and phonological processors' (p. 70).

As this particular study failed to test younger children of the same reading age, it is difficult to know whether these deficits are a cause or a consequence of the dyslexic children's reading difficulties. It is possible that these children's poorer knowledge of the structure of written characters might result from less time spent reading compared to unimpaired readers of the same age. Nevertheless, results from studies such as this one suggest that Chinese children with dyslexia have fundamental impairments in processing the sounds and visual forms of the language, just as dyslexic readers of alphabetic languages do.

A rather different picture emerges from studies of Japanese dyslexic readers. Wydell and Butterworth (1999), for example, described a 16-year-old boy, AS, who was born in Japan to an Australian father (a journalist and writer) and an English mother (an English teacher). AS grew up in Japan to be completely bilingual in English and Japanese. He was among the top 10 per cent of readers of his age in Japanese kanji and kana, reading at a graduate level. However, his performance on tests of English reading, spelling and phonological processing was poorer than that of his Japanese classmates, reflecting his severe dyslexia. Clearly, this boy's phonological difficulties existed whichever language he was reading, yet they only manifested themselves when he read English because it depends on a complex and irregular spelling–sound translation. The regularity and consistency of Japanese presents no such difficulties.

To explain this dissociation, Wydell and Butterworth suggested that languages could be classified along two dimensions, representing (1) the transparency of the language—from transparent (shallow) to opaque (deep) languages, and (2) the granularity of the language—from fine (where words are read by breaking them down into letters that represent individual sounds) to coarse (where words are read as whole units). These dimensions are illustrated in Figure 7.4, with transparency on the x axis and granularity on the y axis.

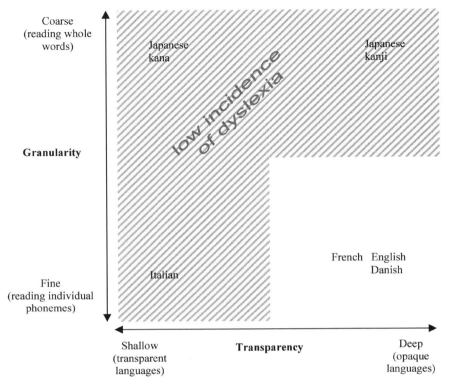

Figure 7.4 The incidence of dyslexia in languages that differ in transparency and granularity (adapted from Wydell & Butterworth, 1999).

The incidence of dyslexia will be low in: (1) any transparent orthography, whether its granularity is fine (such as Italian), coarse (such as Japanese kana) or anywhere in-between; and (2) any language with a coarse granularity, whether the degree of transparency is high (e.g., Japanese kanji) or low. These combinations of transparency and granularity are illustrated by the hatched sections in Figure 7.4.

By contrast, the incidence of dyslexia will be high in relatively opaque languages, particularly those that rely on moderate and fine grain sizes. This combination is illustrated by the non-hatched section of Figure 7.4.

Because of its particular combination of transparency and granularity, Japanese is considered by some to be a perfect language for dyslexic readers to learn. This notion has been adopted enthusiastically by some schools in the United Kingdom that have selected Japanese to be their second language of choice, in preference to more traditionally taught European languages, such as French, German or Spanish. This move has been hailed a success, with many dyslexic pupils attaining a level of proficiency with their foreign language studies that their predecessors had failed to reach.

Conclusion

Learning to read in any language builds upon existing spoken language skills. Children who come to the task of reading with well-developed language skills—with an awareness of phonemes, syllables, rhymes, onsets and rimes and with a good spoken vocabulary—will more readily acquire early literacy skills than will children with poorer language skills. While there is overwhelming evidence that phonological awareness is a good predictor of early reading development across languages, the role that phonological skills play in reading development beyond the earliest stages depends on the nature of the language—whether it is deep or shallow, alphabetic or non-alphabetic.

Similarities and differences in unimpaired reading development are also reflected in dyslexia across languages. While impaired phonological processing, slow object naming and poor verbal memory are commonly found in dyslexic readers of many languages, the effect that these difficulties have on the individual's reading ability differs. Phonological deficits cause relatively few problems for readers of languages with transparent grapheme–phoneme mapping, or with a coarse granularity at the level of whole characters or whole words. In these languages the incidence of dyslexia is low, with dyslexic readers being identified primarily by their slow but *accurate* reading and spelling. By contrast, phonological deficits cause tremendous difficulties for readers of languages with opaque grapheme–phoneme mapping, particularly those with a fine granularity at the level of individual graphemes. In these languages the incidence of dyslexia is high, with dyslexic readers being identified by their slow and *inaccurate* reading and spelling.

The influence of orthography on the prevalence and nature of developmental dyslexia is explored in greater depth through the remainder of this section, while the chapters in the final section of this volume consider the possibility of a universal neurocognitive basis for dyslexia.

Notes

1 This test consists entirely of irregular words including *psalm*, *bouquet* and *campanile*.
2 In the RAN task participants name letters, numbers or objects rapidly and accurately; this provides an index of processing speed.
3 In the Spoonerism task participants exchange the initial sounds of two heard words: for example, *doctor–window* becomes *woctor–dindow*; this provides an index of the ability to segment and manipulate the constituent sounds of words.

References

Assink, E. M. H., Van Bergen, F., Van Teeseling, H., & Knuijt, P. P. N. A. (2004). Semantic priming effects in normal versus poor readers. *Journal of Genetic Psychology*, *165*, 67–79.

Bachmann, F. (1927). *Über die kongenitale Wortblindheit* [On congenital wordblindness]. Berlin, Germany: Karger.

Baluch, B., & Besner, D. (1991). Visual word recognition: Evidence for strategic control of lexical and non lexical routines in oral reading. *Journal of Experimental Psychology: Learning, Memory, and Cognition, 17*, 644–651.

Barca, L., Burani, C., Di Filippo, G., & Zoccolotti, P. (2006). Italian developmental dyslexic and proficient readers. Where are the differences? *Brain and Language, 98*, 347–351.

Barry, C., & de Bastiani, P. (1997). Lexical priming of nonword spelling in the regular orthography of Italian. *Reading and Writing: An Interdisciplinary Journal, 9*, 499–517.

Benuck, M. B., & Peverly, S. T. (2004). The effect of orthographic depth on reliance upon semantic context for oral reading in English and Hebrew. *Journal of Research in Reading, 27*, 281–299.

Besner, D., & Smith, M. C. (1992). Models of visual word recognition: When obscuring the stimulus yields a clearer view. *Journal of Experimental Psychology: Human Perception and Performance, 3*, 389–401.

Bridgeman, B. (1987). Is the dual route theory possible in phonetically regular languages? *Behavioral and Brain Sciences, 10*, 331–332.

Brizzolara, D., Pecini, C., Chilosi, A., Cipriani, P., Gasperini, F., Mazzotti, S., et al. (2006). Do phonological and rapid automatized naming deficits differentially affect dyslexic children with and without a history of language delay? A study on Italian dyslexic children. *Cognitive and Behavioural Neurology, 19*, 141–149.

Brunswick, N. (2009). *A beginner's guide to dyslexia*. Oxford, UK: Oneworld Publications.

Burani, C., & Arduino, L. S. (2004). Stress regularity or consistency? Reading aloud Italian polysyllables with different stress patterns. *Brain and Language, 90*, 318–325.

Cappa, S. F., Nespor, M., Ielasi, W., & Miozzo, A. (1997). The representation of stress: Evidence from an aphasic patient. *Cognition, 65*, 1–13.

Caravolas, M., & Volin, J. (2002). Phonological spelling errors among dyslexic children learning a transparent orthography: The case of Czech. *Dyslexia, 7*, 229–245.

Caravolas, M., Volín, J., & Hulme, C. (2005). Phoneme awareness is a key component of alphabetic literacy skills in consistent and inconsistent orthographies: Evidence from Czech and English children. *Journal of Experimental Child Psychology, 92*, 107–139.

Colombo, L., & Tabossi, P. (1992). Strategies and stress assignment: Evidence from a shallow orthography. In R. Frost & L. Katz (Eds.), *Orthography, phonology, morphology and meaning* (pp. 319–340). Amsterdam: Elsevier.

Coltheart, M., & Coltheart, V. (1997). Reading comprehension is not exclusively reliant upon phonological representation. *Cognitive Neuropsychology, 14*, 167–175.

Cossu, G., Gugliotta, M., & Marshall, J. C. (1995a). Acquisition of reading and written spelling in a transparent orthography: Two non-parallel processes? *Reading and Writing: An Interdisciplinary Journal, 7*, 9–22.

Cossu, G., Shankweiler, D., Liberman, I. Y., & Gugliotta, M. (1995b). Visual and phonological determinants of misreadings in a transparent orthography. *Reading and Writing: An Interdisciplinary Journal, 7*, 237–256.

Critchley, M. (1970). *The dyslexic child*. London: Heinemann Medical.

Cuetos, F. (1993). Writing processes in a shallow orthography. *Reading and Writing: An Interdisciplinary Journal, 5*, 17–28.

de Bree, E., Janse, E., & van de Zande, A. M. (2007). Stress assignment in aphasia:

Word and non-word reading and non-word repetition. *Brain and Language*, *103*, 264–275.

Defior, S., Martos, F., & Cary, L. (2002). Differences in reading acquisition development in two shallow orthographies: Portuguese and Spanish. *Applied Psycholinguistics*, *23*, 135–148.

de Jong, P. F. (2003). Problems in the acquisition of fluent word decoding in Dutch children. In N. Goulandris (Ed.), *Dyslexia in different languages: Cross-linguistic comparisons* (pp. 33–52). London: Whurr Publishers.

de Jong, P. F., & van der Leij, A. (2003). Developmental changes in the manifestation of a phonological deficit in dyslexic children learning to read a regular orthography. *Journal of Educational Psychology*, *95*, 22–40.

Di Filippo, G., De Luca, M., Judica, A., Spinelli, D., & Zoccolotti, P. (2006). Lexicality and stimulus length effects in Italian dyslexics: Role of overadditivity effect. *Child Neuropsychology*, *12*, 141–149.

Frith, U., Wimmer, H., & Landerl, K. (1998). Differences in phonological recoding in German- and English-speaking children. *Scientific Studies of Reading*, *2*, 31–54.

Frost, R. (1994). Prelexical and postlexical strategies in reading: Evidence from a deep and shallow orthography. *Journal of Experimental Psychology: Learning, Memory, and Cognition*, *20*, 116–129.

Frost, R. (2005). Orthographic systems and skilled word recognition processes in reading. In C. Hulme & M. Snowling (Eds.), *The science of reading: A handbook* (pp. 272–295). Oxford, UK: Blackwell Publishers.

Galante, E., Tralli, A., Zuffi, M., & Avanzi, S. (2000). Primary progressive aphasia: A patient with stress assignment impairment in reading aloud. *Neurological Science*, *21*, 39–48.

Goswami, U., Gombert, J. E., & de Barrera, L. (1998). Children's orthographic representations and linguistic transparency: Nonsense word reading in English, French and Spanish. *Applied Psycholinguistics*, *19*, 19–52.

Goswami, U., Porpodas, C., & Wheelwright, S. (1997). Children's orthographic representations in English and Greek. *European Journal of Psychology of Education*, *12*, 273–292.

Goswami, U., Ziegler, J. C., Dalton, L., & Schneider, W. (2001). Pseudo-homophone effects and phonological recoding procedures in reading development in English and German. *Journal of Memory and Language*, *45*, 648–664.

Ho, C. S.-H., & Bryant, P. (1997). Phonological skills are important in learning to read Chinese. *Development Psychology*, *33*, 946–951.

Ho, C. S.-H., Chan, D. W.-O., Lee, S.-H., Tsang, S.-M., & Luan, V. H. (2004). Cognitive profiling and preliminary subtyping in Chinese developmental dyslexia, *Cognition*, *91*, 43–75.

Ho, C. S.-H., Chan, D. W.-O., Tsang, S.-M., & Lee, S.-H. (2002). The cognitive profile and multiple-deficit hypothesis in Chinese developmental dyslexia. *Developmental Psychology*, *38*, 543–553.

Ho, C. S.-H., & Lai, D. N.-C. (1999). Naming-speed deficits and phonological memory deficits in Chinese developmental dyslexia. *Learning and Individual Differences*, *11*, 173–186.

Ho, C. S.-H., Law, T. P.-S., & Ng, P. M. (2000). The phonological deficit hypothesis in Chinese developmental dyslexia. *Reading and Writing: An Interdisciplinary Journal*, *13*, 57–79.

Holopainen, L., Ahonen, T., & Lyytinen, H. (2001). Predicting delay in reading achievement in a highly transparent language. *Journal of Learning Disabilities, 34,* 401–413.

Hoosain, R. (1991). *Psycholinguistic implications for linguistic relativity: A case study of Chinese.* Hillsdale, NJ: Lawrence Erlbaum Associates, Inc.

Huang, H. S., & Zhang, H. R. (1997). An analysis of phonemic awareness, word awareness and tone awareness among dyslexic children. *Bulletin of Special Education and Rehabilitation, 5,* 125–138.

Janssen, U. (2003). Stress assignment in German patients with surface dyslexia. *Brain and Language, 87,* 114–115.

Jespersen, O. (1982). *Growth and structure of the English language.* Oxford: Blackwell.

Juul, H., & Sigurdsson, B. (2005). Orthography as a handicap? A direct comparison of spelling acquisition in Danish and Icelandic. *Scandinavian Journal of Psychology, 46,* 263–272.

Kang, J. S. (1993). Analysis of semantics of semantic–phonetic compound characters in modern Chinese. In Y. Chen (Ed.), *Information analysis of usage of characters in modern Chinese* (pp. 68–83). Shanghai, China: Shanghai Education Publisher.

Katz, L., & Feldman, L. B. (1983). Relation between pronunciation and recognition of printed words in deep and shallow orthographies. *Journal of Experimental Psychology: Learning, Memory, and Cognition, 9,* 157–166.

Katz, L., & Frost, R. (1992). The reading process is different for different orthographies: The orthographic depth hypothesis. In R. Frost & L. Katz (Eds.), *Orthography, phonology, morphology and meaning* (pp. 67–84). Amsterdam: Elsevier.

Laganaro, M., Vacheresse, F., & Frauenfelder, U. H. (2002). Selective impairment of lexical stress assignment in an Italian-speaking aphasic patient. *Brain and Language, 81,* 601–609.

Landerl, K. (2000). Influences of orthographic consistency and reading instruction on the development of nonword reading skills. *European Journal of Psychology of Education, 15,* 239–257.

Landerl, K. (2001). Word recognition deficits in German: More evidence from a representative sample. *Dyslexia, 7,* 183–196.

Landerl, K., Wimmer, H., & Frith, U. (1997). The impact of orthographic consistency on dyslexia: A German–English comparison. *Cognition, 63,* 315–334.

Lepschy, A. L., & Lepschy, G. (1981). *La lingua Italiana* [The Italian language]. Milan: Bompiani.

López, M. R., & Jiménez Gonzáles, J. E. (2000). IQ vs. phonological recoding skill in explaining differences between poor readers and normal readers in word recognition: Evidence from a naming task. *Reading and Writing: An Interdisciplinary Journal, 12,* 129–142.

Lukatela, G., & Turvey, M. T. (1994). Visual lexical access is initially phonological: 2. Evidence from phonological priming by homophones and pseudohomophones. *Journal of Experimental Psychology: General, 123,* 331–353.

Lyytinen, H., Eklund, K., Erskine, J., Guttorm, T. K., Laakso, M.-L., Leppänen, P. H. T., et al. (2004). The development of children at familial risk for dyslexia: Birth to school age. *Annals of Dyslexia, 54,* 185–220.

Marcolini, S., Burani, C., & Colombo, L. (2009). Lexical effects on children's pseudoword reading in a transparent orthography. *Reading and Writing: An Interdisciplinary Journal, 22,* 531–544.

Miceli, G., & Caramazza, A. (1993). The assignment of word stress in oral reading: Evidence from a case of acquired dyslexia. *Cognitive Neuropsychology, 10*, 273–296.

Miles, T. R. (2004). Some problems in determining the prevalence of dyslexia. *Electronic Journal of Research in Educational Psychology, 2*, 5–12.

Nelson, H. E., & Willison, J. (1991). *National Adult Reading Test (NART): Test manual*. Windsor, UK: NFER Nelson.

Nergård-Nilssen, T. (2006). Developmental dyslexia in Norwegian: Evidence from single-case studies. *Dyslexia, 12*, 30–50.

Nyikos, J. (1988). A linguistic perspective of illiteracy. In S. Empleton (Ed.), *The Fourteenth LACUS Forum 1987* (pp. 146–173). Lake Bluff, IL: Linguistic Association of Canada and the US.

Öney, B., & Durgunoğlu, A. Y. (1997). Learning to read in Turkish: A phonologically transparent orthography. *Applied Psycholinguistics, 18*, 1–15.

Orsolini, M., Fanari, R., Tosi, V., De Nigris, B., & Carrieri, R. (2006). From phonological recoding to lexical reading: A longitudinal study on reading development in Italian. *Language and Cognitive Processes, 21*, 576–607.

Patel, T. K., Snowling, M. J., & de Jong, P. F. (2004). A cross-linguistic comparison of children learning to read in English and Dutch. *Journal of Educational Psychology, 96*, 785–797.

Paulesu, E., Démonet, J.-F., Fazio, F., McCrory, E., Chanoine, V., Brunswick, N., et al. (2001). Dyslexia: Cultural diversity and biological unity. *Science, 291*, 2165–2167.

Paulesu, E., McCrory, E., Fazio, F., Menoncello, L., Brunswick, N., Cappa, S. F., et al. (2000). A cultural effect on brain function. *Nature Neuroscience, 3*, 91–96.

Pei, M. (1967). *The story of the English language* (2nd ed.). New York: J.B. Lippincott Company.

Plemmenou, E., Bard, E. G., & Branigan, H. P. (2002). Grammatical gender in the production of single words: Some evidence from Greek. *Brain and Language, 81*, 236–241.

Porpodas, C. D. (1999). Patterns of phonological and memory processing in beginning readers and spellers of Greek. *Journal of Learning Disabilities, 32*, 406–416.

Porpodas, C. D., Pantelis, S. N., & Hantziou, E. (1990). Phonological and lexical encoding processes in beginning readers: Effects of age and word characteristics. *Reading and Writing: An Interdisciplinary Journal, 2*, 197–208.

Ramus, F. (2003). Developmental dyslexia: Specific phonological deficit or general sensorimotor dysfunction? *Current Opinion in Neurobiology, 13*, 212–218.

Rastle, K., & Coltheart, M. (1999). Lexical and nonlexical phonological priming in reading aloud. *Journal of Experimental Psychology: Human Perception and Performance, 25*, 461–481.

Sebastián-Gallés, N. (1991). Reading by analogy in a shallow orthography. *Journal of Experimental Psychology: Human Perception and Performance, 17*, 471–477.

Seidenberg, M. S. (1992). Beyond orthographic depth in reading: Equitable division of labor. In R. Frost & L. Katz (Eds.), *Orthography, phonology, morphology, and meaning* (pp. 85–118). Amsterdam: Elsevier.

Serrano, F., & Defior, S. (2008). Dyslexia speed problems in a transparent orthography. *Annals of Dyslexia, 58*, 81–95.

Seymour, P. H. K., Aro, M., & Erskine, J. M. (2003). Foundation literacy acquisition in European orthographies. *British Journal of Psychology, 94*, 143–174.

154   *Brunswick*

Seymour, P. H. K., & Dargie, A. (1990). Associative priming and orthographic choice in nonword spelling. *European Journal of Cognitive Psychology*, 2, 395–410.

Spencer, L., & Hanley, J. R. (2003). Effects of orthographic transparency on reading and phoneme awareness in children learning to read in Wales. *British Journal of Psychology*, 94, 1–28.

Sprenger-Charolles, L., Colé, P., Lacert, P., & Serniclaes, W. (2000). On subtypes of developmental dyslexia: Evidence from processing time and accuracy scores. *Canadian Journal of Experimental Psychology*, 54, 87–103.

Thornton, A. M., Iacobini, C., & Burani, C. (1997). *BDVDB—Una base dati sul vocabolario di base della lingua Italiana* [A database on basic vocabulary in the Italian language]. Rome: Bulzoni Editore.

Turvey, M. T., Feldman, L. B., & Lukatela, G. (1984). The Serbo-Croatian orthography constrains the reader to a phonologically analytic strategy. In L. Henderson (Ed.), *Orthographies and reading: Perspectives from cognitive psychology, neuropsychology, and linguistics* (pp. 81–89). London: Lawrence Erlbaum Associates, Inc.

van Daal, V., & van der Leij, A. (1999). Developmental dyslexia: Related to specific or general deficits? *Annals of Dyslexia*, 49, 71–104.

Voga, M., & Grainger, J. (2004). Masked morphological priming with varying levels of form overlap: Evidence from Greek verbs. *Current Psychology Letters*, 13, 2. Published 19 May 2004. URL: http://cpl.revues.org/document422.html

Wimmer, H. (1993). Characteristics of developmental dyslexia in a regular writing system. *Applied Psycholinguistics*, 14, 1–33.

Wimmer, H. (1996). The non-word reading deficit in developmental dyslexia: Evidence from children learning to read German. *Journal of Experimental Child Psychology*, 61, 80–90.

Wimmer, H., & Goswami, U. (1994). The influence of orthographic consistency on reading development: Word recognition in English and German children. *Cognition*, 51, 91–103.

Wimmer, H., & Hummer, P. (1990). How German speaking first-graders read and spell: Doubts on the importance of the logographic stage. *Applied Psycholinguistics*, 11, 349–368.

Wolf, M., & Bowers, P. G. (2000). Naming speed processes and developmental reading disabilities: An introduction to the special issue on the double-deficit hypothesis. *Journal of Learning Disabilities*, 33, 322–324.

Wydell, T. N., & Butterworth, B. (1999). An English–Japanese bilingual with monolingual dyslexia. *Cognition*, 70, 273–305.

Ziegler, J. C., & Goswami, U. (2005). Reading acquisition, developmental dyslexia and skilled reading across languages: A psycholinguistic grain size theory. *Psychological Bulletin*, 131, 3–29.

8 Reading acquisition and dyslexia in Spanish

Robert A. I. Davies and Fernando Cuetos

Introduction

It is well known that alphabetic languages vary in the predictability of spelling–sound mappings (Seymour, Aro, & Erskine, 2003). English has a relatively opaque orthography with lower spelling–sound predictability, containing numerous inconsistencies in how similar spellings are pronounced. Examples of how difficult it is to predict the pronunciation of similarly spelled words include *bough*, *cough*, *though*, and *hint*, *pint*. In contrast, some other European languages have orthographies that are highly consistent across words. Spanish is one such language. One would expect these differences in the consistency of spelling–sound predictability to affect reading development. This chapter discusses current evidence relating to this expectation.

Key features of Spanish orthography

Spanish orthography is highly transparent, with no variation between words in the pronunciation of vowels or in the pronunciation of all but a subset of consonants. That subset consists of the letters 'c', 'g' and 'r'. The letters 'c' and 'g' are read aloud in different ways depending on the following vowel. If they appear before an 'a', 'o' or 'u', they are given a hard sound, for example, *casa* → /kasa/ (/k/ as in the English *kilo*) or *gota* → /gota/ (/g/ as in the English *gun*), but if they appear before 'e' or 'i', they are given a softer sound, for example, *cena* → /thena/ (/th/ as in the English *think*) or *giro* → /hiro/ (/h/ as in the English *hill*). The letter 'r' is read differently depending on its position in a word. If it appears at the beginning of a word, it is given a hard rolling sound, for example, *rey* → /rrey/, but if it appears in the middle of a word or at the end, it is given a softer sound equivalent to that used in English, for example, *arpa* → /arpa/ (/r/ as in *army*). These more complex ways of pronouncing letters are consistent throughout the language.

What are the implications of variation in orthographic transparency for how reading develops?

Variation in orthographic transparency means that learning to read in different languages poses divergent challenges for developing readers. We argue, however, that despite learning to read differently, there are likely to be many similarities in the cognitive architecture that supports reading in adults. We believe that, for the skilled reader, key aspects of reading are universal across languages, especially the need to read aloud fluently and the need to extract meaning quickly from print. We think that a broader, but still developmental, perspective taking into account these demands motivates expectations of eventual convergence in the shape of the cognitive architecture supporting reading in different languages.

Our review discusses findings from reading in Spanish and considers the following questions: First, what is the evidence for convergence across alphabetic languages, towards a common cognitive architecture of reading in adults? Second, how do beginning readers compare with adult readers of Spanish, and what is the course of development for reading in Spanish? As part of our treatment of the second question, we discuss how reading-specific difficulties like dyslexia are revealed in Spanish. Of course, we are at an early stage in the development of an adequate cross-linguistic description of reading. Hence we conclude by discussing ways forward in the further investigation of reading in Spanish.

Theories explaining adult reading

Two theories have been influential in the discussion of cognitive processes involved in reading—that is, the spoken production of word pronunciations in response to their printed forms. The first theory is the dual-route account (Coltheart, 1984; Coltheart, Curtis, Atkins, & Haller, 1993; Coltheart, Rastle, Perry, Langdon, & Ziegler, 2001). The second is the connectionist 'triangle' or single-route account (Harm & Seidenberg, 1999; Plaut, McClelland, Seidenberg, & Patterson, 1996; Seidenberg & McClelland, 1989). There are, of course, other theories (e.g., Ans, Carbonnel, & Valdois, 1998), but it is fair to say that debate about the cognitive processes of reading has been dominated by the dual-route and triangle accounts of reading in English.

There are two key differences between the accounts. The first is that the dual-route account makes a distinction in the cognitive mechanisms it assumes between (1) those mechanisms that support the reading aloud of words new to the reader (or invented words, called non-words) and words that obey the rules of English spelling pronunciation (regular words), and (2) those that support the reading of words containing letters or letter sequences that are pronounced in an exceptional fashion (irregular words). The triangle account assumes no such distinction: the same mechanisms support the reading of regular words, non-words, and irregular exception words. The second key difference between the accounts lies in the fact that, in recent work, both accounts have been implemented as computational simulations, but from its earliest versions onwards the triangle model was designed to learn from experience (Seidenberg & McClelland, 1989), while the model of the dual-route account does not (Coltheart et al., 2001).

Computational simulations of human behaviour take the form of software applications written to mimic human behaviour. Such applications work by processing information corresponding to the information used in reading, completing transformation in steps proposed in theories of the cognitive reading system. Numerous assumptions must be made in building the applications, and important differences can arise between simulations as a result of differences in assumptions.

The dual-route theory of reading

The dual-route approach builds on a long tradition of theorizing about reading (reviewed in Coltheart et al., 2001). It proposes that the adult reader has learned the rules about how individual letters are pronounced in English—that is, grapheme–phoneme correspondences, where graphemes refer to letters or combinations of letters (e.g., 'th') that map onto the basic unit of sounds in words (phonemes). The dual-route account also assumes that the adult reader has learned how the spelling patterns for whole words map onto their sounds, for example, *pint* → /pInt/. The use of grapheme–phoneme correspondences serves the reader well for words with regular pronunciations (e.g., *hint*) but the system of lexical spelling–sound mappings is required for the pronunciation of words with exceptional pronunciations (e.g., *pint*).

In the computational simulation of the dual-route account (Coltheart et al., 2001) it is assumed that there are representations in memory for letters, the sounds of letters, spelling patterns for words (lexical orthography) and sound patterns for words (lexical phonology). The work of the system is done through the transfer of information between different levels of representation. In discussions of computational models the amount of information that exists in the system about, say, the presentation of a word to a reader is described using the term *activation*. This mirrors the idea that brain cells involved in performing a task are more active than are uninvolved cells (see Figure 8.1).

The rules system, or non-lexical route, works by coding the phonology of the letters in a word (or non-word) serially from left to right. Perception of each letter (or grapheme[1]) causes the activation of the corresponding letter representation. This activates the corresponding phoneme through the use of knowledge about the rules of pronunciation. Because the non-lexical route assembles phonology in response to print letter-by-letter, the model predicts a marked length effect in reading aloud non-words. This is indeed what is observed (Weekes, 1997). The lexical route runs in parallel to the non-lexical route. Activation of letter representations by visual presentation of words leads to the activation of corresponding lexical orthographic representations,

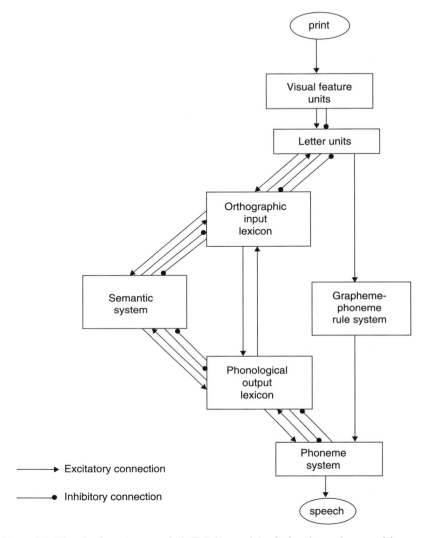

Figure 8.1 The dual-route cascaded (DRC) model of visual word recognition and reading aloud (from Coltheart et al., 2001).

which in turn leads to the activation of lexical phonological representations. The whole-word basis of the spelling–sound mapping completed by the lexical route means that no length effect is expected for reading words. This has also been observed by Weekes (1997; but see Cumming, Patterson, Verfaillie, & Graham, 2006).

Some characteristics of reading behaviour have been observed repeatedly in experimental research. For example, words that appear frequently in everyday language use (e.g., *the*) are read more quickly than words that appear less frequently (e.g., *thence*; Andrews, 1989). This frequency effect is explained in the dual-route model by assuming that the speed with which lexical orthographic representations are activated rises more quickly (information accumulates more quickly) in proportion to how often the word appears in the language. Similarly, low-frequency words with irregular pronunciations (e.g., *comb*) are read more slowly than words with regular pronunciations (e.g., *pet*; Taraban & McClelland, 1987). The dual-route explanation is that because the lexical and non-lexical routes run in parallel, there is interference between the phonological information activated by the rules, which suggests the regular pronunciation (*sew* → /su/), and the phonological information activated by the lexical spelling–sound mapping, which suggests the correct pronunciation (*sew* → /so/). This interference is less of a problem for high-frequency words because the activation of the orthographic and phonological representations for these words happens quickly.

The triangle theory of reading

The triangle theory of reading is so called because it assumes a cognitive system composed of sets of representations encoding knowledge about the orthography, semantics and phonology of words (the apices of the triangle—see Figure 8.2). While there have been antecedents for the theory (e.g., Glushko, 1979), we are really only concerned with the theory as it has been implemented in computational models. The triangle model of reading has been investigated through a number of revisions, each marking an improvement in the capacity of the model to account for observations about human reading behaviour (Harm & Seidenberg, 1999; Plaut et al., 1996; Seidenberg

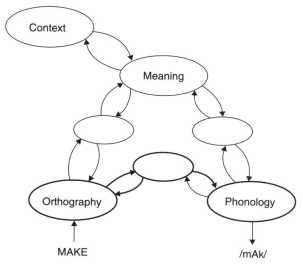

Figure 8.2 The 'triangle model' (from Harm & Seidenberg, 1999).

& McClelland, 1989). All versions are members of the class of computational model called connectionist simulations or networks (which the dual-route model is not).

The key insight from connectionist simulations is that human behaviour can be simulated by networks of simple processing units that resemble neurons at an abstract level (McClelland, Rumelhart, & the PDP Research Group, 1986; Rumelhart, McClelland, & the PDP Research Group, 1986). The evidence suggests that quite complex behaviours can be reproduced using networks of simple processing units. In studies of reading, the units are arranged to deal with information about orthography, semantics or phonology. They are connected so that cooperative and competitive interactions are possible. In the simulations, the completion of spelling–sound mapping for many words can depend upon the activity of the same few units, while many units can be involved in the mappings for any single word. In sum, the representation of information is said to be distributed. In the dual-route model, by contrast, there are lexical orthographic and phonological representations, each uniquely dedicated to one word. For any single word, some units in a connectionist network will be more active in response to the word than others, and comparing the reading of different words, the sets of units that are active may overlap (if the words have similar spellings and pronunciations) or be quite distinct (if the words are different). This means that the network must learn to find a balance in how units cooperate, so that all the words it encounters can be read correctly. The network can learn to do this through the gradual adjustment of the strengths of connections, assimilating repeated experience of how a spelling pattern maps to its sound.

This learning is the crucial feature of connectionist simulations. The simulations of reading have shown that frequency effects arise naturally when networks learn through a gradual process of change in the connections between distributed orthographic and phonological representations, in reaction to reading experience (Plaut et al., 1996; Seidenberg & McClelland, 1989). This is because words that are encountered more often have more opportunity to shape the connection weight changes that occur during learning.

Recent experimental work has shown that, in addition to frequency, the age at which a word was first learned (its age of acquisition, AoA) also affects how easily that word can be read (Gerhand & Barry, 1998; Morrison & Ellis, 1995, 2000). Words acquired earlier tend to be read more quickly and accurately than words acquired later. The dual-route model does not yet have the capacity to explain the AoA effect. However, recent work with connectionist simulations shows that it can be explained by the fact that the connections between units in learning networks are more malleable early in the development of the network's capacity to perform a task like reading (Ellis & Lambon Ralph, 2000). This means that earlier-acquired words are learned at a time when their acquisition shapes the network's connections to suit them, to a greater degree than is possible for later-acquired words.

The triangle account reframes the effect of regularity of pronunciation in

English in terms of consistency. It was initially assumed that differences in difficulty seen in pronouncing, for example, the regular word *hint* and the irregular word *pint* stemmed from the ambiguity of the pronunciation of the letter 'i'. However, later work showed that what really matters is consistency (Glushko, 1979) because irregular words and regular words often belong to families of words with similar spellings (*pint, hint, mint, lint*) and what makes it difficult to say /pInt/ is that a reader is influenced by the differing pronunciations of other words with similar spellings (Jared, McRae, & Seidenberg, 1990). This consistency effect is explained naturally by the triangle model and takes the same form as the account of the frequency effect: the critical factor is experience (Plaut et al., 1996). When the developing reader (human or network) learns the pronunciations of consistent spelling patterns (e.g., *dish*, *fish*), changes in human memory or in the network's connections caused by the experience of reading one word (*fish*) help in reading the other word (*dish*). However, when the developing reader has learned words with similar spellings but differing pronunciations (e.g., *hint, pint*), changes caused by experience in reading one word will actually support the production of a pronunciation different from that required to read the other word. The experience of the network for inconsistent spelling–sound mappings points it in different directions when a reading response is required, slowing it down, though it can still produce the correct pronunciation.

Evidence for convergence in adult reading

Theories of reading in English and cross-linguistic variation in orthographic transparency

Just like regular words in English, words in languages with transparent orthographies can be read in a manner dependent on the non-lexical reading route (Ziegler, Perry, & Coltheart, 2000). The greater simplicity of spelling–sound correspondences in a transparent orthography means that a Spanish-speaking child could learn to read aloud simply by coding the phonology of a word letter by letter (Ziegler & Goswami, 2005). This leads to the prediction that one would be unlikely to find Spanish-speaking acquired dyslexic patients who can read words but not non-words (Ardila, 1991). By the same logic, one would be less likely to find that healthy adults or children are affected in their reading performance by the influence of lexical knowledge (e.g., by frequency or AoA).

Connectionist simulations indicate that AoA and frequency effects should be reduced when spelling–sound mappings are consistent compared to when they are inconsistent (Lambon Ralph & Ehsan, 2006; Monaghan & Ellis, 2002; Zevin & Seidenberg, 2002). The reasoning is that for items with similar spellings and similar pronunciations (e.g., *large* and *barge*) later-acquired or less frequently encountered items like *barge* can be processed using the network structure established for earlier or more frequently encountered items like *large*. This leads to the prediction that frequency or AoA effects will be reduced (Lambon Ralph & Ehsan, 2006; Zevin & Seidenberg, 2002) or absent (Monaghan & Ellis, 2002) in reading aloud in highly consistent orthographies. This is because if the same sets of units and connections can be used to read different but consistent words, then differences in frequency or AoA are much less relevant.

Adult reading in different languages

What do observations about reading in different languages tell us? Usually, we investigate how different attributes of words (item characteristics) affect performance in tasks like reading aloud. Researchers have focused on reaction time as an index of reading behaviour—this is the time from when a word is presented to the moment the participant begins their pronunciation of the word. Much of the investigation of reading has been concerned with which item characteristics affect reading and what shape the effects have.

Item characteristics—e.g., word length and orthographic neighbourhood (N-size)—can be measured directly (Coltheart, Davelaar, Jonasson, & Besner, 1977). Other item characteristics must be estimated. Lexical frequency is usually estimated by counting the number of times a word occurs in a very large sample of text or speech (Baayen, Piepenbrock, & van Rijn, 1993). Characteristics like AoA are usually estimated by asking volunteers to rate when they learned a word, though recent studies have shown that such ratings actually mirror more objective measures (Morrison & Ellis, 2000).

When we consider onset and rime consistency, we are looking at whether sounds of letters, or the way sounds are spelled, are the same or different between words in the language. For words of one syllable, the onset is the letter–sound (or letters–sounds) that begins a word (e.g., 'c' in *cat*), and the rime is the combination of vowel and final consonant (or consonants) that ends a word (e.g., 'at' in *cat*). In English, both pronunciation consistency and spelling consistency may be important.

Observations in English

Recent large-scale studies of reading in English indicate that variation in word naming latencies can be predicted by word length, lexical frequency, N-size, onset and/or rime consistency and AoA (Balota, Cortese, Sergent-Marshall, Spieler, & Yap, 2004; Cortese & Khanna, 2007). These are the characteristics of words that make them harder or easier to read so that, in the laboratory, volunteers take longer or shorter times to prepare responses when they are asked to read the words aloud.

Observations in Spanish and other languages

Spelling–sound relationships for words in Spanish are consistent across the language, so we should not expect effects of pronunciation consistency.

Spanish is also largely consistent in sound–spelling relationships, but there are some exceptions—for example, the sound /b/ can legally be spelled as 'v', as in *votar*, or as 'b' as in *botar*. Our expectation is that effects of spelling consistency are unlikely in Spanish because these effects appear to be tenuous in English (Kessler, Treiman, & Mullenix, 2007). However, the greater complexity involved in the pronunciation of the letters 'g', 'c' and 'r' is highly likely to be important because in Italian, a language with an orthography similar to that of Spanish, variation in the pronunciation of the letters 'c' and 'g' according to the following vowel affects both adults' (Burani, Barca, & Ellis, 2006) and children's reading of low-frequency words (Barca, Ellis, & Burani, 2007).

Observations from Spanish show that reading is also affected by word length, N-size and AoA (Cuetos & Barbón, 2006), and that these effects go in the same directions. The important point is that healthy adult reading is affected by the same mix of factors, irrespective of orthographic transparency. This conclusion is consistent with evidence that frequency or AoA also affects reading performance in other alphabetic languages of varying orthographic transparency, including Italian (Barca, Burani, & Arduino, 2002), French (Bonin, Barry, Méot, & Chalard, 2004), Dutch (Brysbaert, Lange, & van Wijnendaele, 2000) and Turkish (Raman, 2006). In our view, there is cross-linguistic convergence in skilled reading with respect to the effects of key item characteristics. This is not generally recognized in the reading literature.

Comparing the size of effects between languages

One question immediately arises, however. Does the size of the effects observed vary between languages? We believe that the evidence is not sufficient to support firm conclusions at present. The problem is that although the effects of variation in item characteristics can be investigated, the extent to which these effects are observed may vary depending on the context in which the investigation occurs. We are referring in particular to effects due to word list composition (Davies, Burani, & Cuetos, 2010a). Our analyses have shown that some differences between the patterns of reading behaviour observed in different languages can be attributed to demands placed on the volunteers by varying the difficulty of words in each language.

Davies et al. (2010a) report an intriguing discrepancy between findings in Spanish and in Italian (both of which stem from Latin). The discrepancy is this: in Spanish-speaking adults reading is affected by AoA but not by frequency (Cuetos & Barbón, 2006) but in Italian-speaking adults reading is affected by frequency but not by AoA (Barca et al., 2002). What could have caused this difference? If orthographic transparency alone determines how reading happens, both languages should be affected by the same item characteristics in the same way. Our argument is that the cited studies could have differed critically in the demands they placed on participants. The Spanish-speaking volunteers were asked to read a fairly homogenous set of relatively easy words—short, frequent words referring to common objects—while the Italian-speaking volunteers were asked to read a more diverse set of words including some that were long, infrequent and abstract.

The effect of frequency on reading in Italian can be easily explained. In the dual-route model lexical orthographic representations, and hence lexical phonological representations, are activated more quickly because the frequency of words is built into the speed of reaction of processing units (Coltheart et al., 2001). This is the explanation favoured by researchers reporting the Italian frequency effect (Burani et al., 2006). We are sympathetic to this view but suggest that the triangle model can also explain the effect as the consequence of experience in shaping connections between orthographic and phonological processing units (Plaut et al., 1996; Seidenberg & McClelland, 1989; Zevin & Seidenberg, 2002).

Davies et al. (2010a) propose that the Spanish-speaking readers showed a greater effect of AoA because the relative ease of the words they were given invited a faster reading strategy that lowered reaction times. The reaction times reported by Cuetos and Barbón (2006) were shorter than those reported by Barca et al. (2002) because phonological coding was speeded up through a greater dependence on lexical-semantic knowledge in the preparation of the reading response (Kello & Plaut, 2003). This increased the likelihood that factors like AoA would be observed (in a following section we discuss why). How the reader translates a perception of the demands imposed by a task into an adjustment of reading must be investigated in further research. However, it is already clear, not just in our own work, but also in the results reported by other authors (e.g., Baluch & Besner, 1991; Monsell, Patterson, Graham, Hughes, & Milroy, 1992; Raman, Baluch, & Besner, 2004), that the effects of item characteristics are significantly modified by the context of other words.

What this means for researchers is that the words presented to participants must be matched between languages on the speed of response they elicit. A study that did just this is reported by Ziegler, Perry, Jacobs, and Braun (2001). The authors compared the reading performance of German and English adults (university students) on the same set of cognate words (words that look similar, sound similar and have the same meaning in different languages, e.g., *night* in English and *Nacht* in German). Thus, the words presented the same demands in both languages. In fact, reading reaction times were found not to differ between languages. The key finding of this study is that the German readers were more affected by the lengths of words than were the English readers, even though both groups were reading the same words.

Ziegler and Goswami (2006) argued that the cross-linguistic difference in the size of the length effect is evidence that the effect of high spelling–sound consistency in German persists into skilled adult reading. We have reported that reading in Spanish is affected by the length of words such that longer words elicit longer reading latencies (Cuetos & Barbón, 2006). We hypothesize that a significant component of reading aloud in alphabetic languages involves letter-by-letter conversion of word spellings into word pronunciations, and that the tendency to read in this way may be greater in languages like German or Spanish, which have consistent orthographies.

How does lexical knowledge affect adult reading in different languages?

The effect of word length on reading may be greater in Spanish than in English. Does this mean that reading aloud in Spanish is done entirely through letter-by-letter phonological coding? The answer is 'no', due to the observation of the AoA effect we have already mentioned. It seems most likely that adult reading aloud in Spanish depends on a mixture of knowledge about letter-by-letter phonological coding and knowledge about words. How does lexical knowledge come into the picture? While we have focused on the explanation of the effects on reading aloud in terms of orthography and phonology and the mappings between these domains, it is also theoretically possible to read by first accessing concepts (meaning) from print perception, then deriving the phonology of the names of these concepts. Our focus in the present section is on how the need to access meaning quickly provides a motive for establishing the cognitive mechanisms that could support phonological coding via meaning.

If one imagines the process of silently reading for meaning, it is possible to envisage two methods of getting from the perception of print (i.e., the spelling patterns for different words) to the semantics of the words being read (i.e., the meaning or knowledge associated with the words). For example, one could recognize that the string of letters 'c–a–t' is the spelling for the word *cat* and then access knowledge about cats (that they are furry, often pets, etc.) either by gaining access to the meaning directly, having identified the word from its spelling, or by first working out the word's pronunciation, /cat/. We can characterize the first form of meaning access as orthography-to-semantics mapping. The second form of access can be characterized as orthography-to-phonology-to-semantics mapping, where the process of reading involves two steps: the transformation of spelling information into the pronunciation or phonology of a word, and the use of that phonological information as a key to access knowledge about the meaning of the word.

In gaining access to meaning via phonology, the extra step involved in deriving the phonology of a word is relatively straightforward for most words, especially for words with consistent pronunciations in English, or all words in consistent orthographies. But it is still an extra step. This means that there is some advantage in being able to gain access to meaning immediately, as a result of recognizing that the letters 'c–a–t' spell the word *cat*. Connectionist simulations reported by Harm and Seidenberg (2004) provide evidence that the need to access meaning quickly during reading can drive the development of orthography-to-semantics mappings.

Harm and Seidenberg (2004) showed that because orthography-to-phonology-to-semantics mappings are easier to learn, it is likely that early in reading development, activation of meaning from printed words will tend to result from the output of phonological coding. The relationships between semantics and orthography, or between semantics and phonology, are arbitrary in the sense that knowing, say, that *bat* and *pat* sound or look similar does not allow you to predict what *pat* means, given knowledge about what *bat* means. The initial reliance on the orthography-to-phonology-to-semantics route in reading for meaning is driven by the relative arbitrariness of the orthography-to-semantics relationship compared to the systematicity of the orthography-to-phonology relationship. Knowing how the spelling pattern *bat* is pronounced does allow one to predict the pronunciation of *pat*.

However, Harm and Seidenberg (2004) showed that if slow activation of semantics is penalized, orthography-to-semantics mappings grow in importance over time. The penalization of slow access to meaning is readily appreciable in the human situation because rapid comprehension of meaning in reading is useful. Harm and Seidenberg assessed the network as performing less well if it activated meaning more slowly. This is not to say that they, or we, conclude that a developing reader shifts over time from a reading strategy based on orthography-to-phonology-to-semantics mappings to a strategy based on orthography-to-semantics mappings. The idea is that both routes are used cooperatively to gain access to meaning in reading, but that the orthography-to-semantics route grows in importance with increasing reading practice because it results in faster access to meaning.

We have spent some time discussing the ideas behind recent work on how meaning is accessed in reading because we think that variations in orthographic transparency do not provide the whole story of how reading occurs in different languages. The fact that anyone reading in any language must learn to read so that meaning is accessed as quickly as possible gives us a major reason for expecting to see common patterns of behaviour in reading performance despite variations in orthographic transparency. Assuming, as we do, that there is development of orthography-to-semantics mappings to support reading for meaning, we think that the computational mechanism is made available, as a side-effect, for semantics to influence phonological coding in reading aloud.

There is some evidence showing that Spanish-speaking readers read aloud by completing the mapping from orthography to semantics and then from semantics to phonology. We and others have reported evidence from studies of acquired dyslexia, where previously literate patients present with reading difficulties following brain injury. It has been argued that patients presenting with acquired dyslexia in a transparent orthography should only show symptoms commensurate with a reliance, prior to injury, on grapheme–phoneme correspondences (Ardila, 1991). Yet a number of Spanish-speaking patients have presented with preserved lexical reading despite impairment of their capacity to read non-words, which, since they are unfamiliar, are read using grapheme–phoneme correspondences (see Davies & Cuetos, 2005). This preservation of lexical reading must reflect the use of lexical mappings because non-word reading is assumed to depend on sub-lexical mappings. Moreover, all but one of the patients was found to produce semantic errors in reading. The observation of semantic reading errors in acquired dyslexia demonstrates that Spanish speakers can read aloud via semantics.

When might a semantic influence be observed in the reading of unimpaired Spanish-speaking adults? There are two possibilities. The first relates to what might be termed the response of the reader to the demands imposed by a task, as we have discussed in relation to the Cuetos and Barbón (2006) data. The second relates to the intrinsic ease with which each word, treated alone, can be read.

We have suggested that Cuetos and Barbón (2006) observed an AoA effect on reading in Spanish because the adults they tested were motivated to read more quickly and achieved the greater speed through an increased reliance on lexical-semantic knowledge. It has been argued that at least part of the AoA effect involves the semantic system (e.g., Belke, Brysbaert, Meyer, & Ghyselinck, 2005; Zevin & Seidenberg, 2002). Certainly our analyses have shown that for the items presented by Cuetos and Barbón (2006), words that are acquired earlier in life tend to name concepts that are easier to imagine (Davies et al., 2010a). This quality is termed imageability (estimated through the collection of ratings), and the overlap between AoA and imageability suggests a possible semantic origin for the AoA effect on reading.

The simple relationship between Spanish spelling–sound mappings means that letter-by-letter phonological coding should be highly efficient. We would argue, however, that gains in reading speed can still be made. Despite the fact that the activation-flow from orthography to phonology via semantics involves an extra step, we propose that semantics can nevertheless influence phonological coding. This is because adult readers do not need to complete detailed analyses of the spelling patterns of words to access meaning. This has been demonstrated by recent work showing the ease with which skilled readers can recognize words, even where the order of letters has been scrambled (e.g., Perea & Lupker, 2003), as when one 'raeds emials' about the imperviousness of text comprehension to letter scrambling. With information reaching phonology through both orthography-to-phonology and orthography-to-semantics-to-phonology mappings, phonological encoding can be completed more quickly.

Another possible reason why semantics might be involved in reading in Spanish relates to the intrinsic ease or difficulty with which individual words can be read. In English-speaking adults the influence of semantics on reading, which has been measured in terms of the effect of imageability (Strain, Patterson, & Seidenberg, 1995), is only really observed for those words where the phonological coding process is more difficult—for example, words that are low in frequency and contain components with irregular pronunciations (Strain et al., 1995). This is because the extra difficulty allows time for a semantic influence to occur. In the triangle account of reading the reader learns to rely on the lexical-semantic mapping to read low-frequency exception words (Plaut et al., 1996). This reliance on semantic input leaves the adult reader vulnerable to brain injury in one key respect. If semantic knowledge is impaired, as happens—for example—in the condition of semantic dementia, then a patient would have difficulty reading low-frequency words with exceptional pronunciations. This is exactly what has been observed in a large number of cases (Woollams, Lambon Ralph, Plaut, & Patterson, 2007).

Of course atypical spelling–sound mappings are not present in transparent orthographies, but we suggest that the critical construct here is reading difficulty. Low-frequency exception words are difficult in English, but the characterization of what determines relative difficulty in reading should be extended to encompass item characteristics that might hinder reading in other languages. One candidate dimension of reading difficulty for Spanish—and similar languages—is word length. This is because, first, English-speaking patients with semantic dementia are not only impaired at reading low-frequency irregular words, but they also show an abnormally large length effect (Cumming et al., 2006). The length effect has been hypothesized by Cumming et al. (2006) to arise from a reduction in top-down support from semantics to orthographic processing, but there is no reason to exclude the possibility that semantics could also be drawn into the completion of phonological coding. Second, a substantial proportion of words in Spanish and Italian are multisyllabic, and a length effect on reading latencies has frequently been observed in both languages (e.g., Barca et al., 2002; Cuetos & Barbón, 2006). We hypothesize that the greater time required to encode longer words permits semantic activation to influence reading aloud, in a manner analogous to the longer time required to encode low-frequency English exception words phonologically.

This line of reasoning leads to the prediction that we should observe an interaction between length and factors such as imageability or AoA that are associated with semantic processing. The prediction is strongly supported by two observations. First, we have found that an interaction between length and imageability predicts the reading accuracy of MJ, a patient with deep dyslexia (Davies, Cuetos, & Rodríguez-Ferreiro, 2008). Second, we have found that reading latencies in Spanish are predicted by a set of semantic factors, including AoA and an interaction between word length and AoA (Davies et al., 2010a). Thus we submit that semantic information about words does influence reading in Spanish, by both unimpaired readers and by patients, but that this semantic influence is most apparent for difficult-to-read longer words.

Conclusions about the effects on adult reading in different languages

By beginning with adult readers, we started with the end of the developmental process. We took this approach because we think that a broader perspective on development, encompassing adult and childhood reading, supports a more accurate account of the similarities and differences between languages. What are our conclusions concerning the architecture of the reading system in mature, skilled, readers of Spanish? There is no question that the consistency of spelling–sound mappings produces a high level of efficiency in their use. Such efficiency suggests an important role for a letter-by-letter phonological coding mechanism. It also makes it likely that the length effect seen in reading in Spanish would be greater than that seen in languages with opaque orthographies, such as English. However, the observation of the AoA effect in Spanish, and the frequency effect in Italian, indicates that adult reading is influenced by lexical knowledge regardless of variation in transparency. Furthermore, our observation of influences on reading due to the effects of AoA, and the interactions of imageability (or AoA) and length, indicates a semantic influence on reading that arises when the reading system is pressured by the need to work quickly, or by the need to read words that present difficulties for phonological encoding. We turn now to the early part of reading development.

Spanish reading acquisition and dyslexia

A key observation in the cross-linguistic study of reading has been the finding that English-speaking primary school children are less accurate and slower than children of similar school-grade reading in languages with more transparent orthographies, such as Italian or Spanish (Seymour et al., 2003). This observation has been used as evidence that English-speaking children are slower to 'acquire' reading because to do so they must master a more complex set of spelling–sound mappings (Ziegler & Goswami, 2005, 2006). Consider the inconsistent pronunciation, for example, of *bough*, *plough* and *cough*. In comparison, children learning to read highly transparent orthographies need only establish grapheme–phoneme correspondences to read words as diverse as (in Spanish) *rama* [branch], *arar* [to plough] and *toser* [to cough]. However, the exponents of this view have acknowledged that it does not account for the complete picture of reading behaviour (Ziegler & Goswami, 2006).

The idea that skilled readers can use lexical knowledge in reading, even in transparent orthographies, fits the observations of frequency and AoA effects that we have discussed. We believe that the latter findings are best understood within a theory of reading development based on a combination of the ideas discussed in the preceding sections (in relation to the work of Harm & Seidenberg, 2004, for instance) with a very influential theory of literacy acquisition: the idea that children progress through self-teaching by phonological recoding, proposed by Share (1995).

Share's phonological recoding self-teaching theory of reading acquisition

Share (1995) argued that phonological recoding of print serves as a means of self-teaching through which the learner can acquire the orthographic representations necessary for visual word recognition. The child must begin by establishing the simple one-to-one relationships between letters (or graphemes) and their sounds (phonemes), which we have referred to as grapheme–phoneme correspondences. Equipped with such correspondences (the 'sine qua non of reading acquisition', Share, 1995; p. 156), the developing reader can identify and piece together the component sounds of the pronunciation of words encountered in print. Phonological recoding of printed words provides access to the child's verbal vocabulary and is also a means of supporting the development of orthographic representations useful for recognizing those words.

Over time, increasing frequency of experience in phonological coding, and the expanding set of words encountered, supports the capacity to grasp useful regularities about spelling patterns and spelling–sound mappings which encompass collections of letters. In many words in English, and even in languages with transparent orthographies like Italian or Spanish, the pronunciation of some letters depends on the other letters that appear nearby. This increasing knowledge of orthographic conventions feeds back into the capacity of the developing reader to learn through self-teaching, by improving the accuracy of phonological recoding over time.

This emphasis on the frequency of experience means that the developing reader's approach to reading is item-specific. The developing reader is not expected to move through stages characterized by different methods for reading the words in his/her vocabulary (e.g., Frith, 1985). Rather, a child may vary in the way s/he reads different words depending on the frequency with which s/he has encountered and successfully coded those words. Share (1995) proposed that because the evidence suggests that knowledge about word spellings is learned quickly, high-frequency words will tend to be acquired early, and so will come to be visually recognized early in development.

The influences on reading development in transparent orthographies

Findings concerning early Spanish reading development indicate a strikingly rapid transition to mastery in the accurate phonological coding of print. Seymour et al. (2003) reported that Spanish-speaking children in the first year of primary school achieved 95.6 per cent accuracy on a test of letter–sound knowledge, 94.7 per cent accuracy on known word reading and 88.8 per cent accuracy on non-word reading.

It has been shown that the high level of reading performance recorded by Seymour et al. (2003) emerges quite rapidly following a period of greater individual variation prior to primary school entry. Tests conducted on Spanish-speaking children attending kindergarten indicate substantial individual variation in phonemic awareness, letter–sound knowledge and spelling skills (Borzone de Manrique & Signorini, 1998). The data illustrate the variety of proficiencies brought to formal schooling by different children. Extensive evidence from studies with typically developing and dyslexic children indicates that those with more knowledge of how the pronunciations of whole words can be analysed as component sounds (phonological awareness) perform better in tests of reading (Jiménez, 1997; Jiménez et al., 2007; Jiménez & Ortiz, 2000).

A longitudinal study of reading development in Italian (Orsolini, Fanari, Tosi, de Nigris, & Carrieri, 2006) has shown how reading acquisition in Spanish might attain the high accuracy noted in the first year of primary school. Orsolini et al. (2006) found that three months into the first grade, Italian children showed a variety of reading strategies, some producing pronunciations that were related to word targets by the sounds of one or two shared letters, and others producing pronunciations that successfully encoded target word graphemes but varied in fluency. Of the latter, there were some who could decode graphemes but were unable to blend them, and others who were able both to decode graphemes and to blend them as onset–rime units, syllables or even as whole words. Four months later, the heterogeneity was markedly reduced. Together with a much higher rate of word recognition accuracy, the children were found to produce word pronunciations only as onset–rime units, syllables or whole words. In addition, Orsolini et al. (2006) found that the proportion of words that were successfully produced as (blended) whole-word utterances was lower for longer words but higher for more frequent words.

The changes in reading performance observed over time, and the reported frequency effects, are entirely consistent with the item-based view of development proposed by Share (1995). This also fits with the insights produced by connectionist simulations of reading development (e.g., Harm & Seidenberg, 2004; Plaut et al., 1996). Practice in completing tasks like reading aloud drives changes in the connections between the simple processing units thought to underlie a reader's response to orthography. This adaptation typically includes establishing the capacity to deal with context-specific dependencies in phonological correspondences, allowing the developing reader to pronounce, for example, the letter 'c' in the words *cena* (→ /thena/) or *casa* (→ / kasa/), as discussed earlier. We argue that it also serves the capacity to process orthography more efficiently, with greater efficiency marked by a decreased reliance on letter-by-letter coding.

Recent evidence suggests that the development of orthographic representations in Spanish-speaking children is rapid and results in a mature reader who can recognize words based on multiple-letter spelling patterns rather than having to identify individual letters in their fixed positions in printed words. Acha and Perea (2008; see also Perea & Estévez, 2008) report that both children and adults show the capacity to recognize words on the basis of orthographic information where letter identity is important but letter position is not as important as might be thought (unless one 'raeds a lot of emials').

The implication is that more experienced, typically developing children should show less evidence of letter-by-letter phonological coding of printed words. Indeed, Zoccolotti et al. (2005) have reported that older Italian-speaking children showed a decreased length effect on word reading latencies. We have examined this question in Spanish.

In Davies, Cuetos, and Glez-Seijas (2007) we compared the reading behaviour of developmental dyslexic and typically developing children, testing both chronological-age-matched (CA) and younger, reading-ability-matched (RA) control groups. Following previous researchers (e.g., Seymour et al., 2003; Wimmer, 1993), we presented words in lists, and reading was monitored for accuracy and speed. This is because it is commonly observed that reading difficulty in transparent orthographies is usually marked by slow reading speed (long reaction times or slow list reading speeds), while accuracy is comparatively high (e.g., Wimmer, 1993). In terms of the earlier discussion, slower reading would be expected to result where either phonological or orthographic coding was based on letter-by-letter phonological coding.

In our study, the dyslexic readers and RA groups were matched on speed and accuracy using a standardized test of word reading (PROLEC–R; Cuetos, Rodríguez, Ruano, & Arribas, 2007). We presented the children with word lists that varied on lexical frequency, length and N-size. There were very few errors overall, but the dyslexic readers made more errors than did the RAs, who made more errors than the CAs. More errors were made to low-frequency than to high-frequency words. Errors consisted mostly of non-words (e.g., *bigote* [moustache] → /bixote/), though word substitutions (e.g., *nube* [cloud] → /nueve/ [nine]) and some stress errors (e.g., *café* → /cáfe/) also occurred. Word and non-word errors were found to be orthographically similar to target items. Reading speed was affected by frequency, neighbourhood size and length. More importantly, while the dyslexic readers' average reading speed was longer than that of the CAs, they were not slower than the RAs.

Our observations tend to confirm the view that reading difficulty in transparent orthographies is not primarily a deficit of accuracy (Wimmer, 1993). The effects of frequency and orthographic neighbourhood on reading speed indicate that, as was found for adults (Cuetos & Barbón, 2006), Spanish-speaking children are influenced by lexical knowledge in reading aloud. That reading speed was also massively affected by word length simply confirms that the grapheme-level orthography-to-phonology mappings acquired by Spanish-speaking children in the first year of primary school (Borzone de Manrique & Signorini, 1998; Seymour et al., 2003) remain important five to six years later. Finally, the pattern of no difference between dyslexic and RA reading speed, but significant difference between dyslexic and CA speed, is consistent with the view that dyslexic children's reading resembles that of younger typically developing learners (e.g., Pugh, 2006).

In sum, the findings from Spanish suggest a picture of reading development that can be related to an account informed by the self-teaching theory (Share, 1995) as well as by recent connectionist models of reading development (e.g., Harm & Seidenberg, 2004; Plaut et al., 1996). In our view, the typical course of reading development is as follows:

1 Children arrive at primary school with a range of proficiency in the skills vital to reading development: letter–sound knowledge and phonemic awareness. The consistency of Spanish orthography ensures that establishment of grapheme–phoneme correspondences is very rapid and at a quite uniformly high level throughout the population by late in the first year of primary school. The course of development from that point on is determined by the pressure to read fluently and the pressure to access meaning quickly. The goal of development shifts from accuracy to speed.

2 Regularities that encompass patterns of spelling and spelling–sound mappings are assimilated as the learning reader's reading experience widens (as vocabulary increases) and deepens (as frequencies grow). Hence, frequency and neighbourhood effects on reading speed are observed.

3 Growth in knowledge about orthography, brought about through successful phonological recoding, is expected to feed an increase in the possibility that semantics might influence reading performance. In terms of Harm and Seidenberg's (2004) account, these semantic influences are rendered possible if orthography-to-semantics mappings are established to meet the need to access meaning quickly during reading. Such influence has been observed in healthy Spanish-speaking adults and in acquired dyslexic patients and is demonstrated as AoA and imageability effects. We are currently completing an investigation of reading development in Spanish in which we are testing whether similar effects can be seen in children's reading (Davies, Suarez, Rodríguez-Ferreiro, & Cuetos, 2010b).

Reading development and dyslexia in Spanish

Given this account of reading acquisition in Spanish, what does the evidence say about dyslexia? As others have reported, we found that the differences between typically developing and dyslexic children are more marked in relation to measures of reading speed rather than of accuracy (Davies et al., 2007). Dyslexic children read more slowly than chronological-age-matched controls but not more slowly than children matched on reading-age. This observation supports the view that reading acquisition in Spanish-speaking dyslexic children is delayed rather than deviant. Consistent with this conclusion, dyslexic children were found to show effects of frequency, neighbourhood and word length on reading speed, just as control children did. However, current data do not allow us to attribute the character of reading difficulties in Spanish to any one of the current theories of dyslexia.

There are two main strands of thinking about the causes of dyslexia. The most dominant view in recent years is that dyslexia is the result of problems in phonological processing (e.g., Ramus et al., 2003; Snowling, 2000; Vellutino, Fletcher, Snowling, & Scanlon, 2004). Increasingly, however, attention has also been paid to the possibility that the reading difficulties of dyslexia may be related to problems in orthographic or visual processing (e.g., Bosse, Tainturier, & Valdois, 2007).

It is difficult to judge exactly what the predictions of the dual-route account would be in relation to developmental dyslexia in Spanish because the model does not learn (Coltheart et al., 2001). Broadly speaking, however, our expectation would be that impairments at either the orthographic or the phonological level should lead to slowed reading performance. This is because either impairment would make it difficult for children to acquire the experience necessary to establish multiple-letter sequence representations of orthography, or multiple-letter orthography-to-phonology mappings (in dual-route terms, lexical mappings), tending to restrict dyslexic reading to a more letter-by-letter style. Evidence for this in Italian has been reported by Zoccolotti and colleagues (Zoccolotti et al., 1999).

In the triangle account, the impact of phonological impairment can be likened to reduced precision in the ability of the connectionist network to process phonology (Harm & Seidenberg, 1999). Word or non-word reading accuracy is less likely to be affected by phonological impairment in transparent orthographies because of the high consistency of spelling–sound mappings, however (Miceli, Capasso, & Caramazza, 1994). Spanish-speaking dyslexic children will tend to read accurately but slowly, as we have observed, but this slowness is perhaps better addressed from the orthographic than the phonological side of the reading process. If an interactive system like the triangle model is the basis for understanding reading then it is difficult to separate orthographic and phonological processing. Accurate, precise phonological processing would tend to support, and be supported by, accurate and precise orthographic processing (Harm & Seidenberg, 2001). However, connectionist simulations have shown that if errors are deliberately introduced into the way the simulated reader perceives a word's orthography (Plaut, 1999), or if the simulated reader's capacity to pay attention to visually presented information is restricted (Bosse et al., 2007), it will read aloud in a letter-by-letter phonological coding mode. Such an approach to reading would tend to be marked by greater effects of word length and by a substantially slowed reading speed overall.

Ways forward

We have discussed effects on reading performance relating to knowledge about words or knowledge about letters, graphemes and grapheme–phoneme correspondences. Recent evidence from studies conducted in Italian indicates, however, that we should also attend to the impact of knowledge about morphemes. Burani and colleagues (Burani, Marcolini, De Luca, & Zoccolotti, 2008; Burani, Marcolini, & Stella, 2002), among others, have shown that non-words that can be decomposed into morphemes are read more quickly by adults and children than can non-words that are not decomposable, while dyslexic children show this effect even in real word reading. We predict that the same morphological effects will be found in mature and developing readers of Spanish because, like Italian, it is rich in morphology.

In order to probe the factors that shape reading development, we have tested children's capacity to analyse the component sounds of words (Davies et al., 2010b). However, the importance of variation in how much different individuals read is clearly indicated by the theories we have discussed. Children cannot develop through self-teaching without the experience to support learning. Developing readers cannot improve without practice. Tellingly, it has been shown that orthographic processing skill can account for a portion of variance in word recognition performance that is independent of the contribution of phonological processing skill, and this orthographic component can be predicted in turn by degree of print exposure (Cunningham, Perry, & Stanovich, 2001). The contribution of the orthographic component may be due to the fact that readers with high print exposure can more quickly and strongly activate orthographic representations of common words (Chateau & Jared, 2000). This is something we are now in the process of testing.

Finally, we acknowledge that we have framed much of the discussion of our findings in relation to the self-teaching theory of reading development and to the connectionist models reported by Harm, Seidenberg and colleagues (Harm & Seidenberg, 1999, 2004; Plaut et al., 1996). As yet, no computational model of reading in Spanish exists. Notwithstanding the efforts of researchers to extend current models of reading to German (Ziegler et al., 2000), it remains to be seen whether similar extensions can be successfully made to Spanish. Our recent findings suggest that any forthcoming model must take into account the emergence of effects due to lexical factors as the developing reader approaches maturity.

Note

1 We generally refer to 'letters', but this is not strictly correct since the non-lexical reading route will convert strings of letters (e.g., 'th') where they form graphemes into single phonemes.

Acknowledgements

This research was supported by grant MEC–SEJ2006–06712 from the Spanish Government. Robert Davies and Fernando Cuetos are members of a Marie Curie Research and Training Network: Language and Brain (RTN: LAB) funded by the European Commission (MRTN–CT–2004–512141) as part of its Sixth Framework Programme.

References

Acha, J., & Perea, M. (2008). The effects of length and transposed-letter similarity in lexical decision: Evidence with beginning, intermediate, and adult readers. *British Journal of Psychology*, *99*, 245–264.

Andrews, S. (1989). Frequency and neighbourhood effects on lexical access: Activation or search? *Journal of Experimental Psychology: Learning, Memory, and Cognition, 15,* 802–814.

Ans, B., Carbonnel, S., & Valdois, S. (1998). A connectionist multiple-trace memory model for polysyllabic word reading. *Psychological Review, 105,* 678–723.

Ardila, A. (1991). Errors resembling semantic paralexias in Spanish-speaking aphasics. *Brain and Language, 41,* 437–445.

Baayen, H., Piepenbrock, R., & van Rijn, H. (1993). *The CELEX Lexical Database* [CD-ROM]. Philadelphia: University of Pennsylvania, Linguistic Data Consortium.

Balota, D. A., Cortese, M. J., Sergent-Marshall, S. D., Spieler, D. H., & Yap, M. J. (2004). Visual word recognition of single-syllable words. *Journal of Experimental Psychology: General, 133,* 283–316.

Baluch, B., & Besner, D. (1991). Visual word recognition: Evidence for strategic control of lexical and nonlexical routines in oral reading. *Journal of Experimental Psychology: Learning, Memory, and Cognition, 17,* 644–652.

Barca, L., Burani, C., & Arduino, L. S. (2002). Word naming times and psycholinguistic norms for Italian nouns. *Behaviour Research Methods, Instruments and Computers, 34,* 424–434.

Barca, L., Ellis, A. W., & Burani, C. (2007). Context-sensitive rules and word naming in Italian children. *Reading and Writing: An Interdisciplinary Journal, 20,* 495–509.

Belke, E., Brysbaert, M., Meyer, A. S., & Ghyselinck, M. (2005). Age of acquisition effects in picture naming: Evidence for a lexical-semantic competition hypothesis. *Cognition, 96,* B45–B54.

Bonin, P., Barry, C., Méot, A., & Chalard, M. (2004). The influence of age of acquisition in word reading and other tasks: A never-ending story? *Journal of Memory and Language, 50,* 456–476.

Borzone de Manrique, A. M., & Signorini, A. (1998). Emergent writing forms in Spanish. *Reading and Writing: An Interdisciplinary Journal, 10,* 499–517.

Bosse, M.-L., Tainturier, M. J., & Valdois, S. (2007). Developmental dyslexia: The visual attention span hypothesis. *Cognition, 104,* 198–230.

Brysbaert, M., Lange, M., & van Wijnendaele, I. (2000). The effects of age-of-acquisition and frequency-of-occurrence in visual word recognition: Further evidence from the Dutch language. *European Journal of Cognitive Psychology, 12,* 65–85.

Burani, C., Barca, L., & Ellis, A. W. (2006). Orthographic complexity and word naming in Italian: Some words are more transparent than others. *Psychonomic Bulletin and Review, 13,* 346–352.

Burani, C., Marcolini, S., De Luca, M., & Zoccolotti, P. (2008). Morpheme-based reading aloud: Evidence from dyslexic and skilled Italian readers. *Cognition, 108,* 243–262.

Burani, C., Marcolini, S., & Stella, G. (2002). How early does morpho-lexical reading develop in readers of a shallow orthography? *Brain and Language, 81,* 568–586.

Chateau, D., & Jared, D. (2000). Exposure to print and word recognition processes. *Memory and Cognition, 28,* 143–153.

Coltheart, M. (1984). Writing systems and reading disorders. In L. Henderson (Ed.), *Orthographies and reading* (pp. 67–79). Hove, UK: Lawrence Erlbaum Associates.

Coltheart, M., Curtis, B., Atkins, P., & Haller, M. (1993). Models of reading aloud:

Dual-route and parallel-distributed processing approaches. *Psychological Review*, *100*, 589–608.

Coltheart, M., Davelaar, E., Jonasson, J. T., & Besner, D. (1977). Access to the internal lexicon. In S. Dornic (Ed.), *Attention and performance VI* (pp. 535–555). Hillsdale, NJ: Lawrence Erlbaum Associates, Inc.

Coltheart, M., Rastle, K., Perry, C., Langdon, R., & Ziegler, J. C. (2001). DRC: A dual route cascaded model of visual word recognition and reading aloud. *Psychological Review*, *108*, 204–256.

Cortese, M. J., & Khanna, M. M. (2007). Age of acquisition predicts naming and lexical-decision performance above and beyond 22 other predictor variables: An analysis of 2,342 words. *Quarterly Journal of Experimental Psychology*, *60*, 1072–1082.

Cuetos, F., & Barbón, A. (2006). Word naming in Spanish. *European Journal of Cognitive Psychology*, *18*, 415–436.

Cuetos, F., Rodríguez, B., Ruano, E., & Arribas, D. (2007). *PROLEC-R*. Madrid, Spain: TEA Ediciones.

Cumming, T. B., Patterson, K., Verfaillie, M., & Graham, K. S. (2006). One bird with two stones: Abnormal word length effects in pure alexia and semantic dementia. *Cognitive Neuropsychology*, *23*, 1130–1161.

Cunningham, A. E., Perry, K. E., & Stanovich, K. E. (2001). Converging evidence for the concept of orthographic processing. *Reading and Writing: An Interdisciplinary Journal*, *14*, 549–568.

Davies, R., Burani, C., & Cuetos, F. (2010a). *Reading in Spanish and Italian: A cross-linguistic mixed-effects analysis of the determiners of reading in different transparent orthographies.* Manuscript in preparation.

Davies, R., & Cuetos, F. (2005). Acquired dyslexia in Spanish: A review and some observations on a new case of deep dyslexia. *Behavioural Neurology*, *16*, 85–101.

Davies, R., Cuetos, F., & Glez-Seijas, R.-M. (2007). Reading development and dyslexia in a transparent orthography: A survey of Spanish children. *Annals of Dyslexia*, *57*, 179–198.

Davies, R., Cuetos, F., & Rodríguez-Ferreiro, J. (2008, October). *What makes reading difficult in transparent orthographies? Longer words are harder and are read using semantics.* Poster presentation at Academy of Aphasia, Turku, Finland.

Davies, R., Suarez, P., Rodríguez-Ferreiro, J., & Cuetos, F. (2010b). *Responsive to task demands and influenced by lexical knowledge: Reading processes in developing Spanish-speaking readers.* Manuscript in preparation.

Ellis, A. W., & Lambon Ralph, M. A. (2000). Age of acquisition effects in adult lexical processing reflect loss of plasticity in maturing systems: Insights from connectionist networks. *Journal of Experimental Psychology: Learning, Memory, and Cognition*, *26*, 1103–1123.

Frith, U. (1985). Beneath the surface of developmental dyslexia. In K. Patterson, M. Coltheart, & J. Marshall (Eds.), *Surface dyslexia: Neuropsychological and cognitive studies of phonological reading* (pp. 301–330). Hove, UK: Psychology Press.

Gerhand, S., & Barry, C. (1998). Word frequency effects in oral reading are not merely age-of-acquisition effects in disguise. *Journal of Experimental Psychology: Learning, Memory, and Cognition*, *24*, 267–283.

Glushko, R. (1979). The organization and activation of orthographic knowledge in reading aloud. *Journal of Experimental Psychology*, *5*, 674–691.

Harm, M. W., & Seidenberg, M. S. (1999). Phonology, reading acquisition, and dyslexia: Insights from connectionist models. *Psychological Review*, *106*, 491–528.

Harm, M. W., & Seidenberg, M. S. (2001). Are there orthographic impairments in phonological dyslexia? *Cognitive Neuropsychology*, *18*, 71–92.

Harm, M. W., & Seidenberg, M. S. (2004). Computing the meanings of words in reading: Cooperative division of labour between visual and phonological processes. *Psychological Review*, *111*, 662–720.

Jared, D., McRae, K., & Seidenberg, M. S. (1990). The basis of consistency effects in word naming. *Journal of Memory and Language*, *29*, 687–715.

Jiménez, J. E. (1997). A reading-level design study of phonemic processes underlying reading disabilities in a transparent orthography. *Reading and Writing*, *9*, 23–40.

Jiménez, J. E., Hernández-Valle, I., Ramírez, G., del Rosario Ortiz, M., Rodrigo, M., Estévez, A., et al. (2007). Computer speech-based remediation for reading disabilities: The size of spelling-to-sound unit in a transparent orthography. *Spanish Journal of Psychology*, *10*, 52–67.

Jiménez, J. E., & Ortiz, M. R. (2000). Metalinguistic awareness and reading acquisition in the Spanish language. *Spanish Journal of Psychology*, *3*, 37–46.

Kello, C. T., & Plaut, D. C. (2003). Strategic control over rate of processing in word reading: A computational investigation. *Journal of Memory and Language*, *48*, 207–232.

Kessler, B., Treiman, R., & Mullenix, J. (2007). Feedback-consistency effects in single-word reading. In E. L. Grigorenko & A. J. Naples (Eds.), *Single-word reading: Behavioral and biological perspectives* (pp. 159–174). Hillsdale, NJ: Lawrence Erlbaum Associates, Inc.

Lambon Ralph, M. A., & Ehsan, S. (2006). Age of acquisition effects depend on the mapping between representations and the frequency of occurrence: Empirical and computational evidence. *Visual Cognition*, *13*, 928–948.

McClelland, J. L., Rumelhart, D. E., & the PDP Research Group. (1986). *Parallel distributed processing: Explorations in the microstructure of cognition: Vol. 2. Psychological and biological models*. Cambridge, MA: MIT Press.

Miceli, G., Capasso, R., & Caramazza, A. (1994). The interaction of lexical and sublexical processes in reading, writing and repetition. *Neuropsychologia*, *32*, 317–333.

Monaghan, J., & Ellis, A. W. (2002). What exactly interacts with spelling–sound consistency in word naming? *Journal of Experimental Psychology: Learning, Memory, and Cognition*, *28*, 183–206.

Monsell, S., Patterson, K., Graham, A., Hughes, C. H., & Milroy, R. (1992). Lexical and sublexical translation of spelling to sound: Strategic anticipation of lexical status. *Journal of Experimental Psychology: Learning, Memory, and Cognition*, *18*, 452–467.

Morrison, C. M., & Ellis, A. W. (1995). Roles of word frequency and age of acquisition in word naming and lexical decision. *Journal of Experimental Psychology: Learning, Memory, and Cognition*, *21*, 116–133.

Morrison, C. M., & Ellis, A. W. (2000). Real age of acquisition effects in word naming and lexical decision. *British Journal of Psychology*, *91*, 167–180.

Orsolini, M., Fanari, R., Tosi, V., De Nigris, B., & Carrieri, R. (2006). From phonological recoding to lexical reading: A longitudinal study on reading development in Italian. *Language and Cognitive Processes*, *21*, 576–607.

Perea, M., & Estévez, A. (2008). Transposed-letter similarity effects in naming pseudowords: Evidence from children and adults. *European Journal of Cognitive Psychology, 20*, 33–46.

Perea, M., & Lupker, S. J. (2003). Does jugde activate COURT? Transposed-letter similarity effects in masked associative priming. *Memory and Cognition, 31*, 829–841.

Plaut, D. C. (1999). A connectionist approach to word reading and acquired dyslexia: extension to sequential processing. *Cognitive Science, 23*, 543–568.

Plaut, D. C., McClelland, J. L., Seidenberg, M. S., & Patterson, K. E. (1996). Understanding normal and impaired reading: Computational principles in quasi-regular domains. *Psychological Review, 103*, 56–115.

Pugh, K. (2006). A neurocognitive overview of reading acquisition and dyslexia across languages. *Developmental Science, 9*, 448–450.

Raman, I. (2006). On the age-of-acquisition effects in word naming and orthographic transparency: Mapping specific or universal? *Visual Cognition, 13*, 1044–1053.

Raman, I., Baluch, B., & Besner, D. (2004). On the control of visual word recognition: Changing routes versus changing deadlines. *Memory and Cognition, 32*, 489–500.

Ramus, F., Rosen, S., Dakin, S. C., Day, B. L., Castellote, J. M., White, S., et al. (2003). Theories of developmental dyslexia: Insights from a multiple case study of dyslexic adults. *Brain, 126*, 851–865.

Rumelhart, D. E., McClelland, J. L., & the PDP Research Group. (1986). *Parallel distributed processing: Explorations in the microstructure of cognition* (Vol. 1). Cambridge, MA: MIT Press.

Seidenberg, M. S., & McClelland, J. L. (1989). A distributed, developmental model of word recognition and naming. *Psychological Review, 96*, 523–568.

Seymour, P. H. K., Aro, M., & Erskine, J. M. (2003). Foundation literacy acquisition in European orthographies. *British Journal of Psychology, 94*, 143–174.

Share, D. L. (1995). Phonological recoding and self-teaching: Sine qua non of reading acquisition. *Cognition, 55*, 151–218.

Snowling, M. J. (2000). *Dyslexia*. Oxford, UK: Blackwell.

Strain, E., Patterson, K., & Seidenberg, M. S. (1995). Semantic effects in single-word naming. *Journal of Experimental Psychology: Learning, Memory, and Cognition, 21*, 1140–1154.

Taraban, R., & McClelland, J. L. (1987). Conspiracy effects in word pronunciation. *Journal of Memory and Language, 26*, 608–631.

Vellutino, F. R., Fletcher, J. M., Snowling, M. J., & Scanlon, D. M. (2004). Specific reading disability (dyslexia): What have we learned in the past four decades? *Journal of Child Psychology and Psychiatry, 45*, 2–40.

Weekes, B. S. (1997). Differential effects of number of letters on word and nonword naming latency. *Quarterly Journal of Experimental Psychology, 50A*, 439–456.

Wimmer, H. (1993). Characteristics of developmental dyslexia in a regular reading system. *Applied Psycholinguistics, 14*, 1–33.

Woollams, A., Lambon Ralph, M. A., Plaut, D. C., & Patterson, K. (2007). SD-squared: On the association between semantic dementia and surface dyslexia. *Psychological Review, 114*, 316–339.

Zevin, J. D., & Seidenberg, M. S. (2002). Age of acquisition effects in word reading and other tasks. *Journal of Memory and Language, 47*, 1–29.

Ziegler, J. C., & Goswami, U. (2005). Reading acquisition, developmental dyslexia, and skilled reading across languages: A psycholinguistic grain size theory. *Psychological Bulletin, 131*, 3–29.

Ziegler, J. C., & Goswami, U. (2006). Becoming literature in different languages: Similar problems, different solutions. *Developmental Science, 9*, 429–453.

Ziegler, J. C., Perry, C., & Coltheart, M. (2000). The DRC model of visual word recognition and reading aloud: An extension to German. *European Journal of Cognitive Psychology, 12*, 413–430.

Ziegler, J. C., Perry, C., Jacobs, A. M., & Braun, M. (2001). Identical words are read differently in different languages. *Psychological Science, 12*, 379–384.

Zoccolotti, P., De Luca, M., Di Pace, E., Gasperini, F., Judica, A., & Spinelli, D. (2005). Word length effect in early reading and in developmental dyslexia. *Brain and Language, 93*, 369–373.

Zoccolotti, P., De Luca, M., Di Pace, E., Judica, A., Orlandi, M., & Spinelli, D. (1999). Markers of developmental surface dyslexia in a language (Italian) with high grapheme–phoneme correspondence. *Applied Psycholinguistics, 20*, 191–216.

9 Lexical reading in Italian developmental dyslexic readers

Despina Paizi, Pierluigi Zoccolotti and Cristina Burani

Introduction

Italian is a language with a transparent orthography characterized by an almost one-to-one grapheme-to-phoneme correspondence. Readers of transparent orthographies can, in principle, process all written words successfully by using grapheme–phoneme correspondences (letter–sound rules) without accessing the lexicon. Recent research suggests that Italian readers consistently read words which they have previously encountered better than non-words, which, by definition, they have never previously encountered (Pagliuca, Arduino, Barca, & Burani, 2008; Paulesu et al., 2000). This suggests that Italian readers do not rely solely on decoding words using grapheme–phoneme correspondences but on stored lexical knowledge of familiar words. These effects are also apparent in comparisons of high- and low-frequency words (Barca, Burani, & Arduino, 2002; Bates, Burani, D'Amico, & Barca, 2001; Burani, Barca, & Ellis, 2006; Colombo, Pasini, & Balota, 2006) and in research examining the morphemic constituents of words, such as roots and affixes (Burani & Laudanna, 2003). Consequently, there is a growing body of evidence indicating that reading in transparent scripts, and specifically in Italian, which is the focus here, is lexical.

Developmental dyslexia in shallow orthographies such as German and Italian is characterized by much slower reading but higher levels of accuracy than are reported for dyslexic readers of deeper scripts such as English (Wimmer, 1993; see also Ziegler & Goswami, 2005). Specifically, Italian dyslexics' reading is characterized by a marked word length effect (with long words yielding much longer reaction times than short words). This results in slow and laborious, but relatively accurate, reading without the deficit being specific to non-word reading (Zoccolotti et al., 1999). Evidence supporting this characterization comes from both reading and eye-movement studies. Italian developmental dyslexic readers have been shown to be markedly sensitive to stimulus length effects, and much slower than typically developing readers at reading aloud words and non-words (Judica, De Luca, Spinelli, & Zoccolotti, 2002; Spinelli et al., 2005; Zoccolotti et al., 2005). Eye-movement studies show a consistent pattern. Developmental dyslexic readers demonstrate extremely fractionated text scanning as they proceed through a stimulus display making a large number of very small saccades; in addition, they show longer fixation durations than typically developing readers. This pattern holds both in reading passages of text (De Luca, Di Pace, Judica, Spinelli, & Zoccolotti, 1999) and lists of words and non-words (De Luca, Borrelli, Judica, Spinelli, & Zoccolotti, 2002). These characteristics point to the serial processing of written stimuli, irrespective of their lexical status.

It has been suggested that developmental dyslexic readers of transparent scripts match the profile of surface dyslexic readers (Zoccolotti et al., 1999). Surface dyslexia has been described in the literature as a selective deficit in reading exception words (Castles & Coltheart, 1993). This hypothesis was framed within the dual-route theory of reading. The dual-route cascaded (DRC) model (Coltheart, Rastle, Perry, Langdon, & Ziegler, 2001) for reading aloud and visual word recognition assumes two distinct procedures that compute orthographic input into output.[1] The lexical route computes word pronunciation by directly accessing the lexicon. Newly encountered stimuli, namely non-words and low-frequency words, are bound to be processed sequentially via the grapheme-to-phoneme conversion rules of the non-lexical route. According to this framework, surface dyslexia constitutes a deficit of one or more components of the lexical route, which is compensated for by heavy reliance on the grapheme-to-phoneme conversion rules of the non-lexical route (Castles & Coltheart, 1993; Coltheart, Masterson, Byng, Prior, & Riddoch, 1983).

In a dual-route framework of reading, Italian developmental dyslexic readers were hypothesized to rely excessively on the non-lexical reading procedure (Spinelli et al., 2005; Zoccolotti et al., 2005). The central question in this review is whether or not lexical reading is available to Italian developmental dyslexic readers just as it is to proficient readers. Previous findings have focused on word length effects as markers of serial recoding and non-lexical processing. We review a series of experiments on (1) lexical effects that are indicative of lexical reading, namely lexicality effects (with words read faster and more accurately than non-words) and word frequency effects (with high-frequency words read faster and more accurately than low-frequency words), (2) rule contextuality effects, limited to low-frequency words and (3) morphemic constituent effects (with non-words that include morphemes being read faster and more accurately than non-words that do not include morphemes). In parallel to presenting evidence against a deficit in lexical processing, reference will be made to stimulus length and rule contextuality effects, typically thought of as markers of non-lexical processing. The presence of lexicality, word frequency and morphemic constituent effects provides evidence of lexical reading by dyslexic readers as well as by typically developing readers: this is contrary to previous assumptions of predominantly non-lexical reading. Additionally, we consider the interpretation of the size of these effects in dyslexic and proficient readers.

Lexical effects

A common assumption in the literature is that for young readers of transparent scripts marked stimulus length effects are an indication of developmental dyslexia (Ziegler, Perry, Ma-Wyatt, Ladner, & Schulte-Korne, 2003; Zoccolotti et al., 1999). The sensitivity of dyslexic readers to stimulus length, combined with slow and laborious reading performance, is taken as evidence for serial and primarily non-lexical reading. Consequently, an important issue is whether developmental dyslexia in transparent scripts is related to a deficit of the lexical route. A straightforward solution would be to investigate the role of lexicality and word frequency effects in dyslexics' reading performance. The presence of these effects would indicate the availability of lexical reading for dyslexic readers just as for proficient readers.

In all studies reported, the reading deficit was established based on a standard Italian reading test—the MT test (Cornoldi, Colpo, & Gruppo, 1981)—which requires the participant to read a passage aloud within a time limit. A performance at least two standard deviations below the normative mean for either accuracy or speed in this test is taken as the cut-off for pathological (impaired) performance. Reading comprehension varied across children, but it was most often within normal limits. All children were within the normal range for non-verbal intelligence on Raven's Coloured Progressive Matrices (Raven, Raven, & Court, 2003) according to normative Italian data (Pruneti, 1985). They also had normal or corrected to normal visual acuity. Unless otherwise specified, both dyslexic and proficient readers were 11–12 years old.

Lexicality effects

The effect of lexicality has been demonstrated convincingly for Italian adult proficient readers (Pagliuca et al., 2008; Paulesu at al., 2000). Recently, Pagliuca et al. (2008) demonstrated that Italian proficient readers read aloud both high- and low-frequency words faster and more accurately than non-words. This study is the first systematic investigation of lexicality effects in reading the Italian transparent script aloud. The authors employed two lists of short (4- and 5-letter) words—a list of high- and a list of low-frequency words—and two lists of non-words derived from these words. The stimuli were matched on orthographic neighbourhood size (N-size = the number of words from which they differ by only one letter; see Coltheart, Davelaar, Jonasson, & Besner, 1977), summed neighbours' frequency, bigram frequency,[2] number of letters and initial two phonemes. List composition was manipulated to investigate whether lexicality effects could also be present in the context of non-words. The insertion of non-words in the experimental list could potentially have increased the possibility of non-lexical processing (Tabossi & Laghi, 1992). In the Italian transparent script, both real words and non-words can be processed successfully by the non-lexical reading procedure, especially when lexical stress assignment is not required (as is the case for words of more than two syllables).

The results showed that words were read aloud faster and more accurately than their corresponding non-words. This was the case for both high- and low-frequency words, irrespective of list composition. Thus, the effect of lexicality was present both when the words were presented alone (pure blocks) and when they were presented mixed with non-word fillers (mixed blocks). When reading mixed blocks of words and non-words we assume that non-lexical processing is more likely because the lexical status of the forth-coming trial cannot be anticipated, and non-words can only be processed non-lexically (i.e., using grapheme–phoneme correspondences). The latter finding is of great importance as lexicality effects remained present in a context that maximally favoured non-lexical processing. Overall, these findings illustrate that in transparent scripts, just as in deeper scripts, the lexical route is the main route involved in reading aloud (see also Paulesu, 2006; Zoccolotti, De Luca, Judica, & Spinelli, 2008).

Given that reading in Italian could, in principle, be non-lexical, one might assume that Italian dyslexic readers would be more likely to employ non-lexical strategies, particularly since existing evidence suggests that their reading is slower and subject to word-length effects (Zoccolotti et al., 1999). If these readers rely excessively on non-lexical reading, there should be no difference in reaction times for bisyllabic words and non-words, since all types of stimuli would be processed via the grapheme-to-phoneme conversion rules of the non-lexical route. Lexicality effects in developmental dyslexics' reading aloud would advocate against previous assumptions for serial recoding on the basis of small grain size units, as has been suggested for readers of transparent scripts (Ziegler & Goswami, 2005), and by over-reliance on non-lexical processing (Zoccolotti et al., 1999, 2005).

To date, the lexicality effect in reading aloud has been systematically investigated in only one study of dyslexic and typically developing readers (Paizi, De Luca, Zoccolotti, & Burani, 2007). We employed the materials from Pagliuca et al. (2008) in an attempt to replicate the results for dyslexic and typically developing readers. A major difference from the experiments conducted by Pagliuca et al. was that in this study list composition was not manipulated, but words and non-words were presented for reading aloud mixed together in the same blocks to encourage the possibility of non-lexical processing. Nevertheless, the results showed that both high- and low-frequency words were read faster and more accurately than were non-words. The effect of lexicality was significant for both young skilled readers and dyslexic readers. Even though dyslexic readers showed a generally inferior performance in terms of both speed and accuracy, they demonstrated lexicality effects similar to skilled readers. These results are consistent with previous findings (Pagliuca et al., 2008; Paulesu et al., 2000; Zoccolotti et al., 2008) but indicate that the lexical route is the primary reading route for dyslexic readers as well as for adult and young skilled readers.

In the same study, a second experiment (employing the same stimuli with the same participants) assessed the advantage of words over non-words in a visual lexical decision task. A lexical decision, unlike reading aloud, is a task that does not require phonological output, simply a decision about whether an item presented is a word or not. Consequently, if the main deficit in dyslexia is at the level of output phonology, dyslexic and typically developing readers should perform similarly.

To perform well on a lexical decision task, readers need fast and effective access to the mental lexicon (a long-term store of known words). If a difference between participant groups were to occur on this task, it would suggest that dyslexic readers had poorer access to the lexicon. The results from the lexical decision task paralleled those of reading aloud. Both high- and low-frequency words were identified faster and more accurately than non-words by both dyslexic and young skilled readers. Also, high-frequency words were identified faster and more accurately than low-frequency words by both participant groups. However, although the effects of lexicality and frequency were present for dyslexic readers and skilled readers, dyslexic readers were less efficient than skilled readers in that they were much slower and more inaccurate in performing the task.

The advantage of words over non-words has also been reported in another lexical decision experiment carried out with 8- and 9-year-old children (Di Filippo, De Luca, Judica, Spinelli, & Zoccolotti, 2006). However, our study has shown for the first time that low-frequency words also have an advantage over short and quite word-like non-words in lexical decision for both dyslexic and young skilled readers. This finding indicates that the lexicon of dyslexic children includes low-frequency as well as high-frequency words, and implies that dyslexic and skilled readers perform lexical decision in a similar fashion. However, dyslexic and typically developing readers differ significantly in terms of speed and accuracy in accessing the lexicon.

To sum up, lexicality effects are present in Italian reading aloud for proficient—young and adult—and developmental dyslexic readers (Paizi et al., 2007; Zoccolotti et al., 2008). In addition, the advantage of both high- and low-frequency words was confirmed in lexical decision for dyslexic and skilled young readers (Di Filippo et al., 2006; Paizi et al., 2007). Dyslexic readers showed generally inferior performance in terms of both reaction times and accuracy compared to skilled readers. However, the lexicality effect indicates that the lexical route is available for dyslexic readers. This parallels the effects seen in typically developing readers and is consistent with previous findings for proficient adult readers (Pagliuca et al., 2008). This pattern of results strongly suggests that Italian dyslexic children employ lexical reading, at least for short (high- and low-frequency) words, and that they do not rely predominantly on the non-lexical reading procedure.

Word frequency effects

The effects of word frequency have been repeatedly reported for Italian adult proficient readers (Barca et al., 2002; Bates et al., 2001; Burani, Arduino, & Barca, 2007; Burani et al., 2006; Colombo et al., 2006). There is also evidence that word frequency affects reading aloud as well as visual lexical decision of Italian young skilled readers (Burani, Marcolini, & Stella, 2002). However, there are very few demonstrations of word frequency effects on the reading performance of Italian dyslexic readers.

Barca, Burani, Di Filippo and Zoccolotti (2006) investigated the inter-action of word frequency and grapheme-to-phoneme contextuality effects (discussed later) in reading aloud by Italian developmental dyslexic and young proficient readers. Their results showed that reading aloud by Italian dyslexics is affected by word frequency in a similar way to young proficient readers. High-frequency words were read faster and more accurately than were low-frequency words by both groups. Dyslexic children were slower and less accurate than young skilled readers, but frequency effects were also present, strongly suggesting that lexical reading occurred. Word frequency effects were greater in the dyslexic group than in the control group.

We have also investigated word frequency effects in conjunction with length effects, again confirming the influence of word frequency on Italian developmental dyslexic readers' performance, both for reading aloud and for visual lexical decision (Paizi et al., 2007). Two sets of words were used, divided into two frequency conditions (high/low), each containing 15 words per length condition (4, 5, 6, 7 letters). All conditions were matched on initial phoneme, word length (number of letters), bigram frequency and orthographic complexity. The words in each frequency set were matched for frequency, age of acquisition, familiarity and N-size.

The results showed that high-frequency words were read aloud faster and more accurately than low-frequency words by both dyslexic and typi-cally developing readers, clearly indicating that lexical reading occurred. There were also length effects. For typically developing readers the effect of length was limited to significantly faster reaction times for 4-letter words compared to all other lengths. The dyslexic readers were, however, much more affected by stimulus length and showed increasing reaction times for each additional letter. Word frequency interacted with length such that the effect of length was stronger for low-frequency words; this is consistent with the predictions of the DRC model and data from other languages such as English (Weekes, 1997) and French (Ferrand, 2000). Dyslexic children were generally slower and less accurate than were their proficient peers.

The same children were also asked to do a visual lexical decision task to test whether the performance of dyslexic readers would differ from that of typically developing readers in a task that does not require a vocal response. The words used in this experiment were the same as in the reading-aloud task, to which a list of non-words was added. The non-words were derived from the real words and matched with them on length, bigram frequency, N-size and orthographic complexity. The results showed that high-frequency words were identified faster and more accurately than were low-frequency words by both participant groups. Skilled readers showed word frequency effects but not length effects. Developmental dyslexic readers, however, showed both word frequency and length effects.

The co-existence of word frequency and length effects on dyslexic readers' performance in both reading aloud and visual lexical decision cannot be easily interpreted in terms of the (parallel) activation of the two reading routes, as predicted by the standard dual-route model (Coltheart et al., 2001). Different computational approaches such as the connectionist multi-trace memory model for polysyllabic reading—ACV98 (Ans, Carbonnel, & Valdois, 1998)—may provide a better explanation of the data. This model assumes a single processing mechanism and two reading procedures: global and analytic. An important feature of the network is that the two procedures are activated sequentially depending on the visual attentional processing requirements of the input. If the orthographic input is recognized by the network as being familiar, it is processed holistically by the global procedure. If not, the model switches to analytical processing. Since the possibilities for global processing increase with frequency, the model also predicts serial effects for non-words and low-frequency words, but not for high-frequency words (Ans et al., 1998).

The DRC model proposes that a lexical decision is performed by directly accessing word representations in the lexicon, and hence word frequency effects play an important role in this task, but length effects should not be present (Coltheart et al., 2001). However, the results discussed above are more compatible with the predictions of ACV98. For skilled readers the model predicts word frequency but not length effects in lexical decision because the task requires global processing of the stimuli. Dyslexic readers, though, may show sensitivity to length effects due to reduced visual–attentional span. This prediction is supported by findings in deep orthographies such as French (Bosse, Tainturier, & Valdois, 2007; Juphard, Carbonnel, & Valdois, 2004), and shallow orthographies such as Dutch (Martens & de Jong, 2006).

The results discussed in this section are consistent with the predictions of the ACV98 model as well as with data reported for dyslexic readers in other languages (see above). The effect of word frequency was confirmed for long as well as for short words for both dyslexic and skilled readers in reading aloud and visual lexical decision. However, dyslexic readers were slower, less accurate and more affected by stimulus length, which is in line with previously reported data in the literature for Italian developmental dyslexics (Spinelli et al., 2005; Zoccolotti et al., 2005). This pattern of results favours an interpretation in terms of a visual–attentional deficit that may impose processing limitations for the dyslexic readers, as postulated by the ACV98, but clearly the issue is not addressed in the experiments discussed here and requires further investigation.

Rule contextuality effect

Italian is a shallow script from which exception spelling-to-sound correspondences similar to those of deeper scripts (such as English) are essentially absent. In Italian, there is an almost perfect grapheme-to-phoneme correspondence, so that all letter sequences can be read correctly via a limited set of grapheme-to-phoneme conversion (GPC) rules. However, grapheme-to-phoneme correspondence is not entirely perfect because there are certain sequences that require more complex rules than others. For example, the pronunciation of the letters *c* and *g* depends on the letter(s) that follow them. The rules required for the pronunciation of these ambiguous letters are context-dependent and are more complex than other letter sequences that have only one possible pronunciation. For instance, the letter *c* is pronounced 'k' as in *crystal* when followed by a consonant or *a*, *o*, *u*; however, when followed by *e* or *i*, it is pronounced 'ch', as in *church*. The letters *ci* are also pronounced as a single phoneme ('ch' as in *church*) when followed by one of the vowels: *a*, *o* or *u*; whereas when *c* is followed by *h*, the *ch* combination also constitutes a single grapheme pronounced as 'k' (Barca et al., 2006; Burani et al., 2006). The letter *g* follows similar rules.

It has been shown that the presence of the letters *c* and *g* in a word—the presence of complex contextual rules—slows down adult proficient readers' reading compared to their reading of words that contain simple (non-contextual) GPC rules. However, this effect (termed the *rule contextuality effect*) is limited to low-frequency words (Burani et al., 2006). A possible interpretation of this finding within the dual-route computational framework for reading (Coltheart et al., 2001) is that the rule contextuality effect is indicative of the contribution of the non-lexical route in reading low-frequency, but not high-frequency words. GPC rule complexity should not affect lexical processing because it is quite fast in directly accessing the entries of high-frequency words in the lexicon. But for low-frequency words it may be more difficult to distinguish lexical from non-lexical processing. As discussed previously, low-frequency words are more likely than high-frequency words to be processed non-lexically.

These results were replicated for young skilled readers. Barca, Ellis and Burani (2007) examined the role of rule contextuality effects on reading aloud in Italian children (7- and 9-year-olds). The results were remarkably similar to those obtained for adult proficient readers (Burani et al., 2006). Words that contained contextual rules were read more slowly and less accurately than words that did not. In a second experiment it was demonstrated that the rule contextuality effect was significant for reading speed and accuracy, but only for low-frequency and not for high-frequency word reading. As mentioned above, rule contextuality effects appeared to be identical in both adult and young proficient readers. Thus, the effect of complex rules on reading aloud was confirmed despite the transparency of the Italian script. Furthermore, the degree of similarity between the effects reported for adult and young skilled readers demonstrates that from the first elementary grades young readers of transparent orthographies develop a reading system that is as efficient as that of adult proficient readers (Barca et al., 2007).

Barca et al. (2006) focused on the effects of frequency and rule contextuality in the reading performance of dyslexic and typically developing children. If dyslexic readers rely on non-lexical decoding, they should exhibit rule contextuality effects irrespective of word frequency. Typically developing readers, on the other hand, would be expected to show rule contextuality effects only for low-frequency words, similar to adult readers (see above). An experimental design that varied word frequency (high/low) and rule contextuality (contextual graphemes/simple graphemes) was used. The complex rule set contained words with context-sensitive graphemes, whereas words in the simple rule set did not. Both word sets were matched for imageability, N-size, bigram frequency, length and initial phonemes (Barca et al., 2006).

The results demonstrated that words containing complex, context-sensitive rules were read more slowly and less accurately than words that contained simple rules. But the effect was limited to low-frequency words for both groups, paralleling previous findings for adult proficient readers. Even though dyslexic readers showed a generally inferior performance in terms of both reaction times and error rates compared to the skilled readers, both groups were similarly affected by word frequency and rule contextuality effects. Again, these findings suggest that dyslexic readers do employ lexical reading, and this is more likely for high-frequency words, like their proficient peers. If dyslexic readers employed a non-lexical reading strategy for all stimuli to be processed, the rule contextuality effect would be present for both high- and low-frequency words. The effect of word frequency and the limitation of the rule contextuality effect to low-frequency words for dyslexic and skilled readers provide important evidence against a deficit specific to lexical processing for Italian dyslexic readers.

Morphemic constituent effects

In addition to being consistent for orthography-to-phonology conversion, Italian is a language rich in morphology, in that the majority of words are formed by a root and affix (either inflectional or derivational—see examples below). Despite the transparency of the script, the evidence indicates that both skilled and dyslexic Italian readers rely efficiently on word morphemes (roots and affixes) as meaningful lexical reading units of an intermediate size between single graphemes and words.

Italian adult proficient readers read aloud non-words that include morphemes more successfully than non-words that do not (see Burani & Laudanna, 2003, for a review). However, the data on the effects of morphemic constituents on children's reading are scarce. In particular, it has been suggested that during reading acquisition, readers of transparent scripts rely on small grain size reading units, specifically graphemes and phonemes, as opposed to readers of deeper scripts like English, for which multiple grain size mappings are a necessity due to the inconsistencies of the script (Ziegler & Goswami, 2005; see also chapter 2, this volume).

In Italian it has been shown that morpheme-based lexical reading is early and efficient for both reading aloud and lexical decision tasks. Burani et al. (2002) found that novel, non-existent combinations (non-words) made up of a root (e.g., *cod-* [tail]) and a derivational suffix (e.g., *-ismo* [-ism]) resulting in non-existent combinations (morphological non-words, e.g., *codismo* ['tailism']) were read faster and more accurately by both adult and young proficient readers than were non-words that contained neither roots nor suffixes (simple non-words, e.g., *cudosta*). In the same study, a lexical decision task was used to verify that readers would be more likely to recognize as possible words morphological non-words than simple non-words. The results confirmed this hypothesis, thus providing evidence for early and efficient morpholexical reading in Italian.

In the Burani et al. (2002) study it was demonstrated that the presence of morphemes in non-words facilitated the reading performance of young Italian readers, similar to proficient adult readers. A question of interest is whether dyslexic readers can also benefit from the presence of larger than single grapheme lexical units—that is, morphemes. Morphemes are larger reading units than single graphemes, but smaller than words, which dyslexic readers find difficult to process as a whole. This difficulty in whole-stimulus processing has been mainly illustrated by eye movement studies in which dyslexic readers show a high number of fixations and extremely fractionated text scanning (De Luca et al., 2002). Morphemic constituents could have a facilitatory effect on dyslexic readers' reading performance. It could be hypothesized that, if Italian dyslexic readers employ lexical reading, non-words that contain lexical morphemes—roots and affixes—should be read faster and more accurately than non-words that do not.

In a recent study, Burani, Marcolini, De Luca, and Zoccolotti (2008) investigated the role of word morphology in Italian dyslexic readers, reading-skill-matched and chronological-age-matched typically developing readers, and proficient adult readers in reading aloud morphologically complex non-words and words. The first experiment focused on the effect of morphological constituents on non-word reading (morphological/simple). The non-words in the morphological set were constructed from a root (e.g., *donn-* [woman]) and a derivational suffix (e.g., *-ista* [-ist]). New combinations were non-existent in Italian (e.g., *donnista* ['womanist']). Roots and suffixes were of high frequency. The non-words in the simple set did not contain morphemes (e.g., *dennosto*). The two non-word sets were matched on initial phoneme, syllabic structure, length, bigram frequency, orthographic complexity and N-size. All four participant groups read non-words composed of root and suffix (morphologically complex non-words) faster and more accurately than simple non-words (Burani et al., 2008; see Figure 9.1). The results confirmed

a

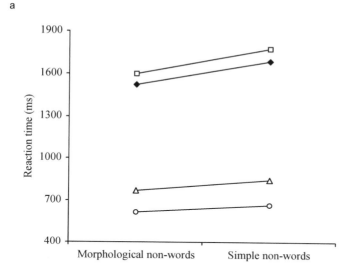

b

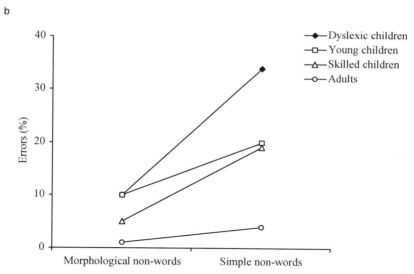

Figure 9.1 Mean reaction times (a) and errors (b) for the reading of morphological
and simple non-words by reader group. (Figures derived from data in
Burani et al., 2008).

previous findings for skilled readers (Burani et al., 2002) and indicated that
dyslexic readers are also sensitive to lexical elements (morphemic constituents) in non-word reading aloud.

According to current theories of reading, real words are processed in a
holistic fashion by directly accessing their representations in the lexicon
(Coltheart et al., 2001) or via stronger connections of the global procedure

(Ans et al., 1998). Consequently, morphemic constituents should not affect the performance of skilled readers, at least not in the case of high-frequency words. However, previous data indicate that whole-word processing may be challenging for Italian dyslexic children, and thus it could be hypothesized that the presence of morphemic constituents in words will be more beneficial for dyslexic readers than for skilled readers.

Burani et al. (2008) assessed the effect of morphemic constituents in reading aloud words in a second experiment using the same participant groups. They employed two sets of words (derived vs. simple). Derived words contained a root and a derivational suffix (e.g., *cass-iere* [cashier]). Simple words could not be parsed as root + derivational suffix (e.g., *cammello*, [camel]). The words were 7–10 letters long, of medium-to-low frequency and the roots and suffixes of the derived words were all frequent. The two word sets were matched on initial phoneme, word frequency, familiarity, length, bigram frequency, N-size and orthographic complexity.

The results showed that morphological structure did not affect word reading of proficient young and adult readers but it was advantageous for both dyslexic and younger reading-skill-matched children (Burani et al., 2008; see Figure 9.2). Overall, these results illustrate that in the absence of available lexical representations, proficient readers took advantage of morphological structure in reading aloud non-words but not in reading words that can be processed holistically, so morphemic parsing is neither necessary nor advantageous. For the unskilled readers, on the other hand, the presence of morphemic constituents proved beneficial for both non-word and real word reading. For dyslexic and younger readers, morpheme-based reading can be efficient for processing words that may not yet be in their orthographic lexicon, or may be too long to be processed as a whole. It is noteworthy that, even though dyslexic and younger readers may have not yet fully mastered whole-word processing, they can rely on smaller than whole-word lexical units—that is, morphemes—to enhance their reading performance.

This is in line with results obtained from languages with deeper orthographies. For both English and Danish, it has been found that only younger readers and dyslexic readers show faster reading times for derived words than for monomorphemic words, whereas reading speed did not differ between the word types for older skilled readers (Carlisle & Stone, 2005; Elbro & Arnbak, 1996). In conclusion, Italian dyslexic readers' reading can be based on grain size units larger than single letters, contrary to assumptions of reliance on small grain size units for readers of transparent orthographies (Ziegler & Goswami, 2005). Similarly, for low-frequency words, especially longer ones that may require serial processing because of their length or their absence from the lexicon, the results demonstrate that the presence of morphemes may facilitate reading for dyslexic readers.

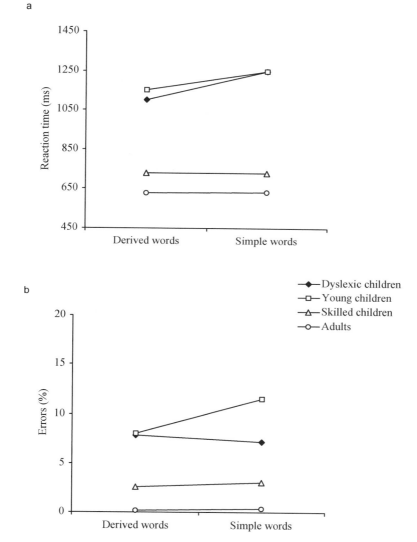

Figure 9.2 Mean reaction times (a) and errors (b) for the reading of derived and simple words by reader group. (Figures derived from data in Burani et al., 2008).

Group differences in effect size: A role for global differences in performance

So far we have focused on the presence of lexical effects, such as lexicality and frequency, in children with or without reading deficits. However, an interesting question concerns the *size* of these effects. In nearly all cited experiments, differences between critical conditions (e.g., high- and low-frequency words) tend to be greater in dyslexic readers than in proficient readers. This is not a new finding. Similar results have been reported for lexicality, length and N-size in a study comparing English and German dyslexic readers (Ziegler et al., 2003). How can these differences in effect size be interpreted?

It is well known that individuals with a generally slower performance tend to produce larger effects, independent of the experimental manipulation (referred to as the over-additivity effect; Faust, Balota, Spieler, & Ferraro, 1999). Consequently, differences in the size of effects between two groups that vary for general processing capacity (such as dyslexic and skilled readers) cannot be directly interpreted as genuine effects. Rather, it has been proposed that such differences may be the result of some combination of (1) a specific effect due to the experimental manipulation and (2) underlying general differences in cognitive speed (Faust et al. 1999). Standard analyses fail to distinguish between these two influences. However, in recent years, various approaches have been proposed to deal with the over-additivity effect (for a discussion see De Brauwer, Verguts, & Fias, 2006). Faust et al. (1999) proposed a model that makes explicit predictions about the global components of individual variation in information processing (the rate-and-amount model, RAM) and offers methods for disentangling the role of global and specific factors. Note that RAM applies only to open scale measures (such as time) and not to closed scale measures (such as accuracy). Therefore, only reaction times may be subject to the data transformations described. Provided that the experimental data fit these predictions, data transformations (such as regression transformations or z-scores) can be used that allow evaluation of the influence of specific task difficulty over and above the effect of the global factor. If an interaction with the group factor (significant in the raw RT data analyses) vanishes when tested with transformed data, this indicates that the increase in size can be explained in terms of over-additivity (i.e., due to global difference in performance between the two groups). Alternatively, if the interaction remains significant, it points to the presence of a specific effect.

Zoccolotti et al. (2008) set out to test the predictions of RAM explicitly in a study on the naming of pictures, words and non-words. One global factor consistently predicted the most individual variation in naming words and non-words, but not pictures. Based on these findings, they tentatively proposed that the global factor contributing to developmental dyslexia indicates slowness in the pre-lexical graphemic analysis of the orthographic input. As in previous experiments, Italian dyslexic readers showed greater lexicality and length effects than did skilled readers in terms of raw reaction times. However, when the z-score transformation was applied to the data, the greater lexicality effect in dyslexic readers vanished, but the greater length effect persisted.

In some of the experiments reviewed above, we have used similar data transformations and obtained quite consistent results. When the effect of the global factor was controlled for, the interaction of the group factor with lexicality and with frequency (present in the raw data) vanished, indicating an over-additivity effect (Di Filippo et al., 2006; Paizi et al., 2007). By contrast, the interactions with the length factor remained significant, pointing to a specific role for this factor in the dyslexic deficit (Di Filippo et al., 2006; Paizi et al., 2007). Overall, these results indicate that the large frequency and lexicality effects present in raw reaction times are most parsimoniously interpreted as being due to over-additivity—that is, global differences in performance between dyslexic and proficient readers. Dyslexic readers' reading performance can be best explained in terms of both a global factor affecting the processing of orthographic material and a specific influence of stimulus length.

Conclusions

The effects of lexicality, word frequency, contextual rules for low-frequency words and morpho-lexical effects on reading for both low-frequency words and non-words demonstrate that Italian dyslexic readers do not exclusively employ a non-lexical reading procedure. Lexical reading is available to them in the same way that it is to young and adult proficient readers. Overall, the evidence regarding lexical effects rules out the possibility of an impairment that selectively affects lexical processing.

It should be noted that, even though Italian dyslexic and typically developing readers are affected similarly by lexical variables in reading, their performance is not identical. All the studies reviewed here demonstrate that dyslexic readers are significantly slower and less accurate than skilled young readers and are, where tested, specifically sensitive to length effects (as also assessed by analyses based on RAM). Yet there were also lexical effects that strongly suggest the presence of lexical processing. The standard dual-route theory does not provide a sufficient explanation for the data on Italian dyslexic readers, especially the parallel existence of both lexical and non-lexical effects in reading aloud and lexical decision. Connectionist dual-route models may provide more compatible predictions.

A recent connectionist network, the CDP+ model (Perry, Ziegler, & Zorzi, 2007), accounts for a series of benchmark effects, including serial effects that have been a challenge for connectionist networks of reading aloud. This model combines the lexical route of DRC with a graphemic buffer that serializes input, resulting in length effects (Perry et al., 2007). The predictions of the CDP+ model account for the effects of lexicality, word frequency and length in reading aloud. Note that the current version of the model does not perform lexical decision, but it is within its capacities as CDP+ includes the lexical route of the DRC model up to the phonological lexicon. The main limitation of both the DRC and the CDP+ models with respect to data from Italian is that they simulate reading of monosyllabic words in English, an opaque orthography.

As opposed to the DRC and CDP+ models, the ACV98 is a connectionist dual-route network for polysyllabic word reading that provides specific predictions for the performance of proficient and dyslexic readers in both reading aloud and visual word recognition (Ans et al., 1998). This model could offer a better account for the data reported here. The ACV98 accounts for the findings observed in our studies and others. These are the advantage of words over non-words in both reading aloud and lexical decision, word frequency effects and the length × frequency interaction, with the effect of length being stronger on low-frequency word reading. The model predicts more pronounced length effects in reading aloud by dyslexic readers than by controls, and most importantly the effect of length in lexical decision only for dyslexic and not skilled readers attributed to reduced visual–attentional span (Ans et al., 1998). A deficit at a visual–attentional level, as proposed by the ACV98 model and reported in the literature for French dyslexic readers (Bosse et al., 2007; Juphard et al., 2004), is compatible with the pattern of results discussed here. However, the visual–attentional components of processing are not addressed here and remain an issue for future research.

Notes

1 See Figure 10.1b in this volume.
2 The frequency with which combinations of letter pairs appear in a language.

Acknowledgements

Cristina Burani, Despina Paizi and Pierluigi Zoccolotti are members of the Marie Curie Research Training Network: Language and Brain (RTN: LAB, http://www.hull.ac.uk/RTN–LAB/) funded by the European Commission (MRTN–CT–2004–512141) as part of its Sixth Framework.

References

Ans, B., Carbonnel, S., & Valdois, S. (1998). A connectionist multiple-trace memory model for polysyllabic word reading. *Psychological Review, 105*, 678–723.

Barca, L., Burani, C., & Arduino, L. S. (2002). Word naming times and psycholinguistic norms for Italian nouns. *Behavior Research Methods, Instruments and Computers, 34*, 424–434.

Barca, L., Burani, C., Di Filippo, G., & Zoccolotti, P. (2006). Italian developmental dyslexic and proficient readers: Where are the differences? *Brain and Language, 98*, 347–351.

Barca, L., Ellis, A. W., & Burani, C. (2007). Context-sensitive rules and word naming in Italian children. *Reading and Writing, 20*, 495–509.

Bates, E., Burani, C., D'Amico, S., & Barca, L. (2001). Word reading and picture naming in Italian. *Memory and Cognition, 29*, 986–999.

Bosse, M.-L., Tainturier, M. J., & Valdois, S. (2007). Developmental dyslexia: The visual attention span deficit hypothesis. *Cognition, 104*, 198–230.

Burani, C., Arduino, L. S., & Barca, L. (2007). Frequency, not age of acquisition affects Italian word naming. *European Journal of Cognitive Psychology, 19*, 828–866.

Burani, C., Barca, L., & Ellis, A. W. (2006). Orthographic complexity and word naming in Italian: Some words are more transparent than others. *Psychonomic Bulletin and Review, 13*, 346–352.

Burani, C., & Laudanna, A. (2003). Morpheme-based lexical reading: Evidence from pseudoword naming. In E. Assink & D. Sandra (Eds.), *Reading complex words: Cross language studies* (pp. 241–264). Dordrecht, The Netherlands: Kluwer.

Burani, C., Marcolini, S., De Luca, M., & Zoccolotti, P. (2008). Morpheme-based reading aloud: Evidence from dyslexic and skilled Italian readers. *Cognition, 108*, 243–262.

Burani, C., Marcolini, S., & Stella, G. (2002). How early does morpho-lexical reading develop in readers of a shallow orthography? *Brain and Language, 81*, 568–586.

Carlisle, J. F., & Stone, C. A. (2005). Exploring the role of morphemes in word reading. *Reading Research Quarterly, 40*, 428–449.

Castles, A., & Coltheart, M. (1993). Varieties of developmental dyslexia. *Cognition, 47*, 149–180.

Colombo, L., Pasini, M., & Balota, D. A. (2006). Dissociating the influence of familiarity and meaningfulness from word frequency in naming and lexical decision performance. *Memory and Cognition, 34*, 1312–1324.

Coltheart, M., Davelaar, E., Jonasson, J. T., & Besner, D. (1977). Access to the internal lexicon. In S. Dornic (Ed.), *Attention and performance VI* (pp. 535–555). Hillsdale, NJ: Lawrence Erlbaum Associates, Inc.

Coltheart, M., Masterson, J., Byng, S., Prior, M., & Riddoch, J. (1983). Surface dyslexia. *Quarterly Journal of Experimental Psychology, 35A*, 469–495.

Coltheart, M., Rastle, K., Perry, C., Langdon, R., & Ziegler, J. C. (2001). DRC: A dual route cascaded model of visual word recognition and reading aloud. *Psychological Review, 108*, 204–256.

Cornoldi, C., Colpo, G., & Gruppo, M. T. (1981). *Prove di lettura MT. Guida all'uso* [The MT reading tests. Users' guide]. Florence, Italy: Organizzazioni Speciali.

De Brauwer, J. D., Verguts, T., & Fias, W. (2006). The representation of multiplication facts: Developmental changes in the problem size, five and tie effects. *Journal of Experimental Child Psychology, 94*, 43–56.

De Luca, M., Borrelli, M., Judica, A., Spinelli, D., & Zoccolotti, P. (2002). Reading words and pseudowords: An eye movement study of developmental dyslexia. *Brain and Language, 80*, 617–626.

De Luca, M., Di Pace, E., Judica, A., Spinelli, D., & Zoccolotti, P. (1999). Eye movement patterns in linguistic and non-linguistic tasks in developmental surface dyslexia. *Neuropsychologia, 37*, 1407–1420.

Di Filippo, G., De Luca, M., Judica, A., Spinelli, D., & Zoccolotti, P. (2006). Lexicality and stimulus length effects in Italian dyslexics: Role of the over-additivity effect. *Child Neuropsychology, 12*, 141–149.

Elbro, C., & Arnbak, E. (1996). The role of morpheme recognition and morphological awareness in dyslexia. *Annals of Dyslexia, 46*, 209–240.

Faust, M. E., Balota, D. A., Spieler, D. H., & Ferraro, F. R. (1999). Individual differences in information-processing rate amount: Implications for group differences in response latency. *Psychological Bulletin, 125*, 777–799.

Ferrand, L. (2000). Reading aloud polysyllabic words and non-words: The syllabic length effect re-examined. *Psychonomic Bulletin and Review, 7*, 142–148.

Judica, A., De Luca, M., Spinelli, D., & Zoccolotti, P. (2002). Training of developmental surface dyslexia improves reading performance and shortens eye fixation duration in reading. *Neuropsychological Rehabilitation, 12*, 177–197.

Juphard, A., Carbonnel, S., & Valdois, S. (2004). Length effect in reading and lexical decision: Evidence from skilled readers and a developmental dyslexic participant. *Brain and Cognition, 55*, 332–340.

Martens, V. E. G., & de Jong, P. F. (2006). The effect of word length on lexical decision in dyslexic and normal reading children. *Brain and Language, 98*, 140–149.

Pagliuca, G., Arduino, L., Barca, L., & Burani, C. (2008). Fully transparent orthography, yet lexical reading aloud: The lexicality effect in Italian. *Language and Cognitive Processes, 23*, 422–433.

Paizi, D., De Luca, M., Zoccolotti, P., & Burani, C. (2007). Lexicality and frequency effects in Italian developmental dyslexia. In *Proceedings of the European Cognitive Science Conference 2007* (p. 945). Mahwah, NJ: Lawrence Erlbaum Associates, Inc.

Paulesu, E. (2006). On the advantage of "shallow" orthographies: Number and grain size of the orthographic units or consistency per se? *Developmental Science, 9*, 443–444.

Paulesu, E., McCrory, E., Fazio, F., Menoncello, L., Brunswick, N., Cappa, S. F., et al. (2000). A cultural effect on brain function. *Nature Neuroscience, 3*, 91–96.

Perry, C., Ziegler, J. C., & Zorzi, M. (2007). Nested incremental modeling in the development of computational theories: The CDP+ model of reading aloud. *Psychological Review, 2*, 273–315.

Pruneti, C. A. (1985). Normative data on the Raven's Coloured Progressive Matrices test from a sample of Italian children. *Bulletin of Applied Psychology, 176*, 27–35.

Raven, J., Raven, J. C., & Court, J. H. (2003). *Manual for Raven's Progressive Matrices and Vocabulary Scales. Section 1: General overview*. San Antonio, TX: Harcourt Assessment.

Spinelli, D., De Luca, M., Di Filippo, G., Mancini, M., Martelli, M., & Zoccolotti, P. (2005). Length effect in word naming latencies: Role of reading experience and reading deficit. *Developmental Neuropsychology, 27*, 217–235.

Tabossi, P., & Laghi, L. (1992). Semantic priming in the pronunciation of words in two writing systems: Italian and English. *Memory and Cognition, 20*, 303–313.

Weekes, B. S. (1997). Differential effects of number of letters on word and nonword naming latency. *Quarterly Journal of Experimental Psychology, 50A*, 439–456.

Wimmer, H. (1993). Characteristics of developmental dyslexia in a regular writing system. *Reading and Writing, 8*, 171–188.

Ziegler, J. C., & Goswami, U. (2005). Reading acquisition, developmental dyslexia and skilled reading across languages: A psycholinguistic grain size theory. *Psychological Bulletin, 131*, 3–29.

Ziegler, J. C., Perry, C., Ma-Wyatt, A., Ladner, D., & Schulte-Korne, G. (2003). Developmental dyslexia in different languages: Language-specific or universal? *Journal of Experimental Child Psychology, 86*, 169–193.

Zoccolotti, P., De Luca, M., Di Pace, E., Gasperini, F., Judica, A., & Spinelli, D. (2005). Word length effect in early reading and in developmental dyslexia. *Brain and Language, 93*, 369–373.

Zoccolotti, P., De Luca, M., Di Pace, E., Judica, A., Orlandi, M., & Spinelli, D. (1999). Markers of developmental surface dyslexia in a language (Italian) with high grapheme–phoneme correspondence. *Applied Psycholinguistics, 20*, 191–216.

Zoccolotti, P., De Luca, M., Judica, A., & Spinelli, D. (2008). Isolating global and specific factors in developmental dyslexia: A study based on the rate and amount model (RAM). *Experimental Brain Research, 186*, 551–560.

10 Dyslexia in Chinese: Implications for connectionist models of reading

I-Fan Su, Kathrin Klingebiel and Brendan S. Weekes

Introduction

A great deal of research has investigated reading processes in languages with alphabetic scripts. Indeed, most theoretical models of oral reading, which can be divided into symbolic (e.g., Coltheart, Curtis, Atkins, & Haller, 1993) and sub-symbolic (e.g., Harm & Seidenberg, 1999; Plaut, McClelland, Seidenberg, & Patterson, 1996; Seidenberg & McClelland, 1989; Van Orden, Pennington, & Stone, 1990) models, have been developed on the basis of studies in English including disorders of reading, such as dyslexia. In our view, data from studies of developmental and acquired dyslexia in Chinese pose a challenge to the generalizability of existing models of oral reading.

In this chapter we examine the extent and nature of this challenge by (1) identifying critical differences between reading in Chinese and reading in alphabetic scripts; (2) reviewing cases of acquired and developmental dyslexia in Chinese; and (3) examining the extent to which existing computational models of reading can account for the reading difficulties observed in case studies of dyslexia in Chinese to date. We focus on a lexical constituency (LC) model developed by Perfetti, Liu and Tan (2005) to ask whether a common computational architecture can be applied universally to reading in alphabetic and non-alphabetic scripts. Our conclusion is that this may not be viable.

To begin our review, we give an introduction to the Chinese language and highlight the differences and similarities to alphabetic languages relevant to models of oral reading. Of special interest is the LC model which is argued to be a universal framework for word reading across writing systems. The computational architecture of the LC model is arguably capable of accommodating alphabetic and non-alphabetic writing systems, as well as explaining how children can learn to read Chinese. We then describe disorders of reading and give a review of cases of acquired and developmental dyslexia in Chinese. Next, we examine whether the LC model predicts such cases and assess whether it accommodates reported reading problems in Chinese. Finally, suggestions for future research are considered.

Differences between alphabetic and non-alphabetic scripts

Chinese orthography differs from alphabetic scripts like English or German in terms of the nature of orthography–phonology correspondences. Alphabetic scripts use a finite number of printed letters (symbols) or letter clusters to produce an infinite number of words. With this finite number of symbols (e.g., English alphabet: 26 symbols, German: 30 symbols, Czech: 41 symbols), a literate individual is able to spell any word. Although complicated by irregularities in the relationships between symbols and sounds, it is usually possible to read any word by mapping its orthography to phonology.

In contrast, the Chinese and Japanese languages use non-alphabetic scripts. These were traditionally defined as logographic, since the basic unit of writing is associated with a unit of meaning (the morpheme) in the spoken language. Chinese script is represented by a vast number of visually complex characters (see Table 10.1).

Table 10.1 Description of Chinese writing

	Definition	*Examples*		
Alphabetic script	A writing system where the basic unit is based on letters (graphemes). Each letter is essentially a phoneme	Letters → Words 'T' 'r' 'e' 'e' → *tree* 'W' 'i' 'n' 'd' → *wind*		
Morpheme	Smallest meaningful unit of a language	*Run* in English (part of *running* and *runner*) Radicals in Chinese (see further below in table)		
Morphographic script (also referred to as logographic or morphosyllabic script)	A writing system whereby the smallest pronounceable unit is a character (grapheme) and represents a morpheme as well as a syllable	本 /běn/ *root*	上 /shàng/ *up*	下 /xià/ *down*
Pictograph	Characters that were derived through pictures of the object corresponding to the meaning	Oracle bone inscription (1200–1045 BC) ㅂ 食	Modern character (420 AD onwards) 口 魚	/kǒu/ *mouth* /yú/ *fish*
Strokes	Lines that characters are made up of. A cluster of combined strokes form stroke-patterns and act as a constituent unit	文 文 文 文 1 2 3 4		

Radicals	Sub-units of the character	氵 water	艹 plant	扌 hand
Tones in Mandarin	First tone: /mā/, 妈 [*mother*] Second tone: /má/, 麻 [*flax*] Third tone: /mǎ/, 马 [*horse*] Fourth tone: /mà/, 骂 [*curse*]	Articulation of tones: 1st 2nd 3rd 4th		
Semantic radical	The semantic radical give clues to the meaning of a character	Semantic radical 土 /tǔ/ *earth*	Radical 也 /yě/ *also*	Character 地 /dì/ *earth*
Phonetic radical	The phonetic radical gives clues to the pronunciation of a character	Phonetic radical 忝 /tiān/ *disgrace*	Radical 氵 *water*	Character 添 /tiān/ *add*
Semantic-phonetic compound characters	Includes a semantic and phonetic radical	Phonetic radical 风 /fēng/ *wind*	Semantic radical 木 /mù/ *tree*	Compound-character 枫 /fēng/ *maple*

Chinese is a morphosyllabic writing system where the basic unit, the character, represents a morpheme as well as a syllable (Shu, Meng, Chen, Luan, & Cao, 2005a). The great majority of characters represent a morpheme in Chinese, making the script morphographic; this means that the smallest pronounceable unit that is associated with meaning is a character. This contrasts with the letters in an alphabet that do not represent meaning. Hence Chinese orthography is considered morphosyllabic given that characters can be segmented using orthographic, morphological and syllabic information (Leong & Tamaoka, 1998; Shu & Anderson, 1997).

Chinese script uses a large number of characters to represent an individual word or parts of words (morphemes/syllables). Each character is built up of simple strokes (24 in total), which can be combined to form a component, also known as a radical (541 in total). The Chinese writing system contains sub-lexical components, generally referred to as semantic radicals, that are associated with meaning, and phonetic radicals that are associated with the sound of the character (Ho & Bryant, 1997). The phonetic radical component of a character contains information about the actual pronunciation of the character or analogy cues in terms of similar-sounding characters. DeFrancis (1989) suggested that pictographs have been estimated at less than 1 per cent of the character lexicon, and Shu and Wu (2006) and Zhu (1988) have shown that between 80 and 90 per cent of all modern characters are phonetic compounds. Shu, Chen, Anderson, Wu, and Xuan (2003) analysed characters taught in elementary-school textbooks prepared by the Ministry of Education in the People's Republic of China and found that approximately 72 per cent of the characters children learn in primary school are semantic–phonetic compounds. These compounds contain two or more distinct radicals that are configured into certain positions within the character (semantic and phonetic radical), which can be organized into a left–right structure, a top–bottom structure or circular/semicircular structure (Zhu, 1988). Furthermore, within the structure of characters, the individual radicals have fixed or legal positions (left, right, top or bottom), and violation of position creates an illegal character (Taft, 2006; Taft & Zhu, 1997; Taft, Zhu, & Peng, 1999b).

The phonological structure of a Chinese syllable differs from the English syllable structure. Syllables in languages using an alphabet tend to have consonant clusters (sequences of consonants) in the onset or the rime position of the syllable. However, phonetic information in Chinese is not encoded sub-syllabically and does not contain consonant clusters. Rather, Chinese has 22 onsets and 37 rimes (Li & Thompson, 1981). In total, there are only 420 syllables but, in addition, syllabic tones are used to differentiate between the meaning of syllables (this duplicates the number of syllables to 1200). According to Li and Kang (1993) there are about 1300 phonetics among the 5631 compound characters. Tones can be classified as having a level contour (first tone, e.g., ē), rising (second tone, e.g., é), first falling then rising (third tone, e.g., ě) or falling (fourth tone, e.g., è), and a high, middle and low register. The registers are typical in both Mandarin and Cantonese, where these combinations result in nine possible tones.

According to the *Xiandai Hanyu Pinlu Cidian* [Modern Chinese Frequency Dictionary] (Beijing Language Institute,1986), in modern-day usage there are 4574 characters, which make up the 1,800,000 character Chinese corpus. However, as there are only about 420 syllables (disregarding tone), 11 characters on average share one pronunciation. Thus, it is important to realize that the Chinese script has many heterographic homophones in addition to visually similar characters (there are also visually similar characters that are not homophonous). This makes Chinese very different from English which contains few words that are visually similar but which have a different pronunciation (e.g., *your/hour*) and even fewer heterographic homophones (e.g., *you/ewe*; *I/eye*).

As mentioned earlier, phonetic radicals can give clues to the pronunciation of a character. According to Zhu (1988) the predictive accuracy of the pronunciation of a compound from its phonetic radical is approximately 40 per cent (see also Yin, 1991). These characters have been called 'regular characters'. A regular character has the same pronunciation as its phonetic radical when it functions as a simple character—for example, 清 /qīng/ with the phonetic 青 /qīng/. In contrast, irregular characters are those that are pronounced completely differently from the radical, meaning that no component has the same pronunciation as the whole character—for example, 猜

/cāi/. Shu et al. (2005a) further proposed a classification of semi-regularity, where the phonetic radical provides only partial information about the pronunciation of the whole character—for example, 精 /jīng/ and its phonetic 青 /qīng/.

Our discussion so far makes it clear that there is a considerable amount of phonological information available in what is primarily seen as a morphemic/ logographic script. However, further consideration of the mix of phonological and semantic information available suggests that oral reading is primarily a lexical event. A lexical event here refers to the fact that pre-existing knowledge of word form and meaning is necessary to name the character aloud. There are two additional unique characteristics of Chinese orthography:

1   Phonetic radicals may have different meanings depending on their position. For example, the phonetic radical 其 /qí/ is on the right in the character 棋 /qí/ [*chess*], but it is on the left in the character 期 /qí/ [*a period of time*].
2   Character components can act as both the phonetic radical and the semantic radical for different words. For example, the character 木 /mù/ [*wood*] is a semantic radical in over 1500 Chinese characters, including 棋 /qí/ (see above). However, it is also a phonetic component in the character 沐 /mù/ [*to wash*] (Weekes, 2006).

This demonstrates that it is often difficult to know which component in a compound is the phonetic or the semantic component. To read a character aloud correctly, the reader must know the pronunciation of the character as a whole. Some homophonic characters share one pronunciation without being semantically related to each other. For example, the characters 呈, 成, 丞, 乘, 盛 are all pronounced 'chéng'. In our view, such features of the script make correct oral reading in Chinese primarily a lexical event, as well as a phonological process. This is because the Chinese writing system does not reflect the segmental structure that is fundamental to alphabetic scripts (Leong & Tamaoka, 1998). Therefore, prior knowledge of the character's word form and meaning are needed to select the correct pronunciation of the character.

This introduction has described many elements of Chinese that are qualitatively different from alphabetic scripts relevant to developing reading models. The nature of orthography–phonology correspondences differs in terms of the basic units, which are represented as radicals; these radicals can exist as semantic or phonetic radicals (or as stand-alone characters), and phonetic information is not encoded sub-syllabically as a sequence of consonant clusters. As all theorists agree that a model of reading needs to be able to explain normal oral reading as well as data from reading disorders such as developmental and acquired dyslexia, we now present these data from Chinese speakers and give a brief overview of dyslexia in Chinese.

Dyslexia in Chinese

There are two types of dyslexia: *acquired*, where people who once were able to read fluently lose this ability due to brain damage, and *developmental*, where children struggle to learn to read. Developmental dyslexia is a specific impairment of reading ability that cannot be explained by any kind of deficit to general intelligence, learning opportunity, general motivation or sensory acuity (World Health Organization, 1993). The British Dyslexia Association (BDA) describes dyslexia in greater detail. They elaborate upon the specific learning difficulty that affects the development of literacy and language-related skills throughout life. It is characterized by difficulties with phonological processing, rapid naming, working memory, processing speed and the automatic development of skills that may not match up to an individual's other cognitive abilities (British Dyslexia Association, 2007). Similarly, the International Dyslexia Association (IDA) and Lyon, Shaywitz, and Shaywitz (2003) agree that difficulties result from a deficit in phonological aspects of language that is often unrelated to other cognitive abilities. However, their definition argues for a neurological basis of dyslexia that is further characterized by difficulties with accurate and/or fluent word recognition and by poor spelling and decoding abilities (International Dyslexia Association, 2002; Lyon et al., 2003). Dyslexia is relatively common: between 5 and 10 per cent of school-age children have exceptional difficulty learning to read, despite conventional instruction and average intelligence. Stevenson et al. (1982) demonstrated that the prevalence of dyslexia is comparable among American, Japanese and Chinese children, and Zhang, Zhang, Yin, Zhou, and Chang (1996) identified between 4.5 and 8 per cent of children in Mainland China as having dyslexia. Developmental dyslexia has also been observed across languages, including Dutch, French, Italian, Japanese and Spanish (see Weekes, 2005, for a review), although the pattern of impairment depends on features of the language and script.

Cognitive neuropsychologists differentiate between three types of dyslexia: deep, surface and phonological dyslexia. Surface dyslexia in alphabetic languages refers to a selective impairment to reading aloud irregularly spelled words, particularly if items are low in word frequency (e.g., *indict*). When an exception word is misread, oral reading is characterized by regularization errors (e.g., *pint* is pronounced as though it rhymed with *mint*). In pure cases this impairment is accompanied by preserved reading of regularly spelled words and non-words (e.g., *zint*) (Weekes, Yin, Su, & Chen, 2006). Table 10.2 summarizes different types of dyslexia observed in Chinese. In Chinese, surface dyslexia is characterized by regularity effects in reading regular characters better than irregular characters, and by phonetic-related errors —for example, reading 暗 /àn/ [*dark*] as 音 /yīn/ [*music*] (note that the two characters share a common phonetic radical; Shu et al., 2005a).

A different pattern of reading impairment is phonological dyslexia, which refers to relatively impaired reading of non-words together with a preserved

Table 10.2 Types of dyslexia in Chinese

Dyslexia type	Manifestation
Dyslexia	Specific reading deficit with difficulties in phonological, orthographic and morphological processing, rapid naming, working memory and processing speed.
Developmental dyslexia	Children who struggle with learning to read that cannot be explained by any kind of deficit to general intelligence, learning opportunity, general motivation or sensory acuity.
Acquired dyslexia	Adults who once were able to read fluently lose this ability as a result of brain injury or disease.
Phonological dyslexia	Impaired reading of non-words together with preserved ability to read aloud irregular and regular words. However, this cannot be observed in Chinese (as there is no orthographic representation of phonemes). Instead, tonal dyslexia has been reported where an incorrect tone is assigned to a syllable such as reading 马 /mǎ/ (third tone) meaning *horse* as /mà/ (fourth tone).
Surface dyslexia	Selective impairment to reading aloud irregularly spelled words, especially when they are low in frequency, and phonetic related errors such as reading 暗 /àn/ [*dark*] as 音 /yīn/ [*music*] as they both share the same radical.
Deep dyslexia	Individuals produce semantic and phonological reading errors, such as reading 煎 /jiān/ [*fry*] as 炖 /dùn/ [*braise*], and visual errors such as reading 赴 /fù/ [*go*] as 处 /chù/ [*place*]. They find abstract words especially difficult to read.

ability to read aloud regular and irregular words. The features of phonological dyslexia are impaired decoding of letter-strings into constituent phonemes and difficulty with assigning phonemes to graphemes and with blending sequences of phonemes into an integrated pronunciation. Chinese contains no orthographic representations of phonemes, only phonetic radicals and tones: therefore, strictly speaking, phonological dyslexia cannot be observed in Chinese speakers. However, one type of acquired phonological dyslexia in Chinese is known as 'tonal dyslexia' (Luo & Weekes, 2004). This refers to the assignment of an incorrect tone to a syllable when reading a character aloud. As tone is a sub-syllabic feature of the Chinese language, this form of acquired dyslexia could be considered to be a type of phonological dyslexia. However, this is not equivalent to the pattern of impaired oral reading of non-words that defines phonological dyslexia in languages with alphabetic scripts.

Deep dyslexia is a severe form of phonological dyslexia (even though some researchers might argue that it is a separate disorder) whereby individuals produce semantic reading errors (e.g., *arm* read as *finger*); visual errors (e.g., *bus* read as *brush*); and morphological errors (e.g., *run* read as *running*). Individuals with deep dyslexia also read concrete (highly imageable) words (e.g., *tulip*) better than abstract words (e.g., *idea*). Reading of non-words and function words (e.g., *and, or*) is also impossible, as in cases of phonological dyslexia. The difference between phonological dyslexia and deep dyslexia is subtle. Individuals with phonological dyslexia do not make semantic errors when reading aloud. In Chinese, semantic reading errors such as producing 煎 /jiān/ [*fry*] as 炖 /dùn/ [*braise*] are observed in adults with brain damage (Yin, 1991) and in children with reading problems (Shu et al., 2005a). However, deep dyslexia in alphabetic languages and in Chinese cannot be compared directly.

Only a few studies of developmental dyslexia exist in Chinese. Recent studies have explored the *causes* of dyslexia rather than analysing the error types of the developmental disorder itself. These studies concentrate on correlations between scores on cognitive tasks in children with reading difficulties. Research suggests that phonological awareness at the level of onset and rime is related to early Chinese reading (Ho & Bryant, 1997; McBride-Chang & Ho, 2000). Difficulties in developing lexical skills for irregular characters could be related to dyslexic children's deficit in phonological memory. Clinical observations by Lam and Cheung (1996) showed that about one-third of those having early language or phonological problems were later found to have reading and writing disabilities. Ho and Ma (1999) trained 8-year-old dyslexic children with phonological strategies and found that they could significantly improve their Chinese character reading performance. This suggests that phonological awareness is necessary for skilled reading in Chinese. Ziegler, Tan, Perry, and Montant (2000) confirmed this by showing phonological frequency effects in skilled character recognition: that is, characters with a high phonological frequency were processed faster than characters with a low phonological frequency. Also Zhu (1988) found that the regularity effect is significant for reading low-frequency Chinese characters only, suggesting that Chinese readers use the phonetic components for sound cues mainly in reading unfamiliar characters.

However, other researchers have argued that phonological awareness is not the only predictor of successful reading in Chinese. For example, Ho, Chan, Lee, Tsang and Luan (2004) repeated the study of Ho, Chan, Tsang, and Lee (2002) but using a larger sample size. They found that as well as a dominant phonological deficit, called a rapid naming deficit, orthographic deficits were a predicting factor. Skilled readers also outperformed poor readers on tasks assessing morphological awareness—that is, the ability to combine familiar units of meaning or morphemes to create new meanings (e.g., 'say *split* without the /p/ sound').

Shu et al. (2005a) described subtypes of developmental dyslexia in Chinese showing characteristics of developmental surface and developmental deep dyslexia. The following error types were classified while the children had to name a character and explain its meaning:

1   *Analogy errors*: child read 跌 /diē/ [*fall*] as 铁 /tiě/ [*iron*], explaining the meaning as 钢铁 /gāng tiě/ [*steel*].

2   *Homophone errors*: naming 驯 /xùn/ [*training animals*] as its phonetic 川 /chuān/, explaining its meaning as 穿 过 /chuān guò/ [*pass through*].

3   *Selection errors*: naming 萄 /táo/ as 葡 /pú/, as 葡 and 萄 form a high-frequency word in Chinese: 葡萄 /pú táo/ [*grape*].

4   *Semantic errors*: child named the target character as a semantically related character—for example, 喊 /hǎn/ [*shout*] as 嚷 /rǎng/ [*loudly*].

5   *Phonetic errors*: child named an irregular character after its phonetic—for example, 暗 /àn/ [*dark*] as 音 /yīn/ [*sound*] and then explaining it as 音 乐 /yīn yuè/ [*music*].

6   *Visual errors*: child confused a character with a visually similar character—for example, reading 赴 /fù/ [*go*] as 处 /chù/ [*place*] and explaining it as 到 处 /dào chù/ [*everywhere*].

Phonetic errors and analogy errors were combined as phonetic related errors.

One of Shu et al.'s (2005a) participants, *L*, demonstrated characteristics of surface dyslexia. He was able to use phonological information to pronounce a character, but he was poor at understanding its meaning. The other two participants, *J* and *Q*, showed characteristics of deep dyslexia. Both understood the meaning of characters that they named correctly, leading Shu et al. (2005) to argue that they were able to obtain character meaning but had some difficulty distinguishing the target from semantically related characters or other characters that form a compound word with the character. (For a review of developmental dyslexia in Chinese, see Klingebiel & Weekes, 2009.)

Several patterns of acquired dyslexia have been reported in Chinese (Law, 2004; Law & Or, 2001; Weekes & Chen, 1999; Yin & Butterworth, 1992). Yin and Butterworth (1992) reported aphasic Mandarin speakers who displayed patterns of impaired and preserved oral reading that resembled features of deep and surface dyslexia in other languages. For example, one group showed a tendency to produce semantic errors on reading tasks, and they produced more errors with low-imageability characters than with high-imageability characters when matched for word frequency. Some individuals, whom they termed deep dyslexic, produced semantic errors when reading aloud. For example, *ZSP*, a 36-year-old male, produced semantic errors such as reading 风 /fēng/ [*wind*] as 刮 /guā/ [*blow*]; visual errors, e.g., 木 /mù/ [*wood*] as 才 /cái/ [*just*]; and mixed-target with errors sharing a radical, e.g., reading 狗 /gǒu/ [*dog*] as 猪 /zhū/ [*pig*]. He also read nouns better than verbs (a grammatical class effect). Other dyslexic individuals produced 'regularization' errors—or, more precisely, Legitimate Alternative Reading of Component (LARC) errors—when reading irregular characters. A LARC error in Chinese is an incorrect pronunciation of an irregular character that is appropriate in other characters containing the same component. So, for example, if 秤 /chèng/ is read as /píng/, this is a LARC error because its component 平 is pronounced /píng/. Chinese surface dyslexic individuals also tend to mis-read homographic heterophones (characters that have more than one pronunciation) out of context, for example pronouncing the character 茄 as /jiā/ in 蕃茄 *tomato*, as reported in Law (2004). The character 茄 is a heterophone as it can be pronounced as /qié/ in 蕃茄 /fān qié/ [*tomato*] or /jiā/ in 雪茄 /xuě jiā/ [*cigar*], depending on the lexical context in which it appears. This pattern of reading errors suggests that characters are read without semantic support (Patterson & Hodges, 1992). However, Yin and Butterworth (1992) reported a positive association between semantic impairment and production of LARC errors, suggesting that lexical–semantic knowledge has an impact on the ability to read irregular characters in Chinese.

Weekes and Chen (1999) also reported a Chinese speaker with surface dyslexia. Following the results of Yin and Butterworth (1992), they formulated a hypothesis about their patient's reading based on reports of associations between surface dyslexia and lexical–semantic impairment in Chinese and other languages. Weekes and Chen (1999) reasoned that correct reading of irregular low-frequency abstract characters requires support from semantic memory, and LARC errors result from sudden loss of semantic support from the lexical–semantic pathway used to read in Chinese. This hypothesis was motivated by theoretical accounts of reading in English that assume that knowledge of word meaning—accessed via a lexical–semantic pathway—inhibits LARC errors produced when reading words that have unpredictable components (see, for example, Patterson & Hodges, 1992). Weekes and Chen (1999) found that semantic impairment was associated with poor reading of irregular characters, particularly if the characters were low in word imageability and frequency.

Another type of dyslexia reported in Chinese is tonal dyslexia. This describes the phenomenon of preserved oral reading of a character at the syllable level but incorrect assignment of tone for that syllable. Some individuals produce tonal errors in writing words even though segmental phonology is preserved in their responses (Law & Or, 2001). Others produce tonal errors in addition to errors at the level of the onset (the optional initial consonant or consonant cluster of the syllable) and rime (errors may occur at both levels). The results from these individuals suggest that sub-syllabic information is represented by components in the Chinese phonological output lexicon, since vowel and onset errors are observed, and that tonal information can be dissociated from the syllable level.

Models of oral reading in Chinese

One goal of cognitive neuropsychological studies of individuals with acquired and developmental dyslexia in Chinese has been the development of cognitive models that can be used in the assessment and rehabilitation of reading and writing impairments (Weekes et al., 2006). Although some models of reading in Chinese have been developed directly from studies of these individuals (e.g., Weekes, Chen, & Yin, 1997), other models are motivated by computational principles that can be implemented as connectionist models (Perfetti et al., 2005; see also Taft, 2006; Taft, Liu, & Zhu, 1999a; Zhou & Marslen-Wilson, 1999, 2000). Although cognitive neuropsychological and connectionist models make different assumptions about the cause of impairment in dyslexia, both types of model assume that selective damage to independent pathways linking orthography and phonology is possible, and that damage will lead to different patterns of acquired dyslexia (Friedman, 1996; Graham, Patterson, & Hodges, 1997, 2000; Houghton & Zorzi, 2003). An example of a cognitive neuropsychological reading model that has been widely accepted in alphabetic scripts (e.g., English and German) is the dual-route computational (DRC) model (Coltheart, Rastle, Perry, Langdon, & Ziegler, 2001, see Figure 10.1b); this model was developed and tested largely on the basis of data from studies of impaired oral reading (for connectionist models, see Harm & Seidenberg, 2004; Plaut et al., 1996). It should be noted that some regard the DRC model as a 'hybrid' model combining computational and neuropsychological approaches.

One question of interest is whether these widely accepted models explain oral reading in non-alphabetic scripts. For example, the logographic nature of characters makes it likely that lexical knowledge (orthographic or phonological) can be used to read characters aloud correctly. This is because Coltheart et al.'s (2001) non-lexical pathway (grapheme–phoneme rule system) is redundant for oral reading in Chinese since graphemes are orthographic representations of phonemes that are used in alphabetic scripts only (see Figure 10.1b). By this definition, grapheme representations may not exist in Chinese. Moreover, the logographic nature of Chinese characters makes it difficult to test non-word reading in an equivalent way in alphabetic and non-alphabetic scripts. Similarly, as the Plaut et al. (1996) model does not contain lexical representations, only sub-word components, it is not clear how their model would explain oral reading in Chinese given that sub-word components are not depicted in print. We note however that functional units such as the rime may be important for oral reading in both scripts.

Other models of reading in Chinese are limited in their capacity to explain how reading develops. Weekes et al. (1997) argued that normal oral reading in Chinese proceeds via two separate pathways: a lexical-semantic pathway that supports reading for meaning, and a non-semantic pathway that connects representations of orthography (i.e., strokes, radicals and characters) to their phonological representations including syllables, rimes and tones (see also Klingebiel & Weekes, 2009). The Weekes et al. framework for oral reading in Chinese is depicted in Figure 10.1a.

In our view, computational models advance traditional frameworks because they require a more precise set of parameters and constraints than those specified in cognitive neuropsychological models. For example, although different levels of units are assumed in Weekes et al.'s model in Figure 10.1a, not enough details are given. For instance, is the phonological representation of the morpheme 糖 /táng/ [*candy*] represented twice, once alone as /áng/ and

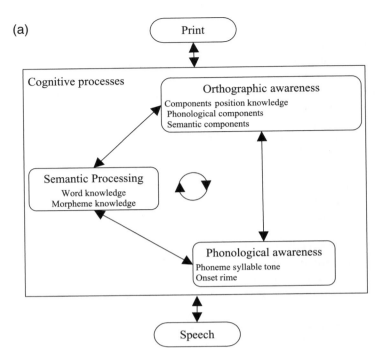

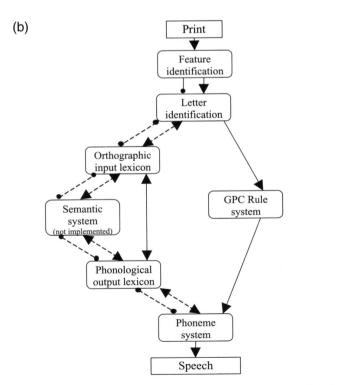

Figure 10.1 (a) Model of reading in Chinese (adapted from Klingebiel & Weekes, 2009); (b) the dual-route cascade model of reading (adapted from Coltheart et al., 2001).

once within the syllable /táng/? When reading 糖, are both /áng/ and /táng/ activated, and how is the correct representation eventually selected? These questions require a set of parameters to be specified for the reading researcher to understand how cognitive processes are used to read aloud in Chinese. Computational models, such as those developed by Coltheart et al. (2001) and by Seidenberg and colleagues, explain the development of literacy—instantiated in terms of learning mechanisms connecting input (orthography) with output (phonology)—in addition to impairments to reading and writing. As progress in understanding the cognitive processes used to read and write in Chinese is likely to come from models instantiating computational properties, we now turn to an evaluation of computational models of word identification and oral reading in Chinese.

Computational models proposed by Coltheart et al. (2001) and by Plaut et al. (1996) were not designed to explain oral reading in Chinese, and we have argued that there are potential problems extending these models to explain reading in Chinese. Perfetti et al. (2005), however, proposed a general computational framework for reading across writing systems called the lexical constituency (LC) model, and they described in detail an implementation of their model for oral reading in Chinese. This model is illustrated in Figure 10.2.

As in the framework shown in Figure 10.2, the LC model assumes two pathways from orthography to phonology. One pathway links orthography to phonology via semantics, comprising connections from orthography to semantics and connections from semantics to phonology (similar to the lexical-semantic pathway in Figure 10.1), the other links orthography to phonology directly (as in the non-semantic pathway in Figure 10.1). However,

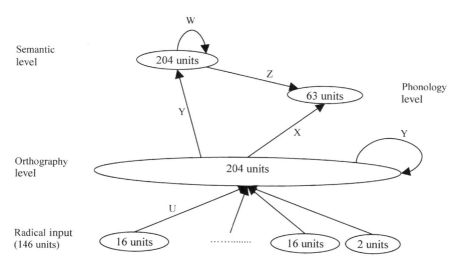

Figure 10.2 The lexical constituency (LC) model of reading in Chinese (from Perfetti et al., 2005). Letters U–Z correspond to the weights within and between separate levels.

unlike the frameworks in Figure 10.1, the LC model assumes a level of representation called radical units. These units map directly to an additional level of orthography representing characters. One reason for assuming that radicals are necessary to read in Chinese is that the script is not systematic enough to support a component approach to reading—unlike letters in an alphabet. Also, contact between radical units and semantic and phonological knowledge is necessarily mediated by character knowledge. Computational models of oral reading in English assume that sub-word knowledge is available in normal oral reading—whether it is symbolic (e.g., grapheme-to-phoneme correspondence rules) or sub-symbolic (e.g., orthographic units in parallel distributed processing models). However, Perfetti et al. (2005) argue that separate levels of representation in alphabetic scripts (a letter versus a word level) are redundant in Chinese due to the lack of component productivity.

According to the LC model, characters are decomposed into radical units to enter the input level during the process of reading aloud. At input, the LC model has 146 input units, with 144 units representing the radicals and the remaining two units representing the spatial relationship between the shared radical structure. The radical level is then connected to 204 character units at the orthography level. As a radical slot is activated, characters in the orthography level that possess this radical become activated until a threshold is reached (0.8 for all units). At the orthography level, the character units are locally represented, with inhibitory connections between them to reflect competing units at the input level. Once a character unit has reached threshold, activation passes along the weighted connection between orthography and phonology, and orthography and semantics. Unlike the representations at the orthography level, the phonology level is distributed. The syllable is coded by three units representing onset (23), vowel (34) and tone (5) across 63 units. Because this level is distributed, there are no within-level connections that compete. Similar to the orthography level, the semantic level is localized with 204 units that correspond to the specific meaning of each individual character. Perfetti and colleagues emphasize that the semantic level only represents meaning of the characters and not character components. Furthermore, the connections within the semantic level share a weight of 0.2 (fixed arbitrarily) to reflect the spread of activation to other characters that are related to its meaning. It is also possible to activate phonology via the semantic system. Once the character has activated the semantic level, the semantic units are then connected to the phonological units with a weight of 1 and other connections set to zero.

The LC model and impaired oral reading in Chinese

The question we pose here is whether the LC model can explain the impairments seen in developmental and acquired disorders of reading in Chinese. As the reader may have realized, the LC model is limited in its ability to explain the data from impaired oral reading. We will begin with cognitive neuropsychological data that challenge this model.

The LC model needs to explain why some individuals produce semantic reading errors and others produce LARC errors (Weekes & Chen, 1999; Yin & Butterworth, 1992, 1998) and mis-read homographic heterophones out of context (Law, 2004). Semantic, LARC and out-of-context errors are revealing because they suggest that oral reading in Chinese involves multiple levels of cognitive processing. Semantic errors show that knowledge about character meaning is activated, whereas LARC and out-of-context errors show that knowledge about the mappings between orthography and phonology in character components is activated during oral reading—albeit at a level that is insufficient to support correct oral reading in individuals with dyslexia. The LC model assumes that character recognition involves lexical identification at both semantic and phonological levels. Therefore, the model accommodates semantic errors as reading via meaning—that is, without access to the mappings between orthography and phonology. Conversely, LARC and out-of-context errors are evidence of oral reading via those mappings without support from the semantic system. By assuming two independent pathways, the model can also explain the phenomenon of *anomia without dyslexia.* Such patients have an impairment in the recall of spoken words but no impairment to word comprehension, the capacity to repeat words or oral reading as a consequence of reading via the non-semantic pathway (see Weekes et al., 1997).

Any model of oral reading in Chinese must also explain effects of tone on literacy. Tone awareness is one predictor of literacy for Chinese-speaking children (Siok & Fletcher, 2001) and is independent of syllabic knowledge and orthographic awareness. Chen, Chen, and Dell (2002) observed priming effects on adult reading for syllables but not for tone (and vice versa), suggesting that there may be independent representations for syllable and tone. The LC model has the potential to explain the features of tonal dyslexia, but currently it does not. The model assumes that phonology is a fully distributed representation that is implemented with the Chinese pinyin system instantiated as a set of phonological representations for onset, vowel and tone and represents Mandarin syllables for which 23 onsets, 34 vowels and 5 tones are sufficient. There are no within-level linkages in the phonological system. This means that lateral inhibition is not possible. This is in contrast to the representations for orthography (specifically radicals and characters) as well as presumed semantic representations at the level of meaning. There are also no local representations for whole words and no representations of rime-level units. The most striking feature of tonal dyslexia is that errors occur with onset and rime intact, suggesting that tone is dissociated from the syllable. At present the LC model can explain some aspects of tonal dyslexia as a consequence of damage to the tone layer of representation.

Nevertheless tonal dyslexia generates several unresolved questions. First, all tones are given equal status in the model, and no consideration is given to the weight assigned to each tone. Luo and Weekes (2004) found a tendency for their patient *ZW* to assign the fourth tone and proposed an economy principle to explain this effect: that is, if the tonal system is disrupted following brain damage, the Chinese speaker adopts the fourth tone as a default, since the fourth tone takes least time to produce in Chinese. The LC model has difficulty accounting for this observation since a model with phonological representations that are fully distributed should produce tonal errors with the same frequency. Second, although the LC model can explain some of the characteristics observed in individuals with tonal dyslexia, it cannot completely explain the desirability of a rime level of representation in the phonological system. The LC model assumes a distributed level of representation for onset and vowel in the phonological output system. This assumption is supported by data from Chinese dyslexic individuals who show selective impairment in the production of the onset relative to the tone and rime (Shu, Xiong, Han, Bi, & Bai, 2005b). However, Luo and Weekes (2004) reported evidence of whole rime substitution errors, suggesting that the rime is represented by components in the lexicon and assignment of tone with the syllable. Thus a rime-level representation independent of tone is needed (see also Law & Or, 2001).

The LC model also cannot explain data from cases of surface dyslexia. For example, Yin and Butterworth (1998) reported radical-by-radical reading, whereby character components including semantic and phonetic radicals were read instead of the name of the character. The critical result from radical-by-radical reading is that character components can be read aloud without contacting character knowledge. Since the model assumes that reading of radicals is mediated by access to characters, it cannot explain this phenomenon. One objection to our claim is that some radicals act alone as characters (i.e., they represent a morpheme) and hence have a legitimate pronunciation. However, individuals who have surface dyslexia produce LARC errors, showing that components can also be read aloud without contacting character knowledge. Taken together, the data from radical-by-radical reading and surface dyslexia show that access to phonological output from radical representations can bypass character representations containing the radical. This is assumed in cognitive neuropsychological frameworks as depicted in Figure 10.1 (see also Law, Yeung, Wong, & Chiu, 2005) but not in the LC model.

A lesion simulation of the LC model would refute our contention that the model cannot account for surface dyslexia (see, for example, Plaut et al., 1996). This could be done via reducing activation in the LC model so that alternative and higher-frequency syllables representing a component replace the target. Reduced activation could occur at several levels including orthographic input, the mappings between orthography and phonology, or mappings from semantic to phonological levels. Another possibility is to instantiate within-level competition at the character level to prevent character reading but allow reading of components. However, it is unclear how this would work, since radicals are mediated by character units. Note also that this would require within-level competition at the phonological level, and it is not clear how the LC model would allow this. For example, if all the phonological representations are activated at once, what criterion would be used to produce a correct response?

One response to the observation of preserved reading of character components coincident with impaired character reading might be to assume independent mappings connecting orthography and phonology at the sub-character level (Han, Bi, Shu, & Weekes, 2005; Luo & Weekes, 2004; Weekes & Chen, 1999), by which we mean below the character (not the word) level. For example, if radical units were connected to phonological output directly, this would allow reading of a component when whole character reading is not possible (see, for example, Taft et al., 1999b; Taft & Zhu, 1997, who propose a model that assumes sub-character representations). Although the adaptation of the LC model to oral reading in Chinese is an attempt to show that the same computational architecture can be applied universally to oral reading across alphabetic and non-alphabetic scripts, we question whether this is viable. There are simply too many unique properties of the Chinese script that need to be accommodated within a lexical constituency framework for this enterprise to be successful.

Conclusion

Chinese is different from languages that use alphabetic scripts, and it is not straightforward to adapt reading models from one writing system to the other. Studies of dyslexia in Chinese suggest that there are at least two independent pathways available for normal reading in Chinese. If these pathways are labelled lexical-semantic and non-semantic, then differences between non-alphabetic and alphabetic scripts—such as whether reading via non-lexical mechanisms is necessary—informs the development of cognitive models of reading and writing across scripts. However, the unique properties of a script require modification to this basic framework. In our view the key theoretical question that needs to be addressed in computational modelling of reading in Chinese is what the relevant units for reading are. One response might be that the minimal unit of orthographic representation represents a syllable. The LC model assumes independent units of representation at the character and radical levels. However, in our view the inclusion of a radical level representation that is independent of other orthographic representations is an error of commission.

We have illustrated similarities between dyslexia in Chinese and alphabetic languages. However, this should not imply that disorders of reading should be viewed as universal (Beland & Mimouni, 2001; Eng & Obler, 2002; Miceli & Caramazza, 1993; Raman & Weekes, 2005). In fact, patterns of dyslexia in Chinese cannot be identical to patterns observed in alphabetic languages, because properties of Chinese script do not allow direct comparisons between disorders. The LC model has the potential to explain reading disorders, although it is in an early stage of development. No doubt further work, including simulations of impaired reading, will refine the explanatory power of the model, allowing a contribution to the understanding of disorders of oral reading in Chinese.

References

Beijing Language Institute. (1986). *Xiandai Hanyu Pinlu Cidian* [Modern Chinese Frequency Dictionary]. Beijing: Beijing Language Institute Press.

Beland, R., & Mimouni, Z. (2001). Deep dyslexia in the two languages of an Arabic/French bilingual patient. *Cognition, 82*, 77–126.

British Dyslexia Association. (2007, September 21). *What is dyslexia?* Retrieved on 12 September, 2008, from http://www.bdadyslexia.org.uk/whatisdyslexia.html

Chen, J. Y., Chen, T. M., & Dell, G. S. (2002). Word-form encoding in Mandarin Chinese as assessed by the implicit priming task. *Journal of Memory and Language, 46*, 751–781.

Coltheart, M., Curtis, B., Atkins, P., & Haller, M. (1993). Models of reading aloud: Dual-route and parallel-distributed-processing approaches. *Psychological Review, 100*, 589–608.

Coltheart, M., Rastle, K., Perry, C., Langdon, R., & Ziegler, J. C. (2001). DRC: A dual route cascaded model of visual word recognition and reading aloud. *Psychological Review, 108*, 204–256.

DeFrancis, J. (1989). *Visible speech: The diverse oneness of writing system.* Honolulu, HI: University of Hawai'i.

Eng, N., & Obler, L. K. (2002). Acquired dyslexia in a biscriptal reader following traumatic brain injury: A second case. *Topics in Language Disorders, 22*, 5–19.

Friedman, R. B. (1996). Recovery from deep alexia to phonological alexia: Points on a continuum. *Brain and Language, 52*, 114–128.

Graham, N. L., Patterson, K., & Hodges, J. R. (1997). Progressive dysgraphia: Co-occurrence of central and peripheral impairments. *Cognitive Neuropsychology, 14*, 975–1005.

Graham, N. L., Patterson, K., & Hodges, J. R. (2000). The impact of semantic memory impairment on spelling: Evidence from semantic dementia. *Neuropsychologia, 38*, 143–163.

Han, B. Z., Bi, Y. C., Shu, H., & Weekes, B. S. (2005). The interaction between semantic and sublexical routes in reading: Converging evidence from Chinese. *Brain and Language, 95*, 235–236.

Harm, M. W., & Seidenberg, M. S. (1999). Phonology, reading acquisition, and dyslexia: Insights from connectionist models. *Psychological Review, 106*, 491–528.

Harm, M. W., & Seidenberg, M. S. (2004). Computing the meanings of words in reading: Cooperative division of labor between visual and phonological processes. *Psychological Review, 111*, 662–720.

Ho, C. S.-H., & Bryant, P. (1997). Phonological skills are important in learning to read Chinese. *Developmental Psychology, 33*, 946–951.

Ho, C. S.-H., Chan, D. W.-O., Tsang, S.-M., & Lee, S.-H. (2002). The cognitive profile and multiple-deficit hypothesis in Chinese developmental dyslexia. *Developmental Psychology, 38*, 543–553.

Ho, C., Chan, D. W.-O., Lee, S.-H., Tsang, S.-M., & Luan, V. H. (2004). Cognitive profiling and preliminary subtyping in Chinese developmental dyslexia. *Cognition*, *91*, 43–75.

Ho, C. S. H., & Ma, R. N. L. (1999). Training in phonological strategies improves Chinese dyslexic children's character reading skills. *Journal of Research in Reading*, *22*, 131–142.

Houghton, G., & Zorzi, M. (2003). Normal and impaired spelling in a connectionist dual-route architecture. *Cognitive Neuropsychology*, *20*, 115–162.

International Dyslexia Association. (2002, November 12). *What is dyslexia?* Retrieved 12 September, 2008, from http://www.interdys.org/FAQWhatIs.htm

Klingebiel, K., & Weekes, B.S. (2009). Developmental dyslexia in Chinese: Behavioural, genetic and neuropsychological issues. In S. P. Law, B. S. Weekes, & A. Wong (Eds.), *Disorders of speech and language in Chinese* (pp. 138–168). Clevedon, UK: Multilingual Matters.

Lam, C. C. C., & Cheung, P. S. P. (1996, November). *Early developmental problems as indicators for specific learning disabilities among Chinese children*. Paper presented at the 47th Annual Conference of the Orton Dyslexia Society, Boston, MA, USA.

Law, S. P. (2004). A morphological analysis of object naming and reading errors by a Cantonese dyslexic patient. *Language and Cognitive Processes*, *19*, 473–501.

Law, S. P., & Or, B. (2001). A case study of acquired dyslexia and dysgraphia in Cantonese: Evidence for nonsemantic pathways for reading and writing Chinese. *Cognitive Neuropsychology*, *18*, 729–748.

Law, S. P., Yeung, O., Wong, W., & Chiu, K. M. Y. (2005). Processing of semantic radicals in writing Chinese characters: Data from a Chinese dysgraphic patient. *Cognitive Neuropsychology*, *22*, 885–903.

Leong, C. K., & Tamaoka, K. (Eds.). (1998). Cognitive processing of Chinese characters, words, sentences and Japanese kanji and kana: An introduction. *Reading and Writing: An Interdisciplinary Journal*, *10*, 155–164.

Li, C. N., & Thompson, S. A. (1981). *Mandarin Chinese: A functional reference grammar*. Berkeley, CA: University of California Press.

Li, Y., & Kang, J. S. (1993). Analysis of phonetics of the ideophonetic characters in Modern Chinese. In Y. Chen (Ed.), *Information analysis of usage of characters in Modern Chinese* (pp. 84–98) [In Chinese]. Shanghai, China: Shanghai Education Publisher.

Luo, Q., & Weekes, B. S. (2004). Tonal dyslexia in Chinese. *Brain and Language*, *91*, 102–103.

Lyon, G., Shaywitz, S. E., & Shaywitz, B. A. (2003). A definition of dyslexia. *Annals of Dyslexia*, *53*, 1–14.

McBride-Chang, C., & Ho, C. S. H. (2000). Developmental issues in Chinese children's character acquisition. *Journal of Educational Psychology*, *92*, 50–55.

Miceli, G., & Caramazza, A. (1993). The assignment of word stress in oral reading: Evidence from a case of acquired dyslexia. *Cognitive Neuropsychology*, *10*, 273–296.

Patterson, K., & Hodges, J. R. (1992). Deterioration of word meaning: Implications for reading. *Neuropsychologia*, *30*, 1025–1040.

Perfetti, C. A., Liu, Y., & Tan, L. H. (2005). The lexical constituency model: Some implications of research on Chinese for general theories of reading. *Psychological Review*, *112*, 43–59.

Plaut, D. C., McClelland, J. L., Seidenberg, M. S., & Patterson, K. (1996). Understanding normal and impaired word reading: Computational principles in quasi-regular domains. *Psychological Review, 103,* 56–115.

Raman, I., & Weekes, B. S. (2005). Acquired dyslexia in a Turkish–English speaker. *Annals of Dyslexia, 55,* 71–96.

Seidenberg, M. S., & McClelland, J. L. (1989). A distributed, developmental model of word recognition and naming. *Psychological Review, 96,* 523–568.

Shu, H., & Anderson, R. C. (1997). Role of radical awareness in the character and word acquisition of Chinese children. *Reading Research Quarterly, 32,* 78–89.

Shu, H., Chen, X., Anderson, R. C., Wu, N., & Xuan, Y. (2003). Properties of school Chinese: Implications for learning to read. *Child Development, 74,* 27–47.

Shu, H., Meng, X., Chen, X, Luan, H., & Cao, F. (2005a). The subtypes of developmental dyslexia in Chinese: Evidence from three cases. *Dyslexia, 11,* 311–329.

Shu, H., & Wu, N. (2006). Growth of orthography–phonology knowledge in the Chinese writing system. In P. Li, L. H. Tan, E. Bates, & O. Tzeng (Eds.), *The handbook of East Asian psycholinguistics: Vol. 1. Chinese* (pp. 103–113). Cambridge, UK: Cambridge University Press.

Shu, H., Xiong, H. Z., Han, Z. H., Bi, Y. C., & Bai, X. L. (2005b). The selective impairment of the phonological output buffer: Evidence from a Chinese patient. *Behavioural Neurology, 16,* 179–189.

Siok, W. T., & Fletcher, P. (2001). The role of phonological awareness and visual-orthographic skills in Chinese reading acquisition. *Developmental Psychology, 37,* 886–899.

Stevenson, H. W., Stigler, J. W., Lucker, G. W., Lee, S. Y., Hsu, C. C., & Kitamura, S. (1982). Reading disabilities: The case of Chinese, Japanese and English. *Child Development, 53,* 1164–1181.

Taft, M. (2006). Processing of characters by native Chinese readers. In P. Li, L. H. Tan, E. Bates, & O. Tzeng (Eds.), *The handbook of East Asian psycholinguistics: Vol. 1. Chinese* (pp. 237–249). Cambridge, UK: Cambridge University Press.

Taft, M., Liu, Y., & Zhu, X. (1999a). Morphemic processing in reading Chinese. In J. Wang, A. W. Inhoff, & H. C. Chen (Eds.), *Graphonomics: Contemporary research in handwriting* (pp. 321–327). Amsterdam: Elsevier Science Publishers.

Taft, M., & Zhu, X. P. (1997). Submorphemic processing in reading Chinese. *Journal of Experimental Psychology: Learning, Memory, and Cognition, 23,* 761–775.

Taft, M., Zhu, X., & Peng, D. (1999b). Positional specificity of radicals in Chinese character recognition. *Journal of Memory and Language, 40,* 498–519.

Van Orden, G. C., Pennington, B., & Stone, G. O. (1990). Word identification in reading and the promise of subsymbolic psycholinguistics. *Psychological Review, 97,* 488–522.

Weekes, B. S. (2005). Acquired disorders of reading and writing: Cross-script comparisons. *Behavioural Neurology, 16,* 51–57.

Weekes, B. S. (2006). Deep dysgraphia: Evidence for a summation account of written word production. *Brain and Language, 99,* 21–22.

Weekes, B. S., & Chen, H.-Q. (1999). Surface dyslexia in Chinese. *Neurocase, 5,* 161–172.

Weekes, B. S., Chen, M. J., & Yin, W. (1997). Anomia without dyslexia in Chinese. *Neurocase, 3,* 51–60.

Weekes, B. S., Yin, W., Su, I. F., & Chen, M. J. (2006). The cognitive neuropsychology of reading and writing in Chinese. *Language and Linguistics, 7,* 595–617.

World Health Organization. (1993). *ICD-10: Classification of mental and behavioral disorders* (10th rev.). Geneva, Switzerland: World Health Organization.

Yin, W. (1991). *On reading Chinese characters—an experimental and neuropsychological study*. Unpublished PhD thesis, University of London, UK.

Yin, W. G., & Butterworth, B. (1992). Deep and surface dyslexia in Chinese. In H. C. Chen & O. J. L. Tzeng (Eds.), *Language processing in Chinese* (pp. 349–366). Amsterdam: Elsevier.

Yin, W. G., & Butterworth, B. (1998). Chinese pure alexia. *Aphasiology, 12*, 65–76.

Zhang, C., Zhang, J., Yin, R., Zhou, J., & Chang, S. (1996). Experimental research on reading disability of Chinese students. *Psychological Science, 19*, 222–256.

Zhou, X., & Marslen-Wilson, W. (1999). The nature of sublexical processing in reading Chinese characters. *Journal of Experimental Psychology: Learning, Memory, and Cognition, 25*, 19–37.

Zhou, X., & Marslen-Wilson, W. (2000). Lexical representation of compound words: Cross-linguistic evidence. *Psychologia, 43*, 47–66.

Zhu, X. (1988). Analysis of cueing function of phonetic components in modern Chinese. In X. Yuan (Ed.), *Proceedings of the symposium on the Chinese language and characters* [In Chinese]. Beijing, China: Guang Ming Daily News Press.

Ziegler, J. C., Tan, L. H., Perry, C., & Montant, M. (2000). Phonology matters: The phonological frequency effect in written Chinese. *Psychological Science, 11*, 234–238.

11 Dyslexia in biscriptal readers

John Everatt, Dina Ocampo, Kazuvire Veii,
Styliani Nenopoulou, Ian Smythe,
Haya al Mannai and Gad Elbeheri

Introduction

The informed early assessment of potential areas of difficulty and strength is of central importance in efforts to support children with specific learning difficulties or dyslexia. Early identification typically leads to more effective outcomes in remediation, particularly in the areas of reading and writing (Torgesen, 2004), whereas a failure to recognize difficulties can often lead to an individual becoming anxious or depressed and suffering serious losses in self-esteem, confidence and motivation (see Edwards, 1994; Miles & Varma, 1995; Riddick, 1996). Objective assessment procedures and tools are essential to educational practitioners in their initial identification of those at risk and their formation of an education plan designed for the needs of the individual.

In the United Kingdom a working group of the Division of Educational and Child Psychologists of the British Psychological Society (BPS), one of the bodies representing those who perform special needs assessments, defined dyslexia as 'evident when accurate and fluent word reading and/or spelling develops very incompletely or with great difficulty' (Working Party of the British Psychological Society, 1999). However, as recognized by the authors of the report, the view that dyslexia can be assessed simply by measuring levels of literacy attainment needs to be tempered by a consideration of the background of the child. A child who has experienced a problematic educational background may lack reading and writing skills but would not necessarily be considered dyslexic. Hence, although the working party's report does not ascribe a particular cause to the literacy difficulties of dyslexic individuals, it recognizes that there may be other factors that lead to the same, or similar, observable difficulties to those experienced by dyslexic readers. In order to identify dyslexia reliably, therefore, we need assessment procedures that can distinguish those presenting literacy problems consistent with dyslexia from those showing similar difficulties resulting from an educational background in which literacy would be difficult to acquire. The focus of the present chapter is on another factor that may lead to poor scores on measures of literacy, but which would not normally be considered as dyslexia.

An individual who has learned to speak a different language from that in which they are expected to be literate will, at least for some period of second-language learning, show evidence of poor literacy skills. It would be highly dubious, however, to describe this individual as dyslexic until the point when second language acquisition meant that they were reading at age-appropriate levels, particularly if they had been shown to be literate in their first language. Similarly, evidence of literacy learning in the first language cannot be used necessarily as the only evidence that the individual is not dyslexic. This pre-supposes that literacy acquisition and literacy learning difficulties will be the same across all languages—a proposal that is discussed in the following pages. Finally, it may be the case that literacy learning in the first language has not commenced, making the search for evidence of first language literacy acquisition meaningless. Hence, as with poor educational experiences, reli-able identification of dyslexia needs to be able to differentiate dyslexic readers from 'inexperienced' second language learners.

One possibility is that the assessment of underlying cognitive/linguistic pro-cesses, particularly those related to phonological skills, affords the potential to distinguish dyslexic individuals from those who are reading in an additional language, despite equally poor literacy skills being presented by both groups (see Everatt, Smythe, Adams, & Ocampo, 2000; Everatt, Smythe, Ocampo, & Veii, 2002; Frederickson & Frith, 1998). This chapter, therefore, presents a discussion of data pertinent to this topic by considering predictors of literacy across different orthographies, and by focusing on findings from studies of individuals learning to read in two languages. Investigations of biscriptal chil-dren in particular can be informative since they allow for the control of individual differences that can be a problem for cross-language studies in which one group of children learning to be literate in one language is com-pared against another group learning to be literate in a different language. Although bilingual data can bring its own difficulties (for example, in terms of generalization), consistent findings across different types of studies argue for effects being due to language rather than alternative explanations. For example, a child showing literacy difficulties in one language but not another (referred to as 'differential dyslexia' in this chapter) can be used to support arguments that dyslexia is specific to certain languages. We return to a discus-sion of this towards the end of the chapter. In addition to data on children learning literacy in two languages, the chapter will also present findings from work conducted with adult second-language learners to discuss the effect of language experience and cultural background on assessment practices. The aim of the chapter is to present an overview of these data to inform the devel-opment of assessment tools for literacy difficulties that are appropriate for use with individuals learning to speak, read and write in different languages.

Literacy assessment in more than one language

With increasing awareness of dyslexia and the literacy difficulties associated with it, and with increased mobility of people between language communities, there is need for assessment procedures that are applicable across many language contexts. In the United Kingdom, screening/assessment tools have been developed to aid the process of identifying/predicting literacy difficulties in people with dyslexia and other special educational needs. However, most assist in identifying the needs of monolingual, predominantly English-speaking children. Although a number have now been used in non-English settings, there is still a need to consider the appropriateness of test materials across a range of language contexts, and to redress the lack of suitable procedures for use within a multilingual context (see Cline & Reason, 1993; Cline & Shamsi, 2000; Peer & Reid, 2000; Smythe & Everatt, 2002).

Given the availability of English-language screening tools, simply translating tests from one language to another may provide the quickest, most cost-effective method of providing multi-language assessment tools (Everatt et al., 2000). However, the development of test procedures based solely on factors related to one language can lead to disadvantages. For instance, learning to read in one language is not necessarily the same as learning to read in another (see differing viewpoints expressed in: Goulandris, 2003; Katz & Frost, 1992; Smythe, Everatt, & Salter, 2004; Ziegler & Goswami, 2005). There is no reason to believe that the best predictors of literacy will be the same across all languages or scripts, and aspects of the language or culture within which an individual is immersed may make an assessment measure inappropriate. Similarly, the cognitive causes of literacy difficulties may vary between languages, meaning that an assessment procedure focusing on one potential cause and shown to be effective with one language group may not be appropriate for individuals from another language context. These points are discussed below with reference to the dominant causal viewpoint within dyslexia research—that is, the phonological deficit viewpoint.

Despite the large body of research that identifies a phonological deficit as a core causal factor in the literacy problems faced by children with dyslexia (Snowling, 2000; Stanovich, 1988), this has yet to be confirmed across languages (see discussions in: Cossu, Shankweiler, Liberman, Katz, & Tola, 1988; Geva & Siegel, 2000; Goswami, 2000; Ho & Lai, 1999; Katz & Frost, 1992; Smythe et al., 2004; Wimmer, 1993). An isolated phonological perspective needs to be shown to provide an assessment framework that works across a range of languages and scripts. Children learning a script (orthography) with a more consistent relationship between written symbols (letters/graphemes) and sounds (phonemes) than that found in English seem to progress in literacy faster, and process words at the level of the phoneme earlier, than those learning a less regular (or less transparent) orthography (see Goswami, 2000; see also chapters 2 and 3, this volume). Compared to children learning to read in English, phonological awareness deficits may be less of a problem when learning a regular orthography with simple rules or correspondences (Wimmer, 1993). Deficits in other areas associated with phonological processing, such as speed of access or short-term storage, may explain more of the variability in literacy ability among children learning more transparent orthographies (Landerl, Wimmer, & Frith, 1997). The transparency of the script, therefore, seems to be a factor that may lead to variation between languages in the ease of literacy acquisition, the manifestation of literacy deficits and the appropriateness of particular assessment procedures.

In our own work investigating the impact of orthography on potential predictors of literacy levels, we compared the performance of English, Hungarian and Chinese Grade 3 children (Everatt, Smythe, Ocampo, & Gyarmathy, 2004; Smythe, Everatt, Gyarmathy, Ho, & Groeger, 2003). English and Hungarian were chosen to assess the impact of variations in orthographic transparency, Hungarian orthography being much more transparent than English orthography (indeed, Hungarian has an almost one-to-one correspondence between letters and sounds). Chinese was chosen to contrast predictors of alphabetic scripts (English and Hungarian, in this case) against predictors of Chinese characters that do not follow the same principles as alphabetic scripts—that is, a Chinese character cannot be broken down into letters (or letter combinations) that represent basic sound units (such as phonemes); rather, a character represents meaning and provides a guide to pronunciation. These languages enable contrasts between orthographies where decoding, in the sense of translating from letters to sounds, (1) should be highly effective (high-transparency Hungarian) (2) is possible, but subject to large numbers of exceptions (low-transparency English) and (3) is not possible, and larger units of translation from written to verbal forms will be needed for accurate pronunciation (Chinese). If phonological processing is predictive of literacy levels due to its influence within letter–sound decoding strategies, then these orthographic differences should lead to changes in the relationship between literacy and phonological processing.

The results of these comparisons indicated differences in the ability of measures to distinguish between those with good and those with poor literacy skills. The English children with poor literacy skills showed deficits on a range of phonological processing measures compared to their peers with good literacy skills. However, Hungarian children with evidence of weak literacy skills performed as well as children with good literacy levels on measures of phonological awareness, although they showed comparative weaknesses in phonological short-term memory and rapid naming (i.e., the ability to repeat non-words and name line drawings of familiar objects as rapidly as possible). These differences between language groups were consistent with predictions based on the relative transparency of the two orthographies (Landerl et al., 1997; Smythe et al., 2008; Wimmer, 1993). Hungarian is highly transparent, and hence deficits in phonological awareness may be less apparent than in English, which is highly opaque. In addition, Chinese children with low literacy scores on tasks measuring the processing of Chinese characters were more likely to differ from their higher achieving peers on tasks of rapid naming and visual short-term memory (i.e., naming line drawings of familiar objects as rapidly as possible and indicating whether an abstract line drawing was the same as one presented a few seconds earlier).

Although further work is necessary, these data imply that Hungarian will be better assessed by phonological measures that focus on the short-term retention of novel phonological sequences (non-words), as well as the fluent accessing of known phonological forms. This interpretation argues that phonological skills are still important for the processing of the Hungarian orthography, but measures requiring the simple identification of sounds within words may not be sensitive enough to detect variations in phonological processing level (i.e., most children have reached competency levels appropriate for the Hungarian orthography in the skills associated with these tasks). Chinese may also require the ability to access known phonological forms fluently, but in addition literacy levels seem to be related to the ability to retain visual information over a short period of time. The importance of the latter skill, rather than a phonological retention task, may be because the strategy of translating letters into sounds for storage cannot be used with Chinese characters, as it can for Hungarian and English, meaning that visual retention strategies are required while Chinese character processing is undertaken.

Further variations in the ability of typical assessment measures to differentiate between good and poor readers/spellers can be found in comparisons of Arabic and English. Although highly transparent for initial literacy learning, Arabic orthography becomes much more opaque in many texts encountered by Grade 4 children and above, mainly due to the exclusion of short vowel markers from these texts. In the Arabic orthography, short vowels are represented by marks presented above or below letters—short vowels do not have independent letters themselves. When these short vowel marks are excluded, words can be interpreted/pronounced in context, even though they are ambiguous in isolation (in English, a single missing vowel would mean that 'bt' could be *bat*, *bet*, *bit* or *but*, even though it can be interpreted from context: *He held the cricket/baseball bt firmly*). Pronunciation and meaning therefore have to be inferred from context when the less transparent form of the orthography is experienced. In studies of children in Grade 4 and above, phonological awareness measures have been found to be reasonable predictors of Arabic literacy levels (Elbeheri & Everatt, 2007), though this level of prediction may be lower than that found for comparison English language groups (Elbeheri, Everatt, Reid, & Al Mannai, 2006). However, this Arabic–English difference was less marked than that in the English–Hungarian comparisons described above (see Figure 11.1), potentially due to the Arabic children having experienced a mixture of relatively transparent and opaque texts. Such findings are consistent with the interpretation that variability in transparency across orthographies is related to the ability of measures of phonological awareness to identify poor literacy levels from the norm.

Geva and colleagues (Geva & Siegel, 2000; Geva & Wade-Wooley, 1998; Geva, Wade-Wooley, & Shany, 1997) have proposed that two viewpoints—the central processing hypothesis and the script-dependent hypothesis—dominate descriptions of the reading process among second language readers. The

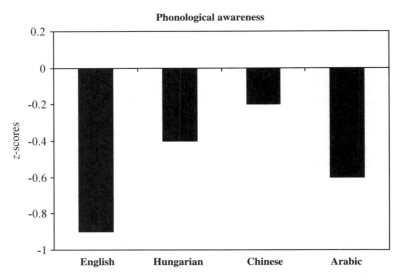

Figure 11.1 Comparative phonological awareness weaknesses (represented by z-scores away from the norm of zero) shown by groups of children with poor literacy skills across four languages.

central processing perspective argues for a focused number of factors that will predict reading ability no matter which language or script is the basis of literacy. The script-dependent perspective derives from the view that different languages/scripts will make different demands on the cognitive system of the learner and, therefore, different processes will determine learning: a predictor of reading ability in one language may well not predict reading in a second. The two views can be contrasted in terms of the rate of learning a written form, whether there are common or different predictors of literacy acquisition, and whether difficulties in one script are independent of difficulties in another. Given that script transparency has been suggested as an important factor in literacy acquisition, the script-dependent hypothesis can be assessed by contrasting languages whose written forms vary in the level of consistency between written symbol and verbal sound. A more transparent script should be acquired faster, show more benefit from skilled phonological processing in the early years of acquisition and is more likely to be free from learning difficulties.

From an assessment perspective, these positions are important since they will determine the extent to which an assessment process is applicable across languages. For example, a strict interpretation of the script-dependent hypothesis predicts that we should find children who are learning two different scripts showing evidence of dyslexia in one but not in the other. As such, an assessment in one language cannot be used as evidence of dyslexia in another. In contrast, a strict interpretation of the central processing viewpoint argues that an underlying cognitive factor (such as poor phonological processing) leads to literacy deficits across languages and, hence, an assessment process that reliably identifies this causal factor is applicable to all languages. A child with an assessment of dyslexia in their first language who moves to an area where literacy in a second language is required would be treated differently depending on which viewpoint is considered correct. Under the script-dependent hypothesis, the first assessment is irrelevant to a decision about dyslexia in the second language and further assessments will be necessary prior to the implementation of any dyslexia-specific educational processes. Under the central processing hypothesis, however, further assessment would be deemed to be unnecessary and support procedures related to a dyslexia assessment can be implemented immediately. Evidence for both hypotheses potentially makes neither process appropriate. That is, given some level of independence between scripts, further assessment may be necessary. However, where commonalities exist, first language assessments may be informative, which should reduce assessment time and resources. For example, an assessment of phonological awareness in one language may be highly predictive of the same skill in a second language, meaning that measures in both languages need not be performed. However, rapid naming levels in one language may not be informative of time to perform a parallel task in a second language, meaning that if this skill has to be assessed in the second language, the first language assessment cannot be used. This conclusion requires that assessors know what to look for across languages, and what modifications to assessment procedures will be needed to accommodate first language evidence. Clearly, the resolution of these differing theoretical positions will aid the development of effective tools for predicting reading difficulties, and techniques for remediating problems among bilingual populations.

The work discussed in this chapter aimed to inform these theoretical positions by testing children who are following a bilingual curriculum as part of normal schooling. Such a bilingual learning environment may lead to different findings from those found in learning contexts where one language is used in compulsory schooling and another is used outside the compulsory system (e.g., via parental instruction or weekend schools—see Gholamain & Geva, 1999). In the bilingual context assessed in the Filipino study referred to in this chapter, literacy learning was concurrent in the two languages from Grade 1. This is in contrast with contexts where literacy in the second language will probably be learned later and over a longer period than in the first language, potentially making second language literacy learning dependent on the processes developed with the first orthography. For example, in the Namibian study discussed in this chapter, literacy learning in the first language (L1) was more likely to start earlier than literacy learning in English, the second language (L2). Consistent findings between the Filipino and Namibian contexts would argue against the interpretation that the level of interdependency found between literacy learning is simply due to L2 literacy using those processes already developed in earlier L1 literacy acquisition.

Bilingual/biscriptal measures and samples

Given that differences between language groups were evident in measures of phonological processing, and that phonological ability has been the core of theoretical models of literacy acquisition and dyslexia, it was the process chosen for particular scrutiny in the present work (Tables 11.1, 11.2 and 11.3 give an overview of the measures and participants in the studies reported below). Therefore, the test battery incorporated measures of the three areas of phonological processing that have been identified as predicting independent amounts of variability in literacy ability (see also Wagner & Torgesen, 1987).

The first of these was the ability to identify and manipulate units of sound within a word, typically referred to as phonological awareness. Measures assessed the biscriptal child's ability to identify individual phonemes within spoken words via tapping tasks (i.e., producing a tap with a pencil for each sound within a word) or odd-one-out tasks (i.e., stating which word in a triplet of spoken words had a different beginning or end sound from the others).

The second phonological area derived from processes related to the storage of phonological units for a brief period of time. Such tasks are often referred to as phonological (or auditory) short-term memory tasks. In the tests used in the current research, children were required to repeat increasingly long sequences of familiar words (the names of objects or digits) that were verbally presented by the assessor.

The final aspect of phonological processing assessed in the test battery was

Table 11.1 Measures used with Filipino–English bilingual children

Grade	Age	N	Measures (used across all grades)			
			Non-language		Filipino and English	
1	7–8	81	Block design	(NV Reas)	Listening comprehension	(List comp)
2	8–9	89	Visual memory	(Visual)	Text reading comprehension	(Text comp)
3	9–10	91			Single word reading	(Reading)
4	10–11	88			Non-word reading	(Non-word)
5	11–12	70			Phonological awareness: phoneme tapping	(Phono)
6	12–13	60			Auditory short-term memory for words	(Aud STM)
					Rapid naming of objects	(Rap Nam)

Note: Age in years.

Table 11.2 Measures used with Namibian Herero–English bilingual children

Grade	Age	N	Measures (used across all grades)			
			Non-language		Herero and English	
2	8–9	22	Raven's Matrices	(NV Reas)	Listening comprehension	(List comp)
3	9–10	41	Visual memory	(Visual)	Single word reading	(Reading)
4	10–11	33			Non-word reading	(Non-word)
5	11–12	20			Phonological awareness: initial/end sound odd-one-out	(Phono)
					Auditory short-term memory for digits	(Aud STM)
					Rapid naming of objects	(Rap Nam)

Note: Age in years.

Table 11.3 Measures used with UK adult students

	Age	N	English only	
English first language non-dyslexic	18+	60	English language experience questionnaire	(bespoke)
English as an additional language			Text reading accuracy, rate and comprehension	(ART)
Low English experience	18+	26	Single word reading	(BAS)
High English experience	18+	29	Phonological fluency: semantic, alliteration and rhyme	(PhAB)
English first language dyslexic	18+	29	Rapid naming of objects and digits	(PhAB)

Note: Age in years.

based on the ability to access quickly a phonological representation from long-term memory. Such tasks have typically been referred to as rapid naming tasks, with the main measure being the time taken to name one or more visually presented familiar objects or grapho-numeric symbols (usually digit names, although rapid letter naming has also been used). In the tasks used in the present work, the children were required to name, as quickly but as accurately as possible, each item in an array of line drawings of familiar objects that were culturally appropriate for the children tested.

The results from these tests provided a detailed assessment of the individual's ability to process phonological forms appropriately. In addition, we included an assessment of the ability to read novel letter strings (i.e., non-words), all of which were pronounceable in the language of assessment and had been derived by rearranging or substituting letters within a real word (e.g., in English, this would involve changing the word *below* into 'bebow' or *window* into 'widnow'). Scores on such non-word reading tasks provide an indication of the individual's understanding of units of sound and how they relate to the written form. This may be particularly pertinent when considering dyslexia, given the evidence that English-language dyslexic readers are poor at applying symbol-to-sound conversion strategies when reading, a deficit that may be related to poor phonological skills (Rack, Snowling, & Olson, 1992; Siegel, 1993; Snowling, 2000; Stanovich, 1988).

The test battery also incorporated measures of visual processing, because deficits in these areas have been found to be related to problems with learning non-alphabetic scripts, as well as with distinguishing between good and poor bilingual readers (Everatt et al., 2000; Yamada, 1998), thereby providing a contrast with the level of prediction provided by the phonological measures. The measures used in the present work required the retention of sequences of spatial movements or the retention of abstract drawings, for a brief period of time, followed by repetition of the movements or identification of the drawings.

The full testing procedure used measures of literacy attainment that had been developed specifically for the present work, since standardized measures did not exist in the non-English languages studied. The focus of the present work was on reading attainment, assessed by requiring children to name individual words presented with no contextual information (although in the Filipino study a measure of text reading comprehension was also included). Again, deficits in word-level reading tasks have been found to be characteristic of dyslexia, leading the Working Party of the British Psychological Society (1999) to conclude that dyslexia is evident at the level of the single word. Indeed, the use of surrounding contextual information to support the decoding of an individual word may be greater among dyslexic than among non-dyslexic readers (Nation & Snowling, 1998).

Additional measures were used with the bilingual children to provide an assessment of the specific nature of any literacy deficits identified. Given that the use of a second language may lead to reduced competence in that language (see Cummins, 1984), low scores on measures of literacy may be due to poor general language skills. The bilingual children were therefore assessed on measures of listening comprehension to provide an indication of language proficiency. Similarly, a measure of non-verbal reasoning was included to ensure that low levels of literacy skills were not due simply to global deficits in test taking (see also Everatt et al., 2000).

All language-based tests were presented in both languages for each cohort of children. One of the guiding principles of the work was the development of measures that could be readily translated and modified for different language environments. In the case of non-verbal measures, translation of test materials was not necessary, although instructions were presented to the child in a form that ensured understanding. In most cases this meant that instructions were given in the first language, with English-language words being used if appropriate in terms of the language context (code-shifting between languages is common/natural in the Philippines, for example) and if pilot work indicated the need (e.g., some terms are better known in their English-language form). Testers were also allowed to vary instructions between languages to reiterate meaning if an individual child was confused or failed on initial practice trials. Recruitment of testers who were themselves bilingual in the languages under investigation allowed instructions to be given in both languages where necessary. In addition, cross-language adaptations of all language-based measures ensured that the measures assessed the skills/processes under investigation. Such adaptations were performed with the aid of practitioners who were native speakers of the languages of assessment and were familiar with current work in dyslexia and literacy assessment. In all cases, materials were piloted prior to their use and tests included worked examples so that children understood what was required of them.

Literacy and phonological skills were also the main measures used to assess adult students with English as an additional language. These measures were specifically targeted since they are the most frequently tested areas of functioning in dyslexia assessment. Measures of literacy assessed the ability to read individual words out of context (taken from the British Ability Scales [BAS], Elliot, 1983). However, measures of text processing (the Adult Reading Test [ART]; Brooks, Everatt, & Fidler, 2004) were included, given that this is more likely to be the primary focus of literacy concerns for an adult reader. Measures of phonological processing covered a range of skills although the focus of the present discussion was on production tasks. These comprised measures of semantic, alliteration and rhyme fluency, as well as measures of rapid naming. These measures were based on those incorporated into tests such as the Phonological Assessment Battery (PhAB; Frederickson, Frith, & Reason, 1997). The fluency tests required the students to name, in 30 seconds, as many words as possible within a particular semantic category (e.g., animals), or beginning with a particular sound (e.g., a /b/ sound) or rhyming with a particular word (e.g., *more*). The rapid naming tasks required the students to name either a series of line drawings of familiar objects (*hat, table, ball, door, box*) or the digits 1–9. Stimulus cards comprised 50 items for each set, presented in a randomly ordered sequence.

The Filipino and Namibian cohorts were chosen to allow the effects of orthographic transparency to be assessed within the same child (for further details, see Everatt et al., 2002; Veii & Everatt, 2005). As explained above, English is a deep orthography with a complex relationship between letters and phonemes. In contrast, the Filipino language of Tagalog and the Namibian language of Herero have relatively shallow orthographies, with highly consistent relationships between sounds and symbols. A strict inter-pretation of the script-dependent hypothesis predicts that children should learn to read Filipino and Herero earlier/faster than English, and that in the initial years of literacy learning phonological processes should be better predictors of Filipino/Herero reading skills than English reading skills. It also suggests that literacy deficits in one language need not be accompanied by literacy deficits in the other, with deficits being more likely in English for both cohorts. The validity of these predictions was assessed in these studies.

The third cohort was chosen from within the United Kingdom (see Everatt et al., 2002) and included adults who had acquired English as an additional language. The variability in English experience among this group provided the opportunity to assess the effects of length of language experience on measures of literacy attainment and phonological processing in a group of individuals with no known literacy learning or phonological processing deficits. Contrasting the performance of this group with that of previously diagnosed dyslexic readers allowed us to determine whether currently used dyslexia assessment measures could distinguish between dyslexic readers with persistent deficits and second language learners with transient deficits that should disappear following increased language experience.

Rate of literacy acquisition

Analyses of variance (ANOVAs) were performed on word reading and non-word reading to investigate the interaction between grade and language within the Namibian and Filipino data sets. When the Namibian data were considered, the interaction between language and grade was significant for word reading, $F(3, 108) = 4.04$, $p < .001$. This finding suggests that Herero word reading skills were improving at a faster rate than English word reading skills across the grades (i.e., the difference between Grade 2 and Grade 5 reading scores was larger for Herero than it was for English, despite the same children being tested in both languages). Although non-significant, non-word reading showed a similar trend for an interaction between language and grade, $F(3, 108) = 2.43$, $p = .07$. Figures 11.2 and 11.3 represent these find-ings, showing steeper lines for Herero reading scores than for the English reading scores.

As with the Namibian data, ANOVAs were performed to assess improve-ments across grades in literacy-related skills for Filipino compared to Eng-lish. These analyses indicated a non-significant interaction between language and grade for word reading, $F(5, 473) = 1.00$, $p = .42$, but a significant interaction between grade and language for non-word reading, $F(5, 473) = 4.66$, $p < .001$, suggesting this time that decoding skills were developing at a faster rate with the more transparent orthography. Taken together with the Namibian data, these results are consistent with the predictions of the script-dependent hypothesis that literacy acquisition varies with orthographic transparency. However, as with any correlational study, there are alternative

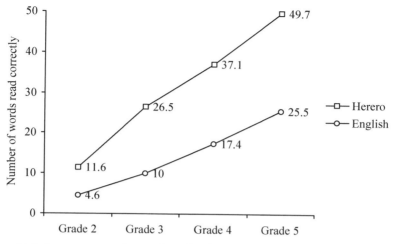

Figure 11.2 Average scores for word reading in Herero and English across the grades. Mean values are presented for each grade in each language task.

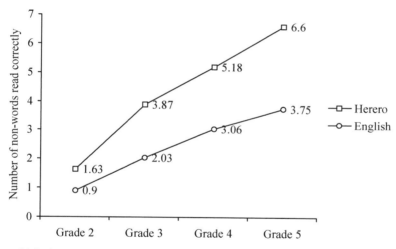

Figure 11.3 Average scores for non-word reading in Herero and English across the grades. Mean values are presented for each grade in each language task.

interpretations. For example, educational experience may differ across the languages (one language may be taught more or better than the other). Although this cannot be ruled out, the Filipino and Namibian contexts varied in educational experience both from each other and from other bilingual contexts (e.g., English may be considered more of a co-experienced language for the Filipino children, but it is much more a second language for the Namibian children, whereas in some studies English is considered the main language of education—see Geva & Siegel, 2000). The Filipino and

Namibian contexts also vary in educational experience from the cross-language between-group work (see Seymour, Aro, & Erskine, 2003). Given that these varying educational contexts show similar results in terms of faster rates of acquisition for the more transparent orthography, the script-dependent viewpoint seems the more likely explanation. However, further data are clearly needed.

Inter-language predictors

Multiple regression procedures were used to investigate the extent to which the cognitive/linguistic measures explained variability in Herero and English word reading. For each analysis, control variables of sex, age and grade were first entered as a block into the analysis. This ensured that any variability explained by the predictor variables could not be due to these control variables. For example, literacy and phonological skills both vary with age, so any relationship between them may simply be due to age—with older children being better than younger children—hence, this regression procedure aims to control for variables such as age prior to assessing the relationship between literacy and phonological skills. The non-verbal reasoning measure and listening comprehension in the language for which literacy was being predicted were then entered into the analysis, again to avoid these measures obscuring the relationship between literacy and the following predictor variables. The potential predictor variables were then added in a stepwise procedure to investigate which variable, or combination of variables, proved to be most predictive (the stepwise procedure adds variables in steps to try to determine the combination of predictors that provide the best level of explanation of literacy).

The first set of analyses focused on within-language predictors of word reading. For Herero word reading, the control variables explained 29 per cent of the variance, with non-verbal reasoning and Herero listening comprehension taking the level of prediction up to 37 per cent. Herero phonological awareness measures accounted for an additional 16 per cent of the variance, with Herero rapid naming and auditory short-term memory collectively adding a further 3 per cent. The corresponding analysis, focusing on within-language predictors of English word reading, indicated that the control variables accounted for 22 per cent of the variance, with non-verbal reasoning and English listening comprehension increasing this to 27 per cent. English phonological awareness added another 20 per cent to the level of prediction, with English auditory short-term memory providing an additional 6 per cent. Taken together, these two analyses indicated that, after the control variables, non-verbal reasoning (as a measure of general non-verbal ability) and listening comprehension (as a measure of language competence) have been taken into account, basic phonological skills were equally reliable predictors of reading ability in both languages. Indeed, it was the ability to recognize sounds within words (phonological awareness) that provided the best level of explanation of word reading level in this biscriptal cohort.

Further analyses combined first and second language measures to contrast listening comprehension and phonological awareness as predictors of reading in L1 and L2. The findings indicated that combining L1 and L2 listening comprehension measures did not increase the level of prediction of reading skills in either the first or the second language over that provided by first language listening comprehension alone. However, second language measures of phonological awareness predicted more variability in both first and second language literacy than first language phonological awareness measures alone; indeed, L2 phonological awareness predicted equal levels of variability in Herero and English word reading to that explained by combining both phonological awareness tasks. These findings indicate that L1 and L2 reading skills seem to be best predicted by L1 comprehension and L2 phonological processing. Such evidence for common underlying predictors of literacy skills is more consistent with the predictions of the central processing viewpoint.

As with the Namibian data, regression analyses were performed to assess whether within-language and between-language measures of underlying cognitive/linguistic skills predicted reading ability in Filipino and English. In these analyses, Filipino word reading was best predicted by non-word reading in English, followed by non-word reading in Filipino, rapid naming in Filipino and auditory short-term memory in Filipino. In total, some 55 per cent of the variance in Filipino word reading was predicted by this mixed-language model. English word reading was also best predicted by non-word reading in English, which, together with rapid naming in English, non-word reading in Filipino and rapid naming in Filipino, predicted approximately 70 per cent of the variability. As with the Namibian findings, cross-language predictions of literacy were identified, consistent with the predictions of the central processing hypothesis. Indeed, in this cohort, where literacy acquisition was concurrent, the best predictor of a literacy-related measure in one language was the analogous measure in the other language.

The inclusion of Grade 1 children in the Filipino study allowed the assessment of an additional prediction of the script-dependent hypothesis. This argues that the level of prediction of reading ability in the early years of learning provided by measures of phonological processing should vary across orthographies with different levels of transparency. Basically, it would be predicted that phonological processes should support the initial learning of a transparent orthography more clearly than a less transparent orthography. In this case, Filipino literacy skills in Grade 1 should be specifically supported by phonological processes, whereas English literacy skills at the same stage are less likely to benefit from good phonological skills. However, for both languages, equivalent amounts (more than 70 per cent) of the variability in reading among the Grade 1 children could be predicted by phonological processing measures of decoding, phonological awareness, rapid naming and auditory short-term memory. These findings are inconsistent with a strict interpretation of the script-dependent viewpoint.

Dual language assessment

A key question in the assessment of literacy difficulties among bilingual individuals is the language in which the assessment should be performed. Should this be in the language with which the child feels most comfortable (often the first language), or in the language in which literacy has to be acquired (often the second language) and where difficulties might already have been detected? Although there is no definitive answer to this question, the data derived from these studies suggest that assessment of L1 cognitive/ linguistic skills may support the identification of difficulties in L2 literacy. For example, in an analysis that focused on the 91 Grade 3 children in the Filipino data set, children scoring in the bottom 15 per cent of the distribution on measures of English word reading, but average on English listening comprehension and non-verbal reasoning, were selected. This procedure lead to the identification of seven children with specific literacy acquisition difficulties in English that could not be explained by their general English language or non-verbal abilities. These seven children were matched with 20 children who showed average profiles on all these measures (i.e., within the average range for English literacy, general language and non-verbal abilities). Comparisons indicated significant differences between the groups in terms of English literacy skills, $t(25) = 7.30$, $p < .001$, but not on measures of English listening comprehension, $t(25) = 1.25$, $p = .22$, or of non-verbal reasoning, $t(25) = 0.67$, $p = .67$.

Further analyses indicated that for the English language tests, those with good and poor literacy skills differed on non-word reading ability, $t(25) = 9.26$, $p < .001$, rapid naming, $t(25) = 5.06$, $p < .001$, and auditory short-term memory, $t(25) = 2.26$, $p = .03$, but not on phonological awareness, $t(25) = 1.01$, $p = .32$. In contrast, all tasks, including those requiring an awareness of phonemes within spoken words, showed significant differences between the groups when the Filipino language tests were used—for non-word reading: $t(25) = 5.46$, $p < .001$; for phonological awareness: $t(25) = 2.50$, $p = .02$; for rapid naming: $t(25) = 2.18$, $p = .04$; and for auditory short-term memory: $t(25) = 2.51$, $p = .02$. Figure 11.4 presents the average scores on the phonological awareness tasks.

Despite children having been selected on good versus poor English literacy skills, tests of English phonological awareness were less able to distinguish between the groups and may therefore be less able to identify a difficulty. However, when tests were performed in Filipino (which would be most likely considered as the children's L1), differences between these same groups in terms of phonological awareness emerged. Combining findings from L1 and L2 leads to profiles similar to those typically found among monolingual English children—that is, showing deficits in most areas of phonological processing. The most likely explanation for the results is that inexperience in the English-based tasks leads to under-performance among control children, reducing the likelihood of identifiable differences. Simply using English language norms in this bilingual context may not be appropriate to separate

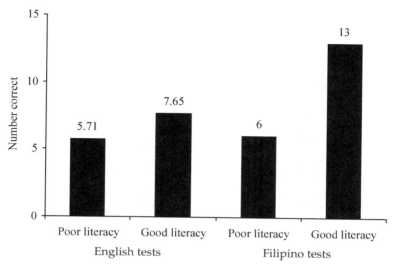

Figure 11.4 Average scores produced by the good and poor English literacy children on the measure of phoneme awareness in each of the languages of testing (English and Filipino).

those with and without underlying phonological awareness deficits. Even with bilingual children experiencing English as a language of instruction, testing in the more dominant home language may be necessary to identify underlying areas of weakness. Although it has been argued that testing in the language of literacy is all that is required to identify literacy difficulties among multilingual children (see Everatt et al., 2000), assessments that aim to propose potential causes for those literacy deficits need to consider whether such a limited testing procedure will be adequate.

This problem is even more evident when comparing bilingual adult tertiary education students with groups of monolingual dyslexic and non-dyslexic students. The bilingual adults in these studies had learned English as an additional language, and typically when they were much older than the children in the Namibian and Filipino studies. However, the majority had been using English for several years prior to testing and had experienced at least one year of tertiary education in English. Data reported in Everatt et al. (2002) indicated that such bilingual adults produced scores on literacy measures that were on average equivalent to those of students who had been diagnosed as dyslexic and who had a history of specific literacy deficits. Both these dyslexic and bilingual students were worse than their monolingual non-dyslexic peers on these tasks, although the difference between the non-dyslexic readers and bilinguals was related to experience of English (see Figure 11.5, which contrasts bilinguals with seven or more years of English experience with those with less than seven years' experience—criteria based on the work of Cummins, 1984).

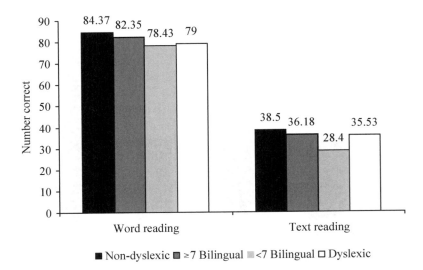

Figure 11.5 Average performance of groups of monolingual non-dyslexic adults, monolingual dyslexic adults and bilingual non-dyslexic adults (with up to 7 years of English experience, or more than 7 years' experience) on the reading tasks.

However, when these groups were tested on measures of phonological processing skills, particularly measures of auditory short-term memory and decoding skills, the bilingual students outperformed the dyslexic readers and achieved scores similar to those of the non-dyslexic readers. Hence, although literacy measures may not support the identification of specific literacy deficits among bilingual students due to poor L2 proficiency, such poor literacy levels in conjunction with poor phonological skill may provide a means to develop appropriate educational plans.

However, the general conclusion derived from the data presented by Everatt et al. (2002) may depend crucially on the measure or measures of phonological processing used. For example, Figure 11.6 presents scores on measures of phonological fluency. When using an alliteration fluency task to contrast the phonological abilities of bilingual students with their dyslexic and non-dyslexic monolingual peers, the bilingual students performed at a higher level than did the dyslexic individuals. In the rhyming fluency task, however, the bilingual students performed at a level much worse than both groups of monolinguals (i.e., the dyslexic and non-dyslexic readers). The same caution may be required when considering the use of rapid naming measures. For both rapid naming tasks (objects and digits), the bilingual students performed at speeds more consistent with those of the dyslexic readers (see Figure 11.7). These rapid naming findings are consistent with those reported in Everatt et al. (2002) and suggest that not all measures of phonological processing will distinguish between those with English literacy

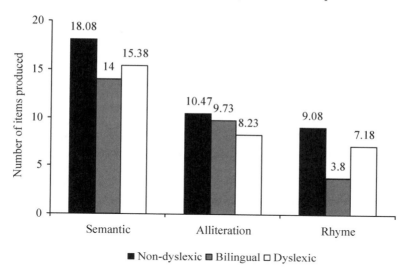

Figure 11.6 Average performance of groups of monolingual non-dyslexic, mono-lingual dyslexic and bilingual non-dyslexic adult college-level students on the fluency tasks.

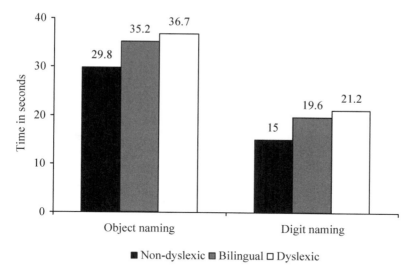

Figure 11.7 Average performance of groups of monolingual non-dyslexic, bilingual non-dyslexic and monolingual dyslexic adult college-level students on the rapid naming tasks.

dyslexia and those who have learned English as an additional language. As with the Filipino children's data, these adult data indicate that further work is required before determining the precise measures to use in an assessment tool designed to distinguish different causes of literacy difficulties.

Differential reading deficits

In this section, case studies are presented as graphical profiles of the scores produced by an individual child on the measures used in the assessment procedures. In these profiles, raw scores have been converted to z-scores based on the means and standard deviations produced by children within the same class. The further away from zero a child scores in the negative direction, the more problems the child may be experiencing in the area of functioning assessed by the measure. Each of the z-scores reported here is a combination of measures of the same underlying factor.

Figure 11.8 presents the results of a single Grade 4 Namibian child but shows two lines to represent, where applicable, this child's performance in the Herero and English versions of the same skills. Consideration of the profile presented in Figure 11.8 indicates that this child shows evidence of literacy

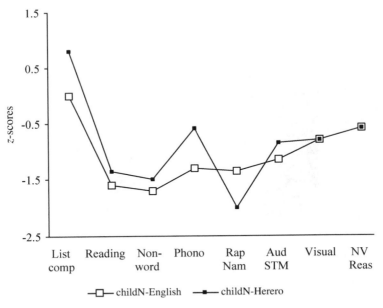

Figure 11.8 Profile of a Namibian Herero–English bilingual child presenting evidence of difficulties in literacy skills in both languages. Note: *childN* refers to a Namibian child and that child's scores on English measures (open squares) or Herero measures (filled squares), with Visual and NV Reas being the same in both languages. The key for the measure names on the x-axis can be found in Table 11.2.

problems in both their L1 and L2, the potential underlying reason being weaknesses in phonological processing. This pattern is representative of a typical profile presented by children with evidence of literacy learning difficulties: that is, word-level literacy weaknesses in addition to some evidence of poor phonological processing skills.

Within the data there were few cases of children whose literacy skills were good in one language and poor in another, which could not be explained by low listening comprehension scores. However, several cases in the Filipino cohort showed different manifestations of literacy deficits dependent on the language of assessment. Figure 11.9 presents one of these cases. Assessment of single-word reading would have indicated this child as dyslexic in English but not in Filipino, consistent with a strict interpretation of the script-dependent viewpoint. However, the profile shows that this child may be struggling in Filipino literacy beyond the level of the single word. When combinations of words are required, as in the sentence comprehension task, this child shows deficits in both English and Filipino—indeed, the performance in Filipino is worse than that in English. One explanation of this profile is that few problems are encountered when learning to decode Filipino words, due to

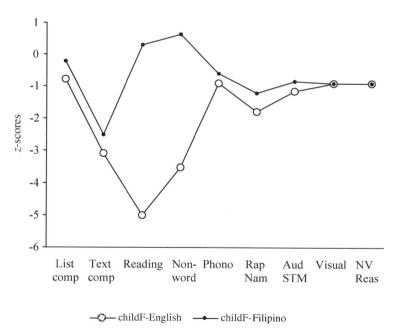

Figure 11.9 Profile of a Filipino Tagalog–English bilingual child presenting evidence of difficulties primarily in English. Note: *childF* refers to a Filipino child and that child's scores on English measures (open circles) or Filipino measures (filled circles), with Visual and NV Reas being the same in both languages. The key for the measure names on the *x*-axis can be found in Table 11.1.

the regularity of the association between letters and sounds; if given enough time, the child can make a good stab at decoding. However, weak fluency in decoding skills may still lead to deficits beyond single-word processing. For example, multi-word text processes may be compromised if the child requires large amounts of time to decode individual words. Note that this is not a general comprehension deficit, as listening comprehension was good in both languages. Comprehension is only poor when required from written text, again in both languages. Therefore, the conclusion that this child will be able to acquire full literacy competence in Filipino may be overly optimistic. Basic word reading may be within normal levels in the regular orthography, but underlying deficits that may lead to poor word processing in a less regular language may still impact on literacy acquisition in both languages.

Conclusions

Overall, the findings discussed in this chapter present evidence for both the central processing and script-dependent hypotheses, similar to the conclusions derived by Geva and colleagues (Geva & Siegel, 2000; Geva & Wade-Wooley, 1998; Geva et al., 1997). The main finding consistent with the script-dependent view was the evidence for differential rates of reading acquisition, which were associated with the transparency of the script. Evidence of variation across languages in predictors of literacy levels can also be interpreted as support for this position. However, this variation was less clearly associated with orthographic transparency in the bilingual data. When a relatively transparent script was learned in conjunction with English, phonological awareness was a good predictor of literacy levels in both English and the more transparent orthography. One explanation is that it is harder to detect the relationship between literacy levels and phonological awareness scores when a regular orthography is being learned, potentially due to faster acquisition of word decoding skills and of the awareness of basic sounds within words. However, when the regular orthography is learned at the same time as an opaque script, acquisition may be slowed allowing the relationship to be evident for longer among biscriptal groups. Strong relationships between phonological awareness measures in the two languages, in addition to cross-language relationships between phonological awareness and literacy, are consistent with a correspondence in skills acquisition across languages. This may lead to the slower acquisition of skills when learning a more regular orthography, although it could also mean that acquisition of skills when learning a more opaque orthography could be accelerated. Such inter-relationships, and this potential explanation of variations in predictors, seem to be more consistent with a central processing explanation that allows for differential manifestations of effects across scripts.

Although the majority of the evidence presented in this chapter supports the view that phonological deficits can be an underlying cause of literacy problems across languages and among bilingual populations, factors related to the script(s) and/or language(s) used by the learner need to be considered, particularly for the practical purpose of developing assessment measures. Given that literacy deficits vary across scripts/languages, whether due to different causes or differential manifestations, assessment measures need to be translated effectively and normed appropriately for the context in which the test is used, otherwise literacy difficulties may be misidentified or mis-interpreted, leading to inappropriate educational support. Such a conclusion argues for the need for assessment tools to be developed that can be used across language and bilingual contexts. Despite the focus of this chapter being on the identification of literacy difficulties, the evidence also suggests that bilingualism need not be a barrier to literacy acquisition. Indeed, the gains in literacy shown by children learning a highly regular orthography coupled with the transfer of skills between scripts may mean that bilingual-ism could, under the right learning conditions, provide an opportunity for more effective literacy acquisition: learning a more regular orthography might lead to faster acquisition of phonological awareness skills that may support the learning of a less regular orthography. Assessment measures may need to be developed with such cross-script effects in mind.

References

Brooks, P., Everatt, J., & Fidler, R. (2004). *Adult Reading Test (ART)*. London: Roehampton University of Surrey.

Cline, T., & Reason, R. (1993). Specific reading difficulties (dyslexia): Equal opportun-ities issues. *British Journal of Special Education, 20*, 30–34.

Cline, T., & Shamsi, T. (2000). *Language needs or special needs? The assessment of learning difficulties in literacy among children learning English as an additional lan-guage: A literature review*. London: DfES Publications.

Cossu, G., Shankweiler, D., Liberman, I. Y., Katz, L., & Tola, G. (1988). Awareness of phonological segments and reading ability in Italian children. *Applied Psycho-linguistics, 9*, 1–16.

Cummins, J. (1984). *Bilingualism and special education: Issues in assessment and pedagogy*. Clevedon, UK: Multilingual Matters.

Edwards, J. (1994). *The scars of dyslexia*. London: Cassell.

Elbeheri, G., & Everatt, J. (2007). Literacy ability and phonological processing skills amongst dyslexic and non-dyslexic speakers of Arabic. *Reading and Writing, 20*, 273–294.

Elbeheri, G., Everatt, J., Reid, G., & Al-Mannai, H. (2006). Dyslexia assessment in Arabic. *Journal of Research in Special Educational Needs, 6*, 143–152.

Elliot, C. D. (1983). *British Ability Scales (BAS)*. Windsor, UK: NFER-Nelson.

Everatt, J., Smythe, I., Adams, E., & Ocampo, D. (2000). Dyslexia screening measures and bilingualism. *Dyslexia, 6*, 42–56.

Everatt, J., Smythe, I., Ocampo, D., & Gyarmathy, E. (2004). Issues in the assessment of literacy-related difficulties across language backgrounds: A cross-linguistic comparison. *Journal of Research in Reading, 27*, 141–151.

Everatt, J., Smythe, I., Ocampo, D., & Veii, K. (2002). Dyslexia assessment of the bi-scriptal reader. *Topics in Language Disorders, 22*, 32–45.

Frederickson, N., & Frith, U. (1998). Identifying dyslexia in bilingual children: A phonological approach with inner London Sylheti speakers. *Dyslexia, 4*, 119–131.

Frederickson, N., Frith, U., & Reason, R. (1997). *The Phonological Assessment Battery (PhAB)*. Windsor, UK: NFER-Nelson.

Geva, E., & Siegel, L. S. (2000). Orthographic factors in the concurrent development of basic reading skills in two languages. *Reading and Writing: An Interdisciplinary Journal, 12*, 1–30.

Geva, E., & Wade-Wooley, L. (1998). Component processes in becoming English–Hebrew biliterate. In A. Y. Durgunoğlu & L. Verhoeven (Eds.), *Literacy in a multilingual context—cross-cultural perspectives* (pp. 85–110). Mahwah, NJ: Lawrence Erlbaum Associates, Inc.

Geva, E., Wade-Wooley, L., & Shany, M. (1997). Development of reading efficiency in first and second language. *Scientific Studies in Reading, 1*, 119–144.

Gholamain, E., & Geva, E. (1999). Orthographic and cognitive factors on the concurrent development of basic reading skills in English and Persian. *Language Learning, 49*, 183–217.

Goswami, U. (2000). Phonological representations, reading development and dyslexia: Towards a cross-linguistic theoretical framework. *Dyslexia, 6*, 133–151.

Goulandris, N. (Ed.). (2003). *Dyslexia in different languages: Cross linguistic comparisons*. London: Whurr.

Ho, C. S.-H., & Lai, D. N.-C. (1999). Naming-speed deficits and phonological memory deficits in Chinese developmental dyslexia. *Learning and Individual Differences, 11*, 173–186.

Katz, L., & Frost, R. (1992). The reading process is different for different orthographies: The orthographic depth hypothesis. In R. Frost & L. Katz (Eds.), *Orthography, phonology, morphology and meaning* (pp. 67–84). Amsterdam: North-Holland.

Landerl, K., Wimmer, H., & Frith, U. (1997). The impact of orthographic consistency on dyslexia: A German–English comparison. *Cognition, 63*, 315–334.

Miles, T. R., & Varma, V. (Eds.). (1995). *Dyslexia and stress*. London: Whurr.

Nation, K., & Snowling, M. J. (1998). Individual differences in contextual facilitation: Evidence from dyslexia and poor reading comprehension. *Child Development, 69*, 996–1011.

Peer, L., & Reid, G. (Eds.). (2000). *Multilingualism, literacy and dyslexia*. London: David Fulton Publishers.

Rack, J. P., Snowling, M. J., & Olson, R. K. (1992). The nonword reading deficit in developmental dyslexia: A review. *Reading Research Quarterly, 27*, 29–53.

Riddick, B. (1996). *Living with dyslexia*. London: Routledge.

Seymour, P. H. K., Aro, M., & Erskine, J. M. (2003). Foundation literacy acquisition in European orthographies. *British Journal of Psychology, 94*, 143–174.

Siegel, L. S. (1993). Phonological processing deficits as the basis of a reading disability. *Developmental Review, 13*, 246–257.

Smythe, I., & Everatt, J. (2002). Dyslexia and the multilingual child. *Topics in Language Disorders, 22*, 71–80.

Smythe, I., Everatt, J., Al-Menaye, N., He, X., Capellini, S., Gyarmathy, E., et al. (2008). Predictors of word level literacy amongst Grade 3 children in five diverse languages. *Dyslexia, 14*, 170–187.

Smythe, I., Everatt, J., Gyarmathy, E., Ho, C. S.-H., & Groeger, J. A. (2003). Short-term memory and literacy: A cross-language comparison. *Educational and Child Psychology, 20*, 37–50.

Smythe, I., Everatt, J., & Salter, R. (Eds.). (2004). *The international book of dyslexia: Part 1. Languages.* Chichester, UK: Wiley.

Snowling, M. J. (2000). *Dyslexia* (2nd ed.). Oxford, UK: Blackwell.

Stanovich, K. E. (1988). Explaining the differences between the dyslexic and the garden variety poor reader: The phonological-core variable difference model. *Journal of Learning Disabilities, 21*, 590–604.

Torgesen, J. K. (2004). Avoiding the devastating downward spiral: The evidence that early intervention prevents reading failure. *American Educator, 28*, 6–19.

Veii, K., & Everatt, J. (2005). Predictors of reading among Herero–English bilingual Namibian school children. *Bilingualism: Language and Cognition, 8*, 239–254.

Wagner, R. K., & Torgesen, J. K. (1987). The nature of phonological processing and its causal role in the acquisition of reading skills. *Psychological Bulletin, 101*, 192–212.

Wimmer, H. (1993). Characteristics of developmental dyslexia in a regular writing system. *Applied Psycholinguistics, 14*, 1–33.

Working Party of the British Psychological Society. (1999). *Dyslexia, literacy and psychological assessment. Report of a working party of the Division of Educational and Child Psychology of the British Psychological Society.* Leicester, UK: British Psychological Society.

Yamada, J. (1998). Script makes a difference: The induction of deep dyslexic errors in logograph reading. *Dyslexia, 4*, 197–211.

Ziegler, J. C., & Goswami, U. (2005). Reading acquisition, developmental dyslexia, and skilled reading across languages: A psycholinguistic grain size theory. *Psychological Bulletin, 131*, 3–29.

Section 3

Neuroimaging studies of reading in different orthographies

12 Cross-cultural differences in unimpaired and dyslexic reading: Behavioural and functional anatomical observations in readers of regular and irregular orthographies

Eraldo Paulesu, Nicola Brunswick and Federica Paganelli

Introduction

The ability to read is of enormous personal, political and economic significance, and it allows access to diverse educational and cultural resources. Reading is not acquired instinctively—it depends on teaching—but once its principles have been mastered, reading becomes effortless for the vast majority of people. Nevertheless, a sizeable minority of intelligent children have problems in learning to read and write despite adequate teaching, and for them reading never becomes effortless. These problems are caused by developmental dyslexia which differs in prevalence across different languages and writing systems.

Some of the world's most common writing systems use an alphabet. Yet not all alphabetic writing systems are alike. Italian, English and German, for instance, show different levels of regularity in the way letters correspond to speech sounds. Italian uses a highly consistent and regular mapping between a small set of speech sounds (phonemes) and a small set of letters or letter combinations (graphemes). English has a highly inconsistent and irregular representation, with more than 1000 possible letter combinations to represent the 40 sounds of the language (Coulmas, 1999; Nyikos, 1988). This makes a huge difference to the ease of acquisition of reading by young children (Frith, Wimmer, & Landerl, 1998; Seymour, Aro, & Erskine, 2003), and to dyslexic readers who fare much better when learning to read a consistent orthography such as Italian than an inconsistent orthography such as English (Barca, Burani, Di Filippo, & Zoccolotti, 2006; Brunswick, 2009; Caravolas & Volin, 2001; Paulesu et al., 2001). It even makes a difference to highly skilled readers at university level. A comparative study of the brain activation patterns of university students (described later in this chapter) has revealed the existence of a multi-component reading system in the brain. This reading system is very similar in different languages, but different emphasis is placed on the sub-components of the system depending on the consistency of the orthography.

In this chapter we discuss the nature of skilled reading in different languages, the manifestation of dyslexia across languages and the results of neuroimaging experiments that show that dyslexia is biologically similar across languages in spite of behavioural differences on reading tasks. In this way, neuroimaging provides an opportunity to extend our knowledge of reading and dyslexia beyond that gleaned from behavioural measures alone.

Prerequisites for fluent reading

What are the building blocks of fluent reading acquisition? In the literature there is widespread agreement on the factors that predict early success in learning to read by young children. The most general prerequisites are good phonological awareness and age-appropriate oral language skills, including a well-developed vocabulary and the ability to name objects rapidly and effortlessly. Likewise, early print awareness and letter recognition skills (before the start of formal teaching of reading) are strong predictors of *reading readiness* of the child—that is, the ease with which the child will learn to read (National Early Literacy Panel, 2004; also review in Ellis, 1993). The development of a mental representation of the alphabetic code (the correspondence between graphemes and phonemes) is a key factor in learning to read, even for inconsistent, complex orthographies like English. This is suggested by the fact that children taught to read through phonics instruction outperform children taught with a global 'look-and-say' method (for a review of the efficacy of different methods of teaching early reading to English-speaking children, see Rose, 2006). By the same token, remediation strategies in dyslexia are essentially based on training phonological skills (see review in Snowling, 2000).

Literacy as brain washing?

Language is a unique faculty of the human mind (Chomsky, 1975; Pinker, 1994), which arises spontaneously even in extremely adverse conditions such as congenital deafness (Petitto & Marentette, 1991; see also chapter 6, this volume). It is generally believed, and it is reasonable to assume, that oral language evolved earlier than any written language. Indeed, the earliest forms of writing date from around 4800 years BC while Homo sapiens were already present about 30,000 years BC (Coulmas, 1999).

However, even a superficial survey of the history of writing suggests that written language is not an artefact that has been imposed on people. Writing has spread quickly through very many cultures, presumably because it serves the practical needs of communication, and through writing communication endures over space and time. It is likely that reading and writing have capitalized on already existing neurocognitive modules other than those used for oral language. For instance, it is possible that the neural naming system for visual stimuli (be they objects, people, colours or shapes) is a crucial pre-requisite to reading. This may have made it possible for reading to achieve a quasi-autonomous space within the cognitive system. The reading system in a mature brain is relatively independent of other brain systems. We can infer that this must be the case since certain types of damage to the brain only impair reading (causing *acquired* dyslexia) and leave other forms of communication comparatively spared (Cappa & Vignolo, 1999; Coltheart, 1982).

Once reading has been acquired, oral language is changed too, as literate individuals become aware of the sounds of language and the way that these sounds can be explicitly manipulated (Castro-Caldas, Peterson, Reis, Stone-Elander, & Ingvar, 1998). For this reason, literacy has been considered an example of 'brain-washing' (Frith, 1998). Also, for readers of a language, the perceived sound of words is affected by the way the words are spelled. Thus, in English, it takes people longer to say that the visually presented (but dissimilarly spelled) words *soap* and *hope* rhyme with each other than the similarly spelled words *rope* and *cope*. Likewise, it takes longer to decide that the words *mint* and *pint* do not rhyme (these words share the orthographic string 'int' but not the sound pattern) than it takes to decide that the words *mint* and *cough* do not rhyme (Seidenberg & Tanenhaus, 1979). This suggests that the skilled reader's brain makes an automatic, and unconscious, connection between the sound of a word and its visual (orthographic) appearance.

Evidence for this can be found in brain activation studies using positron emission tomography (PET) scans. Démonet and colleagues, for example, found activation of visual brain areas associated with reading (particularly the left fusiform gyrus, referred to by some as the 'visual word form area'—see Bolger, Perfetti, & Schneider, 2005; and Cohen et al., 2000) when people were asked to make speech sound judgements of perceptually ambiguous phoneme pairs that they heard but did not see. This finding suggests that participants were visualizing the stimuli—mentally converting phonemes to graphemes—to help them to disambiguate the phoneme pairs (Démonet, Price, Wise, & Frackowiak, 1994).

The vagaries of writing systems

Several kinds of writing system have developed over the years to represent word sounds and/or meaning (see chapter 1, this volume). One of these is a system where the meaning of pictures or of abstract symbols is directly accessible regardless of the sound of the word. This apparently arbitrary (or mostly arbitrary) mapping between pictures/symbols and spoken words is variously referred to as a pictographic, ideographic or logographic writing system. A good example of logographic reading in everyday life is the numbers that we read: the written symbols 1, 2, 3 can be just as easily read as *one*, *two*, *three*; *eins*, *zwei*, *drei*; *uno*, *due*, *tre*; and so on. Similarly, the mathematical symbols that we use (e.g., +, −, =) may be understood by speakers of any language irrespective of the language-specific names (*plus*, *minus*, *equals* in English) that are applied to the symbols. However, in the history of writing, no system has worked completely in this way. Even the Egyptian writing system, with its well-known pictorial (hieroglyphic) elements, has phonetic components. According to Coulmas, 'in Egyptian writing only determinatives— key signs which specify a semantic domain and are not pronounced—can be said to be ideographic' (Coulmas, 1999, p. 225). The Chinese writing system was also traditionally believed (by non-Chinese speakers) to be predominantly ideographic, although this is now known to be false (it is more accurately described as being morpho-syllabic or morpho-graphic—see chapter 10, this volume). It is likely that a component of sound representation was present in writing systems from the beginning, co-existing perhaps with instantly recognizable pictorial symbols for important nouns. Conversely, even highly sound-based writing systems, such as alphabetic systems, may have used instantly recognizable elements. This is seen, for instance, in the frequent abbreviations used in Roman inscriptions (e.g., *D N*, for *dominus noster*, meaning *our emperor*). Modern advertising logos still act in a similar way.

Today the most predominant forms of orthography are alphabetic. There is a basic principle in the use of alphabets that each speech sound in a language can be represented by a letter or string of letters according to a simple set of mapping rules. However, there is a limited set of graphic symbols used for the alphabet regardless of the number of phonemes in a language. In languages such as Italian and Finnish, which consist of relatively few phonemes, this does not cause too many difficulties. There is an almost one-to-one mapping between graphemes and phonemes in these languages, so they come close to having a perfectly transparent (shallow) orthography. However, there are still some minor ambiguities even in these languages. In Italian, these occur primarily at the stage of stress assignment for words with more than two syllables and a consonant–vowel structure. For example, it is not obvious from the written form where to place the stress in the words *tavolo* [table] and *catena* [chain].

By contrast, in languages such as English and French, which consist of many phonemes, having a limited set of alphabetic symbols causes tremendous difficulties. There is a one-to-many mapping between graphemes and phonemes (and vice versa) in these languages, so they have a highly opaque (deep) orthography. English, for example, includes regularly spelled words, such as *dog*, *ship*, and *carpet*, alongside many irregular words, such as *island*, *yacht* and *women*. The latter are spelled in ways that do not allow one to retrieve the word sound by phonological decoding. In these cases, the word sounds can be retrieved only when the entire sequence of letters is recognized. On the other hand, the same sound can be represented by different combinations of letters, like the 'i' sound in *clinical*, *typical* and *women*. As in shallow orthographies, stress assignment in English is largely ambiguous and rarely conveys meaning except in a few cases (e.g., to distinguish between homographs like *con*tent and con*tent*).

Is there a reading instinct?

Remarkably, regardless of the structure of the particular alphabetic orthography, an unimpaired reader can achieve extremely high levels of reading speed and efficiency. Evidence of this efficiency is given by observations of the different speeds with which one can name an object compared with the speed of reading the written name of the same object (even when the written name of the object is highly irregular, such as *yacht*). In an unpublished study, Paulesu and Frith asked fluent readers either to read the names of objects (e.g., *piano, banana, computer*) or to name pictures of these same objects. They were asked to perform both tasks as quickly as possible. The results showed that reading was faster on average by more than 100 ms—with average response times to the pictures of 550 ms and to the words of 430 ms. This was despite the fact that participants were given the chance to practise naming the pictures before the actual reaction time measurements were made. This, and other examples such as the Stroop effect, can be seen as evidence for a reading 'instinct'—that is, a disposition that compels readers to read anything they see in print (even though this is not an innate instinct but one that has been implanted through teaching and learning), and to do it better than other forms of visual naming.

Further evidence comes from functional neuroimaging experiments involving 'implicit' reading that have been undertaken by Price and colleagues (Brunswick, McCrory, Price, Frith, & Frith, 1999; Price, Wise, & Frackowiak, 1996). In these experiments participants were asked to make judgements about written words, non-words and strings of false-fonts (meaningless symbols which are designed to be letter-like). Specifically, they were asked to detect the presence or absence of ascenders within these stimuli. Ascenders are graphic features which rise above the midline of the stimulus (e.g., *b, l, t* as opposed to *s, p, n*). The real words, non-words and strings of false fonts were designed to be as closely matched as possible. Non-words were created from the real words through substitution of the internal consonants, so *cannon* became *caggon*, and *table* became *tagle*; false fonts were created by substituting letters in the real words with letter-like symbols matched for size and the presence or absence of ascenders, so *cannon* became ⵣꟷⵘ ⵘⵝꟷ and *table* became ⵁⵀⵎⵊⵔ. Participants pressed one key of a response box if an ascender was present and another key if no ascender was present. Participants were *never* asked to read the words. Rather, the instructions emphasized the visual feature detection task. If the participants read the words implicitly this was beyond the stated requirements of the task.

Brain activity during the tasks with words and non-words versus false-fonts showed activation of the classic language areas of the left hemisphere involved in reading. These include the inferior frontal gyrus [Brodmann's Area (BA) 44/6], the superior/middle temporal gyrus (BA 21/22), inferior temporal gyrus/fusiform gyrus (BA 37) and parts of the cerebellum (see Figure 12.1).

a

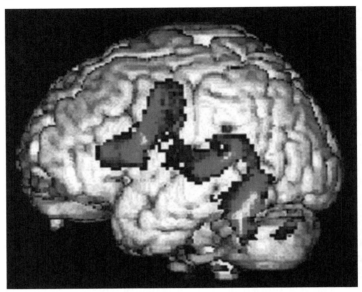

b

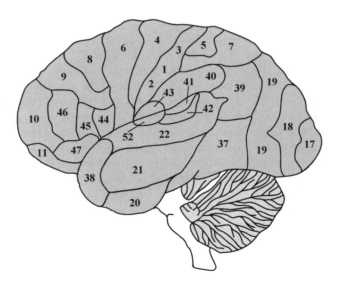

Figure 12.1 (a) Regions of brain activity in skilled readers during a visual feature
detection (implicit reading) task; (b) a map of Brodmann areas (BAs) for
the identification of specific regions in the brain—e.g., Broca's area in the
inferior frontal gyrus is also referred to as BA 44. This figure is published
in colour at http://www.cognitiveneurosciencearena.com/brain-scans/.

It is as if the brains of skilled readers cannot help but read when a written word comes to their attention. Results from a study in which this same task has been used with dyslexic readers are reported later in this chapter.

Cultural diversity in reading

Evidence indicates that the structure of an orthography impacts on the ease and speed with which children learn to read the language. This is the 'cultural' hypothesis of reading, and it is plausible if we consider that young Italian readers can achieve 92 per cent accuracy on word reading tests after only six months of schooling (Cossu, Gugliotta, & Marshall, 1995) while learning to read in English takes considerably longer. For example, accuracy levels in English are lower and reading speed is slower even after three years of schooling when compared to German, another consistent orthography (see chapter 7, this volume; see also Frith et al., 1998; and Landerl, Wimmer, & Frith, 1997). In spite of the evidence of differences in children's reading acquisition, until recently it was unclear whether orthographic complexity also has an impact on the reading performance of adult skilled readers.

To enable us to answer this question, we tested the reading performance of unimpaired adult readers from Italy and the United Kingdom (Paulesu et al., 2000). Volunteers were placed in a PET scanner and asked to read high-frequency regular words from their own language (e.g., the English words: *cottage*, *apron*, *market*, and the Italian words: *carta*, *ponte*, *moto*) and non-words derived from these words (e.g., *connage*, *afton*, *marnet*, and *corla*, *ponda*, *moco*). Participants were also asked to read familiar 'international' words that have the same spelling and meaning in both languages. Half of these words conformed to the English orthography (e.g., *bitter*, *corner*, *basket*), the other half to the Italian orthography (e.g., *pasta*, *villa*, *coma*).

The behavioural results were clear-cut. The Italian adults were consistently faster than the English adults at reading words in their own language, non-words derived both from Italian and from English and international words that conformed to the Italian orthography. It is important to emphasize that the English readers were asked to read regularly spelled words. Therefore the differences observed during reading are not related to the actual complexity of the stimuli. Rather, they are related to the general complexity of the English orthography with its multiple mappings between graphemes and phonemes.

Was there anything special about the Italian readers that made them faster? This possibility was excluded by the fact that their reading performance was identical to that of the English readers when the stimuli were international words from English. Here, Italian readers probably used an 'English' reading strategy and were slowed down. In addition, no differences in response time or accuracy were observed between the two groups in any of the control tasks that did not involve reading. These tasks required participants to name, as quickly as possible, pictures of objects whose names are the same in both languages (e.g., *hamburger*, *piano*, *banana*); to repeat aloud pairs of words common to both languages (e.g., *tennis/polo*) as many times as possible in 15 seconds; and to produce as many words as possible in one minute that either start with a given letter (letter fluency task) or belong to the semantic category 'animals' (semantic fluency task). These results strongly suggest that the behavioural differences observed in the reading tasks were due to the structure of the orthography used in each language rather than to accidental differences in the linguistic skills of the two groups.

These behavioural differences were paralleled by neurophysiological differences measured with PET in the form of local cerebral blood flow increases. These PET data revealed functional commonalities and differences between brain regions involved in reading by English and Italian readers. Both groups showed common activations in cortical language areas of the left hemisphere, as shown in Figure 12.2. These regions include the left inferior frontal gyrus (BA 44), the precentral gyrus (BA 6), the left and right superior temporal gyri (BA 22), the left middle temporal gyrus (BA 21), left inferior temporal gyrus (BA 20), the left fusiform gyrus (BA 37) and the junction of the left and right temporo-parietal cortices (BA 22/40).

Differences in activation were also found between the two groups of readers. It should be stressed, however, that these differences were not in terms of different areas being involved in reading but, rather, the same areas being activated to a greater or lesser extent by readers of English and Italian. Italian readers showed greater activation of the left planum temporale, a region at the temporo-parietal junction (BA 22/42) that has been associated with phonological processing (Démonet et al., 1994; Jacquemot, Pallier, LeBihan, Dehaene, & Dupoux, 2003). In contrast, and for non-words in particular, English readers showed greater activations in the left posterior inferior temporal gyrus (BA 21/37) and anterior inferior frontal gyrus (BA 45), areas that have been associated with word retrieval during reading and naming, and with semantic processes (Poldrack et al., 1999). These findings provide neuroimaging support to the weak version of the orthographic depth hypothesis. Whereas readers of English are more likely to activate the orthographic lexicon to allow them to select the correct pronunciation of words, readers of Italian most likely use all strategies, including sub-lexical mappings, as the operation of lexical and sub-lexical strategies does not produce conflicting results in the way that it would for English readers. These results suggest that within a common brain system for reading there is a different emphasis on the subcomponents of this system that is dependent on the specific demands of the particular orthographic code.

Further light has been shed on the commonalities and differences in brain regions used across languages and writing systems by a meta-analysis of 43 neuroimaging studies of word reading undertaken by Bolger et al. (2005). This analysis combined data from 25 studies of reading in English and other European alphabetic languages, nine studies of reading Chinese, five studies of reading Japanese kana and four studies of reading Japanese kanji. By

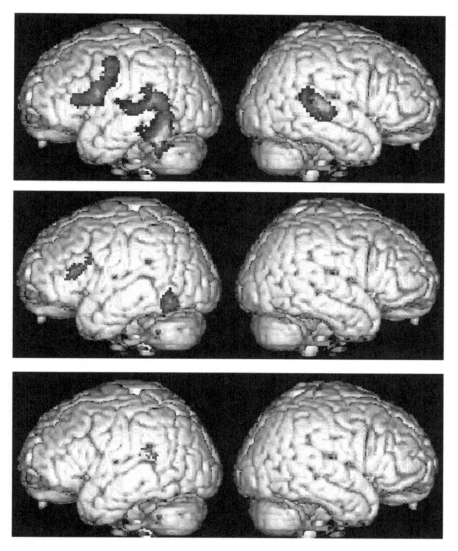

Figure 12.2 Regions of common activation during reading (top row); greater activation in English readers than Italian readers during non-word reading (middle row); and greater activation in Italian readers than English readers regardless of word type (bottom row). This figure is published in colour at http://www.cognitiveneurosciencearena.com/brain-scans/.

averaging across patterns of activation, the authors identified a common network of brain regions, including: the left superior posterior temporal gyrus (BA 22); the left inferior frontal gyrus (BA 6); and the left temporo-occipital cortex—in particular, the posterior fusiform gyrus/inferior occipital cortex (BA 19) and the mid fusiform gyrus (BA 37). These regions were active during word reading across all the languages and writing systems included in the meta-analysis.

Of course, the authors also identified language-specific regions of activity, although these were often in the vicinity of the common reading network. These regions included the superior posterior temporal gyrus (BA 39/40), which was active during the reading of English/European languages and Japanese kana but not during the reading of Chinese or Japanese kanji, and the left dorsolateral frontal cortex and right inferior occipital/posterior fusiform cortices, which were active during the reading of Chinese characters but not during the reading of European or Japanese scripts.

These findings suggest that while there is a strong degree of overlap across writing systems for reading processes—mapping visual features onto phonological and semantic codes—and the brain regions that support them, there are also important language-specific divergences in these processes and regions. The reading of European alphabetic text and Japanese kana involves a greater engagement of brain regions associated with phonological analysis and grapheme–phoneme conversion, while the reading of Chinese characters involves a greater engagement of brain regions associated with the processing of visual features and the 'synchronous processing of semantic and phonological ... connections that mutually constrain the identification of the graphic form' (Bolger et al., 2005, p. 101). Once again, it is important to note that these data demonstrate a strong convergence of activity within a common reading network but differential engagement of neural subcomponents according to the specific demands of the writing system.

In an interesting twist on this type of cross-cultural comparison, a group of French researchers explored commonalities and differences in brain regions involved in reading different languages in a group of monolingual, bilingual and multilingual patients undergoing surgery to remove brain tumours (Roux et al., 2004). Direct cortical stimulation mapping was carried out on the exposed brains of 35 monolingual French speakers and 19 bilingual or multilingual speakers of French plus one or more of English, Spanish, Occitan (a regional French dialect), German, Russian, Chinese or Arabic. Of these patients, 44 had left hemisphere tumours and 10 had right hemisphere tumours. Patients were asked to perform two tasks while their brains were stimulated: reading unrelated sentences (e.g., *the north wind blows strongly*; *the chair is pretty*) and naming objects (e.g., *camera, door, flute*) in each of their languages. Stimulation of brain regions involved in reading and naming caused 'interference' in the patients' ability to perform the reading and naming tasks accurately, typically leading to anomia (a severe naming difficulty), speech/reading arrest, hesitation, paraphasia (the production of inaccurate and often unintelligible speech) or word repetition.

Using this technique, Roux et al. identified reading regions in the left frontal and temporo-parietal lobes, particularly the lower pre- and post-central gyrus, angular and supramarginal gyri and posterior superior temporal gyrus, the posterior part of the inferior frontal gyrus and middle frontal gyrus and the posterior part of the middle temporal gyrus. Brain regions involved in reading extended over a larger area than those involved in naming, although reading and naming regions were usually within the same cortical area, with occasional overlap. Some brain regions (in frontal, temporal and parietal cortices) were language-specific, but most were found to be involved in reading in two, three or four languages. At least one language-specific reading site was found in 8 of the 19 bilingual/multilingual speakers. Overall, however, no differences were found in reading or naming sites between monolingual and bilingual patients. This latter finding supports previous brain imaging studies that have reported that reading/listening to a second language involves largely the same brain regions as does reading/listening to a first language in bilingual speakers of Japanese and English (Nakada, Fujii, & Kwee, 2001), Mandarin and English (Chee, Tan, & Thiel, 1999), Spanish and English (Illes et al., 1999), Italian and English (Perani et al., 1996), Spanish and Catalan (Perani et al., 1998) and Dutch and English (van Heuven, Schriefers, Dijkstra, & Hagoort, 2008).

Clearly, studies of the brain regions used by bilingual and multilingual speakers must be careful to control for the effects of relative proficiency in each language, and the age at which each was acquired, both of which can influence brain activation (Perani et al., 1998). While early bilinguals (who learned their two languages before the age of ten and invariably achieve a high level of proficiency) and proficient bilinguals (whether early or late learners) display similar patterns of brain activation for both languages, late bilinguals who show low or moderate proficiency in the second language tend to display different patterns of brain activation in the two languages.

When reading is problematic: dyslexia across languages

Irrespective of the language(s) that they speak, the majority of children in Europe master the reading process within the first few years of schooling. However, a small proportion of children, estimated at about 5 to 10 per cent of the population of the English-speaking world, find this task terribly difficult; in severe cases, they never become proficient readers. This difficulty—developmental dyslexia—is not due to inadequate educational resources and is largely independent of intelligence (Miles & Haslum, 1986).

The recognition of dyslexia as a neuro-developmental disorder is relatively recent (see reviews by Frith, 1999; and Habib, 2000), although some people doubt the universality and specificity of dyslexia as a single entity because its behavioural manifestations can be so variable. Undoubtedly dyslexia has culture-specific manifestations, and the prevalence of dyslexia differs across languages. For instance, using one behavioural definition of dyslexia—word recognition accuracy in relation to intelligence—Lindgren, De Renzi, and Richman (1985) reported that the prevalence of dyslexia in Italy was half that in the United States.

The effect of language—or, more specifically depth of orthography—on the manifestation of dyslexia has been addressed in an electrophysiological (event-related potential) study comparing the performance of Hebrew/English bilingual adults on a lexical decision task (Oren & Breznitz, 2005). This task included real English and Hebrew words and non-words derived from them. Because Hebrew and English differ in terms of their orthographic depth (unlike English, vowelized Hebrew is shallow), this study enabled its authors to explore the influence of orthography on the speed and accuracy of dyslexic and unimpaired readers of these two languages. On the behavioural task the dyslexic readers were much slower and less accurate than the skilled readers in response to the English words and non-words. They were also much slower (but no less accurate) in response to the Hebrew words and non-words. Furthermore, the dyslexic readers were much slower in response to the English stimuli relative to the Hebrew stimuli than were the skilled readers. The electrophysiological data showed much longer latencies for the dyslexic readers relative to the skilled readers in response to English and Hebrew words and English non-words. Again, these findings highlight the importance of orthographic depth for the manifestation of dyslexia. While the dyslexic readers experienced difficulties in both their languages, these difficulties were more pronounced in response to the irregularity of English than the regularity of vowelized Hebrew. Oren and Breznitz interpreted their findings as reflecting a 'universal basis of dyslexia in the brain' (2005, p. 148), arguing that readers who are dyslexic in one language will experience similar difficulties in any language, although these difficulties will be most pronounced in languages that place the greatest demands on the individual's impaired phonological processing skills.

Several anatomical and functional imaging experiments have been carried out with dyslexic readers (e.g., Brambati et al., 2004; Hoeft et al., 2007; Pugh et al., 2001; Silani et al., 2005; Steinbrink et al., 2008; Temple et al., 2001). As would be expected on the basis of behavioural- and cognitive-level descriptions of dyslexia, these imaging studies support the presence of abnormality within those parts of the brain's language system that are associated with phonological processing and with integrating visual and phonological information during reading (see Habib, 2000). Just as phonological awareness and the depth of a language's orthography impact upon the speed and success of unimpaired reading development, so they also affect the prevalence and severity of dyslexia across languages. This is the 'cultural' hypothesis of dyslexia.

We tested the impact of orthographic effects on behavioural performance and underlying neurophysiology of English, French and Italian dyslexic and unimpaired readers in our study of explicit and implicit reading of real words and non-words (Paulesu et al., 2001). In this study we found that Italian dyslexic readers (using a shallow orthography that facilitates reading) performed more accurately on reading and phonological tasks than did English and French dyslexic readers (see effect sizes in Figure 12.3). This could still be interpreted as evidence that dyslexia is a variable entity across languages.

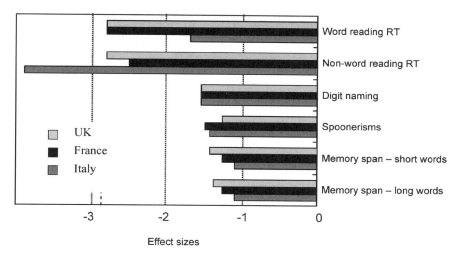

Figure 12.3 Effect size (*z*-scores) of the differences between English, French and Italian dyslexic and control readers on the tests of reading and phonological processing. Negative *z*-scores represent impaired performance by the dyslexic readers relative to control readers of the same language.

However, the difference between the Italian dyslexic and unimpaired readers was just as great as the difference between the English and French dyslexic and unimpaired readers. Overall, these findings support the idea that dyslexia is associated with a phonological deficit. Moreover, they show that this phonological deficit is universal and independent of orthography, at least across the languages investigated in this study.

PET scans recorded during the reading of simple words (concrete bisyllabic nouns such as *window* and *table*) showed the same reduced activity in a region of the left temporal lobe, primarily the middle temporal gyrus and the inferior temporal and fusiform gyri (BA 21/37), in dyslexic readers from all three countries (see Figure 12.4). In view of our previous finding of orthography-specific effects in the brain activation of English, Italian and French skilled readers (Paulesu et al., 2000), we looked for similar differences in the brains of the dyslexic readers, but none were evident. We suggest that this reflects a less developed reading system that is therefore less able (than in skilled readers) to adapt to the specific requirements of the orthography used in each language.

An important aspect of the Paulesu et al. study not considered in some earlier studies of dyslexia (e.g., Rumsey et al., 1997; Salmelin, Service, Kiesilä, Uutela, & Salonen, 1996) is that the dyslexic readers and the unimpaired readers performed this simple reading task equally accurately. Differences in the patterns of neural activation found between the groups could not therefore be attributed simply to differences in task performance. Reduced activation in these regions of the temporal lobe—which have been

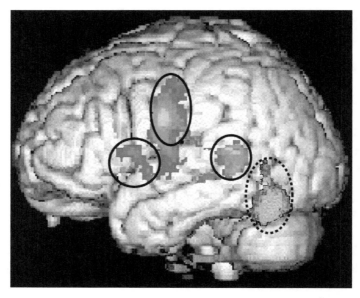

Figure 12.4 Regions of normal brain activation (indicated by the solid lines) and reduced activation (indicated by the dotted line) in English, French and Italian dyslexic readers during the reading of concrete nouns. This figure is published in colour at http://www.cognitiveneurosciencearena.com/ brain-scans/.

implicated in word finding during naming tasks and reading (Brunswick et al., 1999; Price & Friston, 1997)—has been reported in German-speaking dyslexic children (Georgiewa et al., 1999), English-speaking dyslexic adults (Rumsey et al., 1997; Shaywitz et al., 1998) and Finnish-speaking dyslexic adults (Salmelin et al., 1996).

This latter study, using magnetoencephalography (MEG), found that while skilled readers of Finnish show strong activation of the left inferior temporo-occipital region within 200 ms of silently reading real words and non-words, Finnish dyslexic readers fail to activate this region within this time window (Salmelin et al., 1996). Some of the dyslexic readers displayed a late response in the inferior temporo-occipital region (400–700 ms post stimulus onset), albeit to a much lesser extent than the skilled readers. Other dyslexic readers failed to show any such activation within the left temporal lobe. Conversely, the dyslexic readers showed activation in the left inferior frontal lobe (approximately corresponding to Broca's area) while the skilled readers did not. The majority of the skilled readers produced greater activation in response to non-words than real words (in the left middle temporal lobe and central sulcus), as did half of the dyslexic readers (in the temporo-parieto-occipital region). This pattern suggests that in dyslexic readers the modality-independent naming system, of which the temporal gyrus forms a part (see

Price & Friston, 1997), is failing to activate or at least is activating much more slowly than in the skilled readers.

A follow-up study by the same group investigated Finnish dyslexic readers' contextual processing of words within sentences (Helenius, Salmelin, Service, & Connolly, 1999). In this study participants read sentences in which the last word was either (1) expected (e.g., *The piano was out of tune*), (2) semantically appropriate but unexpected (e.g., *When the power went out the house became quiet*), (3) semantically anomalous but phonologically similar to the expected word (e.g., *The gambler had a bad streak of luggage*) or (4) semantically anomalous and phonologically dissimilar to the expected word (e.g., *The pizza was too hot to sing*). Contrary to the earlier results, conditions (1), (2) and (4) elicited anatomically similar responses from skilled and dyslexic readers. In the majority of respondents from both groups a region of the left superior temporal cortex was activated. However, a difference was observed between the groups in their response to the sentences in which the final word was semantically anomalous but phonologically similar to the expected word (Condition 3). The dyslexic readers showed weaker activations to these sentences than to any of the others, and mirroring the findings of the previous study, their activations were delayed by approximately 100 ms relative to those of the skilled readers. The authors suggest that although the sentences provided contextual support for word identification, thus facilitating reading for the dyslexic readers and making the process more cortically similar to that of the skilled readers, the responses of the dyslexic readers were not typical. Unlike the skilled readers who identified words as wholes, the dyslexic readers seemed to rely on sublexical reading processes; these processes caused them unexpected difficulty in the reading of semantically inappropriate words that started with the same letters as the expected words.

Although some studies have shown that dyslexic readers produce little or no activation, or delayed activation, of the temporal-occipital cortex, McCrory, Mechelli, Frith, and Price (2005) found that English-speaking skilled and dyslexic readers both showed activation in this region during word reading and picture naming. However, the dyslexic readers showed relatively less activation than did the skilled readers. Since this region is located between the visual cortex and the anterior temporal cortex, and it has connections to the frontal cortex, this may be where visual, phonological and semantic information is integrated (McCrory et al., 2005). Dysfunction of this region might therefore reflect impairment to this integrative process and may explain the reading and naming deficits of dyslexic readers.

Dyslexia and disconnection

Impairment in the process of integrating different types of information that are necessary for reading may be due not only to dysfunction within specific brain regions, but also to poor connectivity within the brain's language network. This suggestion was made by Paulesu and colleagues following a study in which they observed striking differences in the pattern of brain activation recorded from adult dyslexic and non-dyslexic readers during the performance of a visual rhyme judgement task and a short-term memory task (Paulesu et al., 1996). While the non-dyslexic readers activated anterior and posterior language regions (Broca's area and Wernicke's area) and the insula irrespective of task, during the memory task the dyslexic readers activated only Wernicke's area, and during the rhyming task they activated only Broca's area. In neither condition did they activate the insula. This lack of connection between the anterior and posterior language regions, via the insula and sub-cortical connecting white matter bundles, may reflect a lack of automaticity in the processing of language by the dyslexic readers—i.e., while non-dyslexic readers automatically activate brain regions across the language network when processing language, dyslexic readers do not do this, they only activate those brain regions that are necessary for performing the task.

Abnormal patterns of activation within the left frontal and temporal lobes of dyslexic readers' brains may be explained in terms of the microscopic structure of these regions and the integrity of the connections between them. For example, Silani et al. (2005) compared the density of grey matter and white matter in the brains of English, Italian and French dyslexic and non-dyslexic readers whose behavioural and PET activation data had previously been reported by Paulesu et al. (2001). They found a significant reduction in grey matter density in the left middle temporal gyrus (BA 21) and a significant increase of grey matter density in the left middle posterior temporal gyrus (BA 37) in the brains of all three groups of dyslexic readers. They also found a common reduction in white matter density in the left arcuate fasciculus (a tract of fibres that connects anterior and posterior language areas) and the left post-central gyrus in these individuals. Interestingly, the greater the increase of grey matter density in BA 37 in each dyslexic reader, the worse that individual's performance on a test of reading speed. Silani and colleagues suggest that the increase in grey matter density in BA 37 reflects the presence of cortical abnormalities in this region of the brain (which Pugh et al., 2000, have identified as being a key region necessary for skilled reading). Klingberg et al. (2000) have reported similar anatomical differences in the brains of dyslexic and non-dyslexic readers bilaterally within the white matter of the temporo-parietal region. Once again, a significant relationship was reported between the microstructure of this white matter in the left hemisphere temporo-parietal cortex and non-word reading ability.

Together, these anatomical and functional findings help to explain the reading, naming and phonological processing difficulties of dyslexic readers. As Silani et al. suggest:

The coexistence of local cortical changes together with abnormality of cortico-cortical connectivity within the language network offers a more realistic description of the neurology of dyslexia at a systems level and may explain why tasks like reading or naming, which require the integration of multiple visual, phonological and articulatory codes, are sensitive in revealing a dyslexic brain to teachers and parents.

(2005, p. 2459)

It remains to be seen whether this explanation also holds true for readers of non-alphabetic orthographies like Chinese. Indeed, given the different cognitive demands of the orthography, some differences should be expected. A functional magnetic resonance imaging (fMRI) study by Siok and colleagues with Chinese dyslexic children has identified a region in the left middle frontal gyrus (BA 9) that differentiates these children from age-matched unimpaired readers during the performance of a visual rhyme judgement task (Siok, Niu, Jin, Perfetti, & Tan, 2008). Significantly less grey matter volume was also observed in this region in the brains of the dyslexic children relative to the unimpaired readers.

This region in the left middle frontal gyrus that differentiated between the dyslexic and non-dyslexic children is believed to be involved in the allocation of cognitive resources for working memory and in the control of the right hand for handwriting. Learning to read Chinese involves memorizing fairly arbitrary associations between complex written characters and their pronunciations, and Chinese children spend a great deal of time learning characters by writing them out repeatedly. It is therefore possible that this difference in grey matter volume (and in functional activation) may reflect nothing more than that Chinese dyslexic readers are less likely than their non-dyslexic peers to spend time writing because it is a task that they find frustrating and difficult. However, since no reading-age match comparison was made in this study to see if less experienced, younger readers showed activation in this region, it was not possible to test this hypothesis.

A difference has also been found between Chinese dyslexic and unimpaired readers in the left fusiform gyrus, i.e., in the same posterior brain region associated with dyslexic readers of English, Italian, French and Finnish. However, this difference was only found when the children performed a lexical decision task but not a homophone decision task (Siok, Perfetti, Jin, & Tan, 2004). These two tasks go beyond mere reading, and therefore the partially negative finding of Siok and colleagues cannot be interpreted as yet as evidence of 'Chinese' dyslexia being diverse at the biological level from 'alphabetic' dyslexia.

The finding that dyslexia may be associated with slightly different structural and functional characteristics in alphabetic and non-alphabetic languages further highlights the importance of comparisons across different languages and different writing systems, considering the specific orthographic and phonological requirements of each, if we are to understand fully the neurobiological basis of dyslexia. (This topic is considered further in chapter 13, this volume.)

Conclusions

The studies reported in this chapter show how different languages influence the manifestation and severity of dyslexic symptoms and have clear implications for the accuracy of diagnosis of dyslexia in these languages. It is apparent that diagnosis should not be defined in terms of reading performance, as this may lead to an underestimation of the disorder in languages with simple orthographies. Conversely, even very 'mild' dyslexia may manifest itself as a severe reading difficulty in languages with complex orthographies.

The observation of common brain regions showing altered activation in dyslexic readers from different countries is a crucial finding as it suggests that a single neurological disorder underlies dyslexia (at least for alphabetic orthographies) in spite of some superficial behavioural differences across languages. These differences can now be related to cultural factors, particularly those represented by the orthographic structure of a given language. The studies reported in this chapter explain why in languages with a shallow orthography, such as Italian and Finnish, the impact of dyslexia is diminished, with the consequence that the prevalence of dyslexia is probably underestimated. By contrast, the irregular orthographies of English and French cause greater difficulty for people with even fairly mild dyslexia.

The impact of dyslexia on cognitive tasks other than reading is yet to be fully explored. However, there is abundant evidence that a weak phonological system may prevent the fast and fluent acquisition of a foreign language, particularly one with a deep orthography, if learning is mediated by reading (Lundberg, 2002; Simon, 2000). Specialized training in phonological processing may help individuals with mild dyslexia to achieve more in this area. For children growing up in countries where the native language has a complex orthography, the evidence points to an advantage of teaching methods based on phonics. These methods work by emphasizing the correspondences between graphemes and phonemes using regularly spelled words. Brain imaging studies in which dyslexic individuals are scanned before and after a period of intensive phonological training reveal the specific effects that this training has at the neural level (as studies of aphasic adults have also done; e.g., Cappa et al., 1997; Musso et al., 1999).

In one such study, dyslexic children were scanned before and after a period of training in auditory language processing (Temple et al., 2003). The authors observed that not only did this training improve the children's reading performance, it also resulted in increased activation in brain regions including the left temporo-parietal cortex and inferior frontal gyrus. Similarly, Small and colleagues used fMRI to study brain reorganization in a woman with acquired phonological dyslexia, before and after therapy involving the teaching of grapheme–phoneme correspondences (Small, Flores, & Noll, 1998). These authors found that prior to therapy, the patient's brain activation during reading was predominantly in the left angular gyrus, a region perhaps associated with lexical reading, whereas after therapy activation was predominantly in the left lingual gyrus, a region associated with sub-lexical (grapho-phonological) reading.

It should be noted, of course, that structural and functional differences observed between the brains of dyslexic and skilled readers may not necessarily be the cause of dyslexic readers' reading difficulties but, rather, an effect of lack of reading and writing practice; or they may be due to the use of compensatory strategies. Future longitudinal studies of brain development in speakers of different languages who become either dyslexic or skilled readers will enable researchers to identify commonalities and differences in the relative contributions of brain regions as these individuals learn to read. Such studies will contribute greatly to our knowledge of the neural basis of skilled reading development in different orthographies. They will also provide greater insight into the degree of neurobiological unity in dyslexia in the face of cultural diversity.

References

Barca, L., Burani, C., Di Filippo, G., & Zoccolotti, P. (2006). Italian developmental dyslexic and proficient readers: Where are the differences? *Brain and Language*, *98*, 347–351.

Bolger, D. J., Perfetti, C. A., & Schneider, W. (2005). Cross-cultural effect on the brain revisited: Universal structures plus writing system variation. *Human Brain Mapping*, *25*, 92–104.

Brambati, S. M., Termin, C., Ruffino, M., Stella, G., Fazio, F., Cappa, S. F., et al. (2004). Regional reductions of gray matter volume in familial dyslexia. *Neurology*, *63*, 742–745.

Brunswick, N. (2009). *A beginner's guide to dyslexia*. Oxford, UK: Oneworld Publications.

Brunswick, N., McCrory, E., Price, C. J., Frith, C. D., & Frith, U. (1999). Explicit and implicit processing of words and pseudowords by adult developmental dyslexics: A search for Wernicke's Wortschatz? *Brain*, *122*, 1901–1917.

Cappa, S. F., Perani, D., Grassi, F., Bressi, S., Alberoni, M., Franceschi, M., et al. (1997). A PET follow-up study of recovery after stroke in acute aphasics. *Brain and Language*, *56*, 55–67.

Cappa, S. F., & Vignolo, L. A. (1999). The neurological foundations of language. In G. Denes & L. Pizzamiglio (Eds.), *Handbook of clinical and experimental neuropsychology* (pp. 155–179). Hove, UK: Psychology Press.

Caravolas, M., & Volin, J. (2001). Spelling errors among dyslexic children learning a transparent orthography: The case of Czech. *Dyslexia: An International Journal of Research and Practice*, *7*, 229–245.

Castro-Caldas, A., Peterson, K. M., Reis, A., Stone-Elander, S., & Ingvar, M. (1998).

The illiterate brain: Learning to read and write during childhood influences the functional organization of the adult brain. *Brain, 121,* 1053–1063.

Chee, M. W. L., Tan, E. W. L., & Thiel, T. (1999). Mandarin and English single word processing studied with fMRI. *Journal of Neuroscience, 19,* 3050–3056.

Chomsky, N. (1975). *Reflections on language.* New York: Pantheon Books.

Cohen, L., Dehaene, S., Naccache, L., Lehéricy, S., Dehaene-Lambertz, G., Hénaff, M.-A., et al. (2000). The visual word form area. Spatial and temporal characterization of an initial stage of reading in normal subjects and posterior split-brain patients. *Brain, 123,* 291–307.

Coltheart, M. (1982). The psycholinguistic analysis of acquired dyslexias: Some illustrations. *Philosophical Transactions of the Royal Society, B298,* 151–164.

Cossu, G., Gugliotta, M., & Marshall, J. C. (1995). Acquisition of reading and written spelling in a transparent orthography: Two non-parallel processes? *Reading and Writing: An Interdisciplinary Journal, 7,* 9–22.

Coulmas, F. (1999). *The Blackwell encyclopedia of writing systems.* Oxford, UK: Blackwell.

Démonet, J.-F., Price, C. J., Wise, R., & Frackowiak, R. S. J. (1994). A PET study of cognitive strategies in normal subjects during language tasks. Influence of phonetic ambiguity and sequence processing on phoneme monitoring. *Brain, 117,* 671–682.

Ellis, A. W. (1993). *Reading, writing and dyslexia: A cognitive analysis.* Hove, UK: Psychology Press.

Frith, U. (1998). Literally changing the brain. *Brain, 121,* 1011–1112.

Frith, U. (1999). Paradoxes in the definition of dyslexia. *Dyslexia: An International Journal of Research and Practice, 5,* 192–214.

Frith, U., Wimmer, H., & Landerl, K. (1998). Differences in phonological recoding in German- and English-speaking children. *Scientific Studies of Reading, 2,* 31–54.

Georgiewa, P., Rzanny, R., Hopf, J., Knab, R., Glauche, V., Kaiser, W., et al. (1999). fMRI during word processing in dyslexic and normal reading children. *Neuroreport, 10,* 3459–3465.

Habib, M. (2000). The neurological basis of developmental dyslexia: An overview and working hypothesis. *Brain, 123,* 2372–2399.

Helenius, P., Salmelin, R., Service, E., & Connolly, J. (1999). Semantic cortical activation in dyslexic readers. *Journal of Cognitive Neuroscience, 11,* 535–550.

Hoeft, F., Meyler, A., Hernandez, A., Juel, C., Taylor-Hill, H., Martindale, J. L., et al. (2007). Functional and morphometric brain dissociation between dyslexia and reading ability. *Proceedings of the National Academy of Sciences of the United States of America, 104,* 4234–4239.

Illes, J., Francis, W. S., Desmond, J. E., Glover, G. H., Gabrieli, J. D. E., Poldrack, R. A., et al. (1999). Convergent cortical representation of semantic processing in bilinguals. *Brain and Language, 70,* 347–363.

Jacquemot, C., Pallier, C., LeBihan, D., Dehaene, S., & Dupoux, E. (2003). Phonological grammar shapes the auditory cortex: A functional magnetic resonance imaging study. *Journal of Neuroscience, 23,* 9541–9546.

Klingberg, T., Hedehus, M., Temple, E., Salz, T., Gabrieli, J. D. E., Moseley, M. E., et al. (2000). Microstructure of temporo-parietal white matter as a basis for reading ability: Evidence from diffusion tensor magnetic resonance imaging. *Neuron, 25,* 493–500.

Landerl, K., Wimmer, H., & Frith, U. (1997). The impact of orthographic consistency on dyslexia: A German–English comparison. *Cognition, 63,* 315–334.

Lindgren, D. S., De Renzi, E., & Richman, L. C. (1985). Cross-national comparison of developmental dyslexia in Italy and the United States. *Child Development, 56,* 1404–1417.

Lundberg, I. (2002). Second language learning and reading with the additional load of dyslexia. *Annals of Dyslexia, 52,* 165–187.

McCrory, E., Mechelli, A., Frith, U., & Price, C. J. (2005). More than words: A common neural basis for reading and naming deficits in developmental dyslexia? *Brain, 128,* 261–267.

Miles, T. R., & Haslum, M. N. (1986). Dyslexia: Anomaly or normal variation. *Annals of Dyslexia, 36,* 103–117.

Musso, M., Weiller, C., Kiebel, S., Müller, S. P., Bülau, P., & Rijntjes, M. (1999). Training-induced brain plasticity in aphasia. *Brain, 122,* 1781–1790.

Nakada, T., Fujii, Y., & Kwee, I. L. (2001). Brain strategies for reading in the second language are determined by the first language. *Neuroscience Research, 40,* 351–358.

National Early Literacy Panel. (2004). *Report on a synthesis of early predictors of reading.* Louisville, KY: Author.

Nyikos, J. (1988). A linguistic perspective of illiteracy. In S. Empleton (Ed.), *The Fourteenth LACUS Forum 1987* (pp. 146–173). Lake Bluff, IL: Linguistic Association of Canada and the US.

Oren, R., & Breznitz, Z. (2005). Reading processes in L1 and L2 among dyslexic as compared to regular bilingual readers: Behavioral and electrophysiological evidence. *Journal of Neurolinguistics, 18,* 127–151.

Paulesu, E., Démonet, J.-F., Fazio, F., McCrory, E., Chanoine, V., Brunswick, N., et al. (2001). Dyslexia: Cultural diversity and biological unity, *Science, 291,* 2165–2167.

Paulesu, E., Frith, U., Snowling, M., Gallagher, A., Morton, J., Frackowiak, R. S. J., et al. (1996). Is developmental dyslexia a disconnection syndrome? Evidence from PET scanning. *Brain, 119,* 143–157.

Paulesu, E., McCrory, E., Fazio, F., Menoncello, L., Brunswick, N., Cappa, S. F., et al. (2000). A cultural effect on brain function. *Nature Neuroscience, 3,* 91–96.

Perani, D., Dehaene, S., Grassi, F., Cohen, L., Cappa, S., Dupoux, E., et al. (1996). Brain processing of native and foreign languages. *Neuroreport, 7,* 2439–2444.

Perani, D., Paulesu, E., Sebastian Galles, N., Dupoux, E., Dehaene, S., Bettinardi, V., et al. (1998). The bilingual brain: Proficiency and age of acquisition of the second language. *Brain, 121,* 1841–1852.

Petitto, L. A., & Marentette, P. F. (1991). Babbling in the manual mode: Evidence for the ontogeny of language. *Science, 251,* 1493–1496.

Pinker, S. (1994). *The language instinct.* New York: HarperCollins.

Poldrack, R. A., Wagner, A. D., Prull, M., Desmond, J. E., Glover, G. H., & Gabrieli, J. D. E. (1999). Functional specialization for semantic and phonological processing in the left inferior prefrontal cortex. *NeuroImage, 10,* 15–35.

Price, C. J., & Friston, K. J. (1997). Cognitive conjunction: A new approach to brain activation experiments. *NeuroImage, 5,* 261–270.

Price, C. J., Wise, R., & Frackowiak, R. S. J. (1996). Demonstrating the implicit processing of visually presented words and pseudowords. *Cerebral Cortex, 6,* 62–70.

Pugh, K. R., Mencl, W. E., Jenner, A. R., Katz, L., Frost, S. J., Lee, J. R., et al. (2000). Functional neuroimaging studies of reading and reading disability (developmental dyslexia). *Mental Retardation and Developmental Disabilities Research Reviews, 6,* 207–213.

Pugh, K. R., Mencl, W. E., Jenner, A. R., Katz, L., Frost, S. J., Lee, J. R., et al. (2001). Neurobiological studies of reading and reading disability. *Journal of Communication Disorders, 34,* 479–492.

Rose, J. (2006, February). *Independent review of the teaching of early reading: Final report (The Rose Review).* London: Department for Education and Skills (DfES).

Roux, F. E., Lubrano, V., Lauwers-Cances, V., Trémoulet, M., Mascott, C. R., & Démonet, J.-F. (2004). Intra-operative mapping of cortical areas involved in reading in mono- and bilingual patients. *Brain, 127,* 1796–1810.

Rumsey, J., Nace, K., Donohue, B., Wise, D., Maisog, M., & Andreason, P. (1997). A positron emission tomographic study of impaired word recognition and phonological processing in dyslexic men. *Archives of Neurology, 54,* 562–573.

Salmelin, R., Service, E., Kiesilä, P., Uutela, K., & Salonen, O. (1996). Impaired visual word processing in dyslexia revealed with magnetoencephalography. *Annals of Neurology, 40,* 157–162.

Seidenberg, M. S., & Tanenhaus, M. K. (1979). Orthographic effects on rhyme monitoring. *Journal of Experimental Psychology: Human Learning and Memory, 5,* 546–554.

Seymour, P. H. K., Aro, M., & Erskine, J. M. (2003). Foundation literacy acquisition in European orthographies. *British Journal of Psychology, 94,* 143–174.

Shaywitz, S. E., Shaywitz, B. A., Pugh, K. R., Fulbright, R. K., Constable, R. T., Mencl, W. E., et al. (1998). Functional disruption in the organization of the brain for reading in dyslexia. *Proceedings of the National Academy of Sciences of the United States of America, 95,* 2636–2641.

Silani, G., Frith, U., Démonet, J.-F., Fazio, F., Perani, D., Price, C., et al. (2005). Brain abnormalities underlying altered activation in dyslexia: A voxel based morphometry study. *Brain, 128,* 2453–2461.

Simon, C. (2000). Dyslexia and learning a foreign language: A personal experience. *Annals of Dyslexia, 50,* 155–187.

Siok, W. T., Niu, Z., Jin, Z., Perfetti, C. A., & Tan, L. H. (2008). A structural–functional basis for dyslexia in the cortex of Chinese readers. *Proceedings of the National Academy of Sciences of the United States of America, 105,* 5561–5566.

Siok, W. T., Perfetti, C. A., Jin, Z., & Tan, L. H. (2004). Biological abnormality of impaired reading is constrained by culture. *Nature, 43,* 71–76.

Small, S. L., Flores, D. K., & Noll, D. C. (1998). Different neural circuits subserve reading before and after therapy for acquired dyslexia. *Brain and Language, 62,* 298–308.

Snowling, M. J. (2000). *Dyslexia.* Oxford, UK: Blackwell Publishers.

Steinbrink, C., Vogt, K., Kastrup, A., Müller, H.-P., Juengling, F. D., Kassubek, J., et al. (2008). The contribution of white and gray matter differences to developmental dyslexia: Insights from DTI and VBM at 3.0T. *Neuropsychologia, 46,* 3170–3178.

Temple, E., Deutsch, G. K., Poldrack, R. A., Miller, S. L., Tallal, P., Merzenich, M. M., et al. (2003). Neural deficits in children with dyslexia ameliorated by behavioral remediation: Evidence from functional MRI. *Proceedings of the National Academy of Sciences of the United States of America, 100,* 2860–2865.

Temple, E., Poldrack, R. A., Salidis, J., Deutsch, G. K., Tallal, P., Merzenich, M. M., et al. (2001). Disrupted neural responses to phonological and orthographic processing in dyslexic children: An fMRI study. *Neuroreport*, *12*, 299–307.

van Heuven, W. J. B., Schriefers, H., Dijkstra, T., & Hagoort, P. (2008). Language conflict in the bilingual brain. *Cerebral Cortex*, *18*, 2706–2716.

13 Lexical retrieval in alphabetic and non-alphabetic scripts: Evidence from brain imaging

Brendan S. Weekes

Introduction

A key question in reading research is how the brain processes written words. Answers to this question have been appearing rapidly since the turn of the century. Related to this question is how the language environment shapes brain function—specifically, how the type of script that is used in a language has an impact on the cognitive processes engaged by the brain during normal reading and in developmental dyslexia. We know that there is a cultural effect of language on neural processing, which is revealed by differences in how the brain functions in normal reading and in dyslexia across languages (see, for example, Paulesu et al., 2000, and chapter 12, this volume). It is clear from this research that the language environment shapes how the brain recognizes written words. The aim of this chapter is to illustrate how reading researchers can exploit the differences between alphabetic and non-alphabetic scripts to discover how orthography has an impact on brain function. (For a discussion of the properties of non-alphabetic scripts the reader is referred to chapter 10, this volume.) The focus is on two theoretical questions posed by current models of normal and impaired word recognition: (1) whether the age of acquisition (AoA) of a word has an impact on brain functioning that is independent of word frequency; and (2) whether orthography has an impact on spoken word production.

Age of acquisition effects on word recognition

We have known for more than 40 years that low-frequency words (e.g., *snail*) are more difficult to recognize than are high-frequency words (e.g., *mail*; Forster & Chambers, 1973). Neuroimaging studies also show that word frequency has an effect on brain activation during written word recognition in a variety of languages, including English, German and Chinese. These effects of word frequency have been located reliably in frontal occipital and temporal lobe regions of the brain (shown in Figure 13.1). Specifically, in both alphabetic and non-alphabetic languages low-frequency words evoke stronger activations in the left inferior frontal gyrus and the inferior portion

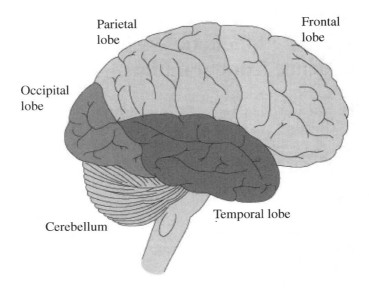

Figure 13.1 Diagram of the human brain showing the four lobar divisions. This figure is published in colour at http://www.cognitiveneurosciencearena. com/brain-scans/.

of the middle frontal gyrus (Chee et al., 2000; Fiebach, Friederici, Müller, & von Cramon, 2002; Fiez, Balota, Raichle, & Petersen, 1999; Keller, Carpenter, & Just, 2001; Kronbichler et al., 2004; Kuo et al., 2003; Lee et al., 2004). These data converge on the view that neural processing of written words reflects the frequency of exposure to written words across languages. However, recent studies have raised the question of whether frequency *per se* modulates brain activation during word identification (Fiebach, Friederici, Müller, von Cramon, & Hernandez, 2003; Tainturier, Tamminen, & Thierry, 2008). This controversy stems from behavioural studies that have reported significant independent effects of *age of acquisition* (AoA) in written word identification tasks, including reading aloud and lexical decision—that is, deciding whether a written stimulus is or is not a word. Words that are acquired early in life (e.g., *cat*) are identified faster than are words acquired later (e.g., *vat*) when variables including word frequency, length and rated imageability— whether visualizing a word is easy (*apple*) or difficult (*justice*)—are controlled. These effects have been reported in alphabetic languages, including Dutch, English, French, Italian, Spanish and Turkish, and in non-alphabetic languages, including Japanese and Chinese (see Juhasz, 2005, for a review).

Estimates of AoA for any word are highly correlated with frequency, since early learned words tend to be more frequent in a language.[1] However, the relative impact of each variable can be isolated experimentally—that is, early- and late-acquired words can be matched for frequency, and low- and high-frequency words can be matched for AoA. In such cases the behavioural results show that frequency and AoA have independent effects on word identification in languages including Chinese (Liu, Shu, & Li, 2007). Fiebach et al. (2003) have also reported AoA effects on brain activation that are independent of frequency. They found that late-acquired words led to greater activation in the left inferior frontal gyrus and anterior insula compared with early-learned words. Of greatest interest is that word frequency had no significant independent effects on brain activation. Fiebach et al. (2003) suggested that the effects of frequency on brain activity reported in previous studies might result from correlations between measures of word frequency and AoA. Clearly, then, it is important to distinguish word frequency effects from possible effects of AoA before concluding that processes in the brain reflect the frequency of exposure to written words.

Most behavioural studies use subjectively rated measures of AoA[2] that are based on adult estimates of the age at which children first learn spoken words (spoken AoA). However, in non-alphabetic scripts it is possible to estimate AoA objectively by measuring the written AoA of characters. Children learn by rote characters that are taught in a specific order with standardized textbooks that are used throughout mainland China. Thus it is possible to know the age at which a character is learned as well as the frequency of a character in printed text. Weekes, Chan, and Tan (2008) took advantage of this fact to examine the hypothesis that there are independent effects of AoA and word frequency on brain activity in Chinese speakers. They tested 12 native Mandarin Chinese speakers in an fMRI study. In this study, 88 highly imageable Chinese words and 88 non-words (formed by juxtaposing legal characters in an illegal way) were shown to participants. Within the 88 words, 22 were early-acquired (e.g., *cat*), 22 were late-acquired (e.g., *vat*), 22 were high-frequency (e.g., *apple*) and 22 were low-frequency (e.g., *melon*). Participants were asked to decide, as quickly as possible, whether each stimulus was a word or a non-word. This task is a lexical decision task. Patterns of brain activity were compared for (1) late-acquired versus early-acquired words, and (2) low-frequency versus high-frequency words. They found that AoA and word frequency predicted visual lexical decision times comparable with behavioural studies (e.g., Liu, Hao, Hua, Tan, & Weekes, 2008; Liu et al., 2007). There were also significant independent effects of AoA and word frequency on brain activity. Activation images were averaged across participants for late-acquired versus early-acquired words, and low-frequency versus high-frequency words (see Figure 13.2). Relative to early-acquired words, brain activity for late-acquired words peaked in left middle frontal gyrus (BA 9), left inferior parietal regions (BA 40/7), bilateral middle temporal gyri (BA 21) and left ventral portion of inferior frontal gyrus (BA 47) (see Figure 12.1b for the location of these regions). Compared to high-frequency words, increased activity for processing low-frequency words was observed only in right occipital sites (BA 18).

These results show that neural processing reflects the age of acquisition of

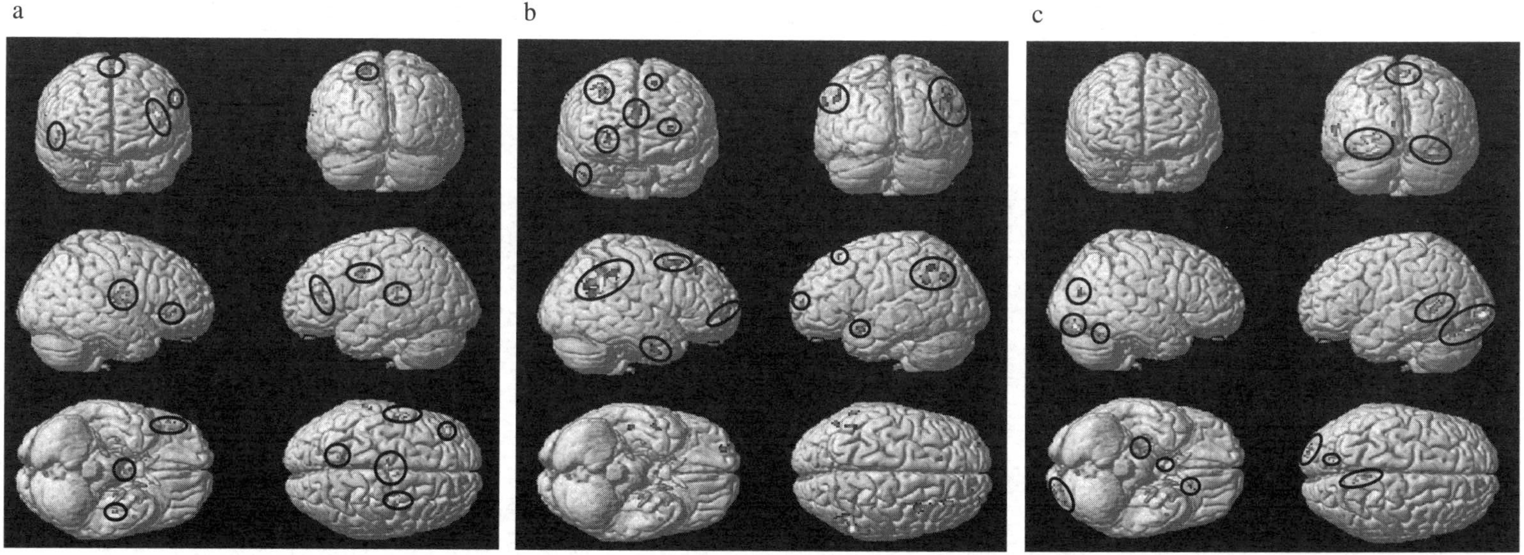

Figure 13.2 Brain images showing contrasts between (a) early-acquired and late-acquired words (highlighting regions of greater activity when people look at words acquired early in life relative to words acquired later in life); (b) late-acquired and early-acquired words (greater activity when looking at later acquired words); and (c) low-frequency words and high-frequency words (greater activity when looking at low-frequency words relative to high-frequency words). This figure is published in colour at http://www.cognitiveneurosciencearena.com/brain-scans/.

a word as well as the frequency of exposure to written words in Chinese. These findings are compatible with results from Fiebach et al. (2002), who found AoA effects in the left mid-inferior frontal lobe in German speakers confirming the importance of these regions in visual word identification in different languages. In addition, brain regions that reflect word frequency such as left mid-inferior frontal lobe (Chee et al., 2000; Fiebach et al., 2002; Fiez et al., 1999; Kuo et al., 2003; Lee et al., 2004) were not active. The left middle frontal gyrus plays a pivotal role in Chinese character processing (Tan, Laird, Li, & Fox, 2005; Tan et al., 2001). AoA effects in this brain region appear to reflect lexical–semantic retrieval. According to Ghyselinck, Lewis, and Brysbaert (2004), late-acquired words occupy a more peripheral position in the semantic network due to weaker connection weights.[3] Since character recognition requires retrieval of lexical–semantic knowledge, we might expect effects of AoA on neural activity in these brain regions. This seems consistent with findings of stronger activity for late-acquired words in the ventral portion of left inferior prefrontal cortex and left inferior parietal lobule, areas that are engaged in the retrieval of phonological and semantic information during lexical–semantic processing (cf. Fiez, 1997; Gabrieli, Poldrack, & Desmond, 1998).

Weekes et al. (2008) also found that word frequency had an independent effect on neural activity but in the right occipital cortex only. However, effects of frequency on brain activity reported in previous studies including activity in the left inferior frontal gyrus and motor cortex were *not* seen. These results differed from Kuo et al. (2003) and Lee et al. (2004) who reported effects of frequency in bilateral medial superior frontal gyri, left precentral motor gyrus, bilateral inferior/middle frontal gyri, bilateral anterior insula, left superior parietal cortex, left inferior temporo-occipital cortex and bilateral anterior lingual gyri. However, the stimuli used in those studies were not controlled for AoA. Therefore the results from Weekes et al. (2008) suggest that reported effects of word frequency on brain activation in Chinese speakers might in fact reflect the impact of AoA on neural functioning.

Independent effects of AoA and word frequency on brain activity should ideally be explained with reference to a neuropsychological model of language processing in Chinese. Weekes, Chen, and Yin (1997) proposed a cognitive neuropsychological framework for understanding word recognition in Chinese that was based on data from individuals who have language disorders resulting from brain damage (aphasia). This framework assumes that oral reading in Chinese can proceed via two pathways: a lexical–semantic pathway in which words can be read aloud via their meaning; and a non-semantic pathway in which orthographic representations (i.e., strokes, radicals and characters) can be read aloud via their direct connections to phonological representations (i.e., syllables, rimes and tones). This framework is shown in Figure 13.3.[4]

According to Weekes et al., characters are processed in both pathways during normal reading. Several representations can thus be activated for a

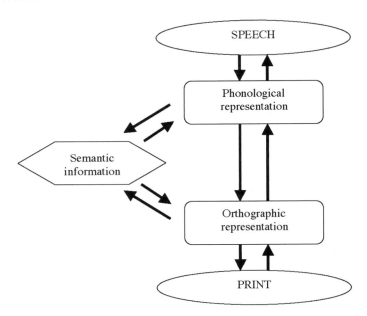

Figure 13.3 Framework for oral reading and picture naming in Chinese (adapted from Weekes et al., 1997).

spoken response. However, oral reading errors are typically not produced, as input from the non-semantic pathway (right side of Figure 13.3) can inhibit semantically related (incorrect) reading responses generated by the lexical–semantic pathway (left side of Figure 13.3). Input from the lexical–semantic pathway can also inhibit phonologically plausible (erroneous) responses generated by the non-semantic pathway.

The effects of frequency can be located at the stage of orthographic input specifically at the level of token exposure to print: that is, the number of times that a printed character is encountered in written text will generate a frequency effect. As the effects of frequency result from token exposure to print, we would expect these effects to be observed at the level of early visual processing. As early visual processing is performed in the occipital cortex, this may explain why the effects of word frequency are observed in these brain regions. The effects of AoA by contrast may reflect the mappings between input and output—that is, the orthography to phonology connections depicted in Figure 13.3. According to the *arbitrary mapping hypothesis* AoA reflects the mappings between input and output representations that are formed during the development of the lexical network (Ellis & Lambon Ralph, 2000; Monaghan & Ellis, 2002; see also Zevin & Seidenberg, 2002). Specifically, if the mappings between input (orthography) and output (phonology) learned on any one trial do not conform to correspondences that have been learned on previous trials, this will produce an AoA effect on subsequent lexical processing. The reasoning is that during lexical development, learning a lexical representation creates a unique mapping in the network if it cannot exploit existing connections within the network. However, if a newly learned lexical representation conforms to existing mappings in the lexical network (e.g., *cat* to *cart*), then a unique mapping in the network is not required, and the AoA of the word should have no impact on subsequent performance.

Zevin and Seidenberg (2002) simulated lexical acquisition by training an artificial learning network to learn mappings between input and output, and they found effects of the point during training when an item was introduced into the network (effectively, representing AoA) on how well the network later recognized words. Critically, however, they also reported that effects of AoA depend on the *nature* of the mappings between input and output that are formed during learning. Specifically, if the mappings between input and output conformed to existing mappings in the lexical network as when learning to read an alphabetic script, AoA had no impact on performance, whereas if the mappings were relatively arbitrary, as in reading Chinese or naming a picture, then AoA *did* have an effect on how well the network recognized words. Within the context of the framework in Figure 13.3, effects of AoA could be located in the mappings between meaning and the phonological output lexicon since these connections are arbitrary in all languages.

In sum, the age of acquisition of a word has an impact on brain functioning that is independent of word frequency in Chinese speakers. Of greatest interest is the fact that the Weekes et al. (2008) results suggest *independent* effects of AoA and word frequency on neural processing. These data also illustrate how reading researchers can take advantage of differences between scripts to discover how orthography impacts on brain function.

Orthographic effects on speech production

Models of spoken word production have been tested and developed in part following the results of behavioural studies using a paradigm called 'picture–word facilitation' (Levelt, Roelofs, & Meyer, 1999). In this paradigm, a phonological (homophonic) relationship between a target picture (e.g., *cat*) and a distracter (e.g., *cap*) speeds responses relative to an unrelated distracter (e.g., *log*) (Glaser & Düngelhoff, 1984; Lupker & Katz, 1981; Schriefers, Meyer, & Levelt, 1990; Starreveld & La Heij, 1996). This phenomenon is called the phonological facilitation effect. One question about this effect concerns the independence of purely sound-based similarity between the distracter and the target (e.g., *cat* and *cap*) from unavoidable similarity between orthographic representations of a distracter and target items in alphabetic languages such as English or Dutch. In all European languages, orthography and phonology are confounded. With the exception of words that have irregular spellings (such as *ate* vs. *eight*), words that are phonologically similar tend to overlap in orthography. A related question concerns whether the reported effects of phonological facilitation on picture naming in brain imaging studies (De Zubicaray, McMahon, Eastburn, & Wilson, 2002) result from the phonological similarity between the spoken forms of distracter and target, or from shared orthography.

Lupker (1982) used a picture–word facilitation task to compare the effects of phonological and orthographic facilitation on picture naming performance. Phonological and orthographic overlap was manipulated by including an orthographic similarity condition (e.g., *year—bear*) as well as a phonological similarity condition (e.g., *brain—plane*), and a condition with orthographic–phonological similarity (e.g., *lane—plane*). Picture name facilitation was greater in the former condition compared to an unrelated control condition, thereby suggesting an independent effect of orthographic facilitation. Similarly, Underwood and Briggs (1984) reported picture–word priming for an orthographic similarity condition with no priming from a phonological similarity condition. Both studies concluded that orthography has an independent effect on picture naming (see also Damian & Bowers, 2003; Damian & Martin, 1999; McCormick, Rastle, & Davis, 2008; Schriefers et al., 1990; Starreveld & La Heij, 1996). Results such as these have consequences for models of speech production. However, it is difficult to make strong claims regarding the effect of orthography on picture naming in alphabetic languages because orthography and phonology are confounded.

In our view, examining differences in the mapping between orthography and phonology across scripts provides a better test of the effects of orthography on speech production. Theories of speech production (e.g., Levelt et al., 1999) can account for effects of orthography because models of oral reading in alphabetic scripts assume that orthographic representations are automatically activated via connections between phonology and orthography (Coltheart, Rastle, Perry, Langdon, & Ziegler, 2001). If orthography automatically activates phonology, then orthographic facilitation can be explained as a result of priming at the level of name retrieval (Starreveld & La Heij, 1996). By contrast, in languages with a non-alphabetic script such as Chinese, representations of orthography and phonology can be independent. For example, a target *bed* 床/chuang2/ has orthographically similar characters 庆 (/qing4/, meaning *celebration*) that are pronounced differently to the target as well as to homophonic characters 创 (/chuang4/, meaning *creation*) that are visually dissimilar to the target. This fact about characters makes it possible to isolate the effects of orthographic and phonological facilitation using a picture–word priming task. Moreover, as shared orthography need not automatically activate target phonology in Chinese, orthographic facilitation effects cannot simply be assumed to result from name retrieval.

Models of oral reading in Chinese allow orthography to have an effect on name production. For example, the triangle framework shown in Figure 13.3 assumes a direct lexical connection between orthography and phonology (as is assumed in models of oral reading in English), as well as a route connecting orthography with phonology via semantic representations. The framework assumes independent representations for orthography and phonology that are linked in a forward direction, so that shared orthography can influence name production. This means that activation of characters with similar orthographic features can flow through to phonological representations to produce picture name facilitation. Critically, the framework in Figure 13.3 allows independent effects of orthographic facilitation and phonological facilitation so that if the target and distracter share orthography but not phonology (or conversely, phonology but not orthography), then facilitation may be observed.

Weekes, Davies, and Chen (2002) investigated the effects of orthographic and phonological similarity on picture naming in Chinese. They found orthographic facilitation effects on naming that were independent of any phonological relationship between a distracter—for example, superimposing the character 庆/qing4/ above a picture of a bed facilitated naming of the picture (*bed*), which is represented by the visually similar character 床 /chuang2/. They also found phonological facilitation effects on naming—for example, superimposing the homophonic character 创/chuang4/ above a picture of a bed also facilitated naming of the picture (*bed*). Weekes and colleagues (2002) reported that orthographic and phonological facilitation did not interact when target pictures and distracters were presented simultaneously, and they suggested that orthographic facilitation effects are due to activation of a target at the level of the orthographic representation, which then feeds forward via the semantic pathway to the target picture to produce facilitation in naming. They also argued that phonological facilitation is due to target name activation via direct lexical mappings between (unrelated) orthography and phonology, as depicted in Figure 13.3 (see also Zhang & Weekes, 2009). In other words they argued for independent effects of orthographic and phonological facilitation on picture naming.

De Zubicaray et al. (2002) investigated phonological facilitation effects on brain activity using a picture–word paradigm with English speakers. They manipulated two levels of distracter (phonologically related and unrelated) and found a decrease in brain activity in the phonological facilitation condition compared to the unrelated condition specifically in Wernicke's area, which is in the vicinity of BA 22 (see Figure 12.1b). De Zubicaray et al. (2002) argued that name facilitation occurs at the level of name retrieval because Wernicke's area is assumed to be necessary for word production (Indefrey & Levelt, 2000; Levelt, 2001). De Zubicaray and colleagues also observed increases in blood flow in brain regions that are not associated with word production. These were exclusively in right hemisphere sites including the anterior cingulate, orbitomedial prefrontal, inferior parietal cortices and the occipital lobe, regions associated with the inhibition of responses that compete with a target for a response. In fact, De Zubicaray et al. suggested that increases in blood flow in these areas result from independent activation caused by orthographic similarity between the distracter and the target, leading to lexical competition via activation of phonologically related word forms. Their claim assumes that the effects of orthographic and phonological similarity have a different locus in the brain.

Weekes et al. (2005) reasoned that some changes in brain activity during phonological facilitation might be due to orthographic similarity between distracter and target. They carried out an imaging study investigating the effects of orthographic and phonological facilitation on picture naming in Chinese. The question they asked was whether the effects of orthographic and phonological similarity have different loci in the brain. They used a design similar to De Zubicaray et al. (2002) which enables the change in brain activity caused by randomly presented individual items to be isolated. Target pictures with monosyllabic names, e.g., 床 /chuang2/ meaning *bed*, were matched in four distracter conditions corresponding to identity, orthographically related, phonologically related and unrelated stimuli. An example from each condition is shown in Figure 13.4. Identity items were the printed names of the target picture. Orthographically related distracters were phonologically and semantically unrelated to the target. Phonologically related distracters shared a syllable with the target but had a different tone. Unrelated items were orthographically and phonologically unrelated to picture names. Distracters in each condition were matched for mean number of strokes and written frequency based on normative information reported in the *Modern Chinese frequency dictionary* (Beijing Language Institute, 1986).

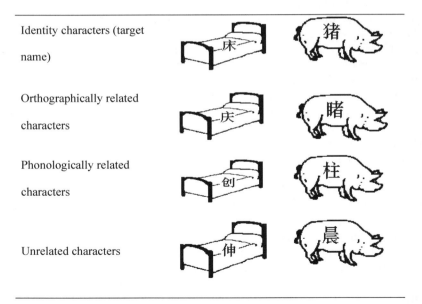

Figure 13.4 Example items used in Weekes et al. (2005).

Participants were familiarized with the set of experimental pictures out of the scanner by viewing each target picture three times with a target name printed on each picture. In the scanner, participants were shown each picture with a distracter superimposed on its centre; they were asked to name the picture as accurately and quickly as possible, while ignoring the distracter. Each trial involved the following sequence: a fixation point (+) was presented in the middle of the screen for 500 milliseconds (ms), followed by a blank screen for 500 ms, followed by a target. The display duration for each target was 750 ms. This was followed by a blank screen for 3.25 seconds and an 11-second inter-stimulus interval (ISI) when participants viewed a fixation point and another scan was acquired. Trials in each distracter condition were presented in random order and randomized between participants to avoid order effects. A total of 80 trials (20 pictures × four distracter conditions) were presented over a 20-minute imaging session. Picture size including background was approximately 10×10 cm. Line drawings and distracters were presented in black on a luminous white background.

We recorded each participant's digital audio file, which was then scored by a native Chinese speaker for response accuracy. Trials in which participants either failed to produce a response or gave an incorrect response were removed from analysis (less than 1 per cent). Participants were shown each picture with a character superimposed on it, and were asked to name pictures as accurately and as quickly as possible while ignoring the characters. The imaging results from this study are summarized in Figure 13.5.

The main findings included spatially segregated facilitation effects in all of the critical conditions at the neural level. Specifically, relative to the unrelated condition, there were significant decreases in blood flow in the orthographically related condition in the left inferior frontal lobe, temporal pole and lingual gyrus, and the right hemisphere thalamus, middle temporal gyrus, temporal pole, angular gyrus and supramarginal gyrus. Increases in blood flow were observed in the orthographic condition in the right hemisphere middle occipital gyrus, inferior parietal lobe, precuneus and supramarginal gyrus (see Figure 13.5). Blood flow decreases in the phonological condition were observed in left hemisphere postcentral gyrus, while *increases* were observed in the precuneus, thalamus and supramarginal gyrus in the right hemisphere.

When blood flow change during phonological processing was compared to orthographic processing directly, the phonological condition produced more activation in the left hemisphere angular gyrus, middle occipital gyrus, insula and hippocampus, and right hemisphere temporal pole and middle temporal gyrus as well as the superior frontal gyrus and thalamus bilaterally (see Figure 13.5). Relative to the phonological condition, the orthographic condition produced more activation in left hemisphere precuneus and supplementary motor area, and the right hemisphere cingulum and middle temporal gyrus as well as supramarginal and angular gyri bilaterally.

The findings from Weekes et al. (2005) supported the prediction that blood

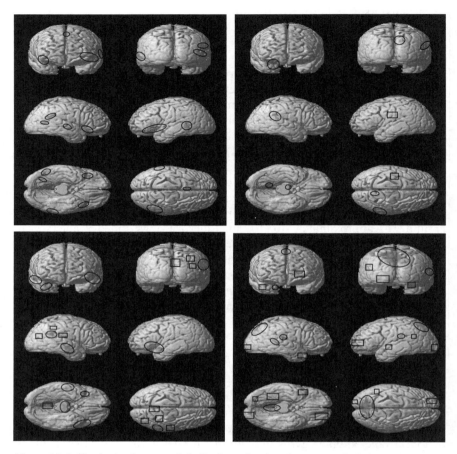

Figure 13.5 Clockwise from top left: Brain activation decreases (circled) and increases (squared outlines) in the identity, phonological and orthographic conditions. Contrasts show differences in brain activation for identity items compared to unrelated items; phonologically related items compared to unrelated items; orthographically related items compared to unrelated items; and orthographically related items compared to phonologically related items. Note that the bottom left panel depicts relatively greater activation in the orthographic condition than in the phonological condition (circled areas) and greater activation in the phonological condition than in the orthographic condition (squared outline areas). This figure is published in colour at http://www.cognitiveneuro sciencearena. com/brain-scans/.

flow changes in the orthographic distracter condition would be observed in brain regions different from those observed in the phonological condition. Although these results are compatible with De Zubicaray et al.'s (2002) claim that orthographic and phonological effects have different neural loci during picture naming, Weekes et al. found blood flow decreases in brain regions different from those reported for English speakers. Specifically, they found evidence of activation in the right precuneus, thalamus and supramarginal gyrus for Chinese speakers, and there was no evidence of blood flow decreases for Chinese speakers in the vicinity of BA 22.

One reason for the observed differences between studies (and therefore across scripts) could be that stimuli used with English speakers do not contain tonal variations, whereas the tone of Chinese distracters and targets differed. Processing of tone causes activation in the precuneus, thalamus and supramarginal gyrus (Gandour et al., 2003), and lateralization of supramarginal gyrus activation is consistent with right hemisphere dominance for the short-term storage of auditory information (Zatorre, Evans, & Meyer, 1994). It is likely, therefore, that differences in language explain the different patterns of neural activation between Chinese and English speakers.

Weekes et al. (2005) also found evidence of blood flow decreases in the orthographically related condition in the right hemisphere (middle temporal gyrus as well as angular gyrus and supramarginal gyrus), whereas De Zubicaray et al. (2002) did not report blood flow decreases in these regions. Assuming that the effect of orthographic facilitation reported by Weekes et al. is independent, blood flow changes in these regions may be a marker of orthographic facilitation effects in other studies, including those employing languages with an alphabetic script. Thus, it is possible that the relative orthographic facilitation effects reported in English by Lupker (1982) will be associated with blood flow decreases in these regions.

As in De Zubicaray et al. (2002), Weekes et al. (2005) observed *increases* in blood flow predominantly in the right hemisphere, including the postcentral gyrus, inferior parietal lobe and occipital lobe. Given that these regions were not active in the phonological condition, the results of Weekes et al. suggest that De Zubicaray's results may reflect the orthographic similarity of phonological distracters in English. Weekes et al. did *not* observe blood flow increases in the right anterior cingulate, inferior temporal gyrus, middle or superior frontal gyri, all areas assumed by De Zubicaray et al. to reflect the inhibition of competing responses. One reason for differences between scripts is that a phonological distracter in English typically automatically activates shared orthography and thus requires the activation of inhibitory processes. Reading in Chinese need not automatically activate phonology, however. If interference from orthography to phonology (and vice versa) is minimal, there is less reason to expect blood flow increases in the frontal cortex.

Independent orthographic facilitation may be unique to Chinese speakers. On the mainland, when children learn characters in elementary school, they are asked by their teachers to write characters first, then to learn the corresponding phonetic pinyin script with considerable emphasis on the learning of unique orthographic combinations (for discussion, see chapter 10, this volume). Orthographic information may be activated automatically in lexical processing as a result. It is not therefore surprising to observe orthographic facilitation given that orthographic awareness is a critical component of lexical processing in Chinese. It is a more open question as to how much orthography contributes to the facilitation effect in picture naming for speakers of languages that use an alphabetic script. If it does have a major effect, then words with irregular spellings in alphabetic languages (e.g., *bear*) may introduce independent effects into the production system in the picture–word task in studies of English speakers. One way to test this hypothesis in English would be to present items with orthographically ambiguous spelling patterns, such as the word *fear* superimposed on a picture of a pear. If orthographically related distracters introduce competition by way of activation of phonologically related word forms, then we may expect inhibitory processing at a neural level.

The results from Weekes et al. (2005) reveal orthographic and phonological facilitation effects in separate brain regions. These independent effects can be located in orthographic and phonological representations shown in Figure 13.3. These results also suggest that models of word production should consider effects of orthography on picture naming. Although the results did not support the view that orthographic similarity leads to inhibition at the neural level, these effects may be stronger in English since competition is more likely when there is a close relationship between orthography and phonology. This is an example of how comparisons across script can lead to testable hypotheses as well as informing development of theoretical models.

Summary

This chapter has illustrated how studies of Chinese character recognition at the neural level can be informative for understanding how the brain processes written words. In doing so, passing reference has been made to how the differences between alphabetic and non-alphabetic scripts can be informative to reading research. It is, of course, necessary to compare languages directly to discover how differences in orthography impact on brain function. However, it is also important to ask whether these differences are meaningful in terms of understanding basic cognitive processes at a theoretical level by asking questions that are relevant to our understanding of how literacy develops. Studies using cross-language comparisons at the neural level must be relevant to models of language processing. Moreover, while comparisons across imaging studies using contrasting languages suggest that reading processes are similar, it does not necessarily follow that equivalent mechanisms are engaged across scripts at either the functional or the neural level. The imaging data reviewed here show that although there are similarities in terms of cognitive processes that are used for lexical retrieval in alphabetic and non-alphabetic scripts, the brain mechanisms that reflect these processes can be quite different across languages. At the same time, differences in brain activation across scripts can be informative in terms of developing models of cognitive processing by formulating hypotheses that may be ideally tested within one language. The conclusion must be that the language environment—specifically the type of script that is used—shapes how the brain recognizes written words.

Notes

1 This is not always the case: e.g., compare *rattle* with *mobile phone*.
2 There is a reliable correlation between subjective and objective measures of AoA (see Juhasz, 2005).
3 In semantic networks, words that are commonly used together have stronger connection 'weights'.
4 Alternative models of reading in Chinese also assume two independent reading pathways (see, for example, Perfetti, Liu, & Tan, 2005).

References

Beijing Language Institute. (1986). *Xiandai Hanyu Pinlu Cidian* [Modern Chinese frequency dictionary]. Beijing, China: Beijing Language Institute Publisher.

Chee, M. W. L., Weekes, B. S., Lee, K. M., Soon, C. S., Schreiber, A., Hoon, J. J., et al. (2000). Overlap and dissociation of semantic processing of Chinese characters, English words, and pictures: Evidence from fMRI. *NeuroImage, 12*, 392–403.

Coltheart, M., Rastle, K., Perry, C., Langdon, R., & Ziegler, J. C. (2001). DRC: A dual route cascaded model of visual word recognition and reading aloud. *Psychological Review, 108*, 204–256.

Damian, M. F., & Bowers, J. S. (2003). Effects of orthography on speech production in a form-preparation paradigm. *Journal of Memory and Language, 49*, 119–132.

Damian, M. F., & Martin, R. C. (1999). Semantic and phonological codes interact in single word production. *Journal of Experimental Psychology: Learning, Memory, and Cognition, 25*, 345–361.

De Zubicaray, G. I., McMahon, K. L., Eastburn, M. M., & Wilson, S. J. (2002). Orthographic phonological facilitation of naming responses in the picture–word task: An event related fMRI study. *NeuroImage, 16*, 1084–1093.

Ellis, A. W., & Lambon Ralph, M. A. (2000). Age of acquisition effects in adult lexical processing reflect loss of plasticity in maturing systems: Insights from connectionist networks. *Journal of Experimental Psychology: Learning, Memory and Cognition, 26*, 1103–1123.

Fiebach, C. J., Friederici, A. D., Müller, K., & von Cramon, D. Y. (2002). fMRI evidence for dual routes to the mental lexicon in visual word recognition. *Journal of Cognitive Neuroscience, 14*, 11–23.

Fiebach, C. J., Friederici, A. D., Müller, K., von Cramon, D. Y., & Hernandez, A. E. (2003). Distinct brain representations for early and late learned words. *NeuroImage, 19*, 1627–1637.

Fiez, J. A. (1997). Phonology, semantics, and the role of the left inferior prefrontal cortex. *Human Brain Mapping, 5*, 79–83.

Fiez, J. A., Balota, D. A., Raichle, M. E., & Petersen, S. E. (1999). Effects of lexicality, frequency, and spelling-to-sound consistency on the functional anatomy of reading. *Neuron, 24*, 205–218.

Forster, K. I., & Chambers, S. M. (1973). Lexical access and naming time. *Journal of Verbal Learning and Verbal Behavior, 12*, 627–635.

Gabrieli, J. D. E., Poldrack, R. A., & Desmond, J. E. (1998). The role of the left prefrontal cortex in language and memory. *Proceedings of the National Academy of Sciences, 95*, 906–913.

Gandour, J., Xu, Y., Wong, D., Dzemidzic, M., Lowe, M., Li, X., et al. (2003). Neural correlates of segmental and tonal information in speech perception. *Human Brain Mapping, 20*, 185–200.

Ghyselinck, M., Lewis, M. B., & Brysbaert, M. (2004). Age of acquisition and the cumulative frequency hypothesis: A review of the literature and a new multi-task investigation. *Acta Psychologica, 115*, 43–67.

Glaser, W. R., & Düngelhoff, F. J. (1984). The time course of picture–word interference. *Journal of Experimental Psychology: Human Perception and Performance, 10*, 640–654.

Indefrey, P., & Levelt, W. J. M. (2000). The neural correlates of language production. In M. Gazzaniga (Ed.), *The new cognitive neurosciences* (2nd ed., pp. 845–865). Cambridge, MA: MIT Press.

Juhasz, B. J. (2005). Age of acquisition effects in word and picture identification. *Psychological Bulletin, 131*(5), 684–712.

Keller, T. A., Carpenter, P. A., & Just, M. A. (2001). The neural bases of sentence comprehension: An fMRI examination of syntactic and lexical processing. *Cerebral Cortex, 11*, 223–237.

Kronbichler, M., Hutzler, F., Wimmer, H., Mair, A., Staffen, W., & Ladurner, G. (2004). The visual word form area and the frequency with which words are encountered: Evidence from a parametric fMRI study. *NeuroImage, 21*, 946–953.

Kuo, W. J., Yeh, T. C., Lee, C. Y., Wu, Y. T., Chou, C. C., Ho, L. T., et al. (2003). Frequency effects of Chinese character processing in the brain: An event-related fMRI study. *NeuroImage, 18*, 720–730.

Lee, C. Y., Tsai, J. L., Kuo, W. J., Yeh, T. C., Wu, Y. T., Ho, L. T., et al. (2004). Neuronal correlates of consistency and frequency effects on Chinese character naming: An event-related MRI study. *NeuroImage, 23*, 1235–1245.

Levelt, W. J. M. (2001). Spoken word production: A theory of lexical access. *Proceedings of the National Academy of Sciences, 98*, 13464–13471.

Levelt, W. J. M., Roelofs, A., & Meyer, A. S. (1999). A theory of lexical access in speech production. *Behavioral and Brain Sciences, 22*, 1–75.

Liu, Y., Hao, M. L., Hua, S., Tan, L. H., & Weekes, B. S. (2008). AoA effects on oral reading in Chinese. *Psychonomic Bulletin and Review, 15*, 344–350.

Liu, Y., Shu, H., & Li, P. (2007). Word naming and psycholinguistic norms: Chinese. *Behaviour Research Methods, 39*, 192–198.

Lupker, S. J. (1982). The role of phonetic and orthographic similarity in picture–word interference. *Canadian Journal of Psychology, 26*, 349–367.

Lupker, S. J., & Katz, A. N. (1981). Input, decision, and response factors in picture–word interference. *Journal of Experimental Psychology: Human Learning and Memory, 7*, 269–282.

McCormick, S. F., Rastle, K., & Davis, M. H. (2008). Is there a "fete" in "fetish"? Effects of orthographic opacity on morpho-orthographic segmentation in visual word recognition. *Journal of Memory and Language, 58*(2), 307–326.

Monaghan, J., & Ellis, A. W. (2002). What interacts with spelling–sound consistency in naming? *Journal of Experimental Psychology: Learning, Memory, and Cognition, 28*, 183–206.

Paulesu, E., McCrory, E., Fazio, F., Menoncello, L., Brunswick, N., Cappa, S. F., et al. (2000). A cultural effect on brain function. *Nature Neuroscience, 3*, 91–96.

Perfetti, C. A., Liu, Y., & Tan, L. H. (2005). The lexical consistency model: Some implications of research on Chinese for general theories of reading. *Psychological Review, 112*, 43–59.

Schriefers, H., Meyer, A. S., & Levelt, W. J. M. (1990). Exploring the time course of lexical access in language production: Picture–word interference studies. *Journal of Memory and Language, 29*, 86–102.

Starreveld, P. A., & La Heij, W. (1996). Time-course analysis of semantic and ortho-graphic context effects in picture naming. *Journal of Experimental Psychology: Learning, Memory, and Cognition, 22*, 896–918.

Tainturier, M. J., Tamminen, J., & Thierry, G. (2008). Age of acquisition modulates the amplitude of the P300 component in spoken word recognition. *Neuroscience Letters, 379*, 17–22.

Tan, L. H., Laird, A. R., Li, K., & Fox, P. T. (2005). Neuroanatomical correlates of phonological processing of Chinese characters and alphabetic words: A meta-analysis. *Human Brain Mapping, 25*, 83–91.

Tan, L. H., Liu, H. L., Perfetti, C. A., Spinks, J. A., Fox, P. T., & Gao, J. H. (2001). The neural system underlying Chinese logograph reading. *NeuroImage, 13*, 836–846.

Underwood, G., & Briggs, P. (1984). The development of word recognition processes. *British Journal of Psychology, 75*, 243–255.

Weekes, B. S., Chan, A., & Tan, L. H. (2008). Effects of age of acquisition on brain activation during Chinese character recognition. *Neuropsychologia, 46*, 2086–2090.

Weekes, B. S., Chen, M. J., & Yin, W.-G. (1997). Anomia without dyslexia in Chinese. *Neurocase, 3*, 51–60.

Weekes, B. S., Davies, R., & Chen, M. J. (2002). Picture–word interference effects on naming in Chinese. In H. S. R. Kao, C. K. Leong, & D.-G. Gao (Eds.), *Cognitive neurosciences studies of the Chinese language* (pp. 101–127). Hong Kong: Hong Kong University Press.

Weekes, B. S., McMahon, K. L., Eastburn, M., Bryant, D., Wang, D.-M., & De Zubicaray, G. I. (2005). Orthographic effects on picture naming in Chinese: A 4 T erfMRI study. *Brain and Language, 95*, 14–15.

Zatorre, R. J., Evans, A. C., & Meyer, E. (1994). Neural mechanisms underlying melodic perception and memory for pitch. *Journal of Neuroscience, 14*, 1908–1919.

Zevin, J. D., & Seidenberg, M. S. (2002). Age of acquisition effects in word reading and other tasks. *Journal of Memory and Language, 47*, 1–29.

Zhang, Q., & Weekes, B.S (2009). Orthographic facilitation effects on spoken word production: Evidence from Chinese. *Language and Cognitive Processes, 24*, 1082–1096.

Glossary

Acquired dyslexia Reading deficit resulting from brain damage or neurological disease, normally in adulthood, usually affecting left-hemisphere brain regions. The precise pattern of impairment varies, but three main types have been identified: deep dyslexia, surface dyslexia and phonological dyslexia.

Age of acquisition (AoA) This refers to the age at which a child learns a concept or word but is often based on retrospective estimates by adults. The age of acquisition effect refers to the fact that words acquired earlier tend to be recognized faster.

Allophone A phonetic variant of a phoneme in a particular language. In English the /t/ sounds in the words *hit*, *tip* and *little* are allophones: phonemically they are considered to be the same sound, although they are different phonetically in terms of voicing and place of articulation.

Alphabetic writing system A writing system in which individual sounds of the spoken language (phonemes) are represented by written letters (graphemes).

Arbitrary mapping hypothesis This argues that the size of the age of acquisition effect is a function of orthographic transparency, and that this varies considerably across languages.

Bigram A pair of written letters or syllables; examples of common bigrams in English are *th*, *er*, *io*, *ea* and *st*.

Bigram frequency The frequency with which combinations of letter pairs appear in a language.

Blending The joining together of individual letter sounds to produce a single spoken word: for example, *cuh*, *ah*, *tuh* are blended together to make the word *cat*.

Blending task A task that typically assesses the ability to blend together spoken sounds to make a word: for example, an individual might be asked to blend the sounds *huh*, *ah*, *tuh* to produce the word *hat*.

Ceiling effect A limitation on the ability to assess a person's performance on a test as they approach the maximum possible score.

Coda The final consonant(s) of a syllable.

Cognate words A word is cognate with another if both derive from the same word in an ancestral language (e.g., *night* in English, *Nacht* in German and Dutch derive from the Proto-Indo-European word *nokt*). However, they do not always mean the same thing: some cognate words have diverged in meaning over time (e.g., *dish* in English and *Tisch* [table] in German).

Concreteness   An indication of how concrete (or abstract) a concept or word is. Concrete words are those that refer to tangible objects in the real world; abstract words refer to concepts that are intangible. This is usually based on subjective ratings from many participants.

Consonant cluster   A group of consonants that has no intervening vowel. In English, *spl* and *ts* are consonant clusters in the word *splits*.

CV units   Consonant–Vowel units; e.g., the word *banana* consists of three CV units: *ba, na, na*, each consisting of a consonant and a vowel.

Decoding   Applying grapheme–phoneme correspondence rules when reading.

Deep dyslexia   Form of acquired dyslexia characterized by semantic errors in reading (e.g., reading *wedding* as *marriage*), and also visual errors (e.g., *sword* read as *word*). Abstract words are particularly prone to such errors. The person with deep dyslexia has almost no ability to read non-words because of disruption to the non-lexical route of the dual route model.

Developmental dyslexia   A specific learning difficulty that primarily affects the skills involved in accurate and fluent reading and spelling. It is characterized by impaired phonological awareness, poor verbal memory and reduced verbal processing speed, and it occurs in children and adults across the range of intellectual abilities.

Devoicing   Pronouncing a normally voiced sound without vibration of the vocal chords so as to make it wholly or partly voiceless: for example, some non-native speakers of English will devoice the normally voiced terminal /b/ so that *bob* sounds like *bop*.

Diacritic   A small symbol added to a letter to alter its pronunciation and/or to distinguish between similar words: for example, the addition of the acute accent to the final *e* changes *lame* to *lamé*.

Digraph   A pair of letters representing a single speech sound, such as the *ph* in *pheasant* or the *ea* in *beat*.

Diphthong   A complex speech sound that begins with one vowel and gradually changes to another vowel within the same syllable, such as the *oi* in *boil* or the *ou* in *loud*.

Dyslexia   See *Acquired dyslexia* and *Developmental dyslexia*.

Elision   The omission or deletion of one or more sounds from a word.

Elision task   Task involving deletion of individual sounds from within words: for example, a person might be asked, 'If you take away the /t/ sound from *stun*, what word is left?' The correct response would be *sun*.

Event-related potential (ERP)   A method of recording electrical activity of the brain in response to a certain stimulus or event. Characteristic ERP waveforms include the P300 (a positive deflection approximately 300 ms after stimulus presentation), which reflects the brain's response to an unexpected event, and the N400 (a negative deflection occurring 400 ms after stimulus presentation), which is thought to reflect semantic integration.

Fixations   As we read, our eyes move across the page in an alternating sequence of scanning movements and pauses. These pauses are known as fixations.

Fixation duration   The time taken for each fixation. The average fixation time is approximately 200 ms but ranges from 50 to 450 ms.

Formant transitions   During the articulation of a stop consonant, the vocal tract is completely closed and no sound escapes through the mouth. However, at the moment of release of the stop constriction, the resonances of the vocal tract change rapidly. These changes are called formant transitions.

Functional magnetic resonance imaging (fMRI)   A technique for measuring brain activity that works by detecting changes in blood oxygenation and flow that occur to meet the demands of increased neural activity. The technique can be used to produce activation maps showing which parts of the brain are associated with a particular mental process.

Glide   Vowels that form diphthongs with full syllabic vowels, characterized by brief duration and a rapid change from one place of articulation to another. In English *w* and *y* are glides, also known as semivowels.

Grapheme   A written letter, or cluster of letters, that corresponds to a spoken phoneme.

Grapheme-to-phoneme conversion   The process of converting strings of written letters (graphemes) into their spoken equivalents (phonemes).

Homographs   Homographs are words that have the same spelling but different meanings and sometimes different pronunciations, e.g., *bow* (front of ship), *bow* (formal bending motion) and *bow* (decorative knot).

Homonyms   Words that have the same pronunciation but different spellings and meanings—e.g., *bear* and *bare*, *two* and *too*—are called homonyms.

Homophones   Words that differ in meaning but are pronounced the same way are known as homophones. They may be spelled the same (homographs) or differently (heterographs).

Iambic stress pattern   This refers to the placement of emphasis or stress on the second syllable of a word (e.g., dis*cuss*).

Imageability   An indication of how easy it is to form a mental image of a concept or word. This is usually based on subjective ratings from many participants.

Irregular language   See *Opaque/irregular orthography*.

Length effect   The effect of word length on the speed with which a word can be read or the accuracy with which it can be recalled.

Lexical decision task   A task requiring participants to indicate quickly and accurately whether a letter string is or is not a real word.

Lexical representation   The spoken or written word form associated with a particular concept.

Lexical stress   The relative emphasis given to a syllable indicated by a change in loudness, pitch or duration (or some combination of these) when articulating a word.

Lexicon   A list of words together with additional word-specific information, e.g., meaning and pronunciation. Lexicon is a word of Greek origin (λεξικόν) meaning vocabulary.

Liquid   The phoneme realized in English as either /l/ or /r/, depending on place of articulation.

Logographic writing system   A writing system in which each symbol represents one word or concept (e.g., numbers or mathematical symbols). This is in contrast to alphabetic writing systems, where each symbol must (usually) be combined with others to form meaningful words.

Magnetoencephalography (MEG)   A non-invasive brain imaging technique that measures the magnetic fields generated by neural activity. The location of brain activity is displayed as it occurs in real time.

Morpheme   The smallest meaningful unit of a language: for example, the word *unhappiness* contains three morphemes: *un* (negation) + *happy* (concept) + *ness* (state or quality).

Morphographic writing system   A writing system such as Chinese in which the smallest pronounceable unit associated with meaning (morpheme) is a character.

Morphological constituents   Aspects of a word that independently carry meaning: for example, in English the prefix *un-* negates a term, while the suffix *-ed* appended to a regular verb denotes past tense.

Morphology   The study of the form or structure of words.

Nasal   This term usually refers to a place of articulation and relates to sounds produced by lowering the soft palate so that air resonates in the nasal cavities and passes out of the nose. Examples in English are the pronunciation of the consonants /m/, /n/ and /ng/ or the nasalized vowel of French *bon*.

Neighbourhood density   Words that share the majority of their constituent phonemes (e.g., *care, hair, bear*) are referred to as phonological neighbours. Words that share the majority of their constituent graphemes (e.g., *cough, bough, though*) are referred to as orthographic neighbours. Words with many neighbours are said to be from a dense neighbourhood.

Neighbourhood size (N-size)   The number of neighbours that a word has (see *Neighbourhood density*).

Non-lexical reading   Reading via grapheme-to-phoneme conversion rather than by accessing the lexicon. This is the only way to read non-words (since by definition they do not have a lexical representation). This is also referred to as the non-lexical route to reading in the context of dual-route models.

Non-words   Novel or nonsense words that do not exist in the lexicon so can only be read non-lexically. Some researchers distinguish between non-words and pseudowords: the former are strings of letters that cannot be pronounced (e.g., *kjoxtgp*), while the latter are letter strings such as *spuff* that can be pronounced. However, in practice the two terms are used interchangeably.

N-size   See *Neighbourhood size.*

Obstruent   A consonant sound formed by obstructing outward airflow; this causes increased air pressure in the vocal tract. Obstruents are subdivided into stops, fricatives and affricates.

Onset   The initial consonant cluster of a word, e.g., *str* in *string.*

Opaque/irregular orthography   A writing system in which the pronunciation of words is not readily predictable from their written form. English uses such an orthography and includes many irregularly spelled words (e.g., *opaque* is pronounced *oh-pake* but could just as easily be pronounced *op-a-cue*, analogous to *barbeque*).

Orthographic analogy   Beginning readers may pronounce unfamiliar words by following the sound pattern of familiar words that share groups of letters: for example, reading the unfamiliar word *glow* by following the sound pattern of the familiar word *blow.*

Orthographic lexicon   The store of all known orthographic forms.

Orthographic transparency   The predictability of the pronunciation of words (their phonology) from their written forms (orthography).

Orthography   The written form of the language.

Over-additivity effect   The observation that individuals with a generally slower reaction time tend to produce larger effects (e.g., priming effects), irrespective of the experimental manipulation.

Phoneme   The smallest linguistic unit, or sound, that distinguishes meaning: for example, the /t/ sound in the words *tip*, *stand* and *cat*. If you remove or replace the /t/ sound, new meanings are created (e.g., *sip, sand, car*).

Phoneme tapping task   A task in which individuals tap out the number of phonemes in a word, e.g., two taps for *in* and three for *door*. Performance on this task provides an indication of the person's ability to identify phonemes.

Phones   Distinct speech sounds: for example, the /p/ sounds in *pit* and *spit*, which differ in the way they are created and in the sounds that they make. The /p/ of *pit* has an extra puff of air after it, which is not found after the /p/ of *spit*.

Phonics   A method of teaching beginners to read by focusing on the spelling–sound relationships of letters, letter groups and syllables.

Phonological dyslexia   A form of acquired dyslexia that is characterized by impaired reading of non-words; it is caused by impairment of the non-lexical route of the dual route model. The person's ability to read real words (regular and irregular) is preserved.

Phonology   The study of the speech sounds in a language.

Phonotactics   The area of phonology concerned with the analysis and description of the permitted sound sequences of a language: for example, a word beginning with the sound /tz/ is not permissible in English (apart from in words such as *tsar* and *tsetse*, which are loaned from other languages).

Place of articulation   For consonants, this is the point in the vocal tract where the flow of air is constricted during pronunciation. There are several of these, ranging from the bilabial (the /b/ in *bun*) to the glottal (the /g/ in *gun*). For vowels, this refers to the arching action of the tongue against the palate to produce front, mid or back vowels (the vowel sounds in *beat*, *up* and *ewe*, respectively).

Plosive   A consonant sound produced by stopping and then suddenly restarting the airflow in the vocal tract, e.g., the /p/ in *pit*. The terms *plosive* and *stop* are often used interchangeably.

Positron emission tomography (PET)   A method of brain imaging that detects radioactively labelled chemicals injected into the bloodstream. Detection of these chemicals in the brain provides an indication of the amount of activity in different regions.

Premorbid   A term used to refer to the time before the onset of an impairment (e.g., a neurological incident such as a stroke) that has subsequently affected language capability.

Prosodic cues   Various acoustic properties of speech such as tone, pitch, accent, etc. (collectively known as prosody), which all provide non-verbal cues to help the listener to identify the meaning of an utterance.

Pseudohomophone (effect)   Written non-words that are constructed to sound like real words, e.g., *soal*, *wurth*; these are typically read faster than standard non-words like *groal* and *surth*. This is known as the pseudohomophone effect.

Pseudowords   See *Non-words*.

Regular language   See *Transparent/regular orthography*.

Regularize   The tendency to pronounce irregularly spelled words (e.g., *yacht*) as though they are spelled regularly (e.g., *yatcht*).

Rime   The end part of a word, including the first vowel and succeeding consonants. In the word *cat*, for example, /at/ is the rime. Two rimes may have the same spelling (e.g., the 'ear' in *bear* and *gear*) but not necessarily the same sound—that is, they do not rhyme.

Rime familiarity effect   The finding that children are more able to read non-words that contain familiar rimes (e.g., *dake*, which shares its rime with many other words, such as *cake*, *lake* and *make*) than rimes that are unfamiliar (e.g., *daik*, which shares its rime with no other English words). This is used as evidence for children's use of orthographic analogy.

Saccades   As we read, our eyes move across the page in an alternating sequence of scanning movements and pauses. The scanning movements are known as saccades.

Segmental information   Information about phonemes, syntax and lexical-semantic representations that is extracted from speech.

Segmentation   The identification of boundaries between spoken words, syllables or phonemes.

Serial stimulus recoding   Alternative term for continuous grapheme-to-phoneme conversion in reading, or phoneme-to-grapheme conversion in writing.

Sight vocabulary   The corpus of words that individuals are able to identify immediately without decoding.

Sonorant   A speech sound that is produced without turbulent airflow in the vocal tract. Essentially this means that a sound is sonorant if it can be produced continuously at the same pitch. Vowels are sonorant, as are consonants like /m/ and /l/.

Sonority profile   The extent to which the vocal tract is constricted during articulation. In general terms, vowels like /a/ have the highest sonority, because the vocal tract is open, while plosives like /p/ have the lowest sonority, because the vocal tract closes.

Speech signal   A general term used to refer to the acoustic profile of the sounds that we perceive when listening to speech.

Stress pattern   The relative emphasis given to the phonemes within words characterized by changes in loudness, pitch or duration: for example, when *present* is used as a noun it is emphasised on the first syllable, but when it is used as a verb it is emphasised on the second syllable.

Sub-lexical reading procedure   See *Non-lexical reading*.

Supra-graphemic level   A subcomponent of a written word that is larger than a grapheme, e.g., a rime or syllable.

Surface dyslexia   A form of acquired dyslexia characterized by an inability to read irregularly spelled words: these words will tend to be regularized (e.g., *yacht* will be read as *yatcht*) as a result of reliance on the non-lexical route of the dual route model.

Transitional probabilities   The likelihood that one speech sound will be followed by another: for example, there is a high probability that if a word starts with the sound /wee/, it will be followed by a /d/ (*weed*), /k/ (*week*) or /l/ (*wheel* or *we'll*), but if it is followed by a /w/ or a /m/, this is likely to indicate the start of a new word (*we would* or *we might*, for example). We therefore learn to identify word boundaries by looking for unlikely (improbable) transitions.

Transparent/regular orthography   A writing system in which the pronunciation of words is readily predictable from their written form. These languages are said to have a transparent or regular orthography.

Visual word form area (VWFA)   An area of the brain in the left midfusiform gyrus where written words are believed to be recognized as whole units instead of as groups of individual letters.

Vocalic interval   The time between the onset of a vowel and the onset of the next consonant.

Voicing   When some speech sounds are articulated, they cause the vocal cords to vibrate: for example, the fricative /f/ is voiced in *van*, but it is voiceless in *fan*. This vibration is known as voicing.

Author index

Aaron, P. G. 18
Abbott, R. D. 118
Abercrombie, D. 51
Acha, J. 171
Adams, E. 222, 223, 230, 237
Ahonen, T. 143
Al-Mannai, H. 225
Al-Menaye, N. 224
Alberoni, M. 266
Alegria, J. 43, 46, 61, 113, 115
Anderson, R. C. 201
Andreason, P. 261, 262
Andrews, S. 158
Ans, B. 16, 156, 187, 192, 195, 196
Anthony, J. L. 29, 44, 46, 47, 52, 58, 62
Ardila, A. 161, 166
Arduino, L. S. 135, 163, 164, 168, 181, 183, 184, 185, 186
Arnbak, E. 192
Aro, M. 9, 10, 11, 38, 56, 69, 75, 82, 88, 93, 132, 133, 136, 155, 169, 170, 172, 234, 249
Arribas, D. 172
Aslin, R. N. 25
Assink, E. M. H. 136
Atkins, P. 156, 199
Auer, E. T. 26
Avanzi, S. 135

Baayen, H. 162
Bachmann, F. 142
Backman, J. 60
Bai, X. L. 214

Baillie, S. 54
Balota, D. A. 162, 181, 186, 194, 274, 277
Baluch, B. 136, 164
Barbón, A. 163, 164, 167, 168, 172
Barca, L. 141, 163, 164, 168, 181, 183, 184, 185, 186, 188, 189, 249
Bard, E. G. 136
Barker, T. A. 46, 47
Baron, J. 29, 48, 60
Barry, C. 136, 160, 163
Bates, E. 181, 186
Beck, I. 32
Beech, J. R. 113
Beers, C. S. 114
Beers, J. W. 114
Beijing Language Institute 9, 282
Beland, R. 215
Belke, E. 167
Bell, L. 32
Benuck, M. B. 134
Berndt, R. S. 36
Berninger, V. W. 118
Bertelson, P. 43, 46
Bertoncini, J. 51
Besner, D. 18, 70, 136, 162, 164, 183
Bettinardi, V. 259
Bi, Y. C. 214, 215
Bindman, M. 112, 114
Bjaalid, I. K. 29, 30, 32
Blair, R. 49, 59
Bolger, D. J. 251, 256, 258
Bolik, F. M. 49
Bonin, P. 163
Borrelli, M. 182, 190

Borstrom, I. 45
Borzone de Manrique, A. M. 170, 172
Bosse, M.-L. 13, 174, 187, 196
Bowers, J. S. 69, 280
Bowers, P. G. 143
Bowey, J. A. 46
Bradley, L. 26, 30, 46, 47, 48, 110
Brambati, S. M. 260
Branigan, H. P. 136
Bråten, I. 19, 63
Braun, M. 164
Breaux, A. M. 48, 60
Bressi, S. 266
Breznitz, Z. 260
Bridgeman, B. 134
Briggs, P. 280
British Dyslexia Association 204
Brizzolara, D. 143
Brooks, P. 231
Bruce, D. J. 29, 48
Bruck, M. 50, 51
Brunswick, N. 17, 70, 82, 137, 140, 141, 143, 181, 183, 184, 249, 253, 255, 260, 262, 264, 273
Bryant, D. 282, 283, 285, 286
Bryant, P. 14, 18, 26, 30, 44, 46, 47, 48, 110, 112, 114, 115, 118, 146, 201, 206
Brysbaert, M. 163, 167, 277
Bülau, P. 266
Burani, C. 135, 137, 141,

163, 164, 167, 168, 174, 181, 183, 184, 185, 186, 188, 189, 190, 191, 192, 194, 195, 249
Burgess, S. R. 29, 44, 46, 47
Burley, J. 101
Burman D. 118, 119, 120
Butterworth, B. 147, 148, 207, 208, 213, 214
Byng, S. 182
Byrne, B. 48, 60

Cahill, M. 3, 9
Campbell, G. L. 8
Campbell, R. 113
Cantor, B. G. 29
Cantor, J. H. 46, 48
Cao, F. 201, 203, 204, 206
Capasso, R. 174
Capellini, S. 224
Cappa, S. F. 17, 70, 82, 135, 137, 181, 183, 184, 251, 255, 259, 260, 261, 266, 273
Caramazza, A. 135, 174, 215
Caravolas, M. 11, 50, 51, 141, 144, 249
Carbonnel, S. 16, 156, 187, 192, 195, 196
Cardoso-Martins, C. 48, 60
Carlisle, J. F. 192
Carpenter, P. A. 274
Carrieri, R. 132, 171
Carroll, J. M. 46, 48, 60
Carter, B. 28, 32, 47, 48, 50, 60, 91
Cary, L. 43, 46, 136
Castellote, J. M. 173
Castles, A. 14, 18, 182
Castro-Caldas, A. 251
Ceci, S. J. 63
Chalard, M. 163
Chambers, S. M. 273
Chan, A. 275, 277, 279
Chan, D. W.-O. 146, 147, 206
Chang, L. 45
Chang, S. 204
Chanoine, V. 141, 143, 249, 260, 264
Chase, E. H. 113

Chateau, D. 175
Chee, M. W. L. 259, 274, 277
Chen, H.-Q. 207, 208, 213, 215
Chen, J. Y. 213
Chen, M. J. 204, 208, 209, 213, 277, 278, 281
Chen, T. M. 213
Chen, X. 201, 203, 204, 206
Cheung, P. S. P. 206
Chilosi, A. 143
Chitiri, H. 75
Chiu, K. M. Y. 214
Chomsky, N. 111, 250
Chou, C. C. 274, 277
Christiansen, M. H. 25
Cipriani, P. 143
Clark, A. 63
Cline, T. 223
Cohen, L. 23, 251, 259
Colé, P. 51, 60, 61, 62, 143
Colombo, L. 135, 137, 181, 186
Colpo, G. 183
Coltheart, M. 15, 18, 46, 69, 70, 134, 156, 157, 158, 161, 162, 164, 174, 175, 182, 183, 187, 188, 191, 199, 209, 210, 211, 251, 280
Coltheart, V. 134
Connolly, J. 263
Conrad, R. 113, 115
Constable, R. T. 262
Content, A. 61
Cornoldi, C. 183
Cortese, M. J. 162
Cossu, G. 29, 32, 37, 50, 52, 88, 132, 136, 223, 255
Coulmas, F. 3, 6, 249, 250, 252
Court, J. H. 183
Cramer, B. B. 46, 48
Critchley, M. 140
Crossland, J. 30, 46
Cuetos, F. 136, 163, 164, 167, 168, 172, 173, 175
Cumming, T. B. 158, 168
Cummins, J. 230, 237
Cunningham, A. E. 46, 48, 175

Curtin, S. 25
Curtis, B. 156, 199

Dakin, S. C. 173
Dalton, L. 37, 38, 136, 137, 139
Damian, M. F. 280
D'Amico, S. 181, 186
Dargie, A. 136
Davelaar, E. 162, 183
Davies, R. 163, 164, 167, 168, 172, 173, 175, 281
Davis, C. J. 69, 82, 83
Davis, M. H. 280
Day, B. L. 173
de Barrera, L. 136
de Bastiani, P. 136
De Brauwer, J. D. 194
de Bree, E. 135
De Cara, B. 26, 27, 33
de Jong, P. F. 69, 143, 144, 187
De Luca, M. 137, 172, 174, 181, 182, 183, 184, 185, 186, 187, 190, 192, 194, 195
De Nigris, B. 132, 171
De Renzi, E. 259
De Zubicaray, G. I. 280, 281, 282, 283, 285, 286
Deacon, S. H. 114, 118
Defior, S. 136, 143
DeFrancis, J. 6, 9, 201
Dehaene, S. 23, 251, 256, 259
Dehaene-Lambertz, G. 251
DeKeyser, R. M. 125
del Rosario Ortiz, M. 171
Dell, G. S. 213
Démonet, J.-F. 141, 143, 249, 251, 256, 258, 260, 264, 265
Demont, E. 30, 32
Desmond, J. E. 256, 259, 277
Deutsch, G. K. 260, 266
Di Filippo, G. 137, 141, 181, 182, 185, 186, 187, 194, 195, 249
Di Pace, E. 172, 174, 181, 182, 183, 184, 187
Dijkstra, T. 259
Ding, B. Q. 43

Diringer, D. 6
Dollaghan, C. A. 24
Donohue, B. 261, 262
Downing, J. 102
Driscoll, K. 29, 44, 47
Duncan, L. G. 46, 47, 49, 50, 51, 54, 59, 60, 61, 62
Düngelhoff, F. J. 279
Dunn, L. M. 101
Dupoux, E. 256, 259
Durgunoğlu, A. Y. 9, 29, 32, 37, 50, 88, 136
Dzemidzic, M. 285

East, M. 49, 59
Eastburn, M. M. 280, 281, 282, 283, 285, 286
Echols, C. H. 25
Edwards, J. 221
Ehsan, S. 161, 162
Eklund, K. 133
Elbeheri, G. 225
Elbro, C. 45, 56, 192
Eleweke, C. J. 115
Elkonin, D. B. 29
Elliot, C. D. . 231
Ellis, A. W. 10, 17, 160, 161, 162, 163, 164, 181, 186, 188, 189, 250, 278
Ellis, N. C. 91, 103, 104, 126
Eng, N. 215
Erskine, J. M. 9, 10, 11, 38, 56, 69, 75, 82, 88, 93, 132, 133, 136, 155, 169, 170, 172, 234, 249
Estévez, A. 171
Evans, A. C. 285
Evans, D. 87, 119, 120
Evans, H, M. 49, 61
Everatt, J. 18, 222, 223, 224, 225, 230, 231, 232, 237, 238
Evett, L. J. 70

Fanari, R. 132, 171
Faust, M. E. 194
Fazio, F. 17, 70, 82, 137, 141, 143, 181, 183, 184, 249, 255, 260, 261, 264, 265, 273
Fear, W. J. 103
Feldman, L. B. 134
Fernald, A. 25

Ferrand, L. 186
Ferraro, F. R. 194
Fias, W. 194
Fidler, R. 231
Fiebach, C. J. 17, 274, 275, 277
Fielding-Barnsley, R. 48, 60
Fiez, J. A. 274, 277
Fischer, F. W. 28, 32, 47, 48, 50, 60, 91
Fletcher, J. M. 173
Fletcher, P. 213
Flores, D. K. 267
Forster, K. I. 273
Fowler, A. E. 44
Fox, B. 29, 61
Fox, P. T. 277
Frackowiak, R. S. J. 251, 253, 256, 264
Franceschi, M. 266
Francis, D. J. 52, 58, 62
Francis, J. 46
Francis, W. S. 259
Frauenfelder, U. H. 135
Frederickson, N. 222, 231
Friederichi, A. D. 17, 274, 275, 277
Friedman, R. B. 209
Friston, K. J. 262, 263
Frith, C. D. 253, 262
Frith, U. 17, 37, 69, 136, 141, 143, 170, 222, 224, 231, 249, 251, 253, 255, 259, 260, 262, 263, 264, 265
Frost, R. 11, 15, 18, 70, 82, 132, 134, 223
Frost, S. J. 260, 264
Frota, S. 54
Fujii, Y. 259
Fulbright, R. K. 262

Gabrieli, J. D. E. 256, 259, 264, 277
Galante, E. 135
Gallagher, A. 17, 264
Gandour, J. 285
Gao, J. H. 277
Garlock, V. M. 45
Gasperini, F. 143, 172, 181, 182, 184, 187
Gates, A. I. 113
Gaustad, M. G. 114

Gelb, I. J. 6
Genard, N. 54
Genesee, F. 51
Georgiewa, P. 262
Gerhand, S. 160
Geudens, A. 59
Geva, E. 223, 225, 227, 233, 242
Gholamain, E. 227
Ghyselinck, M. 167, 277
Giannouli, V. 32
Glaser, W. R. 279
Glauche, V. 262
Glez-Seijas, R.-M. 172, 173
Glover, G. H. 256, 259
Glushko, R. 159, 161
Goldinger, S. D. 26
Goldstein, D. M. 46, 47, 61
Gombert, J. E. 30, 32, 43, 45, 48, 50, 51, 52, 53, 54, 56, 59, 60, 62, 136
Goodacre, E. 115
Goodman, N. 109
Gorard, S. 102
Goswami, U. 11, 18, 23, 24, 26, 27, 28, 31, 33, 34, 35, 36, 37, 38, 43, 44, 46, 49, 50, 59, 60, 69, 82, 91, 115, 136, 137, 138, 139, 161, 164, 169, 181, 184, 190, 192, 223
Goulandris, M. 223
Graham, A. 164
Graham, K. S. 158, 168
Graham, N. L. 209
Grainger, J. 62, 69, 70, 82, 83, 136
Grassi, F. 259, 266
Green, D. W. 70, 71, 72, 73, 74, 76, 79, 80
Groeger, J. A. 224
Gruppo, M. T. 183
Gugliotta, M. 37, 88, 132, 136, 255
Guttorm, T. K. 133
Gyarmathy, E. 224

Habib, M. 259, 260
Hagoort, P. 259
Haller, M. 156, 199

Hammond, E. J. 70, 71, 72, 73, 76, 80
Han, B. Z. 215
Han, Z. H. 214
Hanley, J. R. 87, 90, 95, 136
Hantziou, E. 136
Hao, M. L. 275
Harcum, E. 70
Harm, M. W. 156, 159, 165, 166, 169, 171, 172, 173, 174, 175, 199, 209
Harris, M. 18, 32, 113
Harris, R. 109
Haslum, M. N. 259
Hatano, G. 18
Havelka, J. 18
He, X. 224
Hedehus, M. 264
Helenius, P. 263
Hénaff, M.-A. 251
Henderson, L. 18
Hernandez, A. 260
Hernandez, A. E. 17, 274, 275
Hernández-Valle, I. 171
Hill, S. 46, 47, 49, 59, 62
Hinton, G. E. 63
Ho, C. S.-H. 30, 146, 147, 201, 206, 223, 224
Ho, L. T. 274, 277
Hodges, J. R. 208, 209
Hoeft, F. 260
Høien, T. 29, 30, 32
Holopainen, L. 143
Hoon, J. J. 274, 277
Hooper, A. M. 91, 103, 104
Hoosain, R. 145
Hopf, J. 262
Houghton, G. 209
Hsu, C. C. 204
Hua, S. 275
Huang, H. S. 146
Hughes, C. 32
Hughes, C. H. 164
Hulme, C. 19, 46, 144
Hummer, P. 30, 32, 33, 88, 136
Humphreys, G. W. 70
Hutzler, F. 274

Iacobini, C. 135
Ielasi, W. 135

Illes, J. 259
Indefrey, P. 281
Ingvar, M. 251
International Dyslexia Association 204

Jacobs, A. M. 11, 36, 164
Jacquemot, C. 256
Jaffré, J. P. 109
Janse, E. 135
Janssen, O. 135
Jared, D. 161, 175
Jenner, A. R. 260, 264
Jespersen, O. 131
Jiménez, J. E. 171
Jiménez Gonzáles, J. E. 143
Jin, Z. 265
Jonasson, J. T. 162, 183
Jordan, T. 70
Joshi, R. M. 18
Judica, A. 137, 172, 174, 181, 182, 183, 184, 185, 187, 190, 194, 195
Juel, C. 260
Juengling, F. D. 260
Juhasz, B. J. 274, 287
Juphard, A. 187, 196
Jusczyk, P. W. 25, 43, 44
Just, M. A. 274
Juul, H. 133

Kaiser, W. 262
Kang, J. S. 145, 202
Karan, E. 3, 9
Karmiloff-Smith, A. 45, 63
Kassubek, J. 260
Kastrup, A. 260
Katz, A. N. 279
Katz, L. 15, 18, 29, 32, 50, 52, 70, 71, 82, 134, 223, 260, 264
Kavanagh, J. F. 18
Keller, T. A. 274
Kello, C. T. 164
Kemp, N. 114
Kessler, B. 163
Khanna, M. M. 162
Kiebel, S. 266
Kieslä, P. 261, 262
Kirby, J. R. 118
Kitamura, S. 204
Klingberg, T. 264

Klingebiel, K. 16, 207, 209, 210
Knab, R. 262
Knuijt, P. P. N. A. 136
Kronbichler, M. 274
Ktori, M. 75
Kuhl, P. K. 25
Kuo, W. J. 274, 277
Kwee, I. L. 259

La Heij, W. 279, 280
Laakso, M.-L. 133
Lacert, P. 143
Ladner, D. 183, 194
Ladurner, G. 274
Laganaro, M. 135
Laghi, L. 183
Lai, D. N.-C. 146, 223
Laird, A. R. 277
Lam, C. C. C. 206
Lambon Ralph, M. A. 160, 161, 162, 168, 278
Landerl, K. 30, 32, 33, 37, 69, 136, 141, 142, 143, 224, 249, 255
Langdon, R. 15, 69, 70, 156, 157, 158, 164, 174, 182, 187, 188, 191, 209, 210, 211, 280
Lange, M. 163
Laudanna, A. 181, 189
Lauwers-Cances, V. 258
Law, S. P. 207, 208, 213, 214
Law, T. P.-S. 146
LeBihan, D. 256
Ledgeway, T. 73, 75
Lee, C. Y. 274, 277
Lee, J. R. 260, 264
Lee, K. M. 274, 277
Lee, S.-H. 146, 147, 206
Lee, S. Y. 204
Lehéricy, S. 251
Lenel, J. C. 46, 48
Leong, C. K. 201, 203
Leppänen, P. H. T. 133
Lepschy, A. L. 132
Lepschy, G. 132
Lervåg, A. 19
Levelt, W. J. M. 279, 280, 281
Lewis, M. B. 277
Leybaert, J. 54, 56, 113, 115

Li, C. N. 202
Li, K. 277
Li, P. 275
Li, X. 285
Li, Y. 202
Liberman, I. Y. 28, 29, 32, 47, 48, 50, 52, 60, 88, 91, 136, 223
Lindgren, D. S. 259
Linortner, R. 30, 32, 33
Liow, S. J. R. 72, 74, 79
Liu, H. L. 277
Liu, Y. 16, 199, 209, 211, 212, 275, 287
Lonigan, C. J. 29, 44, 46, 47
López, M. R. 143
Lowe, M. 285
Luan, V. H. 147, 201, 203, 204, 206
Lubrano, V. 258
Luce, P. A. 26
Lucker, G. W. 204
Lukatela, G. 134
Lund, R. 54
Lundberg, I. 266
Lundberg, L. 29, 30, 32
Luo, Q. 205, 214, 215
Lupker, S. J. 167, 279, 280, 285
Lyon, G. 204
Lyytinen, H. 133, 143

Ma, R. N. L. 206
Ma-Wyatt, A. 183, 194
McBride-Chang, C. 45, 206
McClelland, J. L. 63, 69, 156, 157, 159, 160, 161, 164, 168, 171, 172, 175, 199, 209, 211, 214
McCormick, S. F. 280
McCrory, E. 17, 70, 82, 137, 141, 143, 181, 183, 184, 249, 253, 255, 260, 262, 263, 264, 273
McDougall, S. 49, 60
Mackey, A. 126
MacLean, M. 30, 46
McMahon, K. 282, 283, 285, 286
McMahon, K. L. 280, 281, 282, 283, 285, 286
McRae, K. 161

Magnan, A. 51, 60, 61, 62
Mair, A. 274
Maisog, M. 261, 262
Mallery, G. 4
Mancini, M. 181, 182, 187
Marcolini, S. 137, 174, 186, 190, 191, 192
Marentette, P. F. 250
Marschark, M. 113
Marshall, J. C. 37, 132, 136, 255
Marslen-Wilson, W. 209
Martelli, M. 181, 182, 187
Martens, V. E. G. 187
Martin, R. C. 280
Martindale, J. L. 260
Martos, F. 136
Mascott, C. R. 258
Mason, M. 71, 73
Masterson, J. 73, 75, 87, 182
Mayer, C. 110
Mazzie, C. 25
Mazzotti, S. 143
Meara, P. 72, 74
Mechelli, A. 263
Mehler, J. 50, 51, 54
Mencl, W. E. 260, 262, 264
Meng, X. 201, 203, 204, 206
Menn, L. 44
Menoncello, L. 17, 70, 82, 137, 181, 183, 184, 255, 261, 273
Menyuk, P. 44
Méot, A. 163
Merzenich, M. M. 260, 266
Metsala, J. L. 44, 45, 46, 50, 52, 56, 58, 60
Meyer, A. S. 167, 279, 280
Meyer, E. 285
Meyler, A. 260
Miceli, G. 135, 174, 215
Miles, T. R. 140, 221, 259
Miller, S. L. 266
Milroy, R. 164
Mimouni, Z. 215
Mintz, T. H. 25
Miozzo, A. 135
Mitchum, C. C. 36
Monaghan, J. 161, 162, 278
Monsell, S. 164

Montant, M. 206
Morais, J. 43, 46, 48, 61
Moreno, C. 113
Morrison, C. M. 17, 160, 162
Morton, J. 264
Moseley, M. E. 264
Moss, G. 102
Mullenix, J. 163
Müller, H.-P. 260
Müller, K. 17, 274, 275, 277
Müller, S. P. 266
Musselman, C. 113
Musso, M. 266

Naccache, L. 251
Nace, K. 261, 262
Nagy, W. 118
Nakada, T. 259
Nation, K. 14, 18, 230
National Early Literacy Panel 250
Nazzi, T. 51
Neale, M. D. 95, 97, 99
Nelson, H. E. 141
Nergård-Nilssen, T. 143
Nesdale, A. R. 32, 33
Nespor, M. 50, 51, 54, 135
Ng, P. M. 146
Nice, D. 70
Nie, H. Y. 43
Nightingale, N. N. 63
Nittrouer, S. 43
Niu, Z. 265
Noll, D. C. 267
Nunes, T. 14, 18, 112, 114, 118, 119, 120
Nyikos, J. 131, 249

Obler, L. K. 215
Ocampo, D. 222, 223, 224, 230, 231, 232, 237, 238
Oldfield, R. C. 17
Olson, D. R. 7, 18
Olson, R. K. 230
Öney, B. 9, 29, 32, 37, 50, 88, 136
Or, B. 207, 208, 214
Oren, R. 260
Orlandi, M. 174, 181, 182, 183, 184
Orsolini, M. 132, 171
Ortiz, M. R. 171

Pagliuca, G. 181, 183, 184, 185
Paizi, D. 184, 185, 186, 194, 195
Pallier, C. 256
Pantelis, S. N. 136
Pasini, M. 181, 186
Patching, G. 70
Patel, T. K. 69, 144
Patterson, K. 69, 156, 158, 159, 160, 161, 164, 167, 168, 171, 172, 175, 199, 208, 209, 211, 214
Paulesu, E. 17, 70, 82, 137, 141, 143, 181, 183, 184, 249, 255, 259, 260, 261, 264, 273
PDP Research Group 160
Pecini, C. 143
Peer, L. 223
Pei, M. 131
Peng, D. 202, 215
Pennington, B. 199
Perani, D. 259, 260, 264, 265, 266
Perea, M. 167, 171
Peresotti, F. 70
Perfetti, C. A. 16, 32, 113, 199, 209, 211, 212, 251, 256, 258, 265, 277, 287
Perin, D. 48
Perry, C. 15, 69, 70, 156, 157, 158, 161, 164, 174, 175, 182, 183, 187, 188, 191, 194, 195, 206, 209, 210, 211, 280
Perry, K. E. 175
Petersen, D. K. 45
Petersen, S. E. 274, 277
Peterson, K. M. 251
Petitto, L. A. 250
Peverly, S. T. 134
Phillips, B. M. 29, 44, 47
Piepenbrock, R. 162
Pinker, S. 250
Pisoni, D. B. 26
Pitchford, N. J. 73, 75
Pitman, J. 101
Plaut, D. C. 69, 156, 159, 160, 161, 164, 168, 171, 172, 174, 175, 199, 209, 211, 214

Plemmenou, E. 136
Poldrack, R. A. 256, 259, 260, 277
Porpodas, C. 31, 37, 136, 143
Pretzlik, U. 119
Price, C. J. 251, 253, 256, 260, 262, 263, 264, 265
Prior, M. 182
Prull, M. 256
Pruneti, C. A. 183
Pugh, K. R. 172, 260, 262, 264

Quinlan, P. T. 17, 70

Rack, J. P. 230
Raichle, M. E. 274, 277
Raman, I. 163, 164, 215
Ramírez, G. 171
Ramus, F. 50, 51, 54, 143, 173
Rastle, K. 15, 18, 69, 70, 134, 156, 157, 158, 164, 174, 182, 187, 188, 191, 209, 210, 211, 280
Raven, J. 183
Raven, J. C. 56, 101, 183
Read, C. 31, 43, 46, 48
Reason, R. 223, 231
Rees, G. 102
Reggia, J. A. 36
Reid, G. 223, 225
Reis, A. 251
Richardson, U. 26, 34
Richman, L. C. 259
Riddick, B. 221
Riddoch, J. 182
Rijntjes, M. 266
Roberts, L. 49, 60
Robinson, A. 3
Rodda, M. 115
Rodrigo, M. 171
Rodríguez, B. 172
Rodríguez-Ferreiro, J. 168, 173, 175
Roelofs, A. 279, 280
Rose, J. 104, 250
Rosen, S. 173
Rosner, J. 61
Routh, D. K. 29, 61
Roux, F. E. 258
Ruano, E. 172
Ruffino, M. 260

Rumelhart, D. E. 63, 160
Rumsey, J. 261, 262
Rvachew, S. 49, 59
Rzanny, R. 262

Salidis, J. 260
Salisbury, J. 102
Salmelin, R. 261, 262, 263
Salonen, O. 261, 262
Salter, R. 18, 223
Salz, T. 264
Sampson, G. 9
Sandak, R. 113
Sandra, D. 59
Savage, R. 49, 59
Scanlon, D. M. 173
Schmandt-Besserat, D. 6
Schneider, W. 30, 37, 38, 136, 137, 139, 251, 256, 258
Schonell, F. 115
Schoolcraft, H. R. 4
Schreiber, A. 274, 277
Schriefers, H. 259, 279, 280
Schulte-Korne, G. 183, 194
Scott-Brown, K. 70
Scragg, D. J. 11
Sebastián-Gallés, N. 136, 259
Seidenberg, M. S. 69, 134, 156, 157, 159, 160, 161, 162, 164, 165, 166, 167, 168, 169, 171, 172, 173, 174, 175, 199, 209, 211, 214, 251, 278, 279
Sergent-Marshall, S. D. 162
Serniclaes, W. 143
Serrano, F. 143
Service, E. 261, 262, 263
Seymour, P. H. K. 9, 10, 11, 38, 46, 47, 49, 51, 54, 56, 59, 60, 61, 62, 69, 75, 82, 88, 93, 132, 133, 136, 155, 169, 170, 172, 234, 249
Shamsi, T. 223
Shankweiler, D. 28, 29, 32, 47, 48, 50, 52, 60, 88, 91, 136, 223
Shany, M. 225, 242

Share, D. L. 16, 82, 169, 170, 171, 172
Shargorodskii, S. 5
Shaywitz, B. A. 204, 262
Shaywitz, S. E. 204, 262
Shu, H. 201, 203, 204, 206, 214, 215, 275
Siegel, L. S. 223, 225, 230, 233, 242
Signorini, A. 170, 172
Sigurdsson, B. 133
Silani, G. 260, 264
Simon, C. 266
Simon, D. P. 61
Siok, W. T. 213, 265
Small, S. L. 267
Smith, L. B. 43
Smith, M. C. 136
Smolensky, P. 63
Smythe, I. 18, 222, 223, 224, 230, 231, 232, 237, 238
Snowling, M. J. 17, 45, 46, 48, 60, 69, 144, 173, 223, 230, 250, 264
Soon, C. S. 274, 277
Spencer, L. 87, 90, 95, 136
Spieler, D. H. 162, 194
Spinelli, D. 137, 172, 174, 181, 182, 183, 184, 185, 187, 190, 194, 195
Spinks, J. A. 277
Sprenger-Charolles, L. 143
Staffen, W. 274
Stanovich, K. E. 29, 30, 32, 46, 48, 175, 223, 230
Starreveld, P. A. 279, 280
Steinbrink, C. 260
Stella, G. 174, 186, 190, 191, 260
Stevenson, H. W. 204
Stevenson, J. 46
Stigler, J. W. 204
Stone, C. A. 192
Stone, G. O. 11, 36, 199
Stone-Elander, S. 251
Strain, E. 167
Stuart, M. 46
Su, I. F. 204, 208
Suarez, P. 173, 175
Supramanian, S. 73
Sutton-Spence, R. 112, 113

Tabossi, P. 135, 183
Taft, M. 202, 209, 215
Tainturier, M. J. 13, 174, 187, 196, 274
Tallal, P. 260, 266
Tamaoka, K. 201, 203
Tamminen, J. 274
Tan, E. W. L. 259
Tan, L. H. 16, 199, 206, 209, 211, 212, 265, 275, 277, 279, 287
Tanenhaus, M. K. 251
Taraban, R. 159
Taylor, I. 18
Taylor-Hill, H. 260
Temple, E. 260, 264, 266
Termin, C. 260
Thiel, T. 259
Thierry, G. 274
Thomas, S. 70
Thompson, S. A. 202
Thomson, J. 26
Thornton, A. M. 135
Tng, S. K. 72, 74, 79
Tola, G. 29, 32, 50, 52, 223
Tolchinsky, L. 109
Torgesen, J. K. 221, 228
Tosi, V. 132, 171
Tralli, A. 135
Traxler, C. B. 115
Treiman, R. 27, 29, 30, 44, 46, 47, 48, 60, 163
Trémoulet, M. 258
Tsai, J. L. 274, 277
Tsang, S.-M. 146, 147, 206
Tunmer, W. E. 32, 33
Turvey, M. T. 134

Underwood, G. 280
Unger, J. M. 5
Uutela, K. 261, 262

Vacheck, J. 109
Vacheresse, F. 135
Valdois, S. 13, 16, 156, 174, 187, 192, 195, 196
Van Bergen, F. 136
van Daal, V. 141
van de Zande, A. M. 135
van der Leij, A. 141, 144
van Heuven, W. 82, 83, 259
Van Orden, G. C. 199
van Rijn, H. 162

Van Teeseling, H. 136
van Wijnendaele, I. 163
Varma, V. 221
Veii, K. 222, 231, 232, 237, 238
Vellutino, F. R. 173
Venezky, R. l. 10, 18
Verfaillie, M. 158, 168
Verguts, T. 194
Vernon, M. D. 102
Vigário, M. 54
Vignolo, L. A. 251
Vitevitch, M. S. 26
Voga, M. 136
Vogt, K. 260
Volin, J. 141, 144, 249
von Cramon, D. Y. 17, 274, 275, 277

Wade-Wooley, L. 225, 242
Wagner, A. D. 256
Wagner, R. K. 45, 228
Wagstaffe, J. K. 73
Walley, A. C. 43, 44, 45, 46, 50, 52, 56, 58, 60
Wang, D.-M. 282, 283, 285, 286
Webster, A. 115
Weekes, B. S. 16, 157, 158, 186, 203, 204, 205, 207, 208, 209, 210, 213, 214, 215, 274, 275, 277, 278, 279, 281, 282, 283, 285, 286
Weiller, C. 266
Wells, G. 110
Wheelwright, S. 37, 136
Whetton, C. 101
White, S. 173
Whitney, C. 69, 82, 83
Willison, J. 141
Willows, D. M. 75
Wilson, S. J. 280, 281, 285
Wimmer, H. 30, 32, 33, 37, 56, 69, 88, 91, 136, 141, 143, 144, 172, 181, 223, 224, 249, 255, 274
Wingfield, A. 17
Wise, D. 261, 262
Wise, R. 251, 253, 256
Wolf, M. 143
Woll, B. 112, 113
Wong, D. 285
Wong, W. 214

Woollams, A. 168
Working Party of the
    British Psychological
    Society 221, 230
World Health
    Organization 204
Wu, N. 201
Wu, Y. T. 274, 277
Wydell, T. N. 18, 147,
    148

Xiong, H. Z. 214
Xu, Y. 285
Xuan, Y. 201

Yamada, J. 230
Yap, M. 162
Yeh, T. C. 274, 277
Yeung, O. 214

Yin, R. 204
Yin, W. G. 202, 204, 206,
    207, 208, 209, 213, 214,
    277, 278
Yopp, H. K. 46

Zatorre, R. J. 285
Zevin, J. D. 161, 162, 164,
    167, 278, 279
Zhang, C. 204
Zhang, H. R. 146
Zhang, J. 204
Zhang, Q. 281
Zhang, Y. F. 43
Zhou, J. 204
Zhou, X. 209
Zhou, Y. G. 9
Zhu, X. 201, 202, 206,
    209, 215

Ziegler, J. C. 11, 15, 23, 24,
    28, 31, 33, 34, 35, 36,
    37, 38, 43, 46, 50, 59,
    60, 69, 70, 82, 136, 137,
    138, 139, 156, 157, 158,
    161, 164, 169, 174, 175,
    181, 182, 183, 184, 187,
    188, 190, 191, 192, 194,
    195, 206, 209, 210, 211,
    223, 280
Zielisnki, S. 72, 74, 79
Zoccolotti, P. 137, 141,
    172, 174, 181, 182, 183,
    184, 185, 186, 187, 190,
    192, 194, 195, 249
Zorzi, M. 15, 195, 209
Zuffi, M. 135
Zukowski, A. 29, 30, 46,
    47, 48, 60

Subject index

Note: Page numbers in **bold** indicate glossary definitions.

Acquired dyslexia 204, 205, **291**
  Chinese 207–208
  phonological training 267
  Spanish 166–167
  stress assignment 135
Activation 157
ACV98 model 16, 187, 195–196
Age of acquisition (AoA) 160, **291**
  frequency effect 273–279
  non-alphabetic scripts 275
  orthographic transparency 161–162
  reading performance 163–164
  semantic system 167
Akkadian 7–8
Allophone 31, **291**
Alphabetic writing system 7, 8, 9–11,
  252, **291**
American Indians 4, 9
Angular gyrus 258, 283, 285
Anomia without dyslexia 213
Anterior cingulate 281
Anterior inferior frontal gyrus 17, 138,
  256
Anterior lingual gyri 277
Aphasia, stress assignment 135
Arabic
  letter search 74
  orthography 225
Arbitrary mapping hypothesis 278, **291**
Ascenders 253
Auditory short-term memory, bilinguals
  228
Availability problem 35–36, 43, 59–62

Bigram 82, 83, 183, 186–187, 189, 190,
  192, **291**
Bigram frequency **291**

Bilinguals/biscriptal readers
  assessment of literacy difficulties
    236–240
  brain regions involved in reading
    258–259
  central processing hypothesis 225–227,
    235, 242
  education 227
  letter search 74
  literacy acquisition 231–234
  phonological processing 228–230
  script dependent hypothesis 225–227,
    232–234, 235, 242
Blending 29, 46–47, 49, 60, 174, 205, **291**
Blending task 29, 46, 47, 49, **291**
Body units 50
British Sign Language 112, 113
Bullae 6

Cave paintings 4
CDP+ model 15, 195
Ceiling effects 62, **291**
Central processing hypothesis 225–227,
  235, 242
Cerebellum 253
Cherokee script 9
Chinese
  age of acquisition and word frequency
    275–277
  brain regions involved in reading 258
  compound characters 145
  dyslexia 141, 146–147, 204–208, 265
  homophones 9
  letter search 74
  literacy acquisition 224
  neuropsychological model of language
    processing 277–278

onset–rime awareness 30
orthographic and phonological
    facilitation 280–286
phonological awareness 206
reading acquisition 146
reading models 208–212
syllable structure 202
tone awareness 213
visual retention skills 225
writing system 9, 200–203, 252
Cingulum 283
Cochlear implants 120
Coda 26, 27, **291**
Cognate words 164, **291–292**
Common unit tasks 47, 49
Comprehension
    measurement 118–119
    orthographic transparency 95, 97
Computational models of reading 157,
    159–160
Concreteness 103, **292**
Connectionist models 15, 156, 160
Consistency problem 36
Consonant clusters 50, **292**
Consonantal alphabet 8
Contemporary writing systems 8–11
COST A8 study 38
Counting tasks 29, 32
Cultural hypothesis
    dyslexia 260
    reading 255–259
Cuneiform script 6–7
CV units 27, **292**
Czech
    consonant structures 50
    dyslexia 141, 144

Danish
    estimated incidence of dyslexia 141
    morphemic constituent effects 192
    reading acquisition 133, 134
Deafness
    indirect connection between oral and
        written language 111–125
    literacy intervention studies 122–125
    oral vs. British Sign Language
        education 112, 113
    subtitles for 110, 112
    suffix spelling 114–117
    syntax difficulties 112
Decoding 13, 35, 73, 80, 82, 91, 94–95,
    102, 105, 125, 136–137, 181, 189,
    204–205, 224, 230, 232, 235, 238,
    242, 252, **292**

Deep dyslexia 205–206, **292**
Deep orthography 10, 131, 252
    developmental dyslexia 140–145
    reading acquisition 132–134
    serial and parallel processing 70
    see also Opaque orthography
Deep structure of language 111–112
Deletion tasks 29, 47
Developmental dyslexia 204, 205, **292**
    across languages 139–148, 259–266
    assessment 221
    brain activation 260, 261–263
    brain disconnection hypothesis
        263–266
    cultural hypothesis 260
    early identification 221
    event-related potentials 260
    eye-movement studies 181–182
    granularity of language 147–148
    intensive phonological training 266
    neuro-developmental disorder 259
    non-alphabetic languages 145–148
    non-word reading 141–142
    orthographic depth 140–145, 259–260
    orthographic processing problems 173
    phonological deficits 143–145, 173,
        223, 260–261
    rapid naming 143
    reading speed 142–143
    second-language learning 148
    temporal lobe activity 261–263
    visual attention 13, 196
    visual processing problems 173
    see also specific languages
Devoicing 25, **292**
Diacritic **292**
Dictionaries 11
Digraph 88, **292**
Diphthong 88, **292**
Disconnection hypothesis of dyslexia
    263–266
Distributed representation 160
Distributional frequencies 25
Dorsolateral frontal cortex 258
Dual-route account of reading 156,
    157–159
Dual-route cascade (DRC) model 15,
    158, 182, 187, 209
Dutch
    developmental dyslexia 144
    lexical priming and lexical decision
        effects 136
Dyslexia, 204, 205, *see also* Acquired
    dyslexia; Developmental dyslexia

Egyptian writing 252
Elision **292**
Elision task **292**
English
  body units 50
  brain activation during reading 17, 256
  estimated incidence of dyslexia 141
  homophones 9
  item characteristics 162
  letter search 71–81
  literacy acquisition 224
  morphemic constituent effects 192
  non-word reading 136, 141–142
  orthographic depth 131
  phoneme awareness 32, 51–54
  phonological awareness 33–34, 54–58
  phonological neighbourhood density
    26
  positional biases in orthographic
    processing 70
  reading acquisition 133–134
  rhyme awareness 26
  rime awareness 51–54
  speech rhythm 50–51
  stress assignment 252
  syllable awareness 51–54
  syllable structure 10–11, 27, 33
Event-related potentials 260, **292–293**
Eye movements, developmental dyslexia
  181–182

False-fonts 253
Feed-forward inconsistency 36
'Ferrari effect' 138
Filipino–English bilinguals 227, 228,
  231–234, 235, 241–242
Finnish
  dyslexia 262, 263
  reading acquisition 133, 134
  writing system 9
Fixation 190, **293**
Fixation durations 182, **293**
Fluency tests 231
Formant transitions **293**
French
  body units 50
  dyslexia 143, 196, 260–261
  non-word reading 136
  phoneme awareness 32, 51–54
  phonological awareness 54–58
  rime awareness 51–54
  sonority profile 26
  speech rhythm 51
  syllable awareness 30, 51–54

Frequency effect
  age of acquisition 273–279
  dual-route explanation 158–159
  orthographic transparency 161–162
  reading experience 160
  reading performance 17, 163–164
  reading times 94
Frontal cortex 258
Functional magnetic resonance imaging
  (fMRI) 265, 267, 275, **293**
Fusiform gyrus 251, 253, 256, 257

German
  dyslexia 141–143, 144
  length effect 139
  non-word reading 136
  onset–rime awareness 30
  phoneme awareness 32–33
  phonological awareness 33–34
  pseudohomophone reading 136–137,
    139
  reading acquisition 142
  syllable awareness 30
  syllable structure 10, 27
  word recognition 88
Glide 26, **293**
Grain size 23–24, 27–28, 30, 31, 33–35,
  36, 39, 138–139, 148, 190, 192
Granularity problem 36
Grapheme 9, **293**
Grapheme–phoneme correspondence
  34–35, 170
Grapheme–phoneme recoding 37–39
Grapheme-to-phoneme conversion 182,
  188, **293**
Greek
  dyslexia 141, 143
  length effect 37
  letter search 75–81
  lexical priming and lexical decision
    effects 136
  non-word reading 136
  onset–rime awareness 31
  phoneme awareness 32
  vowel sounds 8
Grey matter 264–265

Hebrew 260
Herero–English bilinguals 227, 229,
  231–234, 235, 240–241
Hippocampus 283
Homograph 252, **293**
Homonym **293**
Homophone 9, **293**

Hungarian, literacy acquisition 224

Iambic stress pattern **293**
Icelandic, phonological awareness 54–58
Ideograms 4–6, 251
Imageability 167, **293**
Implicit skills 48, 60–62, 253–255
Infant-directed speech 25
Inferior frontal gyrus 138, 253, 256, 257, 258, 273, 275, 277
Inferior occipital cortex 257, 258
Inferior parietal lobe 275, 281, 283, 285
Inferior temporal gyrus 138, 253, 256, 261
Inflections 112–113
Initial Teaching Alphabet 101–102
Insula 264, 277, 283
Intervention studies
    dyslexia 266–267
    literacy in deaf children 122–125
Invented spellings 31
Irregular orthography **295**
Italian
    brain activation during reading 17, 256
    dyslexia, *see* Italian, dyslexia in
    frequency effect 163–164
    length effect 168, 186
    lexical effect in reading 181, 183–185
    lexical priming and lexical decision effects 136
    morphemic constituent effects 189–193
    non-word reading 136
    orthographic depth 131
    phoneme awareness 32
    reading acquisition 132, 171
    reading speed 137–138, 255–256
    rule contextuality effect 188–189
    stress assignment 135, 252
    syllable awareness 29
    syllable structure 10, 33, 50
Italian, dyslexia in 260–261
    frequency effect 186–187
    incidence of dyslexia 141, 143, 259
    length effect 181, 186–187
    lexicality effects 182, 184–185
    morphemic constituent effects 190–193
    neurophysiology 259
    non-lexical reading 182, 183, 184
    rule contextuality effect 189
Item characteristics 162–164

Japanese
    brain regions involved in reading 258
    dyslexia 141, 147
    kanji and kana 24, 146
    teaching to dyslexic readers 148

Language acquisition device (LAD) 113
Learning to read, *see* Reading acquisition
Left dorsolateral frontal cortex 258
Left fusiform gyrus 251, 253, 256
Left inferior frontal gyrus 253, 256, 257, 258, 273, 275
Left inferior frontal lobe 262, 283
Left inferior parietal region 275
Left inferior temporal gyrus 253, 256
Left middle frontal gyrus 258, 259, 265, 275, 277
Left middle temporal gyrus 253, 256
Left posterior inferior temporal cortex 17
Left posterior inferior temporal gyrus 138, 256
Left precentral motor gyrus 277
Left superior parietal cortex 277
Left superior posterior temporal gyrus 257, 258
Left superior temporal gyrus 253, 256
Left superior temporal region 138
Left temporal lobe 261–262
Left temporo-occipital cortex 257
Legitimate alternative reading of component (LARC) errors 207, 213
Length effect 37, **293**
    dual-route explanation 157, 158
    grain size theory 139
    Italian, dyslexia in 181, 186–187
    semantic system 168
Letter position encoding models 69, 82–83
Letter search 70–81
Letter–sound correspondence 9–11, 109, 110
Letters
    learning about and phoneme awareness 31
    mapping sounds to and orthographic transparency 35–37
    scrambled ordering 167
Lexical constituency model 16, 199, 211–215
Lexical decision effects 136
Lexical decision task 185, 186–187, **293**
Lexical knowledge, reading performance 165–168, 169, 181, 183–185

Lexical priming 135–136
Lexical representations 279, **293**
Lexical restructuring theory 44
Lexical stress 25, 50, 51, **294**
Lexicon **294**
Lingual gyrus 283
Linguistic complexity 10
Liquid 26, **294**
Literacy
  assessment in more than one language
    222–227
  as 'brain-washing' 251
  orthographic transparency 223–224,
    231–234
  phonological development 62–63
Logographic writing system 6–7, 9, 200,
    251, **294**

Magnetoencephalography (MEG) 262,
    294
Matching tasks 46, 47, 48, 49
Mathematical symbols 252
Meaning 111, 165–166
Medial superior frontal gyri 277
Memory, phonological short-term
    memory in bilinguals 228
Mental lexicon 134, 135, 136, 185
Metalinguistic development 45–46
Mid fusiform gyrus 257
Middle frontal gyrus 258–259, 265, 274,
    275, 277
Middle occipital gyrus 283
Middle temporal gyrus 253, 256, 259,
    261, 275, 283, 285
Morpheme 110, 200, **294**
Morphographic writing system 200, 201,
    294
Morphological constituents 189–193,
    294
Morphology **294**
  role in literacy 14, 113–114, 174–175
  second-language learning 125–126
Morphosyllabic script 200, 201
Motherese 25
MT test 183

Nasal 26, **294**
National Adult Reading Test 141
National Literacy Strategy 104
Neighbourhood density 26, **294**
Neighbourhood size (N-size) 183, **294**
Non-letter search 73–74
Non-lexical reading 161, 182, 183–184,
    294

Non-word reading 37–38, 91, 93, 97, 133,
    136, 141–142, 230, **294–295**
Norwegian
  dyslexia 141, 143
  onset–rime awareness 31
  phoneme awareness 32
  syllable awareness 29–30
Notation 109
Numbers 251–252
Nursery rhymes 30

Obstruent 26, **295**
Occipital lobe 257, 258, 275, 281, 285
Oddity tasks 30, 34, 46, 47, 48, 49
Onset 44, **295**
Onset–rime awareness 28, 30–31
Onset–rime grain size 27–28
Opaque orthography, 10, 252, **295**, *see
    also* Deep orthography
Open-bigram model 82, 83
Orbitomedial cortex 281
Orthographic analogy **295**
Orthographic complexity
  rate of learning to read 11
  syllabic complexity and 10
Orthographic depth 10, 131–139
  developmental dyslexia 140–145,
    259–260
  phoneme awareness 32–33
  reading acquisition 33–39, 132–134,
    156
Orthographic depth hypothesis
  strong version 15, 134–136
  weak version 15, 136–138, 256
Orthographic lexicon 23, 256, **295**
Orthographic transparency 147, **295**
  age of acquisition effect 161–162
  frequency effect 161–162
  grapheme–phoneme recoding 38–39
  letter search 74–81
  literacy acquisition 223–224, 231–234
  mapping sounds to letters 35–37
  non-word reading 37–38
  phonological awareness 33–35
  reading acquisition 24, 33–39, 82, 88,
    95, 132–134, 156, 169
  reading comprehension 95, 97
  underachieving readers 95–102
  see also Transparent orthography
Orthography 69, 109, **295**
  depth, *see* Orthographic depth
  derivation 3
  effect on speech production 279–286
  historical perspective 4–8

notational concept 109
phonographic principle 109–110
semiographic principle 109–110
Over-additivity effect 194–195, **295**

Parallel processing 70
Past tense 112
Persian
estimated incidence of dyslexia 141
lexical priming and lexical decision
effects 136
Phoenician language 8
Phoneme 24, **295**
grain size 27
speech signal 25
Phoneme awareness
development of explicit awareness in
English and French speakers 51–54
different languages 28, 31–33
vocabulary 45
Welsh 94–95
Phoneme tapping test 32, **295**
Phones **295**
Phonetic radical 201, 202, 203
Phonics-based teaching techniques
104–105, 142, 250, 266–267, **295**
Phonographic principle 109–110
Phonological awareness
assessment tasks 47
bilinguals 228
distinguishing different types 49–50
large-to-small transition 44, 46–48, 58
levels of awareness in different
languages 28–33, 54–58
orthographic effects 33–35
reading 23, 24–28, 59–62, 171, 206
Phonological development
cross-linguistic perspective 50–58
literacy acquisition 62–63
theories 43–46
Phonological dyslexia 204–205, **295**
Phonological facilitation effect 279–286
Phonological recoding self-teaching
theory of reading 169–170
Phonological representations 24–25
Phonological short-term memory,
bilinguals 228
Phonological task classification 60
Phonology 43, 113, **295**
Phonotactics 25, **295–296**
Pictograms 4–6, 200, 251
Picture–word facilitation 279, 280, 281
Picture writing 4
Place of articulation **296**

Planum temporale 17, 256
Plosive 26, **296**
Plurals 112–113
Portuguese, phonological awareness
54–58
Positron emission tomography (PET)
256, 261, **296**
Postcentral gyrus 258, 283, 285
Posterior fusiform cortex 258
Posterior fusiform gyrus 257
Posterior superior temporal gyrus 258
Practice, reading improvement 175
Precentral gyrus 256, 258, 277
Precuneus 283, 285
Prefix 110
Prefrontal cortex 281
Premorbid **296**
PROLEC–R 172
Pronunciation consistency, reading
experience 160–161
Prosodic cues 25, **296**
Prototypes 31
Pseudohomophone effect 136–137, 139,
296
Psycholinguistic grain size 23–24, 27–28,
30, 31, 33–35, 36, 39, 138–139, 148,
190, 192
Psycholinguistic units 34

Radical-by-radical reading 214
Radicals 201
Rapid naming 143, 229, 231
Rate-and-amount (RAM) model 194
Raven's Progressive Matrices 118
Reaction time, reading 162
Reading
age of acquisition 163–164
comprehension and orthographic
transparency 95, 97
comprehension measurement
118–119
cultural hypothesis 255–259
experience 160, 161
frequency effect 17, 163–164
implicit 253–255
instinct 253–255
item characteristics 162
lexical knowledge 165–168, 169, 181,
183–185
meaning 165–166
morphemes 14, 174–175, 188–193
phonological awareness 23, 24–28,
171, 206
practice effects 175

prerequisites for fluent reading 250–255
reaction time 162
readiness 250
semantic influences 167–168
speech link 23, 251
speed 97, 137–138, 142–143, 255–256
theories 156–161
underachieving readers and orthographic transparency 95–102
Reading acquisition
orthographic transparency 24, 33–39, 82, 88, 95, 132–134, 156, 169
phonics-based techniques 104–105, 142, 250, 266–267, **295**
phonological awareness 23, 59–62
rate 11, 37–39
self-teaching theory 169–170
sex differences 102
typical course 172–173
Record-keeping 6
Regular orthography, **297**, *see also* Transparent orthography
Regularize 135, **296**
Rhyme awareness
orthography and 95
phonological awareness 26, 48
Rhythm of speech
phonological development 50–51
phonotactic learning 25
Right hemisphere, phonological facilitation 281, 283, 285
Right inferior occipital cortex 258
Right superior temporal gyrus 256
Rime 44, **296**
Rime awareness 30–31, 51–54, 58
Rime familiarity effect 37–38, **296**
Rule-based approach 6–7
Rule contextuality effect 188–189

Saccades 182, **296**
Same–different judgement task 29, 30
Schonell Spelling Test 115–116
Schonell Word Reading Test 120
Schwa vowel 110
Script dependent hypothesis 225–227, 232–234, 235, 242
Second-language learning
dyslexia 148
morphology 125–126
see also Bilinguals/biscriptal readers
Segmental information 25, **296**
Segmentation 47, 49, **296**
Self-teaching theory of reading 169–170

Semantic dementia 168
Semantic–phonetic compound characters 201
Semantic radical 201
Semantics, reading 167–168
Semasiographical representation 6
Semiographic principle 109–110
Sentence meaning 111
Serbo-Croatian 132
Serial processing 70, 82
Serial stimulus recoding **297**
SERIOL 82–83
Sex differences, learning to read 102
Shallow orthography 10, 132
developmental dyslexia 140–145
lexical priming and lexical decision effects 135–136
reading acquisition 132–134
see also Transparent orthography
Sight vocabulary 91, 94, **297**
SOLAR 82–83
Sonorant 26–27, 22, **297**
Sonority profile 26, **297**
Sound–spelling correspondence 34–35, 36
Spanish
acquired dyslexia 166–167
age of acquisition effect 163–164
developmental dyslexia 142–143, 172
item characteristics 162–164
length effect 168
letter search 74–75
lexical priming and lexical decision effects 136
non-word reading 136
orthography 155
phonological awareness 54–58
reading acquisition 170–173
semantics and reading 167–168
syllable structure 10
Speech
orthographic effects 279–286
perception 43–44
reading link 23, 251
rhythm and phonological development 50–51
rhythm and phonotactic learning 25
Speech signal 25, **297**
Spelling
phonological awareness 34–35
sound–spelling correspondence 34–35, 36
suffixes 114–122
Spoonerism task 143

Statistical learning 25
Stem 110
Stress pattern 25, 135, 252, **297**
Stress-timed language 50
Strokes 200, 201
Suffix 110
Suffix spelling 114–122
Sumerian cuneiform script 6–7
Superior frontal gyrus 283
Superior posterior temporal gyrus 257, 258
Superior temporal gyrus 253, 256, 258
Superior temporal region 138
Supplementary motor area 283
Supragraphemic level **297**
Supramarginal gyrus 258, 283, 285
Surface dyslexia 182, 204, 205, **297**
Surface of language 111
Swedish, estimated incidence of dyslexia 141
Syllabic writing system 7–8, 9
Syllable awareness 28–30, 43–44, 51–54, 57–58
Syllable grain size 27
Syllable structure 10–11, 27–28, 33, 50, 202
Syllable-timed language 51
Symbol–sound mappings 35–37
Syntax 111–112
System 109

Tallies 6
Tapping tasks 28, 32, 47, 60
Temporal lobe, dyslexia 261–263
Temporal pole 283
Temporo-parietal junction 256
Thalamus 283, 285
Tokens 6
Tonal dyslexia 205, 208, 213–214
Tone 201, 202, 285
Transitional probabilities 25, **297**
Translation pairs 103
Transparent orthography 10, 252, **297**
  reading acquisition 88, 169, 170–173

reading comprehension 95, 97
serial processing 70, 82
see also Shallow orthography
Triangle theory of reading 156, 157, 159–161
Turkish
  non-word reading 136
  phoneme awareness 32
  syllable awareness 29
  syllable boundaries 50
  word recognition 88
  writing system 9

Universal pathway 46, 50

Visual attention, dyslexia 13, 196
Visual processing 230
Visual search 70–81
Visual word form area 23–24, 251, **297**
Vocabulary
  growth 24–25, 44–45
  phonological development 25–26
Vocalic interval **297**
Voicing 31, **297**

Welsh
  estimated incidence of dyslexia 141
  non-word reading 91, 93, 97, 136
  orthography 88
  reading acquisition 87, 90–95
White matter 264, 265
Word frequency effect, *see* Frequency effect
Word length effect, *see* Length effect
Word lists, composition 103–104, 163–164
Word naming latency 162
Writing
  assessment 119
  historical aspects 6–8, 250–251
  systems 8–11, 251–252

Yukaghir 'love letter' 5